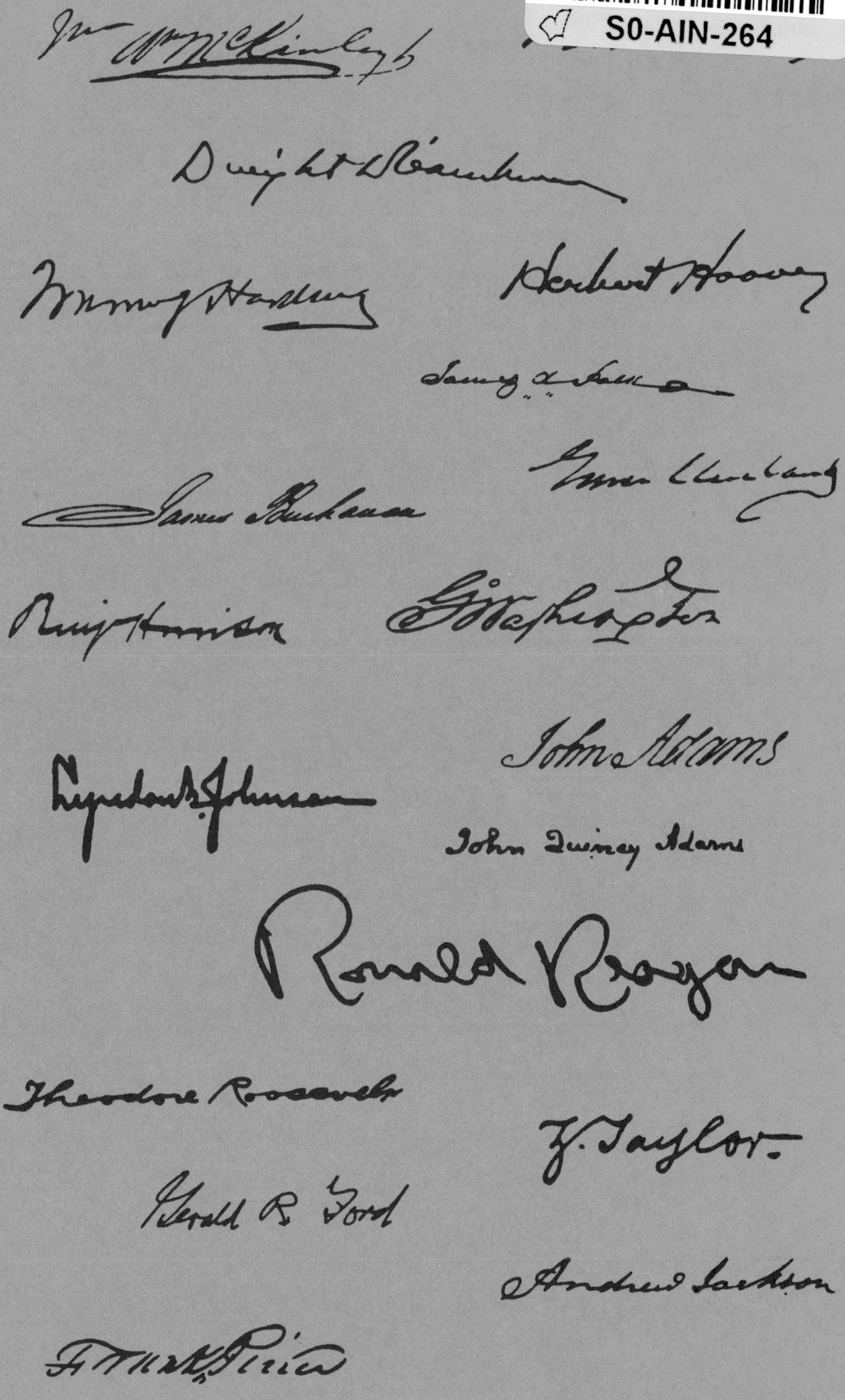
Herbert Hoover
James Buchanan
Benj Harrison
G Washington
John Adams
Lyndon B. Johnson
John Quincy Adams
Ronald Reagan
Theodore Roosevelt
Z. Taylor.
Gerald R. Ford
Andrew Jackson

Records of the Presidency:

Presidential Papers and Libraries from Washington to Reagan

Records of the Presidency:
Presidential Papers and Libraries from Washington to Reagan

By Frank L. Schick
With Renee Schick and
Mark Carroll

Foreword by President Gerald R. Ford

ORYX PRESS
1989

Copyright © 1989 by The Oryx Press
2214 North Central at Encanto
Phoenix, Arizona 85004-1483

Published simultaneously in Canada

Printed and Bound in the United States of America

∞ The paper used in this publication meets the minimum requirements of American National Standard for Information Science—Permanence of Paper for Printed Library Materials, ANSI Z39.48, 1984.

Library of Congress Cataloging-in-Publication Data

Schick, Frank Leopold, 1918–
    Records of the presidency : presidential papers and libraries / by Frank L. Schick, Renee Schick, Mark S. Carroll.
    p.   cm.
    Bibliography: p.
    Includes index.
    ISBN 0-89774-277-X (alk. paper)
    1. Presidents—United States—Archives.   I. Schick, Renee.
II. Carroll, Mark S.   III. Title
CD3029.82.S35 1989   88-28222
353.0085′2—dc19

"...the Past cannot be recovered; but let us save what remains; not by vaults and locks which fence them from the public eye and use, in consigning them to the waste of time, but by such a multiplication of copies, as shall place them beyond the reach of accident."

Thomas Jefferson
February 18, 1791

"The truth behind a president's action can be found only in his official papers, and every presidential paper is official."

Harry S. Truman
1949

To the memory of my father, a distinguished physician whose lifelong interest in history was my inspiration.

Contents

Foreword by President Gerald R. Ford   xi

Introduction   xiii

PART I. Papers and Libraries of the Presidents   1

1. Agencies Responsible for the Maintenance of Presidential
    Records   1
    The Library of Congress   2
    Historical Society and Special Libraries   6
    The National Archives of the United States   7

2. Legislation Relating to Presidential Libraries   13
    The Presidential Libraries Act of 1955 (PL84-373)   14
    The Presidential Recordings and Materials Preservation Act of
    1974 (PL93-526)   16
    The Presidential Records Act of 1978 (PL95-591)   17
    The Presidential Libraries Act of 1986 (PL99-323)   18

3. Guides to Presidential Records   20
    Eighteenth- and Nineteenth-Century Compilations of Presidential
    Papers   20
    The National Historical Publications Commission   21
    The National Union Catalog of Manuscript Collections   22
    Public Papers of the Presidents of the United States and the
    Weekly Compilation of Presidential Documents   22
    The Presidents' Papers Index Series   24
    Other Bibliographic Guides to Presidential Papers   24
    PRESNET: An Automated Information System for Presidential
    Libraries   25

4. Presidential Book Collections at Historic Sites   26
    by Mark Carroll
    Libraries in Presidential Homes   27
    Presidential Book Collections in the Library of Congress   35
    The White House Libraries   36

**PART II. Presidential Papers in the Manuscript Division of the Library of
Congress   39**

5. The Early Presidents   39
    George Washington   39
    Thomas Jefferson   45
    James Madison   53
    James Monroe   56

6. Pre-Civil War Presidents   61
    Andrew Jackson   61
    Martin Van Buren   66
    William Henry Harrison   68
    John Tyler   70
    James K. Polk   72
    Zachary Taylor   75
    Franklin Pierce   77
    Abraham Lincoln   79

7. Post-Civil War Presidents   82
    Andrew Johnson   82
    Ulysses S. Grant   85
    James A. Garfield   87
    Chester A. Arthur   91
    Grover Cleveland   93
    Benjamin Harrison   96

8. Twentieth-Century Presidents   99
    William McKinley   99
    Theodore Roosevelt   101
    William Howard Taft   105
    Woodrow Wilson   109
    Calvin Coolidge   114

**PART III. Presidential Papers in Historical Societies and Special
Libraries   117**

9. Historical Societies   117
    John Adams   117
    John Quincy Adams   118
    The Adams Family Papers in the Massachusetts Historical
        Society   119
    Millard Fillmore   125
    The Fillmore Papers in the Buffalo Historical Society   126
    James Buchanan   128
    The Buchanan Papers in the Historical Society of
        Pennsylvania   130
    Warren G. Harding   133
    The Harding Papers in the Ohio Historical Society   134

10. Special Libraries   139
    Rutherford B. Hayes   139
    The Rutherford B. Hayes Presidential Center   140
    Herbert Hoover   143
    The Hoover Institution and Library on War, Revolution and
        Peace   145

**PART IV. Presidential Libraries Administered by the National
Archives   149**

11. The Franklin D. Roosevelt Library and Museum in Hyde Park, New
        York   149
    Franklin D. Roosevelt   149
    The Planning of the Franklin D. Roosevelt Library   151

The Franklin D. Roosevelt Library and Museum   157
Research Materials in the FDR Library   159
The Museum Area   165
The Franklin and Eleanor Roosevelt Institute   166

12. The Harry S. Truman Library in Independence, Missouri   168
Harry S. Truman   168
The Establishment of the Truman Library   170
The Harry S. Truman Library Building   172
Research Materials in the Harry S. Truman Library   173
The Museum Area   175
The Harry S. Truman Library Institute   176

13. The Herbert Hoover Library and Museum in West Branch,
Iowa   177
The Establishment of the Hoover Library and Museum   177
Research Materials in the Hoover Library   178
The Museum Area   181

14. The Dwight D. Eisenhower Library in Abilene, Kansas   182
Dwight D. Eisenhower   182
The Eisenhower Center in Abilene, Kansas   184
Research Materials in the Eisenhower Library   187
The Eisenhower Museum   190
The Educational Programs at the Library   191

15. The John F. Kennedy Library in Boston, Massachusetts   192
John F. Kennedy   192
The Establishment of the John F. Kennedy Library   194
The Kennedy Library Building   198
Research Materials in the Kennedy Library   198
The Museum Area   201
The Educational Programs at the Library   202

16. The Lyndon B. Johnson Library in Austin, Texas   204
Lyndon B. Johnson   204
The Establishment of the LBJ Library   206
The Johnson Library Complex Buildings   209
Research Materials in the Lyndon B. Johnson Library   210
The Museum Areas   214
The Educational Programs at the Library   215

17. The Gerald R. Ford Library in Ann Arbor, Michigan and the Gerald
R. Ford Museum in Grand Rapids, Michigan   217
Gerald R. Ford   217
The Establishment of the Gerald R. Ford Library and
Museum   220
The Gerald R. Ford Library   223
Research Materials in the Gerald R. Ford Library   224
The Gerald R. Ford Museum   227
Library and Museum Activities   228

18. The Jimmy Carter Center in Atlanta, Georgia   229
Jimmy Carter   229
The Establishment of the Carter Presidential Center   232

The Carter Presidential Center Buildings   235
Research Materials in the Carter Library   235
The Carter Museum   236
Other Parts of the Carter Center   237
19. Presidential Libraries in the Planning Stage: The Richard M. Nixon
and Ronald W. Reagan Libraries   239
Richard M. Nixon   239
The Nixon Presidential Records   242
Research Materials in the Nixon Presidential Materials
Project   244
The Richard Nixon Presidential Archives Foundation   247
Ronald Reagan   248
The Ronald Reagan Presidential Library Plans   249

Appendixes   251
Appendix 1: Statistics for Presidential Libraries   251
Table 1: Actual Costs of Presidential Libraries, FY 1987   251
Table 2: Holdings of Presidential Libraries, Total as of October
1987   252
Table 3: Space Allocations in Presidential Libraries, FY 1987
254
Table 4: Researcher Daily Visits to Presidential Libraries, FY
1946–87   255
Table 5: Museum Visitors to Presidential Libraries, FY 1947–87
256
Table 6: Staff Positions in Presidential Libraries as of October
1987   257
Appendix 2: Directory of Major Presidential Records Collections
258
Appendix 3: Directory of Presidential Historic Sites   260
by Mark Carroll
Appendix 4: Overview of the White House Filing System   263

Chapter Notes   265

Bibliography   279

Index   293

Foreword

When I was planning for the disposition of my presidential records, I found that former presidents and their descendants had made many different decisions concerning their papers. After leaving the government, George Washington took his papers to his home at Mount Vernon, Virginia. After years of delay, his papers and those of twenty-two other presidents came to the Library of Congress which organized them, tried to complete the collections as far as possible, and made them publicly accessible. The papers of John Adams and six of his successors were deposited in state historical societies; the descendants of Hayes and Harding built memorial libraries near their homes. President Hoover deposited all of his papers at the Hoover Institution on War, Revolution and Peace which he founded at his Alma Mater, Stanford University.

President Franklin D. Roosevelt developed the concept of the Presidential Library which is constructed and equipped by private funds, and administered by the National Archives. This pattern was followed by presidents since Roosevelt, and by Mr. Hoover, his only surviving predecessor, who moved his presidential records from Stanford to the Hoover Library in West Branch, Iowa where he was born. I changed this model to the extent that my papers are deposited in the Ford Library on the campus of the University of Michigan and the memorabilia of my administration at the Ford Museum in my home town of Grand Rapids, Michigan.

President Carter was the last Democrat and I the last Republican who were free to dispose of our papers and memorabilia in any way we saw fit. Since 1981, presidential papers are legally the property of the United States; this change in the law limits the options of future presidents. Mr. Reagan will be the first president whose papers will have to be deposited with the National Archives; he and his followers can build with private funds a library and museum at a site of his choice which will be maintained by the Archives.

Presidential libraries are more than brick and mortar—they are living institutions serving all the public. Access to presidential records is of great importance to all those interested in the past of the presidency. Frank Schick, assisted by Renee Schick and Mark Carroll, presents in one volume the history of presidential records and a guide to their contents and to the sites at which they are stored; separate chapters summarize the legislation concerned with presidential libraries and describe the personal libraries of many presidents. All those interested in the past of the presidency will find here a valuable reference and guide for access to presidential records in the original, in print and in microform.

Gerald R. Ford

Introduction

This book is the result of a lifelong interest in the presidency that started when I worked part-time in the Detroit Public Library to earn my way through college. Shifting document boxes in the rare book room, I came across one labeled "Diary of George Washington for the year 1782." As a political science and history major, I was excited about this find and asked my supervisor how Washington's papers had come from Virginia to Michigan. Ever since I have been fascinated with the history and whereabouts of presidential records. Dr. Milo M. Quaife, the historian who edited the diaries of President Polk and wrote many books about American history, had, at that time, a research desk in the Detroit Public Library, and showed endless patience in answering my questions about presidential papers. He, and Professor Maurice M. Ramsey, whose political science classes at Wayne University opened my eyes to the interrelations between political actions, government operations, and historical events, encouraged me to continue my interest in and study of the presidency.

Military service in World War II, the pursuit of academic and government careers, and the raising of a family moved my study of the history of presidential papers into slow gear, although my interest in the topic remained and was further stimulated through an encounter with Senator Estes Kefauver of Tennessee in the early 1960s. Kefauver had visited the Truman Presidential Library in Independence, Missouri, and wanted to explore the possibilities of establishing a similar facility for his papers in his home town in Tennessee. On request of his office, a task force consisting of staff members from the Library of Congress and the National Archives, and of myself, representing the U.S. Department of Education, met several times with the Senator. In preparation for these meetings, I read a great deal about the preservation of the papers of presidents and other famous Americans. As the Democratic candidate for vice president in 1956, Kefauver was not eligible for the provisions of the Presidential Libraries Act of 1955; our job was to recommend a suitable depository for his papers. We suggested that he donate them to the University of Tennessee, his alma mater, rather than establish a library in a small town; this idea was eventually implemented by his widow.

A few years later, when the presidential papers in the Library of Congress were being microfilmed and indexed, I met with David C. Mearns, Chief of the Manuscript Division of the Library of Congress, to whom I mentioned my interest in the history of presidential papers; he showed me with great pride the published volumes of the *Presidents' Papers Index Series,* each of which includes a provenance that discusses the origin of the papers. He encouraged me to complete and publish a history of presidential records and libraries, and suggested that I arrange my study by type of agency of deposit rather than in the chronological order of presidential succession, an arrangement which appealed to me.

The underlying theme of this book is the concept that the personal and public papers of the presidents are crucial to the understanding of this country's history; they are a direct reflection of the problems and pressures that have been faced by the nation's chief executives. Many documents were purposely or accidentally destroyed over the years, and no national policy for their collection, storage, and preservation existed until the later half of the twentieth century. The following pages present, in one volume, the story of presidential papers from their origin to their places of deposit, and a comprehensive guide to their contents and to bibliographic references to them.

The book is divided into four parts. The first part presents a general discussion of the agencies responsible for the maintenance of presidential papers: the Manuscript Division of the Library of Congress, where the bulk of the papers of 23 presidents are stored; the National Archives, which operate the presidential libraries of the last 10 presidents; and historical societies and special libraries, which hold the records of seven presidents. An overview of the extensive federal legislation concerning presidential records is given, with special emphasis on the contributions of presidents Roosevelt, Truman, and Eisenhower in the development of presidential libraries, and on the changes in definition and ownership of presidential records in the aftermath of Watergate. Detailed descriptions of major bibliographies and reference guides to records of the presidency, and a chapter on presidential book collections at historic sites, are also provided in this part.

The other three parts deal with the history of the individual sets of presidential records and a summary of their contents, arranged by their primary place of deposit. Short biographical sketches for each president assist the reader in relating the documents to the history of the nation and to the events in the life of each president. The descriptions of the various sets of records are based on information gathered by visiting the presidential libraries and using the original documents relating to the establishment of these libraries; the provenances in the *Presidents' Papers Index Series* in the Library of Congress; information provided by historical societies, special libraries serving as document repositories, the National Archives Office of Presidential Libraries, and the Manuscript Division of the Library of Congress; and the historical literature.

To help researchers and document collectors locate specific papers of the various presidents, this volume presents abbreviated indexes to the microfilm editions of the papers in the Library of Congress and to the manuscripts in the presidential and special libraries, permitting identification of documents created during specific time periods without making it necessary to consult numerous indexes and finding aids. The book also serves as a guide to the eight presidential libraries that were fully operative in 1988 and to the Nixon Presidential Materials Project of the National Archives; it describes the libraries' development, the main features of the buildings, the museum facilities, and the educational and support activities of the various foundations. Plans for the Nixon and Reagan presidential libraries are sketched out, as they were available in mid-1988.

The four appendixes provide statistical tables, supplied by the Office of Presidential Libraries, which summarize the resources, staff, funding, and use of presidential libraries; a directory of major presidential record collections; a directory of presidential historic sites; and an overview of the White House filing system as described in the presidential libraries' finding aids. The bibliography is a selection of published works consulted in the preparation of the manuscript, and of works by and about various presidents.

My research at the Franklin D. Roosevelt Library was partially supported by a fellowship grant from the Roosevelt Foundation. A great deal of advice, assistance, and support in the preparation of this book was given by many people. While I cannot mention all of them individually, I would like to acknowledge Frank G. Burke, David Van Tassel, William Emerson, John Lorenz, and Daniel Reed, who generously shared their knowledge and expertise with me through the period of developing the manuscript. Others who were very helpful included David Alsobrook, Daniel Fenn, James Hastings, Richard Holzhausen, Richard Jacobs, Judy Kouckey, Philip Lagerquist, William McNitt, James O'Neill, Donald Schewe, Frances Seeber, John Stewart, William Stewart, Diane Van Allsberg, John Wickman, Gary Yarrington, and Benedict K. Zobrist in the National Archives and presidential libraries; Judith Farley, Bruce Martin, James Hutson, Charles Kelly, and Mary M. Wolfskill in the Library of Congress; and Gary Jones and James Whitaker in the Reagan and Nixon presidential library foundations.

Special thanks are due to Carol Hunter and John Wagner, editors at Oryx Press, whose patience and understanding of the subject matter helped greatly in developing and finalizing the manuscript; to Deborah Lazar who deciphered my handwriting and entered the first draft of the book into the computer, so that it could be rearranged and edited; and to Edith Arlen Wachtel for her continued interest in providing relevant resources. Renee Schick and I cooperated in the research for the book and she visited the presidential libraries with me; she wrote a substantial portion of the first part, forged my drafts into a manuscript, and compiled the bibliography. Mark Carroll, author, editor, and publisher, contributed the chapter on presidential book collections and their sites.

Bethesda, Maryland   *Frank L. Schick*
January 1989

Records of the Presidency:
Presidential Papers and Libraries from Washington to Reagan

PART I

Papers and Libraries of the Presidents

1. Agencies Responsible for the Maintenance of Presidential Records

While presidential records began with the official papers of the first president, their history really started on June 15, 1775, when George Washington was appointed commander of the Continental Army. He was an avid correspondent throughout his life and paid great attention to the organization and preservation of his correspondence, to the point of developing a six-part classification system that distinguished between his public and his private papers. In 1776, expecting a British attack, Washington had the various documents collected during the first year of his command of the Continental Army removed to a safe place. He wrote to John Hancock, president of the Continental Congress: "I thought it advisable to remove all papers in my hands respecting the affairs of the States from this place. They are contained in a large box, nailed up and committed to the care of Lieutenant Colonel Reed to be delivered to Congress, in whose custody I would beg leave to deposit them."[1]

When he left office in 1797, George Washington took his papers to his home at Mount Vernon, Virginia. Early in the twentieth century, his papers and those of 22 other presidents finally came to the Library of Congress, where the Manuscript Division organized them, tried to complete the collections, and made them publicly accessible. The papers of John Adams and six other presidents were deposited by their families in state historical societies and special libraries. Franklin D. Roosevelt developed the concept of the presidential library constructed and equipped by private funds and administered by the National Archives. This pattern has been followed by all presidents since Roosevelt. After the passage of the Presidential Libraries Act in 1955, Herbert Hoover, Roosevelt's only surviving predecessor, also established a presidential library.

THE LIBRARY OF CONGRESS

The Library of Congress, one of the largest libraries in the world, serves both as the legislative library for the U.S. Congress and as a national library for the country at large, and is a unique resource for research in all fields of knowledge. Its holdings include many old and rare written and printed records; its intellectual wealth ranges from musical instruments to paintings, posters, and recordings and tapes, and from the Gutenberg Bible and the Declaration of Independence to original musical scores of Beethoven and the handwritten poems of Walt Whitman. The Library administers the U.S. Copyright Office, and has been a pioneer in the preservation of materials, the microfilming and cataloging of printed records, and the development of automated bibliographic data storage and retrieval. It has a multifaceted relationship to many American presidents. Three of its major buildings are named after presidents (Adams, Jefferson, and Madison), and along with its presidential papers collection in the Manuscript Division, it also houses the personal library of Woodrow Wilson.

The history of the congressional quest for knowledge can be traced to 1774 when the director of the Library Company of Philadelphia instructed the librarian to "furnish the gentlemen who are to meet in Congress [the First Continental Congress] with the use of . . . books, as they may have occasion for . . . taking a receipt for them."[2] In this manner the importance of books for Congress received early recognition. On August 6, 1789, when the First Congress of the United States convened in the New York City Hall, Elbridge Gerry, a Massachusetts representative and a signer of the Declaration of Independence, made a motion "that a committee be appointed to report a catalogue of books necessary for the use of Congress with an estimate of expense, and the best mode of procuring them."[3] This motion was tabled, but on April 30, 1790, Gerry's motion was called, and he was appointed to head a committee that recommended on June 23, during the second session of the First Congress, that a library for use of the legislative and executive branches be established. Gerry observed that "without a library, officials will be deprived of necessary books or be obliged at every session to transport to the seat of the General Government a considerable part of their personal libraries."[4]

In 1800, Congress enacted a law, signed by President John Adams on April 24, to move the capital from Philadelphia to Washington. Senator Samuel Livermore of New Hampshire added a section to this act which authorized $5,000 for the purchase of books and for "fitting up a suitable apartment for containing them, and for placing them therein."[5] This established the Library of Congress. In due course, a catalog of needed books was compiled and forwarded to a London bookseller, Cadell and Davies. In a letter of December 11, 1800, Cadell and Davies announced to Senator Bingham and Congressman Waln of Pennsylvania their first shipment of 740 books.[6]

An act of Congress of January 26, 1802, signed by President Jefferson, provided that the Library would be used by both houses of Congress. In addition to some details of what the Library was to purchase, this act provided for a salary for the librarian, spelled out that the Library is to be supervised by a joint committee of three members of the Senate and three members of the House, and that the Library should be placed in the Capitol building. The act also prescribed that the Library's rules and regulations be established by the President of the Senate and the Speaker of the House, and that its use be restricted to members of Congress and the president and vice president of the United States. Three days after Jefferson signed this bill, he approved John J. Beckley, clerk of the House of Representatives, as the first librarian of Congress to serve in both positions concurrently.[7] On January 2, 1805, Jefferson approved an act of Congress that stipulated placement of 300 copies of the laws of the United States and the journals of Congress in the Library of Congress. In November 1807, after the death of John J. Beckley, Jefferson appointed Patrick Magruder, a Washington newspaper writer, as the second librarian of Congress.

In August 1814, the British captured Washington, burned the Capitol, and destroyed the Library of Congress. On September 21, Jefferson offered from his retirement home in Monticello, Virginia, to sell his personal book collection to Congress to "recommence" the Library. He enclosed a catalog with his letter and also explained the condition of his books and how he had brought them together. "I have been fifty years making it and have spared no pains, opportunity or expense to make it what it is. While residing in Paris I devoted every afternoon I was disengaged, for a summer or two, in examining all the principal book stores, turning over every book with my own hand and putting by everything which related to America, and indeed whatever was rare and valuable in every sense." He explained also that he had purchased books in Amsterdam, Frankfurt, Madrid, and London, and goes on to say that "such a collection was made as probably can never be effected, because it is hardly probable that the same opportunities, the same time, industry, perseverance and expense, with the same knowledge of the bibliography of the subject, would again happen to be in concurrence."[8] Joseph Milligan, a Georgetown bookseller, evaluated this collection of 6,487 volumes at $23,950. Majorities in both houses approved this acquisition in the passage of an act on March 3, 1815.[9] In the same month, President James Madison appointed George Watterston as third librarian of Congress; he was the first who did not serve simultaneously as clerk of the House of Representatives.

Jefferson suggested that the book arrangement he had worked out be maintained. Watterston accepted this and invited Jefferson, in a letter of April 26, 1815, to have the books packed up according to that arrangement, because "I have long thought the arrangement of the old Library was incorrect and injudicious."[10] The Jefferson classification scheme followed Francis Bacon's table of knowledge concept, arranged into 44 divisions. The Library of Congress used the Jefferson system with some modifications until the end of the nineteenth century. The first new classification system was published in 1901 under Librarian Herbert Putnam.[11]

In 1851, a fire destroyed 35,000 volumes of a collection that had grown since 1815 to about 55,000 volumes. It also destroyed two-thirds of

Jefferson's library. In 1864, President Abraham Lincoln hired Ainsworth Rand Spofford as librarian of Congress. The first really effective librarian, Spofford served until 1897. He was a personal friend of Rutherford B. Hayes, who gave great assistance to the Library as congressman and president. In 1877, President Hayes agreed to an exchange of books and documents between the White House and the Library and approved $1,000 for the Library to index the "resolves, ordinances, and acts of the Continental Congress and the Congress of the Confederation."[12] In his first annual message to Congress, Hayes recommended the construction of a fireproof building for the Library of Congress. Spofford was also able to enlist the support of presidents Chester A. Arthur and Grover Cleveland and was responsible for the acquisition of many presidential papers and other important collections.

In 1897, President Cleveland approved the Legislative, Executive and Judicial Appropriations Act for 1898; this act expanded the authority of the librarian of Congress and enlarged the Library by adding the Office of Register of Copyright and eight new departments, including one that later became the Manuscript Division. The Library staff was increased from 42 to 108, and the Senate was given power to confirm the president's choice of the librarian. President William McKinley nominated John Russell Young to succeed Spofford in June 1897, and the Library of Congress Building (now the Jefferson Building) was opened to the public on November 1, 1897. In his first annual message to Congress that December, President McKinley expressed the hope that the Library would develop into one "of the richest and most useful libraries of the world."[13]

In February 1903, Theodore Roosevelt approved a law that "authorizes U.S. government agencies to transfer to the Library of Congress any books, maps or other material no longer needed for its use and in the judgment of the Librarian of Congress is appropriate for the uses of the Library."[14] In March, an Executive Order of the president transferred the papers of the Continental Congress; the papers of presidents Washington, Jefferson, Madison, and Monroe; and those of Benjamin Franklin and Alexander Hamilton to the Library of Congress. In 1906, Roosevelt issued another Executive Order transferring papers from the State Department to the Library.

During the Hoover administration, Library staff members were asked to organize, weed, and supervise the development of the White House Library. In 1939, Franklin Roosevelt appointed Archibald MacLeish, a personal friend and prominent writer, librarian of Congress. He was followed in 1945 by Truman appointee Luther H. Evans. In 1954, Dwight D. Eisenhower appointed L. Quincy Mumford, the director of the Cleveland Public Library, as eleventh librarian; Mumford expanded the Library staff of 1,400 to 4,500 and the budget of $9 million to more than $90 million. In 1975, Gerald Ford appointed historian Daniel J. Boorstin librarian; the new Madison Building, dedicated by Ronald Reagan in 1981, was completed under the Boorstin administration. In 1986, the Library's classified book collection consisted of more than 14 million volumes. It held over 70 million items of nonclassified materials including more than 36 million manuscripts. The Library employed a staff of 4,809, and its annual appropriation was over $279 million.[15] Boorstin retired in 1987, and President Reagan appointed James H. Billington of the Woodrow Wilson International Center for Scholars as Boorstin's successor.

The Manuscript Division

In 1867 Librarian Ainsworth Rand Spofford convinced Congress to appropriate $100,000 to purchase the Peter Force Collection, which he described as "the largest and most complete collection of books relating to America in the world which is now gathered on the shelves of the British Museum."[16] In 1882, Spofford persuaded Joseph M. Toner to donate his 40,000-volume collection to the Library of Congress. In the same year, Congress provided $20,000 for the purchase of the Revolutionary War collection of letter books and papers of Comte Rochambeau and also purchased a substantial collection of papers of Benjamin Franklin.

The acquisition of these collections and documents led in 1897 to the founding of the Manuscript Division, which is responsible for the care of and services related to the 23 sets of presidential papers that have been acquired over the years. This action was the result of recommendations made in 1888 by the Joint Congressional Committee on the Library, which noted that a systematic effort should be made to collect and preserve all manuscripts deemed of special value. The recommendations also stated that little had been done by the government regarding the preservation of valuable historical manuscripts, questioned the location of the public and private papers of the presidents of the United States since the time of Monroe, and recommended that when the new library building opened, a department of manuscripts should be established.[17]

The Microfilming Project of Presidential Papers

In 1957, Representative Paul C. Jones of Missouri introduced a bill to give the librarian of Congress the authority and funds to organize, index, and microfilm the presidential papers collections in the Library; because the Van Buren papers had already been indexed in 1910, they were only to be microfilmed. The funds for this project reached the Library of Congress in August 1958. By August 1965, 16 of the 23 collections had been indexed and microfilmed; by 1976 the seven final sets were completed. For each president, the Library of Congress prepared an index, which was published as part of the *Presidents' Papers Index Series*.

To locate individual documents of a particular president, it is essential to use the respective index. The indexes are all identical in arrangement. The introduction to each volume consists of a provenance, a description of the papers, a reel list, and instructions on how to use the index. Each index provides the names of writers and recipients of letters, arranged alphabetically and subarranged chronologically when the same name appears more than once. When a letter is not written by or to a president, it is indexed by the name of the writer and the recipient. The names of writers and recipients, the dates of the letters, and their location on the reels are shown for each entry. The indexes also mention the location of larger collections of presidential papers in other manuscript collections in the Library, and in other depositories. The restrictions to access to the papers in the Library of Congress have all been lifted. The provenances summarize the history of each set of papers, and how they were acquired by the Library. For each of the sets of microfilmed papers described in Part II, the provenances are the primary source of information.

To evaluate the size of the indexing and microfilming operation, one has to keep in mind that the task involved over 2 million documents reproduced on 3,000 reels of microfilm. The microfilm editions and the indexes have made it possible for researchers to examine presidential papers without coming to the Library of Congress. The Library has continued to acquire missing documents for the sets but the later additions have not all been microfilmed.

HISTORICAL SOCIETY AND SPECIAL LIBRARIES

The records of seven presidents are maintained in historical society and other special libraries. Special libraries usually have one primary objective: the support of the information and research needs of their parent organizations. In the case of societies and associations, this may include outside scholars with a serious interest in their special subject area.

The major collections of the papers of John and John Quincy Adams, Millard Fillmore, James Buchanan, and Warren G. Harding are deposited respectively in the historical societies of Massachusetts; Buffalo, NY; Pennsylvania; and Ohio. These societies were organized for the collection, preservation, study, and exhibit of state and local documents and memorabilia.

The Rutherford B. Hayes Library was established as a memorial library by close family members and associates to honor Hayes and to keep his papers, memorabilia, and books available for those who wanted to study his part in and contribution to American history. It was deeded by the president's son, Colonel Webb Hayes, to the Historical Society of Ohio, which maintains the facility. The Hayes Library served as a model for Franklin Roosevelt in the development of his presidential library at Hyde Park, New York.

In 1919, President Herbert Hoover established the Hoover Institution on War, Revolution and Peace Archives at Stanford University, his alma mater. He deposited all his papers in this library, which was by name and subject dedicated to the events preceding, during, and following the First World War. However, when the presidential library program was launched by Franklin D. Roosevelt, Hoover decided to take advantage of its provisions and established the Hoover Presidential Library in West Branch, Iowa, his birthplace. His presidential papers and those concerning his activities as secretary of commerce under the Harding and Coolidge administrations were moved from Stanford to West Branch. As a result, two facilities honor the memory of President Hoover.

THE NATIONAL ARCHIVES OF THE UNITED STATES

The story of official American records starts with the first meetings of the Continental Congress on September 5, 1774, when Charles Thomson was unanimously chosen by the assembly to serve as secretary to the Congress. After the reorganization of the government in 1789, Thomson deposited the congressional records at the Department of State, which became the custodian of essential documents; however, other agencies continued to store their own records.

The greatest dangers to the collection of historic and essential records over the years have been loss, deterioration of paper, and fires. The fires that played havoc with federal records started to attract national attention in the early 1800s when they destroyed valuable records in the War Department and the Treasury. In 1810, Congress showed a concern for archival responsibilities by establishing a Committee on Ancient Public Records and Archives of the United States, which reported that the "papers are in a state of great disorder and exposure; and in a situation neither safe nor convenient nor honorable to the nation."[18] In the end no action was taken, but the idea that the country needed a safe, permanent place to store its records had been born.

On August 24, 1814, the British burned the Capitol and the Library of Congress. In 1836, the Post Office and the Patent Office sustained losses by fire, followed by a Treasury fire in 1838. Louis McLane, secretary of the Treasury, reported to President Andrew Jackson that there was no secure place for documents in the State, War, and Navy departments. Jackson responded by requesting from Congress the erection of a suitable depository. However, before any significant progress was made at the Treasury, a fire at the Post Office received higher repair priority. Building materials already purchased for the Treasury were transferred to the Post Office. Treasury building repair did not reach completion until the early 1860s. In 1870, a fire did great damage to government buildings and records; a congressional committee was appointed and issued a report that aroused the interest of President Hayes, who requested a $200,000 appropriation for the construction of a fireproof building, but again, no action was taken.

A fire in 1877 destroyed part of the Department of Interior and became a landmark because it aroused for the first time a sense of urgency in Congress for a fireproof depository for federal records where different departments could store and retrieve their documents. In 1880 and 1881 fires damaged the War Department; over 40 fires occurred between 1881 and 1912. Delays and indecision finally gave way in 1896 when a bill was passed for a storage facility that was referred to as a hall of records. Funding for this project passed five years later, but construction did not start at the chosen site until 1926 and the National Archives building was not opened until 1934.

The recurring series of delays in establishing the National Archives, despite continual losses to fire or improper storage, is remarkable. Several factors may have been involved: a lack of strong conviction in Congress for its responsibility to preserve historic records; no organized group to keep the preservation issue before Congress long enough to achieve success; and the constant temptation to take the easy and cheap way out by storing documents in a leaky attic or damp basement where conditions would take their toll over time.

During the nineteenth century, while important records were being badly and inefficiently stored and substantially devastated, archival problems were studied but solutions never implemented. Between 1789 and 1903 all congressional records were deposited at the Department of State; in 1903 they were transferred to the Library of Congress and some 30 years later to the National Archives.

Several events strengthened the faltering drive toward the organization of an archives facility. In 1884, the American Historical Association was founded, and six years later it organized its Public Archives Commission. At that time, J. Franklin Jameson, generally considered the father of the American archives movement, came on the scene. Jameson received one of the first American Ph.D. degrees in history, and served from 1905 to 1928 as editor of the *American Historical Review,* and simultaneously as head of the Carnegie Institution's Department of Historical Research. He was president of the American Historical Association and concluded his career as director of the Manuscript Division of the Library of Congress. Jameson studied archives in Europe and was the leading advocate for the establishment of an American National Archives. He was supported by his former student, Waldo Gifford Leland, who, some 35 years later, was involved in the establishment of the Franklin D. Roosevelt Library.

Shortly after the turn of the century, Jameson and some of his colleagues concluded that the essential task for starting an archives movement was to find out where archives already existed in the United States. This investigation was undertaken by Claude H. Van Tyne and Waldo G. Leland in 1906. Their study of existing American archives was published in 1907 by the Manuscript Division of the Library of Congress as *Guide to the Archives of the Government of the United States.*[19]

In 1907, Jameson asked President Theodore Roosevelt, who was interested in the archives project, for space estimates from the secretaries of his administration. Roosevelt also corresponded on this topic with Herbert Putnam, the librarian of Congress, who supported the archives development but stressed that an archival function should not be added to the responsibilities of the Library.[20]

In 1908 the Public Archives Commission of the American Historical Association appointed a committee to study the preservation of federal records. Two years later this group reported that "records are in many cases stored where they are in danger of destruction from fire and in places which are not adapted to their preservation, and where they are inaccessible for administrative and historical purposes. . . . Many of the records of the Government have in the past been lost or destroyed because suitable provisions for their care and preservation was not made."[21] Consequently, the American Historical Association petitioned Congress for the erection of a national archives depository where the records of the government could be concentrated, properly cared for, and preserved.

In 1911, Jameson appeared before a House committee in support of this petition and entered into the records of the hearings a history of the movement for national archives. In 1912, Waldo G. Leland published his article, "The National Archives: A Program," in the *American Historical Review*,[22] continuing the argument that archives are recognized in all civilized countries as a natural and proper function of government.

In 1913, Congress authorized plans for an archives building not to exceed $1,500,000, but the outbreak of the First World War interrupted these plans until 1925, when President Calvin Coolidge recommended construction of a building for the records of the government. By that time, the construction of the building had become a national issue supported by the American Legion and the Daughters of the American Revolution. In 1926, Congress appropriated $6,900,000 and the secretary of the Treasury was authorized to develop contracts for the construction of the facility.

In 1930, estimates made to determine the quantity of government records to be accommodated indicated that over 3.5 million cubic feet were already in existence. When President Hoover laid the cornerstone for the new building on February 20, 1933, he said:

> . . . there will be aggregated here the most sacred documents of our history, the originals of the Declaration of Independence and the Constitution of the United States. Here will be preserved all the other records that bind State to State and the hearts of all our people in an indissoluble union.[23]

On December 9, 1931, Senator Reed Smoot introduced two bills to establish an organizational structure for the archives; they included provisions for the appointment of an archivist by the president with consent of the Senate and the establishment of an Archives Council.[24] Neither bill passed Congress. In 1934, as the new records building neared completion, Senator Henry Keyes of New Hampshire introduced a similar bill that also failed. In that same year, archives legislation introduced by Senator Kenneth McKellar of Tennessee and Congressman Sol Bloom of New York passed on April 16. Bloom's bill originally created a United States Bureau of Archives within the Department of Interior, operating under the administrative authority of an Archives Commission and headed by an archivist appointed by the president with the advice and consent of the Senate. However, with the assistance of J. Franklin Jameson, Senator Thomas P. Martin of New York introduced a bill to create a separate independent agency. The final Senate bill containing this idea passed on June 10, 1934. A compromise bill worked out between the House and Senate, the Archives Act, PL73-432, was signed by President Franklin D. Roosevelt on June 16. Congress also appropriated $50,000 to begin the agency's work during 1935.

While the building was still under construction, the president appointed Robert D.W. Connor as the first archivist. There were about 320 employees to be hired, equipment to be purchased and installed, and regulations to be written for coping with the millions of cubic feet of records scattered throughout the country. In addition, there were almost 18 million feet of motion pictures, 2.25 million photographic negatives, and 5,500 sound records to be dealt with in the Washington area alone, and untold quantities of records not yet counted in other states.

One of the major achievements of the Archives Act was that it broadened the National Archives' responsibility beyond the acquisition of historic documents into other and more modern media. One of the dreams of Jameson, the establishment of the National Historical Publications Committee (NHPC), was also realized; the NHPC received the mandate to make plans and recommendations for the writing and publication of historical works.

In 1941, President Roosevelt spoke at the dedication of the Archives Building in the following unforgettable terms:

> As President I accept this newest house in which the people's record is preserved—public papers and collections which refer to one period in our history. This latest addition to the Archives of America is dedicated at the moment when government of the people by themselves is everywhere attacked. It is therefore proof—if any is needed—that our confidence in the future of democracy has not diminished and will not diminish.[25]

In 1949, in accordance with the Federal Property and Administrative Services Act, the National Archives lost its status as an independent agency and was merged with the General Services Administration. The responsibility for administering presidential libraries was given to the Archives in 1955. The National Archives and Records Administration Act of 1984 re-established the National Archives as an independent agency, an event celebrated at the Archives by the distribution of oversized campaign buttons with the message "Free at Last."

The Office of Presidential Libraries

The Office of Presidential Libraries came into existence in 1964. Until then, the functions of supervision, coordination, and administration of presidential libraries were attended to by the U.S. archivist. Franklin D. Roosevelt had great confidence in Robert D.W. Connor, the first archivist, and selected him as his chief associate in bringing his library into existence. At their first meeting, the President voiced the opinion that "Presidential Papers including those in the Library of Congress as well as his own, should be in the National Archives."[26] Connor kept the development and later the actual management of the Franklin D. Roosevelt Library under his personal direction and saw to it that the position of director was given to Fred Shipman.

The concept that presidential papers should be preserved in presidential libraries that are branches of the National Archives was strengthened by the Roosevelt example. President Truman deplored the loss of presidential papers in the past and said that "such destruction should never again be permitted . . . because the truth behind a President's actions can be found only in his official papers, and every Presidential paper is official."[27] In 1949, he deposited some of his presidential films, scripts, and speeches in the National Archives. In 1950, he asked Archivist Wayne Grover to insert a clause in the draft of the proposed Federal

Records Act that would make it possible for presidents and high government officials to deposit their papers in the National Archives, and began to plan the establishment of his own library following Roosevelt's model.

The Presidential Libraries Act of 1955 empowered the General Services Administrator, to whom the archivist reported, to maintain and operate presidential libraries as presidential archival depositories. Presidents Truman and Eisenhower were assisted by the Archives in the arrangement and storage of their papers, and their libraries were developed with the help of the archivist's office. President Hoover took advantage of the provisions of the Presidential Libraries Act to transfer the papers relating to his federal service from Stanford to the Hoover Presidential Library in West Branch, Iowa. By 1957, the presidential library system had grown to four institutions; when Archivist Wayne Grover and his deputy Robert Bahmer felt that they needed assistance, Karl L. Trevor was appointed as special assistant for presidential libraries, serving from 1957 to 1964.

In January 1964, the Office of Presidential Libraries was established as a permanent entity in the Archives, and Herman Kahn, who had been the director of the Roosevelt Library, was appointed assistant archivist for presidential libraries. His job was to:

> . . . establish and coordinate policies with regard to Presidential Libraries, including programs for acquisition, preservation, and use of historical materials appropriate for deposit in the Presidential Libraries; maintain liaison with the incumbent administration and with officials of former administrations with regard to organization, storage and reference service on Presidential papers and other historical materials prior to the establishment of a Presidential Library . . . .[28]

The Office of Presidential Libraries and the presidential library system grew much more rapidly than predicted. In 1955, when the Presidential Libraries Act was passed, it was estimated that there would be 12 to 15 libraries within 100 years; due to the unusually large number of administrations since 1960, there will be 10 libraries to maintain in just over 30 years. The country's population increased dramatically, and the number of government records in general, and presidential papers in particular, grew exponentially. Computerization of the White House offices, which began during the Carter administration, will eventually reduce the labor intensity of records management, but will take considerable time and effort to implement. While it cost $64,000 to operate the FDR Library in 1955, its fiscal 1985 budget was $569,000.

A small number of Archives staff have maintained liaison between their agency and the White House, assisting the White House staff in the preparation and preservation of presidential records for eventual shipment to the respective presidential libraries, especially since the establishment of the Office of Presidential Libraries. As a result of the cooperation between President John F. Kennedy's staff and the Archives, the Kennedy papers were stored in temporary Archives facilities in Waltham, Massachusetts within two weeks of the assassination, and the organization of the Johnson papers was started. President Richard M. Nixon gave the Archives support functions a more formal setting; the liaison office was named the Office of Presidential Papers and Archives (OPPA) and moved into the White House early in the administration. Nixon was keenly aware of the problems of preservation of records and taken with the idea of recording history in the making, to the extent of establishing the White House taping system. The OPPA staff director, Jack Nesbitt, reported directly to H.R. Haldeman, the President's assistant for domestic affairs. President Nixon's resignation in 1974 resulted in the impounding of his papers by congressional action, in litigation still unresolved in 1988, in the Presidential Recording and Materials Preservation Act of 1974 and in the Presidential Records Act of 1978, all of which impact on the Archives' management of presidential records. Implementation of the Presidential Libraries Act of 1986 will further change the planning and funding of the libraries of future presidents. (See Chapter 2.) President Gerald R. Ford did not maintain the OPPA, but President Carter's papers were controlled very efficiently by Archives staff, resulting in a quick and well organized transfer of his papers to Atlanta after the end of his term. President Ronald Reagan first reduced and later reestablished the formal liaison with the Archives during his second term.

As the presidential library system evolved, each library developed some specialties reflecting their namesakes' interests, such as local and naval history for Franklin D. Roosevelt, America's role in world relief work for Herbert Hoover, and human rights for Jimmy Carter. The Truman Library's theme is the presidency; the Eisenhower Library emphasizes the Second World War; and the Johnson Library stresses education, civil rights, and public administration. These interests are frequently furthered by the private foundations connected with each library, but must be coordinated by the Archives staff. To keep the buildings and programs of the various institutions on a comparable course, the Office of Presidential Libraries follows the *Presidential Libraries Manual* [29] by which it coordinates the management, guidelines, budgets, and general directions of each library, while taking into account areas of diversity. For example, the directors of the libraries can use up to $1000 of their library's gift fund on their own authority, but larger expenses need the approval of the Office of Presidential Libraries. Each library has to submit a five-year program plan, an annual work plan, a quarterly narrative report, a quarterly statistical report, and other reports as required. Fiscal Year 1987 statistics issued by the Office of Presidential Libraries are found in Appendix 1.

Regular meetings of the directors provide cohesion for planning and cooperation on exhibits, research, and educational activities. Budgetary restraint has been stressed since the Office of Management and Budget in the 1970s was critical of some of the libraries' activities.

The Office of Presidential Libraries has been very successful in coordinating a system that maintains uniform operating procedures in attractive facilities staffed by exceptionally competent and helpful personnel; yet each of the libraries looks different, serves different clienteles, shows different exhibits and materials, and, most of all, projects the image and character of each president in a unique way.

2. Legislation Relating to Presidential Libraries

Following the precedent established by George Washington, all presidents have considered presidential papers their personal property to be taken home with them when they left office. They and their families often chose writers and historians to compile the stories of their lives and administrations, but, with few exceptions, they gave little thought to how their papers would be organized and stored to provide access for historical research. Franklin D. Roosevelt, a serious student of history, realized the importance of organizing the massive records of his administration so they would be accessible to historians. He established the concept of building a library to contain his presidential materials and to have this library administered by the National Archives, which came into existence under his administration. On July 4, 1938, he informed Robert D.W. Connor, the first Archivist of the United States, that he wanted to build a facility in Hyde Park which would contain the records of his presidency. The Franklin D. Roosevelt Library was established as part of the National Archives by a joint resolution of Congress in 1939 and became the first of the presidential libraries authorized by the 1955 Presidential Libraries Act (PL84-373). However, Roosevelt did not differ from his predecessors when it came to the question of ownership of the papers; they were his property which he donated to the United States.

The concept that presidential papers are owned by the president was rarely challenged until Richard Nixon tried to withhold some of his records from Congress during the Watergate hearings and after his resignation. These actions prompted the passage of the Presidential Recordings and Preservation Act of 1974 (PL93-526) and of the Presidential Records Act of 1978 (PL95-591); the latter ensures that, starting with President Reagan's administration on January 20, 1981, all presidential papers will be considered government property.

The substantial increase in the amount of records generated by each administration and in the cost of maintaining presidential libraries prompted Congress to set limits to the size of the library and museum complexes that a president can transfer to the National Archives in the future; these limits are spelled out in the Presidential Libraries Act of 1986 (PL99-323).

THE PRESIDENTIAL LIBRARIES ACT OF 1955 (PL84-373)

The National Archives were established as an independent agency in 1934; the Federal Property and Administrative Services Act of 1949 transferred the Archives to the newly created General Services Administration (GSA) as the National Archives and Records Service, placing nearly all archival and records management authority with the GSA Administrator, who delegated it to the archivist of the United States. The Federal Records Act of 1950, which repealed the National Archives Act of 1934, contained a provision, inserted at the request of President Truman, which authorized the National Archives and Records Service to accept the papers of the presidents and other public figures.

President Truman exchanged a number of letters with the General Services Administration in which he expressed his intention "to offer his papers to the Federal Government, either under the Federal Records Act of 1950 or as part of the contents of his Presidential Library, if and when it should be built."[1] As a result of this correspondence, it became possible for the National Archives to provide some assistance to President Truman regarding the arrangement and organization of his papers. Originally, he was not certain whether he wanted to deposit his papers in the National Archives or in a presidential library, but by July 1950, he had made his decision and the Harry S. Truman Library was incorporated.

By 1955, the National Archives and Records Service had developed a plan to standardize the acquisition of presidential papers and the administration of presidential libraries. Such an approach would place the papers under safe and professional management, organize them into a retrievable arrangement, and guard them against pilfering or loss. Their upkeep would be guaranteed in perpetuity and handled through public funds.

The legislative action for implementing such a plan got under way when three identical resolutions were introduced in the House of Representatives in June 1955 by John McCormack, majority leader, Joseph W. Martin, Jr., minority leader, and Congressman Edward H. Rees of Kansas. Representative McCormack summarized the principal benefits of the legislation as follows:

1. It provides a system for the preservation and use of presidential papers that accords with our Constitution and traditions.
2. It enables the government to acquire, as gifts, expensive archival depositories and equipment that can be used not only for Presidential papers, but also for the preservation of valuable federal records accumulated outside of Washington.
3. It gives scholars throughout the country easier access to these manuscripts by establishing resource collections in other parts of the country, stimulating interest in our history and government.[2]

As a result of the legislation, presidential libraries would become field branches of the National Archives; the records of the presidents, the land, and the building would be donated and the maintenance of the buildings would be financed from federal funds, admission fees paid by visitors, and the sale of reproductions of documents and publications.

Edmund F. Mansure, the GSA Administrator, pointed out that the resolutions proposed a foundation for the systematic preservation and use of the papers of the American presidency; while there was nothing mandatory in the legislation, it assured a president of the integrity of his papers, their orderly arrangement, and their eventual availability as historical records to the people.

Dr. Wayne C. Grover, the archivist of the United States, advised that the legislation should not set inflexible criteria for the acquisition of materials for these libraries and should leave specific details for the future. However, he did mention the following general guidelines:

1. The libraries should devote themselves to the acquisition of original source materials in paper and microform;
2. As national institutions they should concentrate on collections relating to national and international affairs for the period of the presidency;
3. As federal institutions they should avoid competition with state and local historical societies and should emphasize federal records and materials collected by the president, reflecting his personal and family interests.[3]

The legislation would authorize the GSA Administrator "to accept for deposit the papers and other historical materials of any President or former President of the United States or of any other official or former official of the Government, other papers relating to or contemporary with any President or former President . . . subject to restrictions agreeable to the Administrator as to their use; and . . . to accept for the United States any land, buildings and equipment offered as a gift for the purpose of creating a Presidential archival depository, and to maintain, operate and protect them as a part of the national archives system."[4]

The administrator would also be authorized to enter into agreements "with any State, political subdivision, university, institution of higher learning, institute or foundation, to utilize as a Presidential Archival Depository land, buildings, and equipment . . . to be made available without transfer of title to the United States, and to maintain, operate and protect such depository as part of the National Archives system."[5] This sentence had considerable impact on several of the future libraries because it allowed university campuses to be considered for sites of presidential libraries, a trend which brought the Johnson papers to the University of Texas in Austin, the Ford Library to the University of Michigan in Ann Arbor, and the Carter Library to Emory University in Atlanta, Georgia.

The legislation would make congressional authorization for each set of presidential papers unnecessary, although it would require the administrator to "submit to Congress a written report concerning any proposed depository with a description of the property and of the papers involved and an estimate of the cost of any additional necessary equipment and the annual cost to the United States for maintaining the depository. This report is to lie before Congress for 60 days before the Administrator may take title to property or enter into any agreement concerning it. Presumably, if Congress has not by the end of that period enacted legislation preventing the Administrator's further action, he may proceed to take title to the property or agree to administer it."[6]

The legislation had full bipartisan support and was so well designed that it encountered no problems in the House or Senate and was hailed by scholars, local advocates of new tourist attractions, and educators who saw in these new institutions significant educational facilities. The Presidential Libraries Act of 1955 (PL84-373) was approved by Congress and signed into law by President Eisenhower on August 12, 1955.

Except for authorizing the Franklin D. Roosevelt Library as part of the Archives' presidential library system, the act applied only to then living (Hoover, Truman, and Eisenhower) or future presidents. The work on the Truman Library in Independence, Missouri, was completed in February 1957. In accordance with the law, the GSA Administrator submitted a report concerning the deed of the site, building, and historical records to Congress; there being no objection, the transfer was completed and the Truman Library was dedicated in July 1957.

THE PRESIDENTIAL RECORDINGS AND MATERIALS PRESERVATION ACT OF 1974 (PL93-526)

After President Richard Nixon was elected in 1968, he immediately started to deposit some of his papers in the National Archives; early in 1969, he indicated plans to establish his own presidential library. A month after his resignation in August 1974, Nixon informed General Services Administrator Arthur F. Sampson that he planned to deed additional documents to GSA and to cooperate in the creation of the Nixon Library. Sampson signed an agreement that gave Nixon legal title and property rights to all papers, files, and tapes of his administration.[7] According to this agreement, Nixon and his heirs would be authorized to destroy documents and tape recordings between September 1, 1979, and September 1, 1984, or following his death, whichever would occur first. This agreement would have given Nixon possession of about 42 million documents. In case of acceptance, the United States would have gained only restricted access to the materials for a short period, and permanent access only to those papers that Nixon cared to designate for donation. Congress objected to this agreement and invalidated it by passing the Presidential Recordings and Preservation Act of 1974 (PL93-526), signed into law on February 11, 1975, by President Ford.

The law was enacted to ensure the preservation and public availability of the Nixon papers and related materials. Under the provisions of the law, the documentary materials that had already been impounded by the government as evidence in the Watergate hearings were transferred to the GSA, prohibiting their destruction. The law also specifically abrogated the Nixon-Sampson agreement, and established the National Study Commission on Records and Documents of Federal Officials to explore topics of ownership, control, disposition, and preservation of historic materials. Nixon challenged this legislation through the courts; the Supreme Court responded with the decision *Nixon v. Administrator of General Services*, in which it upheld the Presidential Recordings and Preservation Act of 1974. Justice Brennan, writing for the 7:2 majority, stated that "Congress can legitimately act to rectify the hit-or-miss approach that has character-ized past attempts to protect these substantial government and public interests in the records."[8] The Court's decision not only upheld the law, but went further by establishing some basic principles to govern the control of and access to presidential papers, taking into consideration the claims raised by Nixon concerning separation of powers, executive privi-lege, right of privacy, first amendment rights, and standards of control and access.

THE PRESIDENTIAL RECORDS ACT OF 1978 (PL95-591)

The report of the National Study Commission on Records and Documents of Federal Officials was completed in March 1977 and made two basic recommendations:

1. All documentary materials received or made by Federal Of-ficials in discharge of their official duties should be considered the property of the United States.
2. Federal Officials should be given the prerogative to control access to their materials up to 15 years after the end of their federal service.[9]

To address these issues, the Presidential Records Act of 1978 (PL95-591) was passed by Congress and signed into law by President Jimmy Carter on August 14, 1978. Taking effect on January 20, 1981, the act established public ownership of presidential records starting with the Reagan administration.

The law has the following major provisions:

* The ownership, possession, and control of presidential records shall be with the United States.
* As far as practicable, documentary materials should be categorized into presidential or personal records as they are produced or received in the White House.
* The president may dispose of presidential records which he consid-ers to have no administrative, historical, informational or evidentiary value, but must obtain the views of the Archivist—giving 60 days advance notice before taking action.
* After conclusion of a president's tenure, the custody, control, pres-ervation and accessibility of presidential records will be transferred to the Archivist.
* The Archivist is directed to deposit presidential records under his control in a Presidential Library or Archival Depository operated by the United States.
* Prior to leaving office, a president may impose mandatory restric-tions up to ten years on the public availability of certain types of information.
* The Archivist is to identify and limit access to the records in accordance with restrictions by a president prior to his leaving office.

- The vice president has the same authority and responsibility with respect to his records as the president.
- As long as the ex-president is living, he is to be consulted concerning the person who is to administer his papers.
- The documents to be considered for deposit include motion pictures, still pictures, and sound recordings from private sources that are appropriate.[10]

THE PRESIDENTIAL LIBRARIES ACT OF 1986 (PL99-323)

In 1979, members of Congress were startled to discover that the amount the country spent on its former presidents during that year exceeded the cost of the entire current White House operation. In 1955, the cost to maintain former presidents had been $64,000; this expense had increased by 1980 to an estimated $18,300,000. Senator Lawton Chiles stated in the first hearings on this subject on November 6, 1979, that the expenditures had grown "in 25 short years over 285 times."[11] He pointed out that this growth was due to new laws Congress had passed in 1964, expanding the services provided to former presidents. The senator stated that the purpose of the hearings was to conform more closely with the taxpayers' interest in economy in government. He was joined in his efforts by Senator David Pryor and the decision was made to draft legislation to reduce the cost of presidential libraries.

The Presidential Libraries Act of 1986 (PL99-323) requests that the U.S. archivist submit to Congress a written report concerning every planned presidential archival depository, describing the land, building, equipment, and papers to be given to the United States, and an estimate of the total annual cost to the government of maintaining, operating, and protecting the depository. No action is to be taken by the archivist regarding an archival depository unless there are sufficient endowments to fund its construction, land, and equipment plus 20 percent. Each facility is limited to a maximum area of 70,000 square feet, unless the donors deposit additional funds to cover the maintenance of a larger facility. Because these requirements do not apply to any president who took his oath of office before January 20, 1985, President Reagan is excluded from the new provision, but will be urged to comply. Proposed changes and additions to the existing presidential libraries will also have to be submitted to Congress for approval.

The law aims to raise additional funds for ongoing operations through endowment requirements, and imposes more effective cost control measures. The act establishes an account in the National Archives Trust Fund to which the archivist may solicit and accept gifts or bequests of money or other property for the purpose of maintaining, operating, protecting, and improving the archival depositories. The archivist may accept private gifts from state and local governments, and may authorize foundations and institutions to operate and maintain presidential libraries, thus privatizing the upkeep of these facilities. Proceeds from the sale of items in the gift shop as well as separate endowments made for the facilities are also to be deposited in this fund.

The 1986 act aims to save tax funds by preventing the erection of large and expensive monuments to presidents that must then be maintained by the government in perpetuity. The 70,000 square feet limit for archival depositories will severely restrict the space available for museum displays in future presidential libraries. The law therefore requires the archivist to consult with the secretary of the Smithsonian Institution and the National Capital Planning Commission to study the demand for, and the cost of establishing, a Museum of the Presidents, and the feasibility of financing and operating such a museum with nonfederal funds.

3. Guides to Presidential Records

Keeping records in order, and providing a method of arranging them in a way so that they can be retrieved, has been a problem throughout history. This chapter summarizes the bibliographic tools that can be used as guides through the maze of presidential papers, from Washington's early classification scheme through the automated information system under development by the Office of Presidential Libraries.

EIGHTEENTH- AND NINETEENTH-CENTURY COMPILATIONS OF PRESIDENTIAL PAPERS

No president was more concerned with the preservation of his own papers and of historical records in general than Thomas Jefferson. On February 18, 1791, he wrote to Ebenezer Hazard, who was engaged in collecting and preparing for publication early Virginia and American documents: "I learn with great satisfaction that you are about committing to the press the valuable historical and State papers you have been so long collecting. Time and accident are committing daily havoc on the originals deposited in our public offices. The late war has done the work of centuries in this business. The lost cannot be recovered but let us save what remains; not by vaults and locks which fence them from the public eye and use in consigning them to the waste of time, but by such a multiplication of copies as shall place them beyond the reach of accident."[1] Ebenezer Hazard's *Historical Collections; consisting of state papers and other authentic documents intended as materials for a history of the United States of America*, was printed in two volumes between 1792 and 1794 by T. Dobson in Philadelphia.

During the 1830s and 1840s Congress acquired the papers of George Washington, James Madison, Thomas Jefferson, and James Monroe. The Washington papers, arranged by the first president's own classification scheme (see Part II), were edited from the original manuscripts by Jared Sparks and published in 12 volumes in the 1830s.[2] In 1838, President Martin Van Buren approved an act of Congress to publish the papers of James Madison under authority of the Joint Library Committee of Congress.[3]

American State Papers. Documents, legislative and executive, of the Congress of the United States, selected and edited under the authority of Congress was published by Gales and Seaton in Washington in 38 volumes between 1832 and 1861. The contents of this publication are divided into 10 classes, covering foreign relations, Indian affairs, finance, commerce, navigation, military and naval affairs, the Post Office, public lands, and claims and miscellaneous topics, covering the period from 1789 to 1838.

Messages and Papers of the Presidents was compiled by James Daniel Richardson under the direction of the Joint Committee on Printing of the House and Senate, pursuant to an act of the 52nd Congress of the United States. This work consists of 20 volumes covering the period from 1789 to 1897.[4]

Messages of early presidents are included in *The Archives of the United States Government; A Documentary History, 1774–1934.* This is a scrapbook collection of 24 loose-leaf volumes of about 4,500 selected photo reproductions and copies of documents of congressional hearings, reports, bills, and presidential messages compiled in 1934 by Percy Scott Flippin under the direction of Robert D.W. Connor, the first archivist of the United States.

THE NATIONAL HISTORICAL PUBLICATIONS COMMISSION

Early in the twentieth century, J. Franklin Jameson urged the establishment of a permanent commission for planning a comprehensive and well-arranged scheme of government publications of historic documents. In 1906, he presented a paper to the American Historical Association entitled "Gaps in the Published Records of the United States History."[5] He persuaded the Carnegie Institution's Department of Historical Research to sponsor the first survey of significant American documents stored in federal facilities used as archives; this survey resulted in the publication of the first guide to federal records, Claude H. Van Tyne's and Waldo G. Leland's *Guide to the Archives of the Government of the United States*, first published in 1904, and revised and enlarged in 1907.[6]

Jameson's idea of a historical publications and research organization, however, was not realized until 1934 when he assisted in the drafting of the National Archives Act and was able to incorporate in this legislation a provision for the establishment of a National Historical Publications Commission (NHPC). Because the commission had no staff, little was accomplished before 1950 when the Federal Records Act was passed, giving the commission the authority to employ an executive director and editorial staff. The NHPC was "responsible for planning and recommending national programs for collecting, preserving and publishing archival and other manuscript materials and for encouraging and facilitating the execution of these programs by appropriate public and private institutions."[7] As a result of this new authority, the papers of Thomas Jefferson were published by Princeton University Press. In addition, NHPC arranged for publication of the presidential papers of John Adams, John Quincy Adams, James Madison, and Andrew Johnson as well as of such other American statesmen as Benjamin Franklin, Alexander Hamilton, John C. Calhoun, and Henry Clay.

THE NATIONAL UNION CATALOG OF MANUSCRIPT COLLECTIONS

In 1949, the Society of American Archivists and the American Association for State and Local History set up the Joint Committee on Historical Manuscripts, which included a representative of the Library of Congress. In 1951, the Library of Congress proposed to this committee the establishment of a national register of historical manuscripts. The NHPC was very supportive of the plan. Rules for cataloging manuscripts had to be developed, and it was decided that the register should include collections of the private papers of families and organizations, as well as of official government manuscripts, on both the national and state levels. By 1952, the *Annual Report of the Librarian of Congress* announced that the register would include all collections of historical manuscripts regardless of their subject. After various test runs and reviews by archivists and librarians, the only major change in the project was its name, which became the *National Union Catalog of Manuscript Collections.*

The first catalog cards for this series were printed in 1959, and the first printed volume of the *National Union Catalog of Manuscript Collections (NUCMC), 1959–1961* appeared in 1962.[8] Its 1,061 pages contained reproductions of cards for nearly 7,300 manuscript collections that were issued by the Library of Congress during 1959, 1960, and 1961, covering about 400 repositories in the United States. The series includes listings of presidential papers and has published 22 volumes, the latest in 1986, for the years 1980 to 1984. It reports on 2,479 collections held by 91 repositories of which 29 are represented for the first time. Since its beginnings, the *Catalog* has published descriptions of almost 55,000 collections located in 1,297 different repositories.

The basic guide to the collections in the Manuscript Division of the Library of Congress is the *Master Record of Manuscript Collections*, a printout that includes for each entry: birth and death dates; span dates of papers; container numbers; index; microfilm availability; restrictions; up to three terms describing the profession of the individual whose papers are collected; and the entry number for the *NUCMC*. The *Master Record* will eventually be available for online searching.

PUBLIC PAPERS OF THE PRESIDENTS OF THE UNITED STATES AND THE WEEKLY COMPILATION OF PRESIDENTIAL DOCUMENTS

The Public Papers and Addresses of Franklin D. Roosevelt, with a special introduction and explanatory notes by the President, were compiled and edited by Samuel I. Rosenman and published in 13 volumes between 1938 and 1950.[9] This scholarly and detailed publication served as a model for the series *Public Papers of the Presidents of the United States,* which was conceived in the fall of 1954 at a luncheon attended by Wayne Grover, Archivist of the United States, historian George M. Elsey, and two former Truman aides, David D. Lloyd and Kenneth Hechler. President Truman had pointed out that while the proceedings of Congress and the decisions of the Supreme Court had long been available in official series, there were, with the exception of Rosenman's work for the papers of Roosevelt, no complete public records of the messages and papers of twentieth-century presidents, such as had been compiled for earlier presidents by Richardson in *Messages and Papers of the Presidents.*[10]

A plan to develop such a series was brought to the attention of President Eisenhower's staff. The NHPC reviewed the proposal; realizing that there was no uniform official publication and that many presidential statements could be found only in the form of mimeographed White House releases or in the daily papers, the NHPC recommended the establishment of an official series in which presidential writings, addresses, and remarks of a public nature could be made available. This recommendation was accepted and appropriate regulations became effective in 1957. The regulations provided for the coverage of the present and preceding years. They stated that the series should only cover oral utterances by the president or writings subscribed to him and the materials must be in the public domain. Other limitations indicated that the releases should be communications to Congress, public addresses, press conferences, public letters, messages to heads of state, formal executive documents, and various other statements of the president. For editorial reasons, not all essential statements of presidents are included, but the coverage is quite complete.

In 1958, the series *Public Papers of the Presidents of the United States* was extended to include the years from 1953 to 1956. In 1959, the publication of additional volumes covering the entire administration of President Truman was authorized. The responsibility for the series rests with the Office of the Federal Register, a unit of the National Archives.[11] As of July 1987, the series consisted of the following sets of presidential papers:

- 4 volumes of Herbert Hoover
- 8 volumes of Harry S. Truman
- 8 volumes of Dwight D. Eisenhower
- 3 volumes of John F. Kennedy
- 10 volumes of Lyndon B. Johnson
- 6 volumes of Richard M. Nixon
- 6 volumes of Gerald R. Ford
- 9 volumes of Jimmy Carter
- 6 volumes of Ronald Reagan

The papers of President Hoover are based on historical materials held in the Herbert Hoover Presidential Library in West Branch, Iowa, and cover the period 1929–1933. Publication began in 1974, commemorating the centennial of Hoover's birth; the foreword is by President Richard M. Nixon. The papers of President Harry S. Truman, covering the period 1945 to 1953, were published between 1961 and 1966. The papers of President Dwight D. Eisenhower, under whose administration this series was begun, were published between 1958 and 1961. The series continued throughout the next administrations, each volume appearing with a one- to two-year delay until publication. The last volume of the

Reagan administration covers the papers through 1984 and was published in 1986.

A companion publication to the *Public Papers* series, the *Weekly Compilation of Presidential Documents,* was begun in 1965 to provide a broader range of presidential materials on a more timely basis. This well-indexed compilation provides the text for the volumes of the *Public Papers* series. Beginning with the Carter administration, the *Public Papers* series expanded its coverage to include all materials printed in the *Weekly Compilation,* such as the president's daily schedule, lists of nominations submitted to the Senate, Office of the Press Secretary releases, and other items of general interest.

THE PRESIDENTS' PAPERS INDEX SERIES

In 1957, Public Law 85-147 was passed to organize, microfilm, and index the papers of the presidents. This legislation resulted in the microfilm publication program of the 23 sets of presidential papers maintained by the Library of Congress. The Library produced a series of indexes describing the papers, listing the contents of the microfilm reels, and providing a subject index.

Similar indexes exist for the papers of the presidents maintained in historical societies and special libraries. The presidential libraries of the National Archives publish brief guides to the historical materials in their collections (see Parts III and IV).

OTHER BIBLIOGRAPHIC GUIDES TO PRESIDENTIAL PAPERS

In 1949, the National Archives published a *Guide to Records in the National Archives,* which was replaced by an updated edition in 1974.[12] The guide is divided into six parts; the fourth part contains records of the executive branch, including some presidential papers.

In 1961, Yale University Press, under the direction of the NHPC, published *A Guide to Archives and Manuscripts in the United States* by Philip M. Hamer.[13] It was designed to assist searchers in locating significant manuscripts, including papers of U.S. presidents, in libraries and archives. In this monumental work, 1,300 repositories in 50 states, the District of Columbia, Puerto Rico, and the Canal Zone are listed. In 1978, the National Historical Publications and Records Commission (previously NHPC) published the *Directory of Archives and Manuscript Repositories in the United States* for the dissemination of information about historical research materials; an updated second edition of the *Directory* appeared in 1988.[14]

In 1985, Dennis A. Burton, James B. Rhoads, and Raymond W. Smock published *A Guide to Manuscripts in the Presidential Libraries.*[15] This publication provides cross-indexed listings and short descriptions of the holdings of the separate presidential library collections from Hoover to Ford, thus, in effect, combining some of the finding aids of seven libraries in one volume.

PRESNET: AN AUTOMATED INFORMATION SYSTEM FOR PRESIDENTIAL LIBRARIES

Voluminous finding aids to each collection of papers are available to scholars using the presidential libraries. Between 1983 and 1985, the Office of Presidential Libraries conducted a feasibility study to determine whether an automated information system could improve access to information about presidential records held in the various libraries, standardize descriptive practices in all libraries, and simplify the chore of producing finding aids. The study determined that a number of archival functions could be automated and that automation would improve access and be cost effective.

An operational prototype of the manuscript processing and reference system, named PRESNET, was designed by a contractor and representatives of the Office of Presidential Libraries; at the same time an initial draft of a subject thesaurus based on the White House Central Files filing manual was prepared by a committee of archivists. In March 1986, the system was installed and a three-month operational test carried out in the Gerald R. Ford Library in Ann Arbor, Michigan. Data for a large number of collections were entered and all modules of the system were tested. The staff also experimented with retrospective conversion of existing finding aids.

Online entry and editing of data, and retrieval of information from PRESNET's automated database, will eventually provide significant efficiencies over manual preparation and searching of finding aids. Retrospective conversion of finding aids in the older libraries will be expensive and time consuming. In preparation for implementing an automated system, the staff of the Carter Library are preparing finding aids on computers in a fielded format that can be easily converted to PRESNET records without rekeying data. Implementation of PRESNET is expected to occur as part of an agencywide automation program of the National Archives and Records Administration that may begin in fiscal year 1989. This will eventually make it possible to access information about presidential as well as other federal records stored anywhere in the Archives system from any computer terminal with access to the Archives network.

4. Presidential Book Collections at Historic Sites

by Mark Carroll

Libraries at homes or places associated with presidents vary enormously in the level and importance of the collection, depending on the existence of a more formal library for that president, on the literary and research interests of the man himself, and on the kind of memorial honoring him.

A large number of the presidential sites are maintained as a public trust by the National Park Service (NPS), as mandated by Congress. Others are owned or maintained by historical societies, state and local governmental bodies, or house associations. Many are registered as National Historic Landmarks by the National Park Service.[1]

The role of books in these national shrines is a varied one, reflecting as far as possible the interests of the illustrious former resident. On a chair in the nursery of John F. Kennedy's boyhood home rests a copy of *King Arthur's Knights*, one of his childhood favorites. A family Bible is on display at the Abraham Lincoln boyhood home. Woodrow Wilson's Bible, on which he took the oath of office as governor of New Jersey, and twice as president of the United States, is in the drawing room of his retirement home in Washington. Other similar displays of actual copies associated with a president, or volumes substituting for them, add verisimilitude to the careful evocation of past eras striven for at these historic presidential sites.

In many of the homes, care is constantly exercised to augment existing collections with books known to have been owned by the president, or books that will enhance and augment knowledge about him and his life and service to the nation.

Of course, the list of sites associated with a president is not limited to birthplaces or residences. Tombs or other burial places and monuments of various sizes, shapes, and styles commemorate the life and service of the honoree to his nation. Although emphasis in this account is on homes, it is interesting to note the range and kind of memorials.

A National Park Service inventory of presidential sites lists the following types of properties: "birthplaces, boyhood homes, wedding sites, law and other professional offices, locations of military service, sites of Inaugurations and Inaugural Balls, official residences, Presidential retreats and private vacation homes, places of death, sites of burial, and memorials. The representative sites in all these categories differ dramatically in character and in state of preservation. The Presidents have lodged in or used log cabins, mansions, apartment houses, farms, roominghouses, and even quonset huts and tents."[2]

Few of these places have libraries or books directly connected with the presidential presence, and some presidents had at least a remote association with a great number of sites. However, given below is a brief outline of the main edifices and any book collections linked to our chief executives.[3]

LIBRARIES IN PRESIDENTIAL HOMES

George Washington (1789–1797) A state; several counties; our nation's capital; and numerous cities, towns, and geographical features throughout the land all commemorate George Washington's name and fame. Washington is most closely associated with Mount Vernon, his gentle Potomac estate, where the Mount Vernon Ladies' Association administers a research library that includes a 12,000-volume reference collection, some 15,000 manuscripts, and an 800-volume rare book collection, including 80 books belonging to Washington. Through gift and acquisition, its holdings are constantly being increased. A modern, climate-controlled library stack houses the collection, and each year the association reports the gift, loan, or purchase of books with known relevance to our first president.[4]

Other books owned by Washington, some 350 of them, are in the Library of the Boston Athenaeum, at 10½ Beacon Street, opposite the Massachusetts State House. Washington had willed his 1,000-volume library to his nephew, Judge Bushrod Washington, who later dispersed it.

Washington's birthplace in Westmoreland County, Virginia, is commemorated by a conjectural restoration built in 1930–32. It is a national monument, administered by the National Park Service, and includes a colonial "living farm" and a Morgan horse farm. The library at the site consists of 700 volumes centered on the years 1730–50.

John Adams (1797–1801) "The Old House," formally known as the Adams National Historic Site, was purchased by Adams 10 years before he assumed the presidency. It is located in Quincy (originally called Braintree), Massachusetts, the town where his birthplace still stands. He and succeeding generations of his family added to The Old House, which was deeded to the nation in 1946. "Whatever you write, preserve," wrote Adams, and the family archives, held by the Massachusetts Historical Society, provide the basis for a series of magisterial volumes illuminating the early life of the Republic. The library at The Old House, a separate building, was erected by Charles Francis Adams on the edge of the garden, and houses books that reflect the tastes and interests of four generations of statesmen and writers in this illustrious family. The National Park Service maintains and administers the property.[5]

Thomas Jefferson (1801–1809) No house in America so well reflects the personality of its builder and owner as does Monticello, that architectural gem that sparkles with the spirit, intellect, and civility of our third president. Set in rolling hills southeast of Charlottesville, Virginia, the estate where Jefferson spent 56 of his 83 years is rightly renowned as the epitome of the American classical revival. Harshly treated after his death, it was rescued in 1924 by the Thomas Jefferson Memorial Association and painstakingly restored to the grandeur invested in it by its creator.

Jefferson's library, situated in the southeastern corner of the mansion, is stocked with the sorts of books that he knew and used. His own holdings were sold to the government to replace the Congressional Library burned by the British in 1814. Ten wagons conveyed the 6,487 volumes to the Capitol after Congress appropriated $23,950 for the purchase.

Shortly after the sale, Jefferson began to assemble a new library, confiding to John Adams that "I cannot live without books." The library Jefferson subsequently assembled is now at the University of Virginia.

James Madison (1809–1817) The Madison family moved to Montpelier, near Orange, Virginia, in 1760. As secretary of state and later president, James Madison spent July through October of every year on the plantation. The house was recently willed to the National Trust for Historic Preservation and is now open to the public daily. Madison's library of several thousand books was bequeathed to the University of Virginia, but today, unaccountably, only 587 pamphlets remain of the collection. An additional collection of more than 700 books was sold at auction in 1854, five years after his wife Dolley's death. The majority of these books have never been located.

James Monroe (1817–1825) While Monroe was serving as U.S. minister to France, his friend Thomas Jefferson supervised the construction of Ash Lawn, south of Charlottesville, Virginia. Monroe used it as his country home for 25 years, through 1824. The house is now owned by the College of William and Mary. Some of Monroe's books, including a family Bible, are in a special collection in the William and Mary library, and copies are sometimes displayed at Ash Lawn. In his retirement, Monroe lived at Oak Hill, near Leesburg, Virginia, in a brick house that Jefferson helped to design.

The law office where James Monroe practiced between 1786 and 1789 is located in Fredricksburg, Virginia, and is open to the public. It contains furniture and belongings of Monroe and his wife, as well as some of the President's papers and books. Of special interest is the desk from his White House office on which he prepared his 1823 message to Congress, which contained what later became known as the Monroe Doctrine. Some 50 years ago, when the desk was moved, several secret compartments were discovered that contained Monroe letters; these are exhibited at the site.

John Quincy Adams (1825–1829) John Quincy Adams was born in Quincy, Massachusetts, in his father's farmhouse, which was deeded to him in 1803. The last 22 years of his life were spent at the family manse, The Old House, sometimes called "Peacefield," where he planted trees and worked the gardens, converting the estate from a working farm to a Victorian country gentleman's seat. Even as a teenager, he was a confirmed book buyer and reader, and his literary legacy includes a wide ranging collection of poetry, essays, and drama.

Andrew Jackson (1829–1837) Some 12 miles northeast of Nashville, Tennessee, set on 600 acres on Old Hickory Boulevard, is the white painted-brick residence of our seventh president. At the end of his presidency, he returned to the property, which he had purchased 33 years earlier, and lived there until his death in 1845. He is buried in the garden beside his wife. In the library of the home are some 600 books belonging to Jackson, including poetry, history, architecture, and military studies, as well as a family Bible. The Ladies' Hermitage Association has operated the estate since the turn of the century.

Martin Van Buren (1837–1841) In 1839 President Van Buren purchased Lindenwald, a New York estate a few miles south of the town of Kinderhook, where he was born. The original building, erected in 1797, metamorphosed from a Federalist into an Italianate style as successive owners adapted it to their particular needs. Van Buren lived there until his death in 1862, and the house has been little altered since then. A four-room library wing was added in Van Buren's day, but the house has only a small collection of letters, documents, and books. The house remained in private ownership until 1975, when it was acquired by the National Park Service. The 22-acre estate has been designated a National Historic Site and has recently been reopened after extensive renovation.

William Henry Harrison (1841) Early in the nineteenth century, while serving as governor of the Indiana Territory, Harrison built Grouseland, a brick Georgian mansion, in Vincennes, Indiana. He lived there while governor and later during periods between military campaigns. The house passed out of the Harrison family in 1850 and was for a time used for grain storage and as a hotel. The Francis Vigo Chapter of the Daughters of the American Revolution saved the house from being razed in 1911 and has maintained it ever since. The house reflects domestic furnishings of the early nineteenth century. There is a small genealogical collection. After 1814, Harrison lived on a 1,000-acre farm in North Bend, Ohio, leaving it in 1841 to serve his single month as president. The house burned in two nineteenth-century fires. The land is unmarked and in private ownership.

John Tyler (1841–1845) While president, Tyler bought a residence on the James River, in Virginia, and retired there to spend the remainder of his life. The home, called Sherwood Forest, is in private hands, owned by a Tyler descendant. There are some original furnishings and mementos of the president's life. It is a National Historic Landmark and is open to the public.

James K. Polk (1845–1849) President Polk's father Samuel built a two-story brick home in Columbia, Tennessee, in 1816. His son lived there only intermittently, and the house is maintained as the James K. Polk ancestral home. It was opened to the public in 1929 and is administered jointly by the State of Tennessee, the Polk Memorial Association, and the Polk Memorial Auxiliary. The small collection at the house museum includes Polk possessions and related artifacts.

Zachary Taylor (1849–1850) The redoubtable warrior who served but briefly in the White House has a number of forts, barracks, and battlefields associated with his life and times, but no major home survives. He lived in his father's house in Louisville, Kentucky, from the age of one year, was married there, and returned often for visits. The house has been restored by its private owners, and is not open to the public. It has been designated a National Historic Landmark.

Millard Fillmore (1850–1853) In his early pre-political career, President Fillmore taught school and practiced law in the village of East Aurora, New York. In the mid-1820s, he built the home that was to become his memorial house museum. He moved out after a few years, and the house was subsequently moved several times. It was acquired by the East Aurora Historical Society in 1975 and has been open to the public since 1979. Among the books furnishing the home are some from the White House, most probably part of the library that his wife Abigail assembled.

Franklin Pierce (1853–1857) The State of New Hampshire administers the Pierce homestead in Hillsboro, built by the President's father in 1804. It is a two-story wooden frame building that has been described as a handsome example of New Hampshire village architecture. It is a National Historic Landmark and is open to the public as a historic house museum.

James Buchanan (1857–1861) When he was secretary of state in 1848, James Buchanan bought the Federal style mansion and estate known as Wheatland, in Lancaster, Pennsylvania. It was to be his permanent home until his death in 1868. The home was the focus of his celebrated "front porch campaign" for the presidency, and today contains many of his household furnishings and books (some signed by him on the title page). It is a National Historic Landmark and is open to the public under the auspices of its owner, The James Buchanan Foundation for the Preservation of Wheatland.

Abraham Lincoln (1861–1865) Several conjectural log cabins symbolize and commemorate the rustic beginnings of our sixteenth president. One is the National Historic Site, south of Hodgenville, Kentucky, on land that his father had farmed. The property was acquired by the government in 1916, and the National Park Service acquired it from the War Department in 1933. A second cabin, about 10 miles away, has been built on the farm where Lincoln lived from 1811 to 1816. It is privately owned, but open to the public.

Another farm, near Gentryville, Indiana, was where Lincoln grew to young manhood, from 1816 to 1830. The log home is a replica representing the frontier life that Lincoln knew and is set in a living historical farm. His mother, Nancy Hanks Lincoln, is buried here. The site has been administered by the National Park Service since 1962.

The only home that Lincoln owned is in Springfield, Illinois, where he lived from 1844 to 1861, practicing law and advancing his political career. It is a two-story frame building near the city center, and has been the focal point of a National Historic Site since its establishment in 1971 under the aegis of the National Park Service.

Numerous other Lincoln memorials throughout the land frequently use books to underscore their Lincoln associations. For example, at Ford's Theater in Washington, DC, a National Historic Site, there is a research library of some 2,000 volumes concentrating on Lincoln's life and times.

Andrew Johnson (1865–1869) The only president who worked at the tailor's trade, Johnson settled in Greeneville, Tennessee, in 1827, and here plied his trade, entered politics, lived in two houses, died, and was buried. His shop is now enclosed within the visitor center of the Andrew Johnson National Historic Site maintained by the National Park Service. Across the street is the house where he lived and worked for two decades. Not far away on South Main Street is a two-story brick house where he lived from 1851 until he died in 1875. Several hundred reference books, plus 100 personal association items, are included in the site's inventory.

Ulysses S. Grant (1869–1877) Like Zachary Taylor, Grant's career is commemorated in many camps, battlefields, and bivouacs. After his noted service in the Civil War, Grant was presented by the citizens of Galena, Illinois, with a furnished two-story Italianate house overlooking the Galena River. Grant lived in it intermittently, and in 1904 his son deeded it to the city as a memorial. The State of Illinois acquired it in 1932 and restored it in the 1950s. There are Grant family items in the home, and the 300-volume book collection centers on the general's life and times and the history of the area. The building is a National Historic Landmark.

Rutherford B. Hayes (1877–1881) The Rutherford B. Hayes Presidential Center, Spiegel Grove State Park, Fremont, Ohio, includes the verandaed brick residence that was the Hayes home during the last two decades of his life, when he served as governor of his state and president. He enlarged the brick residence on several occasions, and he and his wife are buried there. His descendants presented it to the State of Ohio, stipulating that the house be reserved indefinitely for family use and that the state build a memorial library and museum.

The library/museum was opened in 1922, partially funded by Hayes' son Webb. It was enlarged in 1967 and is administered, like the home, by the Hayes family, the Ohio Historical Society, and the Rutherford B. Hayes and Lucy Webb Hayes Foundation.

Although described elsewhere in this volume, the library deserves special mention here, for it is regarded as the first presidential library on a modern scale, setting a useful precedent for later presidential library centers. The extensive collections include several thousand books owned by Hayes, on law, history, and religion, and include *belles lettres* and genealogical works. All are maintained in a special category in the library.

James A. Garfield (1881) The last president born in a log cabin, Garfield served only a few months before his assassination. He is commemorated at Lawnfield, his home in Mentor, Ohio, where he waged his successful "front porch" campaign. After his assassination, his widow completed a library wing. The 2½-story home was acquired from the Garfield heirs in 1936 by the Western Reserve Historical Society, which with the Lake County Historical Society and the National Park Service cooperatively administers the site. The library of this National Historic Landmark contains some 3,000 volumes related to Garfield and his career. On the grounds of the site stands a log cabin similar to Garfield's birthplace, as well as a small building that was once a library and served as his campaign office.

Chester A. Arthur (1881–1885) The National Historic Landmark commemorating this president is a row house on Lexington Avenue in New York City, where he took the oath of office. It is privately owned and not open to the public. A replica of his birthplace is maintained by the State of Vermont at North Fairfield and is open to the public. It is operated as an interpretive center and has no books in its display.

Grover Cleveland (1885–1889; 1893–1897) Many of the buildings associated with President Cleveland have burned or were torn down. The remaining significant home is a National Historic Landmark in Princeton, New Jersey, named Westland. It is a stucco-covered stone structure built about 1847. Cleveland lived in it in his final decade, retired but active in community and university activities. It is privately owned and not open to the public.

Benjamin Harrison (1889–1893) The site of another "front porch" presidential campaign was the Benjamin Harrison home in Indianapolis, Indiana, which Harrison occupied during the last quarter century of his life. He built the red brick house in 1875 and later added to it. The Arthur Jordan Foundation leases it to the Benjamin Harrison Foundation, which opens the house museum for public visits. In Harrison's library is a massive handmade bookcase and other artifacts. The building is a National Historic Landmark.

William McKinley (1897–1901) The only existing home for McKinley, who was gunned down by an assassin in 1901, is in Canton, Ohio. It was built for Mrs. McKinley's grandfather, and she was born there. The future president, then a congressman, and his wife used the house as their legal residence from 1873 until he was elected governor of Ohio in 1892. The building was remodeled several times, but has now been restored to its exterior appearance at the time of McKinley's residence. Privately owned and not open to the public, the house is listed in the National Register of Historic Places. McKinley's tomb is on a hill overlooking the city.

Theodore Roosevelt (1901–1909) The inventory of dwellings associated with our "bully" president is a rich and varied one. His birthplace on East 20th Street in New York City is maintained by the National Park Service with assistance from the Theodore Roosevelt Association. The North Dakota cabin he used while hunting and ranching in the late 1800s has been restored and moved to the Theodore Roosevelt National Park near Medora.

On September 14, 1901, Roosevelt was sworn in as president, just hours after McKinley's death, in the library of the home of Ansley Wilcox on Delaware Avenue in Buffalo, New York. Years later, public-spirited citizens of the city saved the home from demolition. Beginning in 1970 the National Park Service, with assistance from other organizations, began the home's restoration to its 1901 appearance.

Roosevelt's rambling retreat at Sagamore Hill, overlooking Oyster Bay on the north shore of Long Island, New York, was his permanent home. It was the summer White House during his presidency, and reflects his interests in hunting and a full strenuous life. Bookcases and book-shelves throughout the house are filled with volumes revealing the wide range of interests of the President and his family. Roosevelt wrote a great many books on history, hunting, wildlife, and politics, and these may also be seen at the home. In 1950, two years after the death of Mrs. Roosevelt, the property was purchased by the Theodore Roosevelt Association, which presented it to the American people as a gift in 1963.

William Howard Taft (1909–1913) The house in which President Taft was born, on Auburn Avenue, in Cincinnati, Ohio, remained his home until after his marriage. Decades later, like so many other presidential sites, it was considerably changed and fell into disrepair. In 1961, The William Howard Taft Memorial Association sought to rescue it, and in 1969 its administration was transferred to the National Park Service, which exhibits some books associated with President (later Chief Justice) Taft.

Woodrow Wilson (1913–1921) The son of a preacher, Woodrow Wilson was born in the parsonage of the Presbyterian Church in Staunton, Virginia. The brick Greek revival home is open to the public under the auspices of the Woodrow Wilson Birthplace Foundation and is a National Historic Landmark. Its library includes some 2,000 volumes, 1,500 photographs, and 100 letters.

Prospect, the home he occupied while president of Princeton University, still stands. The Tudor-style stone mansion with a four-story tower is used as a faculty dining hall. It is a National Historic Landmark.

Just before the end of his second term as president, Wilson bought a three-story red brick neo-Georgian house at 2340 S Street, in Washington's northwest section. Wilson died here in 1924. After his widow's death, the house and its furnishings were willed to the National Trust for Historic Preservation, which administers it as a historic house museum. One of the features of the house, which is a National Historic Landmark, is an 8,000-volume library.

Warren G. Harding (1921–1923) The 1920 Harding presidential campaign was another "front porch" exercise, the veranda in this instance being at 350 Mount Vernon Avenue, Marion, Ohio. Harding built the house in 1890, when he was the owner-editor of the Marion *Star*. His widow, who died in 1924, willed the house to the Harding Memorial Association, and it has been open to the public since 1926. Since 1979, the State of Ohio has operated the home, which is a National Historic Landmark.

Calvin Coolidge (1923–1929) The Plymouth Notch Historic District is regarded as a prime Vermont example of a turn-of-the-century rural village in a perfect state of preservation. Here, attached to the general store, is the 1½-story wooden house in which Coolidge was born. It has been restored to its appearance in 1872, when Coolidge was born on July 4. Across the street, where he lived from 1876 until graduation from college, is the family home in which he took the oath of office after President Harding died. Both houses are maintained by the State of Vermont and are open to the public. The entire village is listed on the National Register of Historic Places, and the homestead is a National Historic Landmark.

Herbert Hoover (1929–1933) West Branch, Iowa, at the time of Hoover's birth in August, 1874, was a growing farm community of about 350 persons. The two-room board and batten cottage in which he was born was once moved but is now restored to its original location. The National Park Service administers the National Historic Site, which also includes the Herbert Hoover Presidential Library-Museum.

Franklin D. Roosevelt (1933–1945) Like his distant cousin Theodore, Franklin Roosevelt was one of our most energetic and active presidents, despite his poliomyelitis. His birthplace at Hyde Park, New York, which was his lifelong home, was considerably altered after the President's father James acquired it in 1867; it was transformed over the years into a 35-room stone- and stucco-covered Georgian mansion. Franklin Roosevelt donated the property to the nation, and it was opened to the public in 1946 as a unit of the National Park Service. Some 3,000 books are placed throughout the house in brass grilled cabinets, open bookcases, and tables. All have been cataloged. Adjacent to the home is the first of the official presidential libraries established under the auspices of the National Archives.

Harry S. Truman (1945–1953) The main attraction of the Truman Historic District in Independence, Missouri, is the Gates-Wallace-Truman house, President Truman's home for over a half century. Now administered by the National Park Service, the 2½-story frame farmhouse was the home of Truman's wife, Bess Wallace Truman, from her childhood until her death. Mr. and Mrs. Truman lived in the house from their marriage in 1919 until his death in 1972. Furnishings and books reflect their long tenancy. The historic district surrounding the house contains homes and other buildings associated with them. Truman's presidential library contains the office (a replica of his White House Oval Office) he used from the time of its opening in 1957 until his death.

Dwight D. Eisenhower (1953–1961) The only home that General Eisenhower ever owned in his long and distinguished career was the farmhouse in Gettysburg, Pennsylvania, that he purchased in 1950. He used it as a retreat in his presidential years, and it became his retirement home. When asked about which building was significant enough to him to be designated a National Historic Landmark, he wrote that "our farmstead at Gettysburg would be the most suitable spot because it is the only home, truly ours, that has been acquired by us during almost a half century of public service that has led us to many corners of the world." The Eisenhowers deeded their farm to the National Park Service in 1967, and it was turned over to the nation after their deaths. The home contains Eisenhower's personal library of books on history, biography, literature, military doctrine, and art.

John F. Kennedy (1961–1963) The gray 2½-story frame house in which Kennedy was born in the Boston suburb of Brookline in 1917 was his home for the first four years of his life. The National Historic Site was repurchased by the Kennedy family in 1966 and donated to the National Park Service. The home has been restored to its 1917 appearance.

Lyndon B. Johnson (1963–1969) The famed LBJ Ranch, where President Johnson had installed an airstrip and hangar (also used for press briefings) to enhance its use as an alternate White House, is now part of Lyndon B. Johnson National Historical Park. The two-story stone and frame residence is still occupied by his widow, Lady Bird, but the exterior may be viewed from the grounds. The park, at Johnson City, Texas, also contains a reconstruction of his birthplace, a typical late nineteenth-century "dog trot," or center hall two-bedroom house. His boyhood home, also part of the park, has been restored to its 1925 appearance. The study collection at the park numbers some 2,000 volumes.

Richard M. Nixon (1969–1974) The National Park Service has proposed that Nixon's birthplace at Yorba Linda, California, be enhanced by an orchard (replacing a parking lot) so that the grounds could be "restored to the historic citrus-farm environment" of the early years of this century. The home is presently owned by the Nixon Birthplace Foundation, and the seven acres surrounding it are owned by the local school board. The Nixon Presidential Library will be built at this site.

Gerald R. Ford (1974–1977) Ford's birthplace in Omaha, Nebraska, where he was christened Leslie L. King, Jr., after his father, may be commemorated by transparent plastic columns, since the original home was destroyed by fire. A representation of the home, rather than a reconstruction, is the current preference of the planners. A garden now occupies the site. When he was three, Ford assumed his stepfather's name when his divorced mother remarried.

A Gerald R. Ford Museum is in operation at Grand Rapids, Michigan, in the district that he represented in Congress for 27 years. The Ford home in Alexandria, Virginia, which was his Washington residence during most of his congressional years and from which he moved to the White House after the first days of his presidency, has been designated a National Historic Landmark. It remains in private ownership.

Jimmy Carter (1977–1981) A Carter library, museum, and policy center has opened in Atlanta, Georgia. Sites commemorating Carter's birth and life are yet to be designated. The National Park Service's plan is to transform his former hometown of Plains, Georgia, into a memorial that will also celebrate the agricultural, educational, and social life of the South. Included in the plan are a shortline railroad and a campground. Other features would include Carter's current home, two previous residences, the hospital where he was born, his high school, and the Plains railroad station.

Ronald Reagan (1981–1989) Reagan's boyhood home, in Dixon, Illinois, has been acquired by the Ronald Reagan Home Restoration and Preservation Association. The two-story gable roof frame house is being restored to the period of the President's occupancy from 1920 to 1923.

PRESIDENTIAL BOOK COLLECTIONS IN THE LIBRARY OF CONGRESS

There are two notable presidential collections in the Library of Congress: the books of Thomas Jefferson, and the books and personal mementos of Woodrow Wilson.[6]

The Jefferson library, housed in the Rare Book and Special Collections Division, contains volumes purchased from Jefferson in 1815 to replace the books lost when the British burned the Capitol. A number of those 6,487 volumes were themselves lost in another fire in 1851. Those that remain are kept as a unit. Many bear Jefferson's markings and the original Library of Congress classifications and bookplates. With the collection are some books from Jefferson's third and final library, sold at auction in 1829, three years after his death.[7]

The personal library of Woodrow Wilson, installed in the room named for him adjacent to the Rare Book and Special Collections Division, was presented to the Library of Congress in 1946 by Edith Bolling Galt Wilson. It consists of 6,792 volumes and 1,122 pamphlets associated with every period of his life, from childhood books and school texts to monographs and specialized studies. There are also hundreds of inscribed volumes given to him during his presidency and in later years, as well as diplomas, medals, and other momentos. The collection complements the collection of presidential papers donated to the Library by Mrs. Wilson beginning in 1939.

THE WHITE HOUSE LIBRARIES

Every four years, for a half century, representatives of the booksellers of the nation have taken themselves to the White House to present a selection of current American books to the president of the United States. This ceremony, first held in 1930, was to commemorate an addition to a White House library established to provide a resource for the recreational reading of the presidential family.[8]

Before this personal library was established, library resources at the White House were spotty at best. In 1929, Douglas A. Watson visited President Hoover and heard the President deploring the lack of books in the White House. Watson then suggested the library idea to bookman John Howell of San Francisco. The councils of the booksellers' association quickly warmed to the idea, and in 1930, 500 books were selected and donated. After 1933, 200 new books were added every four years until Richard Nixon's second term, when no donation was made.[9] A selection of 250 books was presented to President Ford in 1975. In March 1977 250 carefully chosen volumes were presented to Rosalynn Carter on her husband's behalf. An additional 20 books, especially chosen for the President's daughter Amy, were added to the presidential gift.

In the first term of President Ronald Reagan, it was not possible to schedule an in-person presentation, so the books were shipped to Washington without an attendant ceremony. In his second term, a presentation was made at the White House in May 1987. The gift of 200 books, nominated and chosen by the board of directors and staff of the Booksellers' Association, was designed to be a balanced representation of recently published works.

Before this thoughtful undertaking by the country's booksellers, the place of books in the nation's first residence was minimal. It was Abigail Powers Fillmore who caused the first library to be established in the executive mansion. Congress appropriated $2,000 in 1850, and Mrs. Fillmore, a former schoolteacher, chose a range of books that included British and American literature, American history, politics, and law.

This appropriation continued until 1880, when government funds for the purpose ceased. In the later years of the nineteenth century, presidents often took the books with them when they left the White House. Thus the importance of the booksellers' gift, which routinely provided current reading matter.

Other White House libraries include Mrs. Kennedy's reference and recreational library for residents and staff. Established in 1962, it concentrates on American history and the presidency. An eminent committee of historians and editors of presidential papers chose the original deposit. Many of the books were donated. This collection, which is a responsibility of the White House Historical Association, is cataloged and maintained by the Library of Congress. There are also reference and research libraries, one of them devoted to material relating to the history of the White House and its collections.

In the Old Executive Office Building, that splendid 1889 monument to Victorian grandeur next to the White House, there are also White House libraries. The old War Department Library, an ornate balconied three-story court, now houses the White House Law Library. The general White House Library and Research Center is located in the imposing four-story former State Department.

The buildings associated with our presidents reflect the diverse natures of the heritage, life, and interests of our chief executives, and of the nation they led. They provide a unique approach to the history of our nation, and the study of our presidents and ourselves.

PART II

Presidential Papers in the Manuscript Division of the Library of Congress

5. The Early Presidents

GEORGE WASHINGTON
First President—Federalist
1789–1797

Washington's contributions to American history were uniquely significant; without his military and civilian leadership, personal character and prestige, this Republic would not have come into existence in the form we know today. His military acumen helped win the Battle of Yorktown, from which the British could not recover; the assurance of his leadership helped the Constitutional Convention produce a strong document that could be ratified by the nine participating states; his support was vital to enactment of the Bill of Rights during his first term.

Born February 22, 1732, on Pope's Creek Farm in Westmoreland County, Virginia, Washington moved with his family at the age of two to a farm that later became part of his Mount Vernon estate. When Washington was 11 his father died and his half brother Lawrence became head of the family. Lawrence was 14 years older than George, and was his idol and guide until his death in 1752. At age 16 Washington started to work as an assistant surveyor and did his first large surveying assignment for Lord Fairfax, a relative of Lawrence's wife. In 1753, he requested a military commission from Fairfax and was sworn in as major. There are no records of where he was educated or how much education he received, but he spoke and wrote incisively at an early age, as shown in his diaries and extensive correspondence. He read a great deal to gain information on a variety of topics, writing once: "I conceive a knowledge of books is the basis upon which other knowledge is to be built."[1] From 1754 to 1763 he participated in the French and Indian War, was promoted to colonel in command of all Virginia troops, and served from 1759 to 1769 in the Virginia House of Burgesses until it was disbanded because of its protest against the British Stamp Act. During the same period, Washington managed and expanded his land holdings around Mount Vernon and reluctantly reached the conclusion that cooperation with England had no future.

In 1774 and 1775 he participated in the First and Second Continental Congresses as a member of the Virginia delegation; in 1776 he was elected commander-in-chief of the Continental Army and endured the horrors of Valley Forge in the winter of 1777–78. In 1781, he won the decisive Battle of Yorktown and resigned his commission in 1783 after the Treaty of Paris was signed. When the Articles of Confederation proved ineffective, Washington and other leaders, in search of a stronger central government, hosted the Mount Vernon Conference in 1785, which led to the Annapolis Convention. This latter meeting was poorly attended, but it set the stage for the Constitutional Convention of 1787, over which Washington presided. There was unanimous agreement by all leaders of the Constitutional Convention that Washington should serve as first president of the country.

During his first term, the main task of the president was to appoint competent people to key positions and to have the new machinery of government start to function. Washington's efforts to establish normal trade relations abroad had to wait until his second term. Negotiations with the Indians continued through both of his terms. The Bill of Rights was passed by Congress in 1789 and was ratified by the states in 1791.

His second term saw the resignations of Jefferson and Hamilton from his cabinet; the signing of the Jay Treaty; the outbreak of the Whiskey Rebellion, which Washington put down energetically; and the orderly preparation for his retirement. In May 1797, two months after returning to Mount Vernon, he wrote of his retirement plans, "To make and sell a little flour annually, to repair houses going fast to ruin, to build one for the security of my papers of a public nature, and to amuse myself in agricultural and rural pursuits, will constitute employment for the next few years I have to remain on this terrestrial globe."[2]

When Washington died on December 14, 1799, there was national agreement to Henry Lee's eulogy of Washington as "first in war, first in peace, and first in the hearts of his countrymen."[3]

The Washington Papers

During the Revolutionary War, Washington, always aware of the value of his papers, was concerned for their safety. Because the number of his papers grew steadily, he wrote on April 4, 1781, to John Hancock that the papers had to be kept in order by a competent staff and requested that a "man of character" and a "set of writers" be assigned to work at this task. When Washington received approval for his request, he appointed Lt. Col. Richard Varick as his recording secretary and also gave him the responsibility of organizing his wartime papers. Varick, a former member of Benedict Arnold's military unit, was cleared of any connection with the well-known traitor; he had a solid, though insignificant, military record, and had previously served as secretary to General Philip Schuyler.

To handle the required sorting, copying, and assembling of papers, Varick installed a workshop in Poughkeepsie, New York, which operated from May or June 1781 to January 1784. During this period, his staff arranged all public and private papers of Washington from 1775 to the end of 1783. In order to have the papers properly arranged, Washington developed a classification scheme that he outlined in a memorandum attached to Varick's letter of appointment. The papers were to be grouped in the following classes:

1. All letters to Congress, Committees of Congress, the Board of War, Individual Members of Congress in their public Characters and American ministers Plenipotentiary in Foreign Courts.
2. All letters, Orders, and Instructions to Officers of the line, of the Staff, and all other Military Characters.
3. All letters to Governors, Presidents and other Executives of States, Civil Magistrates and Citizens of every Denomination.
4. Letters to Foreign Ministers, Foreign Officers, and subjects of Foreign Nations not in the immediate service of America.
5. Letters to Officers of every Denomination in the service of the Enemy, and to British subjects of every Character with the Enemy, or applying to go in to them.
6. Proceedings of Councils of War in the Order of their dates.[4]

A seventh class to cover Washington's private correspondence was established later; the issue of separating private from official records has remained a touchy one to this day. Varick was instructed to set up a chronological arrangement within each class and to supervise the recording in uniform "Books of Entries" by clerks. The letters to Washington were to be similarly grouped, recorded, filed, and stored in boxes. A number of clerks were hired who had to sign an oath of office which read in part:

> that I will not read to, or permit to be read by any person not employed in the service of the aforesaid [Varick] any of the said papers or any others in the Office of the said Lt. Col. Varick, and that I will not take or with my privity or knowledge permit to be taken from the office of said Lt. Col. Varick any original Papers or copy or Extract.[5]

On October 1, 1781, Varick wrote to Washington that the task was "a continued series of drudgery" and "two four hour shifts, six days a week were all a transcriber could face." During the next two and a half years, Washington encouraged Varick to complete the work. When Washington spent time in Poughkeepsie, he had discussions with Varick, including complaints from Varick's staff about their compensation. By the end of 1783, 37 folio volumes had been produced, each bound in tooled sheepskin with vellum backs, and each containing its own index. In June 1783, Washington purchased six hair trunks in which he planned to ship his papers. He wrote in November, when the shipment under the direction of Col. Howe, whom Washington put in charge, took place, that "the wagons contain all my Papers, which are of immense value to me."[6] After receiving the volumes at Mount Vernon in early 1784, Washington wrote to Varick that he had earned his "entire approbation and was greatly satisfied in having his papers properly arranged and correctly recorded." He continued to acknowledge that "neither the present age or posterity will consider the time and labor which have been employed unprofitably spent."[7] After completing this task, Varick became Speaker of the New York Assembly, attorney general of New York, and mayor of New York City.

In 1782 and 1783, Reverend William Gordon requested the use of Washington's papers to write a history of the American Revolution; he was turned down by Washington, who explained: "It appears to me impracticable for the best Historiographer living, to write a full and correct history of the present Revolution who has not free access to the Archives of Congress, those of individual states, the papers of the Commander-in-Chief, and Commanding Officers of separate departments. Mine—while the War continues—I consider as a species of Public property, sacred in my hands."[8] During his temporary retirement before his election to the presidency, Washington employed Robert Lewis to transcribe his early letterbooks from the period 1755 to 1758.

When Washington left Mount Vernon for New York City in April 1789 to assume his duties as first president of the United States, his papers were left at his estate. A month after his inauguration, he told Matthew Carey, printer, bookseller, publisher, and author, who wanted to copy some documents relating to the battles of the Revolution, that "all the papers in my possession, relative to the Revolution are packed up in the trunks and boxes in Mt. Vernon."[9] During the presidential years, Washington's correspondence with each of the government departments—State, Treasury, and War—and with Congress, was transcribed in a separate series of letterbooks. At the end of his second term, Washington employed Tobias Lear and Bartholomew Dandridge, two former secretaries, to go over his papers and pull those which should be given to John Adams, his successor. The remainder of his presidential papers were packed and shipped to Mount Vernon. As the first president, many of Washington's actions were precedent setting, so no one questioned his decision to take his presidential papers to his home upon his retirement, just as he had done with his military papers.

In April 1797, Washington wrote to James McHenry that he planned to have a building constructed "for the accommodation and security of my military, civil and private papers which are voluminous and may be interesting."[10] He was never able to carry out this plan. Throughout his short retirement at Mount Vernon, Washington was concerned with bringing the collection of his papers to completion and keeping them in good order. When he found out in 1797 that some of his papers had been borrowed by Charles Lee, his attorney general, he promptly arranged for their return. To get his papers in better order he employed Albin Rawlins as assistant to copy and record letters and other papers, in addition to other duties. Shortly before his death, he asked his friend Tobias Lear to "arrange and record all my late military letters and papers. Arrange my accounts and settle my books, as you know more about them than any one else, and let Mr. Rawlins finish recording my other letters which he has begun."[11]

In his will, Washington left to his nephew Bushrod Washington "all the Papers in my possession, which relate to my Civil and Military Administration of the affairs of this Country ... and such of my private

Papers as are worth preserving."[12] Tobias Lear began to look over and arrange the papers shortly after the President's death, and Bushrod Washington discussed with him the preparation of a biography of his uncle. Lear was to arrange the papers and do the preliminary work and Bushrod Washington would do the writing. Lear spent eight months sorting the papers during which time he came across the personal correspondence between George and Martha Washington, which he turned over to Mrs. Washington. She seems to have burned all but two of these letters, which were saved by accident.

Bushrod Washington and Lear did not proceed with their plans concerning the biography; Bushrod turned the task over to Chief Justice John Marshall, who worked on the biography between 1803 and 1807 at his home in Richmond, Virginia, where many of the president's papers had been sent to him by Bushrod Washington. Many of the papers remained at Marshall's home and others were sent back and forth between Richmond and Mount Vernon while the two men worked on a revision of the biography and, between 1823 and 1825, on what was to be a three-volume edition of Washington's letters.

In 1819, Bushrod Washington complained in a letter to James Madison that "the papers sent to the Chief Justice, and which are still in Richmond, have been extensively mutilated by rats and otherwise injured by damp as he not long since informed me."[13] Marshall returned what he thought was the bulk of the papers to Washington in 1823, but actually kept many others until 1827. Washington, in contrast, took good care of the papers in his possession, which were stored in his offices at Mount Vernon. Unfortunately, he loaned and gave away many papers to close friends of the President, such as General Lafayette, the widow of Alexander Hamilton, and James Madison. Some of these letters were returned—others were not. In some cases original letters were taken away and copies left behind to replace them. William Sprague, who was working on an autograph collection of the signers of the Declaration of Independence and the Constitution, obtained Bushrod Washington's permission to "take whatever letters he might choose from General Washington's voluminous correspondence provided that he would leave copies in their stead."[14]

Jared Sparks, the editor of the *North American Review*, became interested in compiling an edition of Washington's writings in 1824. He asked Bushrod Washington for access to the papers, but at first was refused. In 1827, Washington gave Sparks permission to look through the papers at Mount Vernon, and by 1828, he allowed him to take some of the papers to Boston to work on them. In November of 1829, before Sparks had made much progress with his work, Bushrod Washington died and left a will in which he deeded all papers to his nephew George Corbin Washington, a lawyer and member of Congress, who moved the papers that remained in Mount Vernon to his office in Georgetown. Sparks continued with his project, and his 12-volume edition of *The Writings of George Washington*[15] was published between 1834 and 1837.

Over the years, government officials had often asked permission from Bushrod and George Corbin Washington to consult the Washington papers. In 1833, Secretary of State Louis McLane asked George Corbin

Washington to deposit the papers in the Department of State. On January 3, 1834, Washington answered that he would be willing to deposit the papers, as soon as Jared Sparks had finished with them, for a sum that would be mutually satisfactory, but would withhold those which were "of a private nature, or which it would obviously be improper to make public."[16] McLane reported this to Congress and agreed to pay $35,000 for the papers, an amount which both Houses approved. The papers were delivered in small batches until 1836.

The government checked the Washington papers that had been delivered against Spark's edition of Washington's writings and found that certain items were missing and that some copies had been substituted for originals. In 1849, the Department of State agreed to pay George Corbin Washington an additional $20,000 for the remainder of the papers in his possession. In 1867, the Library of Congress purchased the Peter Force Library, which contained many valuable Washington items. In 1888, President Grover Cleveland and Secretary of State Thomas F. Bayard initiated a plan to publish all historical documents on deposit in the Department of State. As a result, the *Writings of George Washington*, edited by Worthington C. Ford, appeared between 1889 and 1893.[17] Between 1889 and 1892 Congress appropriated $14,000 to restore, bind, and mount the papers of the Continental Congress and those of Washington, Madison, and Monroe.

In 1904, the George Washington papers in the Department of State were transferred to the Library of Congress, except for three letterbooks containing Washington's correspondence with the Department. Many of the Washington manuscripts were separated from the main body of the papers over the years and some of the private papers held by Washington family members were later sold to private collectors, historical societies, and libraries. In the late 1920s and 1930s, the Library of Congress assembled photocopies of Washington manuscripts from other institutional and private collections to supplement the Washington papers. The Library cooperated closely with John C. Fitzpatrick, the editor for the United States Washington Bicentennial Commission of *The Writings of George Washington from the Original Manuscript Sources, 1745–1799*, which was published by authority of Congress in 39 volumes between 1931 and 1944.[18] A microfilm edition of seven series, containing 64,786 documents, was issued in 1964 by the Library of Congress Manuscript Division. More papers have been added since and it is estimated that the Library of Congress has, in originals and reproductions, about 95 percent of extant Washington papers. Other depositories of the original papers are at the Huntington Library in San Marino, California, the Historical Societies of Virginia and Pennsylvania, the Virginia State Library, Yale University, and the Detroit Public Library.

The Washington Papers in the Library of Congress

Series	Reels
1. Exercise Books and Diaries. 1741–99. 43 vols.	
A. Exercise Books. 1741–47, 1748. 3 vols.	1
B. Diaries. 1748–99. 36 vols.	1–2
C. Surveys. 1749–52. 4 vols.	2
2. Letterbooks. 1754–99. 41 vols.	2–14
3. Varick Transcripts. 1775–83. 44 vols.	
A. Continental Congress. 7 vols.	14–16
B. Continental and State Military Personnel. 16 vols.	16–22
C. Civil Officials and Citizens. 5 vols.	22–24
D. Foreign Officers and Subjects of Foreign Nations. 2 vols.	24
E. Enemy Officers and British Subjects. 1 vol.	24–25
F. Continental Army Council Proceedings. 3 vols.	25–26
G. General Orders. 7 vols.	26–28
H. (Originally P.) Personal Correspondence. 3 vols.	28–29
4. General Correspondence. 1697–99. 298 vols.	29–115
5. Financial Papers. 1750–96. 34 containers	115–117
6. Military Papers. 1755–98. 26 containers	
A. Orderly Books and Military Records. 1755–83. 8 containers	117
B. Captured British Orderly Books. 1777–78. 8 vols.	117–118
C. Miscellaneous Military Records. 1769–98. 12 containers	118
7. Applications. 1789–96. 32 vols.	119–124
8. Miscellaneous Papers. ca. 1775–99. 16 containers	
A. Recipients' Copies of Washington Letters. 1 container	124
B. Certificates of Washington's Degrees and Honors. 2 containers	124
C. Surveys. 1 container	124
D. Notes, Extracts, and Forms. 12 containers	124

THOMAS JEFFERSON
Third President—Democratic-Republican
1801–1809

Thomas Jefferson was born in 1743 at Shadwell in Albemarle County, Virginia. He inherited from his father, a planter and surveyor, several thousand acres of land, and from his mother a high social position among the Virginia gentry. He attended the College of William and Mary in Williamsburg, graduated in 1762, and spent the next five years there studying law under George Wythe, one of the foremost legal scholars of the time. He was admitted to the Virginia bar in 1767.

Jefferson's public service career started in 1769 when, at the age of 26, he was elected to the House of Burgesses, where his first action was the introduction of an unsuccessful bill to allow owners to free their slaves. In 1770, a fire destroyed his home, Shadwell; in 1772, he married Martha Wayles Skelton and started to build a new residence at Monticello, not far from his former home. As relations between the colonies and Great Britain deteriorated, Jefferson was increasingly drawn into the conflict and joined a small group of Virginia patriots, including Patrick Henry, in forming colonial committees against Great Britain's political and economic tyranny. Jefferson drafted a number of exceptionally well-written resolutions, among them "A summary view of the rights of British America," which was read at the August 1774 Virginia Convention and considered too revolutionary for adoption, but was widely distributed and launched Jefferson's writing career. When he came to Philadelphia in 1775 as a Virginia delegate to the Second Continental Congress, John Adams commented on his "reputation for literature, science, and a happy talent for composition."[19] Jefferson was appointed to a five-man committee, which included John Adams and Benjamin Franklin, to draft an official declaration of independence from Great Britain. The Declaration of Independence was approved by the Congress on July 4, 1776; while the document underwent various changes, it remained largely the work of Thomas Jefferson.

Jefferson continued to serve in the Virginia legislature until 1779. He worked on the revision of many state laws, including the passage of a bill for religious freedom that later became the basis for the First Amendment. From 1779 to 1781 he held the office of governor of Virginia. His wife's death in 1782 threw him into a deep depression, and he never remarried. He did not return to public life until 1783, when the state legislature elected him again as a delegate to the Confederation Congress. His contribution during these sessions included his "Notes on the establishment of a Money Unit," proposing a sound currency system, and the draft of a bill for organizing the government of the Northwest Territory, which prohibited slavery in the future states. In 1784, Congress sent him to Paris to negotiate commercial treaties with major European countries; he served as minister to France from 1785 to 1789.

During his absence, the Constitution was adopted; soon after his return, he was invited by George Washington to become secretary of state. He served in this position from 1789 to 1793, resigning because of disagreements with Alexander Hamilton. He co-founded with James Madison the Democratic-Republican party and ran for president in 1796. He lost the presidential election by three electoral votes and served as vice president under John Adams from 1797 to 1801. He had hoped that close cooperation with Adams would reduce the influence of Alexander Hamilton and the Federalist party, but political events combined to strengthen the Federalist position.

In 1800, Jefferson won his campaign for the presidency and served two terms. His many successful policies as president included the use of the young navy to defeat the Barbary pirates who had been threatening America's navigation rights. The interference of Great Britain and France with American navigation resulted in the passage of the Non-Intercourse Act of 1806 and the Embargo Act of 1807. He sent the Lewis and Clark expedition to explore the West and negotiated the Louisiana Purchase from France, which doubled the land area of the United States.

After his White House years, Jefferson retired at age 66 to Monticello. There he worked on improving the home he had built with great skill, imagination, and loving care. He also founded the University of Virginia at Charlottesville, designing the buildings, planning the courses of study, and acting as rector. The first state university in the United States, the University of Virginia opened its doors a year before he died. Much of his time during retirement was spent keeping in contact with his friends and associates through correspondence, and in writing on many topics. Having been invited to attend the celebration of the 50th anniversary of American independence, Jefferson, feeling too feeble to accept, wrote: "May it be to the world the signal of arousing men to burst the chains under which monkish ignorance and superstition had persuaded them to bind themselves, and to assume the blessings and security of self-government."[20] He died on July 4, 1826, exactly 50 years after the Declaration of Independence was adopted, and on the same day that John Adams, his predecessor, occasional antagonist, and lifelong friend, also passed away.

The Jefferson Papers

Jefferson was an extensive writer, an avid reader, and a dedicated book collector. As a student and as a member of the Virginia House of Burgesses, he kept a small library and some of his correspondence in his rented quarters in Williamsburg; the remainder of his and his father's papers were kept at Shadwell. The fire at Shadwell in 1770 destroyed most of the papers and Jefferson wrote to his friend John Page that "every paper I had in the world and almost every book was lost . . , of papers of every kind I am utterly destitute. All of these, whether public or private, of business or amusement, have perished in the flames. On a reasonable estimate I calculated the cost of the books burned to have been 200 pounds sterling."[21] Twenty-five years after Jefferson's death, his grandson, Thomas Jefferson Randolph, discovered a few memoranda and account books from that period at the Randolph family home in Edgehill, Virginia. The lack of pre-1770 manuscripts has given historians an incomplete view of Jefferson's formative years, particularly as to his early thoughts and reading matter.

In 1780, during Benedict Arnold's raid on Richmond, Jefferson's letterbooks for the period he was governor of Virginia were also lost. To fill the gap, he borrowed from George Washington the letters he had written to him and copied them for his own files. He also copied his correspondence with Horatio Gates from the general's letterbooks of 1780 and 1781 to complete the record of his gubernatorial correspondence during the last months of the Revolution. There is also a mysterious gap in the Jefferson papers during the 1790s after his resignation as secretary of state; these papers may have been destroyed for political reasons. Jefferson himself burned his correspondence with his wife after her death. Additional losses occurred when Jefferson's papers were edited by George Tucker and Henry A. Washington.

Jefferson considered his letters of great significance in comparison to his other achievements as statesman and writer, and was concerned that they be well organized and preserved. In 1823, he wrote to Robert Walsh: "The letters of a person, especially of one whose business has been chiefly transacted by letters, form the only full and genuine journal of his life."[22] The same year, he mentioned in a letter to Hugh P. Taylor that he wanted to deposit some folio volumes of manuscripts at the library of the University of Virginia, an institution dear to his heart, where they would most likely be preserved with care.[23] Disregarding his legislative and executive documents, public speeches, state papers, architectural designs, and other written documents, his preserved letters alone consist of about 40,000 items written between 1760 and 1826. Jefferson's papers express the mind of the Renaissance man he was, showing his interest in government, politics, law, and history, as well as in agriculture, education, philosophy, music, literature, architecture, mathematics, and most fields of natural history.

In his later years, Jefferson relied increasingly on Thomas Jefferson Randolph, his grandson, to help him care for his estate and his financial affairs. Randolph was named the executor of his grandfather's will and was also given the responsibility of guarding his papers. Jefferson sold his first library to the Library of Congress in 1815; in 1829, under Randolph's supervision, the Library of Congress acquired more of Jefferson's printed books as well as several bound volumes and bundles of manuscripts mainly concerned with Virginia history and some notes and comments on subjects such as philosophy, history, and law.

Randolph used the papers left by his grandfather to prepare and edit *Memoir, Correspondence, and Miscellanies from the Papers of Thomas Jefferson*, which was published by F. Carr and Co. in Charlottesville in 1829.[24] Randolph wanted to keep the papers intact because he felt that the sale of the manuscripts would be one way to raise money to clear the Jefferson estate from debt. He generally refused requests for access to the papers, with the exception of George Tucker, a political economist and author, whom he permitted to study Jefferson's letters in preparation for *The Life of Thomas Jefferson*, a remarkably impartial contribution to early American history published in 1837.[25] Otherwise, no one is known to have made use of the manuscripts until 1848.

Randolph knew that the papers of Washington and Madison had been sold to the government. He wrote to Frederick A. H. Muhlenberg of Lancaster, Pennsylvania: "Many applications are made for copies of letters; to comply would greatly impair their value and I have felt myself reluctantly compelled to decline a compliance. My contemplation is to dispose of the whole in mass where they would be accessible to everyone."[26] Negotiations with Secretary of State James Buchanan regarding the sale were finalized in 1848, and the Congressional Appropriations Act of August 12, 1848, contained the following item: "For paying Thomas Jefferson Randolph, executor of Thomas Jefferson, deceased, the sum of twenty thousand dollars, for all papers and manuscripts of the said Thomas Jefferson: Provided, that said T.J. Randolph shall deposit all the said papers and manuscripts of a public nature in the State Department, and execute a conveyance thereof to the United States."[27]

Buchanan asked Randolph to include in the sale the public as well as the private papers of his grandfather. When Randolph delivered the papers to the Department of State, he asked that the private papers be separated from the public ones and returned to the family. He described the state of his grandfather's papers at the time of their sale to the government in a letter to Henry A. Washington, then librarian of the Department of State:

> The letters written by Mr. Jefferson are all arranged together in chronological order. The papers, documents, official correspondence, notes of transactions while Secretary of State to General Washington, are bound in three volumes of marbled paper, marked A.B.C.: The letters received are in three series alphabetically arranged—The first, received during his residence in Paris; the second, during his residence in Philadelphia and Washington as Secretary of State, Vice President and President; the third, after his return home. These are contained in paper boxes, open at top and back, the width and breadth of letter paper folded lengthwise; the name of the writer and date endorsed across the end, added to these are packages with the contents endorsed on the wrapper. There is also an index containing some 40,000 entries of letters written and received, partly in a bound volume and continued on loose sheets stitched together. The arrangements for reference is very convenient and it would be desirable to preserve it. His private family letters were in three square boxes and not intended to be sold, but the Secretary of State Mr. Buchanan expressed a doubt as to the law and advised their deposit. These I wish to reclaim as of no public value and interesting only his family.[28]

Henry Washington was selected by Congress's Joint Committee on the Library to prepare Jefferson's papers for publication by the government. Washington moved the papers from the Department of State to Williamsburg, where he was then a professor at the College of William and Mary. He worked on the selection, separation, and collation of the papers between 1850 and 1854. Unfortunately, he went very rapidly through the approximately 40,000 letters turned over to him to search for items suitable for his publication. He also took some of the documents to the offices of the publisher, Taylor and Maury, in New York City, and loaned others to his assistants. He divided the manuscripts into five series, thereby destroying Jefferson's original arrangement. Further damage was done by retracing faded parts of the manuscripts, often inaccurately, probably with a sharp steel pen. A nine-volume work, *The Writings of Thomas Jefferson,* was published between 1853 and 1854 under congressional sponsorship.[29] Washington also proposed to Congress that he select all papers worthy of preservation and arrange and index them. In a letter to Edward Stelle, assistant librarian of Congress, Washington reported that "having selected, arranged, and indexed the manuscripts, they are now ready for the hands of the binder, leaving in my possession a mass of refuse matter nearly twice as large as that which has been selected for preservation which will be placed at the disposal of the Library Committee."[30] Much later, it was discovered that Washington was guilty of many omissions, inaccuracies, and garbled extracts and that the 134 volumes of Jefferson manuscripts that he turned over to a Washington binder did not include all the papers in his possession.

The tragedy of the Jefferson papers is that their author, concerned with their preservation for posterity, left them in such good order and that they were completely dispersed and frequently damaged after his death. The number of Jefferson manuscripts that were mutilated, discarded, misfiled, or disappeared in the processes of editing, collating, copying, printing, and binding is beyond anyone's knowledge.

The selection of the private papers was apparently overlooked at the Department of State until 1869 when Randolph reminded Hamilton Fish, then secretary of state, that these papers belonged to the heirs of the President. On February 17, 1870, the Committee of the Library decided that Librarian Ainsworth Rand Spofford should examine the Jefferson papers and be authorized to turn over to the executor of Thomas Jefferson "such of the papers as upon examination shall be deemed of a private character."[31] In 1871, these papers were sent to the executor of the estate, a fact which Sarah N. Randolph, acting for her aged father, acknowledged in June of that year. Spofford recognized that the division of Jefferson's letters into those of a public and private nature was difficult because many of the documents were partly public and partly private. For this reason it was decided to return to the heirs only those papers that were unquestionably private to them, retaining for the Department of State letters considered to be partly public and partly private.

In 1875, before all the private papers had been returned, Thomas Jefferson Randolph died and the Jefferson papers in his possession passed to his daughter Sarah. In a letter to Congress in 1888, she offered to re-edit all Jefferson papers that had been improperly and inaccurately edited by Henry Washington. As a witness before the Committee on the Library, Miss Randolph pointed to various inaccuracies and tampering with the documents and proposed to prepare not only a new, correct, and thorough edition but to include documents in her family's possession which "would throw much light upon the private and public life of the great statesman, and present him in many phases of life, heretofore unknown and therefore more interesting to the world."[32] As a result of this hearing, the committee members directed Spofford to investigate Miss Randolph's allegations and to report back to them at their next meeting. Spofford's report of March 8, 1888, includes the following comments: "The deficiencies of this edition are so great as to impair, and in some cases to destroy its value as an index to true opinions of Mr. Jefferson, and his relation to the men and events of his time. The fact remains that the writings of one of the foremost statesmen in American history have been given to the world in a most incomplete form, omitting far more than they contain."[33]

As a result of Spofford's evaluation, the Joint Committee agreed to sponsor a new edition of Jefferson papers to be undertaken by Miss Randolph under the supervision of Spofford and to purchase the papers that had remained in her possession. Before Congress reached a final decision as to how the editing should be done and which papers were to be returned to Sarah Randolph, she died in 1892, leaving the papers to her sister Caroline Ramsey Randolph. The next edition of Jefferson's papers, considered the most scholarly to appear in the nineteenth century, was *The Writings of Thomas Jefferson*, edited by Paul Leicester Ford and published in 10 volumes between 1892 and 1899.[34]

In 1897, when the Library of Congress moved from the Capitol to its new building (now called the Jefferson Building), Spofford came across some papers which the government had retained during the 1871 dispute over which of the letters were of a public or private nature. Spofford reported this find in December 1897 to Secretary of State John Sherman, ending with the following paragraph:

> This deposit, with the multitude of others, was completely overlooked by me in the multiplicity of increasing cares and labors pressing upon the librarian in the Copyright Bureau and the Library proper, and their discovery, after so many years enables me to perform a most gratifying though tardy act of justice in restoring them to the Department. They are believed to be wholly intact.[35]

The collection of public papers was bound and added as the sixth series to the five bound series which Henry Washington had turned over to the Department of State in 1854. In 1904, the Department transferred almost all Jefferson letters to the Library of Congress, retaining only official letters as minister to France from May 11, 1785, to August 6, 1787; letters to Secretary of State John Jay; and a few other papers.

In 1898, Thomas Jefferson Coolidge, a great-grandson of the President, purchased approximately 7,000 items from Caroline Randolph and presented them to the Massachusetts Historical Society. In 1902, Miss Caroline Randolph passed away and left the remaining papers in her possession to three nieces. A fire consumed most of the papers of Mrs. William Mann Randolph, one of the nieces. Thomas Jefferson Coolidge, Jr. purchased a large group of Jefferson's architectural drawings for Monticello from the nieces in 1911, which he also deposited in the Massachusetts Historical Society. The remaining papers were eventually given to the University of Virginia, along with many papers of the Randolph family at Edgehill.

In 1912, about 2,500 of Jefferson's papers appeared on the market, offered for sale by George P. Coleman, a descendant of both George Tucker and Henry A. Washington. They were bought by William K. Bixby, a prominent St. Louis collector who wanted to share them with the public. He presented 1,100 items to the Missouri Historical Society; the rest were distributed among many individuals and repositories, including the Library of Congress, which bought 137 letters from Bixby. In 1917, the Library of Congress bought 300 letters from another source and received three Jefferson memoranda books. In August 1922, the Department of State transferred to the Library of Congress another set of letters, Jefferson's annotated draft of the Declaration of Independence, Jefferson's directions for his epitaph and gravestone, and several other items covering the period from 1790 to 1816.

On the occasion of the bicentennial of Thomas Jefferson's birth in 1943, Congress authorized the preparation of *The Papers of Thomas Jefferson*, sponsored by Princeton University, published by Princeton University Press, and supported by the New York Times Company, the Ford Foundation, and the National Historical Publications Commission. This edition is projected to appear as a series of 40 to 50 volumes. Professor Julian P. Boyd assumed editorial responsibility; Volume 1, which covers the years 1760–76, appeared in 1950. Volume 20, the last edited by Boyd, was published in 1982, covering the period of April 1 to August 4, 1791. When concluded, this will be the most complete, correct, and scholarly collection of Jefferson papers in print, combining papers from all repositories. A microfilm index of the Princeton control files is available.[36]

The collection of approximately 25,000 Jefferson papers at the Library of Congress is complemented by the papers at the University of Virginia, which holds about 3,400 items consisting mostly of original documents or contemporary transcripts made by secretaries and family members and some recent transcripts or photocopies of documents that remain in private hands or in less readily accessible repositories. All documents are by or to Jefferson and bear a direct relationship to him. The university entered upon the deliberate collection of Jefferson papers only in the present century. A small collection, mainly archival in nature, had accumulated in the Rotunda, the central University of Virginia building that Jefferson had designed as the library. An inventory in 1928–29 showed that the University then held only 175 manuscripts and 111 copies. By 1934, the Jefferson collection numbered 634 items. In 1942, the Edgehill Randolph family papers came to the University and the collection has grown considerably since then. A calendar of the collection, *The Jefferson Papers of the University of Virginia*, was issued in 1950 and updated and indexed in 1973.[37] A microfilm edition was prepared in 1977, consisting of a series of drawings, a special series, and a main series, all arranged in chronological order.[38]

The Massachusetts Historical Society in Boston holds in its Coolidge Collection approximately 7,000 items, mainly private papers. A microfilm edition of 31 rolls was issued in 1944. The National Archives in Washington holds the *Papers of the Continental Congress Relating to Jefferson*, consisting chiefly of transcripts of diplomatic correspondence (12 rolls of microfilm); other items include letters of application and recommendation during the two administrations of Thomas Jefferson.

Other collections are at the Missouri Historical Society, St. Louis, Missouri; the Historical Society of Pennsylvania in Philadelphia; the College of William and Mary in Williamsburg, Virginia; the Henry E. Huntington Library in San Marino, California; the American Philosophical Society in Philadelphia; the New York Historical Society; the Virginia State Library in Richmond; the William L. Clements Library in Ann Arbor, Michigan; Yale University; and in many other repositories and private hands.

The Jefferson Papers in the Library of Congress

Series	Reels
1. General Correspondence and Related Materials. 1651–1826. 236 vols.	1–57
2. Gates Letterbook Correspondence. 1780–81. 1 box	57
3. District of Columbia Miscellany. 1790–1808. 3 boxes, 1 portfolio	58
4. Account Books. 1767–82. 3 vols.	58
5. Commonplace Books. 2 vols.	59

6. Randolph Family Manuscripts. 1790–1889. 1 box   59
7. Miscellaneous Bound Volumes and Clippings. 8 vols.   59–60
8. Virginia Records. 1606–1711. 19 vols.   60–65
9. Collected Manuscripts. 1783–1822. 1 box   65
10. Addenda. 1735–1902 and undated.

JAMES MADISON
Fourth President—Democratic-Republican
1809–1817

Born on March 16, 1751, at Port Conway in King George County, Virginia, Madison was part of the same planter aristocracy as Washington and Jefferson. He grew up in his parents' home at Montpelier in Orange County, Virginia, was educated by tutors, and attended a private school. He graduated from the College of New Jersey (now Princeton University) where he studied history, government, and theology. Madison, commonly referred to as the "Father of the Constitution," was a great political philosopher, had a brilliant mind, and was a skillful practical politician. He started his political career at age 24 when he served on the Orange County Committee of Safety. In 1776 and 1777 he served in the Virginia House of Delegates, and assisted in the writing of the Virginia Constitution. His friendship with Thomas Jefferson and admiration for his democratic ideals began at that time. He was also attracted by some of Alexander Hamilton's ideas, especially his advocacy of a strong central government.

Possibly because of his short stature, inborn reticence, and personal modesty, Madison relied more on written than oral expressions. He represented Virginia in the Continental Congress from 1780 to 1783 and helped organize the national government under the newly adopted Articles of Confederation. As a delegate to the Annapolis Convention in 1786, he and Hamilton called for a revision of the Articles. Washington approved, writing to Madison: "Without some alteration in our political creed, the superstructure we have been seven years raising at the expense of so much blood and treasure, must fall."[39]

Madison was among the leaders who convened the Constitutional Convention in Philadelphia in 1787, served on a number of its committees, and took it upon himself to keep complete records of the debates. He wrote that he had decided to "preserve as far as I could an exact account of what might pass in the Convention. I chose a seat in front of the presiding member, with other members on my right and left, hearing all that passed. I noted what was read from the chair or spoken by the members . . . and losing not a moment unnecessarily between adjournment and reassembly I was enabled to write out my daily notes during the session or within a few days after its close."[40] His journal of the Convention is considered the most significant record of its proceedings. He drafted a plan for the new government, the Virginia Plan, which was patterned after the Virginia Constitution and became the basis for the United States Constitution. Together with Alexander Hamilton and John

Jay, Madison wrote, under the nom de plume "Publius," 85 essays in defense of the Constitution; these appeared first in the New York press between 1787 and 1788, were published in book form as *The Federalist: A Commentary on the Constitution of the United States*, in 1788, and are a key contribution to American political theory.[41]

Patrick Henry thwarted Madison's attempt to run for the U.S. Senate, but he was elected to the House where he served from 1789 to 1797. He helped to frame the Bill of Rights, to draft the legislation to establish various government departments, and to enact the first revenue legislation. He also acted as an advisor to George Washington and helped to prepare both his Inaugural and his Farewell Address. In 1794, at the age of 43, he married Dolley Payne Todd, a widow. When Federalist John Adams became president, Madison returned to plantation life at Montpelier and served as a member of the Virginia legislature. He campaigned for Jefferson in 1800 and served as his secretary of state from 1801 to 1809.

As Jefferson's chosen successor, Madison easily won the presidential election of 1808 as the Democratic-Republic candidate. His presidency was overshadowed by friction with Great Britain, which culminated in the War of 1812 and the burning of the Capitol in 1814. Federalism failed to maintain itself as a strong national party, and Madison easily won re-election to a second term in 1812. He established the Second Bank of the United States and advocated protective tariffs. The war ended with the signing of the Treaty of Ghent in 1814.

Madison left office pleased with the election of James Monroe as his successor. During his retirement he succeeded Jefferson as rector of the University of Virginia in 1826, and served as co-chairman of the 1828–29 Virginia Constitutional Convention that revised the state constitution he had helped to write 50 years earlier. Together with his wife, he selected and edited his papers in preparation for publishing them. He died on June 28, 1836, and bequeathed his papers to his wife.

The Madison Papers

Madison was known to give manuscripts as mementos to his friends and family and to clip the signature off his letters to send them to autograph collectors. He or one of his friends also frequently wrote explanatory notes on his papers and revised some words or sentences, altering the original text. He rarely retained full copies of his own letters while serving in the Continental Congress, and often included among his papers undated sheets with rough notes on various items, such as summaries of books and pamphlets he was reading, speeches to be delivered or that had already been made, letters to be written or already received. Unfortunately, Madison was also of the opinion that the only papers worth saving were those of a public nature and therefore discarded most that dealt with private subjects.

Shortly after Madison's death, Mrs. Madison, who was always in precarious financial condition, sold the papers which, according to her, had been selected for publication by Madison, to the government for $30,000. They were published by Langtree & O'Sullivan in 1840 in three volumes[42] and included the previously unknown notes on the Constitutional Convention. In the introduction to the notes Madison had written: ". . . I feel it a duty to express my profound and solemn conviction . . . that there never was an assembly of men, charged with a great and arduous trust, who were more pure in their motives, or more exclusively and anxiously devoted to the object committed to them, than were the members of the Federal Convention of 1787, to the object of devising and proposing a constitutional system which should best . . . secure the permanent liberty and happiness of their country."[43]

During the late 1830s and early 1840s, Mrs. Madison deposited all remaining papers of her husband in a bank vault in Washington. At times these papers were under the sole custody of her son John Payne Todd. In 1848, she sold what she believed to be the rest of her husband's unpublished papers to Congress for $25,000 and delivered them to Secretary of State James Buchanan, not knowing that her son had removed some of the most valuable papers and had sold them to James C. McGuire, a Washington collector who paid Todd's never ending gambling and liquor debts over the years.

The Department of State became aware that the papers it had bought from Mrs. Madison were not all the papers James Madison had bequeathed to her when McGuire published *Selections from the Private Correspondence of James Madison from 1813 to 1836*, in 1853.[44] The Department considered instituting legal proceedings in the name of the United States to recover possession of the missing papers, but Caleb Cushing, the attorney general, decided that this would not be expedient. McGuire made no secret of the fact that he had a considerable collection of Madison papers. He published "Jonathan Bull and Mary Bull,"[45] Madison's allegory on the Missouri question, from these papers, and helped William C. Rives, Madison's first biographer, by letting him examine and even loaning him some papers. The papers in the Department of State were also loaned to Rives. McGuire later cooperated with Rives and Philip R. Fendall on *Letters and Other Writings of James Madison, Fourth President of the United States*, published in Philadelphia in 1865.[46]

After McGuire's death, much of his collection was sold in a series of public auctions by the executors of his estate, including a collection of about 3,000 letters in 1892. While this collection was assumed to consist mostly of the private papers of President and Mrs. Madison, the collection also contained much of Madison's official correspondence from 1780 to his death. Most of these materials were bought by the Chicago Historical Society in 1893 with funds donated by Marshall Field, and were purchased by the Library of Congress in 1910.

The papers that Congress had purchased in 1837 and 1848 from Mrs. Madison were transferred from the Department of State to the Library of Congress in 1905, but the Department of State retained Madison's notes of the debates during the Federal Convention of 1787 and other papers until 1922. In 1881, James Madison Cutts, a greatnephew of the President, donated a copybook of youthful writings to the Library of Congress. Forty-three letters addressed to Madison between 1817 and 1836, which belonged to the American Art Association, were bought by the Library in

1917; other papers were bought in 1921, 1922, 1924, and 1933. In 1940, Mrs. Philip M. Rinelander deposited in the Library of Congress papers that had come through her husband's family from the heirs of William C. Rives. Mixed in with Rives' own papers were almost 900 Madison manuscripts and some papers sent to him by his contemporaries, which Rives had used in the writing of the President's biography. Most of this material had been loaned to Rives by the Department of State. Some gifts in 1924 and 1926 were received from James C. McGuire II, the grandson of the man to whom John Payne Todd had sold so many Madison papers.

Approximately 10,000 Madison papers in the possession of the Library of Congress were microfilmed in six series in 1964. A seventh series has been added since then and an estimated 12,000 items were held by the Library in 1986. Small, but significant Madison collections are held by the University of Virginia, the Huntington Library, the Historical Societies of Virginia and Pennsylvania, the New York Public Library, the William L. Clements Library at the University of Michigan, and Princeton University.

The Madison Papers in the Library of Congress

Series	Reels
1. General Correspondence and Related Items. 1723–1859. 90 vols.	1–24
2. Additional Correspondence and Related Items. 1780–1837. 8 vols.	25–26
3. Madison-Armstrong Correspondence. 1813–36. 1 vol.	27
4. Autobiography. ca. 1751–1852. 1 vol.	27
5. Madison's and Jefferson's Notes on Debates and Related Items. 1776–88. 6 vols.	27
6. Miscellaneous Manuscripts. ca. 1763–1836. 7 containers	28
7. Additions.	

JAMES MONROE
Fifth President—Democratic-Republican
1817–1825

Like Washington, Jefferson, and Madison, James Monroe was the son of a Virginia planter. He was born in Westmoreland County, Virginia, in 1758 and was sent at age 16 to Williamsburg to attend the College of William and Mary. When the Revolution broke out, he quit college to join the Continental Army. He had a distinguished service record and was wounded at the Battle of Trenton. After the war, Monroe studied law under Jefferson's guidance and was elected to the state legislature in 1782. He served as a member of Virginia's delegation to Congress from 1783 to 1786 and helped to write the legislation for the

Northwest Ordinance. When his term in Congress expired, he established a law practice in Fredericksburg, Virginia, married, and later built a beautiful home at Ash Lawn, near Jefferson's Monticello. In 1790, with the support of Patrick Henry, he returned to Congress as a senator.

In the Senate, he became one of the leaders of the Democratic-Republican party and helped fight Alexander Hamilton's Federalist policies. In 1794, George Washington appointed Monroe U.S. minister to France, where he spent two years. In 1799, he was elected governor of Virginia and established a close friendship with Madison, who was serving in the legislature at that time. In 1803, Jefferson sent Monroe to France to help negotiate the purchase of the Louisiana Territory by the United States. After several years as minister to Great Britain, he returned to the United States and his law practice in 1807. He considered running for president against Madison, but the Democratic-Republican party leadership persuaded him to desist; he became governor of Virginia for a second time in 1811, but resigned shortly thereafter to accept Madison's appointment as secretary of state. During the War of 1812, Monroe also held the post of secretary of war. In 1816, he won the Democratic-Republican nomination for president and the presidential election.

In his inaugural address, Monroe commented: "Never did a government commence under auspices so favorable, nor ever was success so complete. If we look at the history of other nations, ancient or modern, we find no example of growth so rapid, so gigantic, of a people so prosperous and happy."[47] He appointed a strong and stable cabinet, with John Quincy Adams as secretary of state, representing New England, and John C. Calhoun as secretary of war, representing the South. Madison stabilized relations with Great Britain through the Rush-Bagot agreement in 1817, which eliminated fortifications along the Canadian border, and successfully negotiated the purchase of Florida from Spain. His most noted effort was the proclamation of the Monroe Doctrine in December 1823, in which he warned the European powers that "we should consider any attempt on their part to extend their system to any portion of this hemisphere as dangerous to our peace and safety."[48] In domestic affairs, Monroe made little effort to lead Congress; he approved the Survey Act of 1824 which provided for planning public works such as roads and canals; he also approved protective tariff acts and the admission of Missouri to the Union as a slave state.

After his second term as president, Monroe retired to Oak Hill, his estate in Loudon County, Virginia. He resumed his friendships with Jefferson and Madison, served as a regent of the University of Virginia, and, in 1829, co-chaired with Madison the Virginia state constitutional convention. The country had experienced great prosperity at home and abroad during his administration, and he had been a very popular president. His retirement, however, was not happy. Financially, he was in extremely strained conditions and he unsuccessfully tried to collect money from the government for expenses he had incurred during his public service. Finally, he was forced to sell some of his properties in Virginia. After his wife died in 1830, he moved to New York City to live with his younger daughter, Maria, and her husband, Samuel L. Gouverneur. He died there on July 4, 1831, the third president to die on Independence Day.

The Monroe Papers

In his efforts to settle his claims against the government, Monroe asked Congress for an investigation of his accounts and used many of the papers he had accumulated during his long years of public service to document his claims. To stimulate action by Congress, he wrote a long paper which he sent to Gales and Seaton in Washington for publication. The "Memoir of James Monroe, Esq. relating to his Unsettled Claims upon the People and Government of the United States" was published in 1826 in three successive issues of the *National Intelligencer*.[49] In 1827, Monroe worked on two papers that he hoped would raise money; one was a comparison of the government of the United States with other republics, and the second was his autobiography. His son-in-law acted as his agent in dealing with his claims to Congress, and Monroe had supplied him with papers concerning these claims. When he moved to New York, he took some of his papers along to complete his autobiography. When he died, some papers were still at Oak Hill, his claims before Congress were unresolved, and the manuscripts he had started remained incomplete. The comparison of governments, *The People, the Sovereigns*, was edited and published by his grandson Samuel L. Gouverneur, Jr. in 1867,[50] and the autobiography, based on his incomplete manuscript and edited by Stuart Gerry Brown, was finally published in 1959.[51]

Monroe left a will dated May 16, 1831, naming Gouverneur as "sole and exclusive executor" and asking him to care for Monroe's older daughter Elizabeth Hay, who had been widowed the previous year. As to his papers, he stated: ". . . with respect to the works in which I am engaged and leave behind, I commit the care and publication of them to my son in law Samuel L. Gouverneur, giving to him one third of the profits arising therefrom for this trouble in preparing them for publication, one third to my daughter Maria and one third to my daughter Elizabeth."[52]

During the next few years, Gouverneur administered the Monroe papers with care. He loaned some papers to President John Quincy Adams who was preparing a eulogy for Monroe in Boston and who returned them within a short time. He did some work toward the publication of the manuscripts in the 1830s but was too busy with other pursuits to accomplish much. Elizabeth, Monroe's older daughter, died in 1840; in the same year, the Gouverneurs moved to Washington and spent parts of each year in Oak Hill. When he was working for the Department of State between 1844 and 1849, Gouverneur became acquainted with Henry O'Reilly, who had been the editor of the *Rochester Daily Advertiser*, and entered into negotiations with him to publish a selection from the papers along with a memoir of Monroe "in case it should be found that a sale of the whole mass could not be made to the Government."[53]

In 1844 or 1845 Gouverneur turned over the major part of Monroe's papers to O'Reilly who stored them somewhere in New York City while he was busy installing telegraph lines from eastern Pennsylvania to St.

Louis and the Great Lakes. In May 1847, Gouverneur wrote O'Reilly about the whereabouts of the papers and the possibility of publishing them. Remaining without answer, he wrote again in October: "I feel some anxiety that all my papers are safely deposited where no accident can befall them."[54]

When Gouverneur learned during 1848 that Congress had purchased the second part of the Madison papers, as well as those of Alexander Hamilton and Thomas Jefferson, he decided to take steps to finally make proper disposition of the Monroe papers. He came to an agreement concerning the proceeds with the executor of Elizabeth Hay's estate and with Henry O'Reilly; on January 1, 1849, he sent a petition to Congress requesting financial assistance to publish Monroe's papers. When he learned that Congress would prefer to buy the papers rather than support their publication, he agreed to sell them after O'Reilly relinquished his rights to the proceeds. On February 28, 1849, the Senate voted to purchase the papers for $20,000 and on March 2, the House concurred. The negotiations specified that the sale would be limited to those papers not of a private character and that they be deposited in the Department of State. On March 13, 1850, Secretary of State John M. Clayton signed a receipt for the material and Samuel L. Gouverneur, as executor of the estate of James Monroe, received $20,000.

In 1882, James Shouler was the first person to use the papers for historical research and described them as "a huge mass of interesting matter relative to our earlier national history, which lies unassorted in the Department of State and for whose editorial supervision and publication it is to be fervently hoped that Congress will some day make suitable provision."[55] In 1889 the papers were finally sorted, repaired, and bound in 22 volumes, and an index to the papers was prepared.[56] Seven years later, the librarian of Congress prepared a seven-volume unofficial edition of the Monroe papers which was published some 70 years after Monroe's death.[57] In 1903, the papers were transferred to the Library of Congress and a list of 2,650 manuscripts was prepared.

Monroe's private papers suffered an even more complicated fate than the public ones. His younger daughter, Maria Gouverneur, died in 1850 at Oak Hill. In 1852, Oak Hill was sold, and in 1853, Samuel Gouverneur married Mary Digges Lee. The couple moved to the home of the second Mrs. Gouverneur at Needwood near Petersville, Maryland, where they lived for the next 12 years. When Samuel Gouverneur died in September 1865, he bequeathed his estate, including the remaining papers in his possession, to his second wife. The following year his son, Samuel L. Gouverneur, Jr., successfully sued his stepmother to recover his mother's furniture, paintings, and other household ornaments, but the papers were not mentioned. Samuel L. Gouverneur, Jr. died in 1880 and Marian Campbell Gouverneur, his widow, inherited his possessions, including a substantial number of Monroe papers. Some of these papers were probably the ones found in secret compartments of the desk on which the address that incorporated the Monroe doctrine was signed. This desk is now in the James Monroe Law Office and Memorial Library in Fredericksburg, Virginia.

In 1888, former President Rutherford B. Hayes called the Gouverneur manuscripts to the attention of the librarian of Congress and the entire collection was deposited at the Library of Congress in 1902, then withdrawn and again deposited between 1922 and 1927 for possible purchase, but the purchase never took place. Mrs. Samuel Gouverneur, Jr. gave the papers to her three daughters prior to her death. Parts of the collection were finally purchased by the Library of Congress from the Monroe heirs in 1931 and in 1950. The papers inherited by Laurence G. Hoes, one of Samuel Gouverneur, Jr.'s grandsons, were given to the James Monroe Memorial Library in Fredericksburg. Other papers are in the library of the College of William and Mary in Williamsburg, and in the University of Virginia and Virginia State libraries. The papers of James Monroe in Virginia repositories were microfilmed and an index was prepared by the University of Virginia in 1969.[58] The Monroe papers that Samuel Gouverneur had taken to Needwood in Maryland and that stayed in the possession of his second wife were eventually given to the New York Public Library (about 1,300 items). It is not known how many Monroe papers are still in private hands. The Library of Congress acquired documents through purchases and gifts, and the microfilm edition made in 1960 contains 3,821 items in four series; additional papers have since been added as a fifth series. According to 1986 estimates, the Library has approximately 5,200 items.

The Monroe Papers in the Library of Congress

Series	Reels
1. General Correspondence. 1758–1839. 37 vols.	1–9
2. Additional Correspondence. 1780–1836.	9–10
3. Letterbooks and Account Book. 1794-1806. 3 vols.	10–11
4. Photocopies. 1797-1824. 1 box	Not filmed
5. Addition.	

6. Pre-Civil War Presidents

ANDREW JACKSON
Seventh President—Democrat
1829-1837

Andrew Jackson, the son of Irish immigrants, was born in 1767 in a log cabin on the border between North and South Carolina. Unlike the first six presidents, he came from a poor family and did not have the opportunities and education of his predecessors. However, his great drive and ambition propelled him to an outstanding career. He joined the militia in his early teens and was captured by the British in 1781. In 1784, he began to study law, and was admitted to the North Carolina bar in 1787. A dashing and daring young man, Jackson was happy to move to the new frontier, the western district of North Carolina, where he became attorney general. He married Rachel Donelson Robards in 1791. They had no children, but he adopted his favorite nephew, Andrew Jackson, Jr. When a constitutional convention was called to organize the new state of Tennessee, Jackson became a member. From 1796 to 1798, he served as the state's first representative to Congress and as U.S. senator, establishing a long-lasting friendship with Senator Aaron Burr of New York.

In 1798, Jackson returned to Tennessee to devote his attention to his personal financial affairs, served as judge of the state Superior Court from 1798 to 1804, and was elected major general of the Tennessee militia. After some financial setbacks, he successfully developed his plantation, the Hermitage, near Nashville. He volunteered his militia unit in the War of 1812 and fought courageously with his men, who nicknamed him "Old Hickory." He crushed the Creek Indians, who were allied with the British, in 1813 and became a national hero when he won the Battle of New Orleans in 1815. Jackson furthered his military and political career by commanding U.S. troops in the Seminole War in Florida, and serving as territorial governor of Florida. He was re-elected U.S. Senator from Tennessee in 1823. In 1824, he ran for the presidency, but lost to John Quincy Adams. After careful preparation and a skillfully planned national campaign, he won the 1828 presidential election by a large majority of the popular vote.

Jackson was the first president to combine the functions of chief executive, chief of state, and chief of party. His policies polarized the country into two parties: his supporters, the Democratic-Republicans (later Democrats), and his opponents, the National Republicans (later Whigs). As president, Jackson ensured his leadership in Congress through party strength and veto action. He fought against the Second Bank of the

United States and was able to prevent its recharter; his firm stand helped to resolve peacefully the South Carolina nullification crisis in 1832–33. He won a smashing victory against Henry Clay in the presidential election of 1832; his loyal supporter, Martin Van Buren, became vice president and succeeded him in the presidency in 1837. Jackson retired to the Hermitage where he died in 1845.

The Jackson Papers

Because of his lack of education, Jackson, as a youth, was quite limited in expressing himself in either writing or speaking. He eventually mastered these skills by sheer determination, though his spelling and grammar remained poor. Despite his terms in the U.S. House and Senate, there are few manuscript sources for his career prior to 1813. Beginning with the Creek War, he started to collect his papers carefully, labeling them "to be kept for the historian," and to file and store them in boxes.[1] He wrote as many as 20 letters a day and urged Andrew Jackson, Jr., a student at West Point, to write letters because "writing letters employs the thoughts, expands the mind, and will give you by a proper attention an easy habit of communicating your thoughts."[2] He accumulated many papers during his military campaigns and hoped that some writer or historian would be anxious to prepare his biography. After the Battle of New Orleans, several well-known contemporaries expressed an interest in doing this.

Among his potential early biographers was Dr. David Ramsay, a physician, Revolutionary patriot, and South Carolina historian who was killed in 1815 before he had a chance to work on the biography. John Reid, Jackson's aide-de-camp and a trusted associate, had furnished papers and information to Ramsay. With Jackson's encouragement, Reid started to work on a biography in 1815, but died suddenly in 1816. Henry John Eaton, an attorney, was chosen by Jackson and the Reid family to complete the manuscript, which appeared in 1817 as *The Life of Andrew Jackson* under the joint authorship of Reid and Eaton.[3] In the second and following editions of the *Life*, Reid's name was omitted from the title page.

In 1819, James Gadsden, a military officer under Jackson, considered writing an updated biography and asked Jackson to supply him with his papers. Jackson wrote to Gadsden that he would have his public papers carefully collated and boxed for him and requested that they be returned to his adopted son. However, there is no evidence that Jackson ever sent Gadsden any of his papers.[4] Henry Lee, son of Light Horse Henry Lee, was the next person to consider a Jackson biography. While he never published anything, he left a manuscript of 78 folio pages after his death in 1837 in Paris. The manuscript is a chronicle of Jackson's early life up to 1813 and is preserved as a separately bound volume in Series 4 of the Jackson papers in the Library of Congress.[5]

During the early days of Jackson's first administration, Amos Kendall, editor of *Argus of Western America*, became a close friend of the President. Kendall had shown some interest in writing a biography as early as 1827 when he began to collect some information and papers.

Jackson thought that Kendall was an able writer and was pleased that he was to start working on this task. Actually, Kendall produced very little because, until 1840, he served as postmaster general, but Jackson continued to favor him as his biographer even after his retirement. In June 1842, Kendall finally seemed ready to work seriously on the biography and requested access to Jackson's papers at the Hermitage. At that time, Francis Blair, editor of the *Congressional Globe*, and a prominent Jacksonian, became concerned with Kendall's progress and wrote to Jackson that Kendall's health was impaired and that "he would not be able to finish the work he had set for himself."[6] For this reason, he urged Jackson "to make a disposition in his will of the papers in Mr. Kendall's hands to assure the fulfillment of the task committed to him in case of his death and failure to perform it."[7] He also assured Jackson that he would see to it that such a trust was faithfully executed and suggested that George Bancroft, an eminent historian, would be the best choice to finish the task should Kendall die or become disabled. Since Kendall could not leave Washington in 1842, he sent James A. McLaughlin, a nephew of his wife, to visit Jackson at the Hermitage. McLaughlin stayed there for several months, sifting through the papers. Because Jackson considered everything "perfectly safe" in Kendall's hands, he and McLaughlin decided not to waste time in making copies but rather to send the boxes of papers directly to Kendall in Washington. In 1843, Kendall worked enthusiastically on the biography and planned "to publish in fifteen or more numbers, the Life on Andrew Jackson . . . starting in May 1843."[8] The first number did not appear until October, but Kendall did produce seven of the projected fifteen numbers during Jackson's life time.[9] Kendall then became preoccupied with marketing the stock of the S.F.B. Morse telegraph company and stopped working on the Jackson biography.

In 1845, Jackson developed increasing apprehension about the state of his own health and began to make arrangements for the safety and preservation of his papers. In April, he wrote to his friend Francis P. Blair, "This may be the last letter I may be able to write to you. But live or die I am your friend . . . and leave my papers and reputation in your keeping, as far as justice is due to my fame, I know you will shield it."[10] In May, Jackson wrote another letter to Blair: "When Mr. Kendall has done with my papers I wish them handed over to you, to whom I will them, for the defense of my reputation. There are many private papers that ought to go into no other hands but a confidential friend."[11] In his last letter of May 20, 1845, Jackson directed Kendall to pass his letters on to Blair when he was done with them and closed with the words that they would "at last meet in a blissfull immortality."[12] Jackson died on June 8, 1845, and Blair's problems concerning Jackson's papers started.

A few days after Jackson's death, Francis Blair wrote to Andrew Jackson, Jr., informing him that Jackson's papers had been willed to Blair. In October and November 1845, Blair and Jackson, Jr. exchanged letters advising Kendall of their agreement to deposit all papers with Blair. By 1849, Martin Van Buren became interested in enhancing his own collection of papers and wrote to Blair that he wanted to preserve his correspondence with Jackson. Blair agreed to this request but told Van Buren that he had not been able to retrieve the papers from Kendall and wrote that he thought he would "never get them till the devil gets him."[13] Several months later some of the Jackson and Van Buren correspondence was returned by Kendall. Another year elapsed before Blair sent the papers to Van Buren.

Van Buren and his heirs carefully selected those papers that should be preserved for posterity and probably burned anything they found incriminating, including some of Jackson's correspondence. Before Kendall died in 1869, he confided to William Stickney, his son-in-law, that he did not complete Jackson's biography because he had been too poor to collect the needed information and that all who had promised him papers, except one, had disappointed him. One may assume that the one was President Jackson, who had shown more faith in Kendall than he deserved.

In 1851, Senator Thomas Hart Benton began to write the memoirs of his own public life. The two-volume *Thirty Years View*, a history of the workings of American government from 1820 to 1850, acknowledged Blair's assistance in providing use of Jackson's papers.[14] In 1857, James Parton began to write a Jackson biography for which he interviewed many of the men who had worked with Jackson; Blair and Kendall gave him some assistance but tended to withhold manuscript sources. In spite of this, Parton's work, which appeared in three volumes in 1859–60, was very successful.[15] Kendall gave up the idea of completing his work.

The records of the seventh president might have fallen into oblivion after the deaths of Kendall (1869) and Blair (1876), had it not been for Col. William G. Terrell, a correspondent of the *Cincinnati Commercial*. In February 1879, Terrell published in his paper 72 letters of Jackson to Kendall. Terrell had discovered these letters in the winter of 1878–79 when he was in Washington visiting William Stickney, Amos Kendall's son-in-law. Stickney had in his possession a package of several hundred Jackson letters and allowed Terrell to take the package home for more careful study. He gave Terrell permission to copy whatever he wanted for publication in his newspaper. Terrell read in the letters references to other papers that Jackson had sent to Kendall. Stickney had never seen these papers and assumed they were in the possession of Montgomery Blair, Francis P. Blair's son, but Blair denied it. At this point, Terrell remembered that he had read in a letter that Mrs. Stickney, Kendall's daughter, had copied some Jackson papers when she was a young girl. Mrs. Stickney remembered having copied the papers in the old *Globe* office. When Terrell investigated this further, he found some old trunks in the attic of the building, two of which contained the missing Jackson papers. In discussions with Montgomery Blair, Terrell learned that after Jackson's death, Francis Blair had visited the Hermitage and had brought a large trunk of papers to his Silver Spring home. The trunk was located at a Blair country house and was filled with Jackson papers, apparently letters not picked up by Kendall.

Almost 40 years after Jackson's death, on February 29, 1884, a Senate resolution was passed to the effect that "the Committee on the Library be instructed to inquire into the propriety and expediency of purchasing said collection of papers from General Jackson's legal heirs, and having the same edited and published as the property of the government for the use of the Congressional Library."[16] This resolution started a belated search for the papers and resulted in a bill of injunction, filed by Andrew Jackson, the son of the President's adopted son, against Woodbury and Mary Elizabeth Blair, the grandchildren of Francis P. Blair. Blair's heirs replied that the papers had been given by Jackson to Francis Blair without any conditions and that the "gift and bequest was absolute and in all respects subject to the control and disposition of the said Francis P. Blair."[17]

Because the trunk with Jackson's letters in the *Globe* office had been forgotten, it was widely believed that a large number of Jackson papers were stored with the Kendall papers at a warehouse in Washington which was ravaged by fire in July 1894. It can be assumed that some of Jackson's papers were destroyed at that time, but in 1931 a substantial number of Jackson papers appeared on the market and were considered to be those that survived the warehouse fire.

In 1903, the Blair heirs sent a letter to Herbert Putnam, librarian of Congress, suggesting that the Jackson papers "should be in a permanent place of deposit where they would be well cared for, properly classified, indexed, filed, and with the aid of experts be made accessible to historical investigators."[18] With this letter, title to the largest collection of the President's papers was conveyed to the Library of Congress. In 1909, papers previously in the possession of Col. Terrell were given to the daughter of Andrew Jackson, Jr. This collection was acquired by the Library of Congress in 1911 and, when added to the Montgomery Blair Collection, made the Jackson papers among the most nearly complete of the presidential collections then in the Library's possession.

In 1911, John Spencer Bassett published his two-volume biography *The Life of Andrew Jackson*, and established himself as the foremost authority on Jackson.[19] In 1919, he was asked by Dr. J. Franklin Jameson of the Carnegie Foundation to prepare an edition of the writings and correspondence of Andrew Jackson. With the help of the Library of Congress, he searched out Jackson letters and papers in institutions and private ownership throughout the country, and some originals and a number of copies were added to the collection. Bassett's first three volumes appeared before his death in 1928; the final three volumes were completed by Jameson.

More Jackson papers were discovered in 1930 by Marquis James when he was working on *Andrew Jackson, the Border Captain.*[20] This set of papers surfaced in Massachusetts and, according to James, was considered part of the bulk of the "Kendall Papers" which had survived the warehouse fire. The origin of this collection could not be traced, but some of the papers had definitely been in the hands of Amos Kendall and bear his annotations and endorsements. The group also includes the letters addressed to Kendall from the Hermitage by James McLaughlin; it was purchased by the Library of Congress in 1932. Occasional gifts and purchases have been added to the Library's collection since then. In 1943, a collection of 600 fragments of deliberately mutilated letters and documents was purchased; another substantial acquisition of papers was made in 1964, some of which had appeared in the *Cincinnati Commercial* and were acquired from Amos Kendall's descendants. As time goes on, other collections may surface, but most of the lost Jackson papers, approximately 26,000 items, seem to have found their way to the Library of Congress. The Tennessee State Library has approximately 1,500 items; smaller collections are in the Tennessee Historical Society, the Chicago Historical Society, the New York Public Library, and the New York Historical Society.

The Jackson Papers in the Library of Congress

Series	*Reels*
1. General Correspondence and Related items. 1775–1860. 119 vols.	1–60
2. Letterbook. 1829–31. 1 vol.	60
3. Letters and Orders. 1813–22. 15 vols.	61–63
4. Record Books. 1800–37. 10 vols.	64
5. Military Papers. 1781–1832. 13 vols.	65–70
6. Additional Correspondence. 1779–1855 and undated. 8 vols.	71–74
7. Miscellaneous Correspondence. 1789–1845 and undated. 3 boxes	75
8. Messages and Speeches. ca. 1829–36. 3 boxes	76–77
9. Miscellaneous Manuscripts. 1795–1856. 1 box	78
10. Nonmanuscript materials. Various dates. 17 boxes	Not filmed
11. Jackson-Kendall Letters. 1827–45. 60 letters.	78
12. Addenda.	

MARTIN VAN BUREN
Eighth President—Democrat
1837–1841

Martin Van Buren was born in 1782 in the old Dutch community of Kinderhook, New York. He was the first president born an American citizen rather than a British subject. He attended local schools, studied law in New York, was admitted to the bar in 1803, and began to practice law in Kinderhook when he was 20 years old. Van Buren was a man of great charm and political talents. Referred to as "the fox of Kinderhook" by his political opponents, he was a leader in the New York political machine, the "Albany Regency." John Randolph once said of him "he rowed to his object with muffled oars."[21] In 1812, he was elected to the New York State Senate, served as state attorney general from 1816 to 1819, and became United States senator in 1821. He worked for Andrew Jackson in the campaign of 1828 and helped to swing 20 of the state's 36 electoral votes to Jackson. He was elected governor of New York in the same year but resigned to accept the appointment of secretary of state in Jackson's cabinet. He also served as U.S. minister to England during the first Jackson administration and as vice president during the second. Van Buren was Jackson's closest adviser and his choice as successor.

In 1836, Van Buren easily won the presidential election; he made it clear that he planned to continue to work in Jackson's shadow, glorying in the prosperity of the country. He even reappointed all the members of Jackson's cabinet. A few months later, the first major U.S. depression began with the Panic of 1837, when banks suspended the payment of silver and gold for paper money. Hundreds of banks and businesses failed, and Van Buren fought for the establishment of an independent treasury system to handle government transactions. Prosperity returned temporarily in 1839, but the depression resumed and persisted until 1845. Van Buren was chosen by the Democratic convention to run for a second term, but was defeated by William Henry Harrison who was portrayed as a man of the people in contrast to Van Buren, who "ate his meals off gold plates."[22] He spent much of his time during the next few years in campaigning for reelection in 1844 and 1848, but was not successful. After an extensive trip to Europe, he retired to his estate near Kinderhook where he died in 1862.

During his retirement, Van Buren wrote many letters to influence politics and prepared two publications, the *Inquiery*[23] and his autobiography.[24] Throughout his life, Van Buren was a controversial personality because so many of his contemporaries saw him either as a wise, genial, and charming man, or as a sly politician given to trickery and the spoils system. Personally, he suffered many reverses; he became a widower at 37 and never remarried. His last years were lonely and he was disappointed by the slow editing of his writings by his son, Smith Thompson Van Buren.

The Van Buren Papers

Van Buren attempted to collect his papers in preparation for his autobiography. Unfortunately, the papers show many gaps as a result of his self-confessed inattention to their care. For example, he had a practice of keeping his files within manageable limits by destroying correspondence considered of little value.[25] After his death, the papers remained in the control of the family until 1904 when they were presented to the Library of Congress by Mrs. Smith Thompson Van Buren and Dr. Stuyvesant Fish Morris who had inherited them from Smith Thompson Van Buren.

The collection of Van Buren papers in the Library of Congress covers the years from 1787 on, but the main part relates to the period from 1820 to 1850. There is a legal record book for the years 1807–13 and an estimate record book for the years 1862–63. The major portion of the papers is correspondence written during his own administration and that of Andrew Jackson. The Library of Congress holds about 6,000 items; small collections are in the New York State Library, the Columbia County Historical Society, the Pierpont Morgan Library, and the Massachusetts Historical Society.

The Van Buren Papers in the Library of Congress

Series	Reels
1. Autobiography. 1854–62. 4 boxes	1–3
2. General Correspondence. 1787–1868. 61 boxes	4–34
3. Additional Correspondence. 1811–53. 1 box	34
4. Messages. 1837–38. 3 boxes	34–35
5. Legal Record Book. 1807–13. 1 box	35
6. Estimate Record Book. 1862–63. 1 box	35
7. Miscellany. 1814–1910. 3 boxes	Not filmed
8. Addendum.	
A. Addenda. 1799–1861.	Not filmed
B. Correspondence. 1799–1861 and undated.	36
9. Addendum. 1839–1947. 1 box	Not filmed

WILLIAM HENRY HARRISON
Ninth President—Whig
1841

William Henry Harrison, the fifth president to come from Virginia, was born in 1773 in Charles City County, the youngest of seven children of Benjamin Harrison, a well-to-do planter and politician, and a signer of the Declaration of Independence. Harrison attended Hampden-Sydney College and studied medicine under Dr. Benjamin Rush in Philadelphia. He left college in 1791 to join the army as an ensign, was assigned to General Anthony Wayne, and fought in several battles against the Indians. In 1798, John Adams appointed Harrison as secretary of the Northwest Territory and later territorial governor, a position he held from 1800 to 1812. In 1811, he first gained national attention when he won the Battle of Tippecanoe. At the outbreak of the war in 1812, he became brigadier general and was given command of the northwest frontier; he won the Battle of the Thames River in Canada in 1813. In 1814, he retired to his farm in North Bend, Indiana, and was elected to the U.S. Congress in 1816 for the 1817–19 term. From 1819 to 1825 he served in the Ohio senate. He became U.S. senator from Ohio in 1825 and resigned in 1828 to accept John Quincy Adams' appointment as U.S. minister to Colombia; he was recalled from that post when Andrew Jackson became president, and lived on his farm during the entire Jackson administration. In the campaign of 1836, he was one of several candidates put up by the new Whig party to run against Martin Van Buren and made a surprisingly good showing. In 1840, the Whigs united behind him and his running mate John Tyler against Martin Van Buren under the slogan "Tippecanoe and Tyler too." Harrison ran primarily on his military record, keeping silent about national issues. He won the election with a large popular vote, but never was able to test his popularity or his administrative skills because he served the shortest term of any president, dying exactly one month after his inauguration from pneumonia, the aftermath of a cold caught while delivering his long inaugural address.

William's son, John Scott Harrison, became the father of Benjamin Harrison, the twenty-third president of the United States.

The Harrison Papers

In 1858, the home of President Harrison in North Bend, Indiana, the "old Log Cabin," which became famous in the campaign of 1840, burned to the ground. According to the *New York Times*, almost everything in the house was lost except some furniture, clothing, and a few paintings. The report goes on to say that ". . . the public has sustained a great loss in the destruction of a mass of valuable correspondence and papers reaching from General Harrison's first entry into public life till the untimely close of his career. These papers were stored in one of the garrets, and only a basketful or two were saved."[26]

In 1896, President Benjamin Harrison wrote to a friend that his grandfather's papers were all destroyed when the residence at North Bend was burned, but that friends had sent him some letters, campaign publications, and published biographies. He goes on to say, "I have not found time to arrange or classify these materials and am not just now in a position to consider the question of attempting to write my grandfather's biography."[27]

In 1910, the Library of Congress first became interested in the William Henry Harrison papers, but was not able to obtain any. In 1915, Mrs. Mary Lord Harrison, the widow of President Benjamin Harrison, started to deposit her husband's papers in the Library of Congress. One of the boxes contained important papers of the ninth president, dating from 1805 to 1841, centering on the War of 1812. In this box were also the papers relating to the 1840 campaign that had been sent to Benjamin Harrison. Mrs. Harrison requested that the papers of her husband and his grandfather be treated as the same collection and that the papers be used only with her or her daughter's permission, which could be withdrawn at any time. Mrs. Harrison made additional deposits in 1928 and 1932; these deposits also contained William Henry Harrison papers along with the Benjamin Harrison papers. In June 1933, Mrs. Harrison donated all the deposited materials to the Library of Congress and requested that the William Henry Harrison papers be bound separately.

Over the years, family members donated small collections of original or photocopied manuscripts. By 1958, the Library of Congress had a collection of almost 1,000 papers preserved in nine volumes and two other containers. A few other William Henry Harrison manuscripts are in the historical societies of Indiana, New York, Pennsylvania, Virginia, and Wisconsin, and at the William Clements and University of North Carolina libraries.

The Harrison Papers in the Library of Congress

	Series	*Reels*
1.	General Correspondence. 1734–1939. 8 vols.	1–2
2.	Letterbook. 1812–13. 1 vol.	2
3.	Miscellany. ca. 1812-1932 and undated.	3–4
4.	Printed Matter. 1815–1922 and undated.	
	A. 4 pamphlets, including 2 addresses by President Harrison.	Not filmed
	B. Pamphlets concerning President Harrison. (Only title pages filmed)	
	C. Miscellaneous newspaper clippings and other printed matter.	Not filmed
5.	Original Correspondence and Photocopies. 1793–1841 and undated.	Not filmed

---

JOHN TYLER
Tenth President—Whig
1841–1845

Born in 1790, John Tyler, the descendant of prosperous Virginia planters, graduated from the College of William and Mary, studied law, and was admitted to the bar in 1809. He became a member of the Virginia legislature in 1811 and served as a captain in the militia during the War of 1812. In 1813, he married Letitia Christian, with whom he had eight children. Tyler was very popular in Virginia, was elected to Congress at age 26, became governor at 35, and U.S. senator at 36. He supported Andrew Jackson in the elections of 1828 and 1832, but broke with him in 1833 over the issues of nullification and secession. Tyler joined the Whig party and was put on the ticket in 1836 as a vice presidential candidate. In 1840, he ran on the Whig ticket with William Henry Harrison, and on April 5, 1841, when Harrison died, he became the nation's first "President by Act of God."

Tyler retained the members of Harrison's cabinet but immediately made it clear that he would be the boss of his administration. When the Whigs wanted to push legislation through Congress for a new national bank to deal with the economic crisis, Tyler vetoed the measure and his entire cabinet, except Secretary of State Daniel Webster, resigned. The Whig party officially expelled Tyler, who then appointed conservative Democrats to his cabinet. In 1842, he again vetoed bills calling for higher tariffs. The Whigs started impeachment procedures, but the House voted against impeachment in 1843 by a vote of 27 to 83.

During Tyler's presidency, Texas joined the Union by annexation and Florida was admitted as the twenty-seventh state. Tyler was widowed while in the White House and subsequently married Julia Gardiner, a New York socialite 30 years his junior, with whom he had seven children. In 1844, neither political party was willing to nominate him; he organized a new states' rights Democratic-Republican party, but when the Democrats nominated James K. Polk, he withdrew at the urging of Andrew Jackson. Tyler retired to his Virginia plantation, Sherwood Forest, where he lived with his growing young family and where he kept his library and papers.

An outspoken pro-slavery and states' rights advocate, Tyler strengthened the presidency as an administrator, but further widened the gap between North and South. In 1860, after Lincoln's election, Tyler proposed that a peace convention be held to try to avert civil war. He headed the delegation from Virginia and was elected president of the convention that met with President Buchanan. The peace conference ended in failure, and Tyler was elected to the Confederate House of Representatives. He died in January 1862 while attending the first session of this Congress.

The Tyler Papers

Tyler valued the papers that he had accumulated during his long career and made a will in 1859 in which he appointed four of his sons and two sons-in-law as his literary executors, "bequeathing to them for revision and publication if they shall think proper all such of my papers as relate to my own times and relate either to my own biography or to public affairs." He stipulated that the "collection of Autographs and all my private papers not relating to public affairs be given to my wife."[28]

In June 1864, Union troops looted his home. According to a letter of Union Col. Mason Tyler, "some books were carried off by soldiers and not a few letters from prominent leaders in the Confederacy to the Ex-President were discovered and appropriated."[29] A letter written by a soldier from Rhode Island states: "In the middle of the largest room was a cartload, more or less, of papers that had apparently been emptied from drawers as rubbish. This pile attracted my attention, and I was very soon absorbed in selecting letters and papers from historic personages."[30] The same soldier also found a package containing copies of telegrams sent to President Tyler while he was presiding officer of the Peace Convention. Other military and civilian travellers reported in their correspondence the looting and destruction of Tyler's home by General Wild's troops, but Captain Daniel R. Larned, General Burnside's secretary, reported that he gathered up the private papers and placed them in a box, and that the house was protected by a guard. Possibly some of these papers remained in the house until Mrs. Tyler returned a year later. Some of Tyler's papers were stored at his summer home, known as "Villa Margaret," in Hampton, Virginia. Mrs. Tyler, who came from New York, spent most of the war years with her mother in Staten Island, but managed to make trips back to Sherwood Forest in 1862 and 1863 and may have taken some possessions and possibly some letters with her to New York. She also deposited some papers at the Farmer's Bank in Richmond, Virginia, where, according to Dr. Lyon G. Tyler, one of the president's 15 children, "President Tyler's correspondence together with an account of his Bank vetoes and notes in extenso were destroyed in the Richmond fire of 1865."[31] Lyon G. Tyler was an ardent collector of his father's remaining papers and became in fact the president's literary executor. Owning a few papers, he contacted his father's friends to get more letters and papers. Slowly and tediously he collected from them whatever he could, and between 1884 and 1896 brought out a three-volume set entitled *Letters and Times of the Tylers*.[32] These papers were sold to the Library of Congress in 1919, and a few papers have been added since. The Library has about 1,450 documents in its collection. Other collections are in the library of the College of William and Mary in Williamsburg, Virginia, in the Gardiner Family Papers Collection at Yale University, at Duke University, and in the Pierpont Morgan Library.

The Tyler Papers in the Library of Congress

Series	Reels
1. General Correspondence. 1710–1861. 4 vols.	1–2
2. Autograph Collection. 1691–1916. 3 vols.	2–3
3. Additional Correspondence. 1844–1918.	3
4. Addenda.	

JAMES K. POLK
Eleventh President—Democrat
1845–1849

James Knox Polk was born in 1795 on a farm in North Carolina, the oldest of 10 children. He lived in Tennessee when he was a child, graduated from the University of North Carolina in 1818, and returned to Tennessee where he studied law and was admitted to the bar. He was elected to the Tennessee legislature at age 28 and became a United States representative at 30. Polk served in Congress for 14 years, four of them as Speaker of the House under the Jackson and Van Buren administrations. He left Congress in 1839 to run for and win the governorship of Tennessee. In 1844, Polk was nominated for president at the Democratic convention—the first "dark horse" presidential candidate of a major party; the Whig campaign slogan was "Who is James K. Polk?"[33] He campaigned for expansion and the annexation of Texas and Oregon and won the election by a very narrow popular and electoral margin. He was the youngest man to hold the office of president up to that time.

John Quincy Adams said of Polk: "He has no wit, no literature, no point of argument, no gracefulness of delivery, no elegance of language, no philosophy, no pathos, no felicitous impromptus; nothing that can constitute an orator but confidence, fluency, and labor."[34] He was a strong and conscientious administrator who kept all the strands of government in his own hands. James Buchanan, his secretary of state, said that Polk was "the most laborious man he had ever known."[35] He was assisted in his work by his wife, Sarah, whom he had married in 1824; theirs was one of the great, but lesser known, presidential partnerships. Polk fulfilled the nation's "manifest destiny" concept by pushing the frontier all the way to the Pacific Coast. He reached agreement on the boundaries of Oregon with Russia and Great Britain, and added New Mexico and California to the Union after a war with Mexico. In spite of the congressional Whig majority during 1847–49, he maintained good relations with Congress. Polk's health deteriorated under the stress of his work and he died in June 1849, only 103 days after leaving office.

The Polk Papers

Shortly before leaving the White House and only a few months before his death, Polk wrote his "Last Will and Testament" in which his papers are not specifically mentioned, but in which he left to his wife Sarah everything not otherwise disposed of, "including personal property of any description."[36] Sarah Childress Polk survived him by 42 years and spent her widowhood in seclusion at Polk Place in Nashville, Tennessee. There, all their possessions, including her husband's papers, remained.

Polk's concern for the collection of his papers started around 1825 when he was elected to Congress. He preserved all his correspondence very carefully during his pre-presidential years. In the beginning of his presidency, Polk was so busy that he had no time for correspondence; there are very few letters preserved from the first few months of his administration. By August 1845, however, he began the unusually meticulous and systematic compilation and preservation of his records that resulted in one of the most complete and thorough collections of the papers of any president. While he was in the White House, his secretaries kept an index of his correspondence and kept letterpress copies of all letters sent out from the White House. Charles G. Sellers, the first major biographer of Polk, referred to the papers as a magnificent collection. Milo Quaife, the editor of the *Diary of James K. Polk*, called Polk's documents "little short of marvelous."[37] Allan Nevins compared them to those of John Quincy Adams and Rutherford B. Hayes.

Shortly before his death, Polk asked William L. Marcy, his secretary of war, to write his biography, stating that the acts of his administration are now "a part of the public history" and recognizing the "great importance of having presented to the country a truthful and reliable history of the remarkable events which were crowded into my Presidential term, and especially in the War."[38] George Bancroft, an eminent historian, who had served Polk as secretary of the navy and as minister to Great Britain, had considered writing a Polk biography even before his inauguration, but the President felt that Marcy would be better suited to the task because his knowledge of the facts was more extensive. Marcy eventually decided not to write the biography, but John S. Jenkins published *The Life of James Knox Polk*, a popular biography, a year after the president's death, without using Polk's papers.[39]

Mrs. Polk continued to be interested in having a responsible author write her husband's biography and negotiated with Henry Stephens Randall and Ransom Hooker Gillet to let them use the papers, but both projects were dropped. John Cadwalader used some of the Polk papers for his biography of James Buchanan. In 1887, George Bancroft decided to work on a Polk biography after all and borrowed the president's papers, but did not get beyond a draft before 1891, when both Bancroft and Mrs. Polk died.

In 1875, Mrs. Polk had agreed to leave the papers to the Historical Society of Tennessee upon her death. However, 10 years later, when Mrs. Polk wrote her will, she stated that "the manuscripts, letters, correspondence, etc. belonging to my late husband, I give for her Sole and Seperate [sic] use to my Niece Mrs. George W. Fall, whom I reared from infancy and who is to me as a daughter."[40]

During the first decade after Mrs. Polk's death, nothing was heard about the papers, but in 1902, an announcement of the Chicago Historical Society appeared which indicated that it had purchased some papers of President Polk, including his 1845 to 1849 diary and some drafts of his messages, speeches, and correspondence between 1826 and 1848. In 1903, Librarian of Congress Ainsworth R. Spofford sent Worthington C. Ford of the Manuscript Division to Nashville when he learned that a substantial part of the Polk papers was in Mrs. Fall's possession. Mr. Fall wrote to Spofford that his wife would be willing to dispose of the papers at "a reasonable figure." Ford found that all the papers, with the exception of about 300 letters that had been sold to the Chicago Historical Society, were still available and that the price was "dirt cheap."[41] In December 1903 the collection of about 10,000 items arrived at the Library of Congress. Arrangement and indexing of the Polk papers began immediately, and the collection was ready for use shortly thereafter. Seven years later, Herbert Putnam, the next librarian of Congress, wanted to complete the collection of Polk papers and arranged for the purchase of the papers held by the Chicago Historical Society.

In 1927, the third and final large collection of Polk papers came to light. Working on an edition of Andrew Jackson's papers, historians J. Franklin Jameson and John Spencer Bassett learned about the existence of a large number of Polk papers in the possession of Mrs. Rollin P. Grant, the daughter of Mrs. George W. Fall. Jameson informed the librarian of Congress of the existence of these papers; Putnam explained to Mrs. Grant that in 1903 the Library of Congress had purchased from Mrs. Fall all the papers of President Polk and convinced Mrs. Grant to have her papers shipped to the Library of Congress. Mrs. Grant agreed to this request but asked that some original letters be sent to the Polk Memorial Room in the War Memorial Building in Nashville, Tennessee, to permit her to keep a promise she had made previously. Putnam was pleased to comply with this condition. Since then some items have been added and the Library of Congress now has a collection of more than 20,500 Polk papers. A few items are held by the Yale University Library and by the Tennessee State Library.

The Polk Papers in the Library of Congress

Series	*Reels*
1. Diaries. 1845–49. 25 vols.	1–3
2. General Correspondence and Related Items. 1775–1849. 132 vols.	4–55

3. Additional Correspondence and Related Material.
   1826–49. 3 boxes   56–57
4. Letter Press Copy Books. 1845–49. 5 vols.   57–59
5. Messages and Speeches. 1833–49. 7 boxes   60–61
6. Notes in Polk's Handwriting and Executive Record
   Book. 1831–47 and undated. 2 boxes, 1 vol.   61–62
7. Account and Memoranda Books. 1820–49. 16 vols.   62
8. Miscellaneous. Broadsides and Broadsheets. 1827–83.
   2 boxes   63
9. Sarah C. Polk Papers. 1838–91. 3 vols.   63–64
10. Printed Matter. 8 containers   Not filmed
11. Omitted Correspondence. 1811–49.   64–67

ZACHARY TAYLOR
Twelfth President—Whig
1849–1850

Zachary Taylor was the seventh Virginian to reach the White House, and the first president elected to office without previous political experience. Like William Henry Harrison, Taylor was chosen by the Whigs as their presidential candidate primarily because he was a war hero. Born in 1784, the son of a Revolutionary War officer, he was brought up on the Kentucky frontier where there were no schools. His rather rudimentary education was provided by tutors his father hired. He was commissioned as a first lieutenant in the U.S. Army at age 23 through the influence of James Madison, who was a relative and was then secretary of state. Taylor spent the next 40 years in the army, fighting successfully against Indians and Mexicans and rising to the rank of major general. He married Margaret Smith in 1810 and had six children with her. Their only son became a lieutenant general of the Confederacy, and one of their daughters married Jefferson Davis, the president of the Confederacy.

After the annexation of Texas in 1845, Taylor was given command of troops on the Rio Grande to defend the territory against Mexican efforts at reconquest. He became famous through the victory at Buena Vista, a battle fought during the Mexican War. The Whig convention in June 1848 nominated Taylor for president because it felt that "Old Rough and Ready's" homespun ways and his long and distinguished military record would be political assets in the North; as a descendant of an old southern family, Taylor was in favor of opening the Southwest territories to slavery, which would help him in the South. He ran against Lewis Cass, a Democratic senator from Michigan. Martin Van Buren ran as the anti-slavery candidate of the Free Soil party and split the Democratic vote, giving Taylor the election by a small margin. Both houses of Congress were controlled by the Democrats.

Taylor had no definite plans for his administration, but controversy erupted in 1849 over whether the new territories acquired from Mexico should be free or slave. To end the dispute over slavery in new territories, Taylor urged settlers in New Mexico and California to draft constitutions and apply for statehood. Southern leaders were furious and threatened secession in February 1850, but Taylor declared that he would command the Army against them in person and hang any man taken in treason. Congress tried to construct a compromise, but Taylor was opposed to it and would have vetoed it had not events taken an unexpected turn. On July 4, 1850, he laid the cornerstone of the Washington Monument and remained out in the hot sun for several hours. He became ill from the heat and died several days later. Daniel Webster was convinced that Taylor's death prevented the outbreak of civil war in 1850.[42]

The Taylor Papers

President Taylor's personal papers were destroyed or dispersed in 1862 when the home of his son, Richard, in St. Charles Parish, Louisiana, was confiscated by the Union Army. Some letters of Union soldiers describe the plunder of the 700-acre plantation and home in which many of the memorabilia, artifacts, and papers taken there by Mrs. Taylor were looted, and the house burned.

When the Library of Congress began to build its collection of presidential papers, it was greatly frustrated in attempts to purchase the Taylor papers. A few Taylor items were purchased in 1904, and the president's grandson, Captain John R.M. Taylor, gave some letters to the Library in 1906. In 1909, Gaillard Hunt, Chief of the Manuscript Division, tried to acquire more Taylor papers and wrote to many people who might have received letters from Taylor and to the President's daughter, Betty Taylor Bliss Dandridge. She replied: "All his papers, both public and private, were stored at my brother General Richard Taylor's Plantation near New Orleans and were destroyed when the house was sacked and burned in 1862 by the Federal troops during the War."[43] In 1919, the small number of items in the Library's possession were bound into one volume. In 1922, Betty Taylor (Mrs. Walter R. Stauffer), daughter of Richard Taylor, added two items as a gift and 11 others as a deposit. In 1944, the Library purchased 64 letters written by Zachary Taylor to Thomas S. Jesup and eight items, dated 1818 to 1840, relating to the Seminole Indian campaign of 1837 and 1838. In 1952, the Stauffer family in New Orleans converted the 1922 deposit into a gift and added nearly 500 items relating to President Taylor and his son. Several additions over the years brought the collection to approximately 650 items. Several collections in the Library contain letters or copies of letters written by or to Taylor and documents referring to him.

Small numbers of Taylor documents, mostly pre-presidential, are widely scattered among collectors and libraries, including the Kentucky Historical Society, the University of Kentucky, the University of North Carolina, and the Huntington Library in California.

The Taylor Papers in the Library of Congress

Series	Reels
1. Autobiographical Account. ca. 1826.	1
2. General Correspondence. 1814–50. 2 boxes	1
3. Family Papers. 1837–87.	2
4. Miscellany. 1820–1931.	2
5. Memorial Volume. 1850. 1 vol.	2
6. Addenda. 1820–50 and undated.	

    A. Correspondence. 1829–50 and undated.
      1 container
    B. Letter Fragment from Zachary Taylor to Jefferson
      Davis. Dec. 1847.

FRANKLIN PIERCE
Fourteenth President—Democrat
1853–1857

Franklin Pierce was born in Hillsboro, New Hampshire, in 1804. He was the son of a Revolutionary War veteran who was a tavern keeper and a leader of the Democratic-Republican party in the state. He graduated from Bowdoin College and was admitted to the bar in 1827, the same year his father was elected governor of New Hampshire. Pierce was elected to the New Hampshire state legislature and became speaker of the lower house in 1830; at age 28, he was elected to Congress and served two terms in the House. In 1837, he became the youngest member of the U.S. Senate. His wife, whom he had married in 1830, suffered from tuberculosis and did not like Washington, which forced him to live a bachelor life. He began to drink heavily. In 1842, he returned to New Hampshire and continued to be politically active in the state. President Polk offered him the position of attorney general in 1845, but he did not accept. In 1847, he accepted a commission as a colonel in the volunteer army to fight in the Mexican War and was promoted to brigadier general within a year. After returning to New Hampshire in 1848, Pierce refused the Democratic nomination for governor, but two years later presided over a convention to revise the state constitution.

Possibly the darkest of dark horses at the Democratic convention of 1852, his name was entered on the thirty-fifth ballot when the contest between Lewis Cass and James Buchanan came to a standstill. He was nominated on the forty-ninth ballot, much to the distress of his wife, who still did not want to move to Washington. Pierce denied that he had sought the nomination and the family discord sharpened when their 11 year old son Benjamin wrote to his mother: "I hope he won't be elected for I should not like to be in Washington and I know you would not either."[44] However, the Whig party was in a state of disintegration, and Pierce easily won the election against Lieutenant General Winfield Scott.

Two months before he took office, Pierce and his wife saw Benjamin, their only surviving child, killed when their train was derailed. Their two other children had died in infancy, so this latest tragedy nearly devastated them. Pierce entered the presidency emotionally exhausted and with his self-confidence destroyed. He had been elected president because he was a northern Democrat who favored the extension of slavery. He attempted to purchase Cuba from Spain and to pressure Great Britain to relinquish its special interests in Central America. These moves toward expansion angered the North. He also supported the Kansas-Nebraska Act of 1854, which repealed the Missouri Compromise, enabling Kansas to become a slave state if the settlers would vote for it. Southerners and northerners vied for control of the territory and shooting broke out in Kansas, a prelude to the Civil War. While aiming to preserve the Union, Pierce tried to maintain a balance between northern nationalism and southern sectionalism. By the end of his administration, peace had been restored in Kansas. Though he did much for the expansion of trade and purchased land across Arizona and New Mexico to be used as a right of way for a new railroad to the Pacific coast, he eventually lost the respect of both sides. His close association with the Kansas issue cost him his renomination in 1856, when the Democrats selected James Buchanan as their candidate. The Pierces retired to New Hampshire at the end of his term.

In 1860, Pierce refused any suggestions about running for president and proposed Jefferson Davis, his former secretary of war, as the best candidate the Democrats could choose. As the Civil War began, Pierce still opposed the use of force by the North and considered the Emancipation Proclamation unconstitutional. He was shunned by his friends because of his political beliefs, and when his wife died in 1863, he began to drink more heavily. He died in 1869. Few presidents had less success in the White House and experienced more tragedy in personal life.

The Pierce Papers

In 1868, a year before his death, Pierce left a will in which he made no reference to his personal papers but bequeathed "all of the rest and of my Estate of every kind and description whether real personal or mixed . . . to my nephew Frank H. Pierce."[45] Frank Pierce served in the diplomatic corps and practiced law in New York. Because of his absence from New Hampshire, his brother, Kirk D. Pierce, had possession of the President's personal papers and sold them to the Library of Congress in 1904. The collection was quite small and probably only a remnant of what must have existed when Pierce left the White House. The Library organized the manuscripts and published a calendar of them in 1917.[46] Roy F. Nichols, the President's biographer, believes that Pierce may deliberately have destroyed most of the papers of his presidential years after he retired, including what must have been a voluminous correspondence between himself and his wife. The prefatory note to the *Calendar* refers to a fire that is said to have destroyed many of the Pierce papers; however, members of the Pierce family do not recall hearing of such a fire.[47]

During 1924 and 1926, the New Hampshire Historical Society purchased some papers from the Pierce family. The society allowed the Library of Congress to obtain photostats of these items. The Henry E.

Huntington Library possesses a diary kept by Pierce during the Mexican War, which it allowed the Library to copy. These items are included in the Pierce microfilm collection and index produced by the Library in 1959. Some items have been added since, totalling approximately 2,300 pages. Letters by, to, or about Pierce can be found in other manuscript collections in the Library. Other Pierce manuscripts are owned by Bowdoin College, the William L. Clements Library, the Concord Public Library, the New York Public Library, and the historical societies of New Jersey and Pennsylvania.

The Pierce Papers in the Library of Congress

Series	*Reels*
1. Diary. May 27–July 30, 1847. 1 vol.	1
2. General Correspondence. 1838–68. 7 vols.	1–3
3. Additional Correspondence. 1820–69. 14 vols.	3–6
4. Miscellaneous Correspondence. 1838–69. 1 box	6
5. Messages to Congress. 1854–56. 3 vols.	7
6. Addenda. Autograph Letters and Manuscripts. 1824–57 and undated. 1 box	Not filmed

ABRAHAM LINCOLN
Sixteenth President—Republican
1861–1865

Born in 1809 near Hodgenville, Kentucky, Abraham Lincoln moved at the age of seven with his parents to Spencer County, Indiana. He lost his mother at the age of 10, and moved with his father to Illinois. Lincoln helped with farm work, did some other semi-skilled jobs, and obtained about a year's worth of formal education. He worked as a clerk in a store in New Salem, Illinois, and, in 1832, served for two months as a volunteer in the Black Hawk War, where he was elected captain of volunteers. To support himself while studying law, Lincoln worked as surveyor and later as postmaster of New Salem. From 1834 to 1842, he served as a member of the Illinois state legislature, was licensed in 1836 to practice law, and married Mary Todd in 1842. In 1843, he ran for Congress as a Whig and was defeated. He served in Congress as representative from Illinois from 1847 to 1849 and practiced law in Springfield between 1849 and 1854. He was an unsuccessful candidate for the Republican vice presidential nomination in 1856, and was defeated in his campaign for the Senate in 1858. However, in this election he won national prominence because of his debates on the slavery issue with Stephen A. Douglas. This exposure won him the Republican presidential nomination in 1860. The northern Democrats nominated Douglas; the southern Democrats nominated John C. Breckenridge; and the remnants of the Whigs and Know-Nothings formed a new Constitutional Union party with John Bell of Tennessee as their candidate. Lincoln won the election and became the first Republican president.

As president, Lincoln built the Republican party into a strong organization and rallied most of the northern Democrats to the Union cause. When he moved into the White House in 1861, seven states had left the Union and others were preparing to do so. Most federal forts in the South had been taken over by the secessionist states, but Fort Sumter in South Carolina still remained in federal hands. When it fell, Lincoln realized that only force could preserve the Union. He called for volunteers to suppress the rebellion and ordered a blockade of all southern ports. In September 1862, Lincoln issued a proclamation ordering the seceded states to return to the Union by January 1, 1863, or all slaves within areas under rebellion would be freed. In 1863, the Emancipation Proclamation was issued accordingly, and in July of that year, the Union forces won the Battle of Gettysburg. In 1864, Lincoln was re-elected. On April 9, 1865, Lee surrendered to Grant at Appomattox Court House; five days later John Wilkes Booth mortally wounded Lincoln at Ford's Theater in Washington.

The Lincoln Papers

After the death of the President, Robert T. Lincoln, his only surviving son, asked Associate Supreme Court Justice David Davis to administer his father's estate. The files of the President were packed by Lincoln's secretaries, John G. Nicolay and Col. John Hay, and were stored at the National Bank of Bloomington until 1874, when Robert Lincoln directed that they be sent to John Nicolay in Washington, who was preparing an authorized Lincoln biography jointly with John Hay.[48] When Nicolay died in 1901, these papers were moved to the Department of State with the approval of then Secretary of State Hay. Herbert Putnam, director of the Library of Congress, contacted Robert Lincoln in December 1901 and suggested that his father's papers be stored in the Library, but Lincoln took no action. After Hay's death in 1905, Lincoln moved his father's papers to his office in the Pullman Building in Chicago. When Robert Lincoln retired to Washington, he took the papers with him and stored them during the winter months in his home in Georgetown, and during the summers in his country home in Manchester, Vermont. In the spring of 1919, 54 years after the President's assassination, Robert finally deposited the papers in the Library of Congress with the provision that their whereabouts should not be announced because he was still worried that the papers, if they fell into the wrong hands, would be damaging to people still alive. In 1923, four years later, he deeded the papers to the Library of Congress with the stipulation that the papers be withheld from inspection for 21 years from the date of his death. He died in July 1926. [49]

Why Robert Lincoln withheld his father's papers from public view for 82 years is not clear; it does not seem that he ever inspected them himself. He wrote in 1865 that the papers relating to the Lincoln administration were in such confused state that they could not be used. He stated in his will "Such of said manuscripts and papers as I shall not have withdrawn from such custody before my death, I hereby give and bequeath to the government of the United States to be kept and preserved in said Library of Congress."[50] The papers were placed in six specially built cases, sealed and placed into a locked compartment in the Manuscript Division of the Library of Congress. In anticipation of the opening, the papers were arranged, indexed, bound, and microfilmed, but the staff working on this task was sworn to complete secrecy. On July 26, 1947, the boxes were opened to the public. They contained over 18,000 individual documents, including some 900 separate memoranda, copies of letters, proclamations, and drafts of speeches written by the President. Over the years, additional papers have been added to the collection, and other manuscript collections in the Library contain letters written by and to Lincoln. The Library holds approximately 42,000 Lincoln items; the Illinois Historical Society and Brown University also have substantial collections.

The Lincoln Papers in the Library of Congress

Series	Reels
1. General Correspondence and Related Documents. 1833–1916. 194 vols.	1–94
2. Additional Correspondence. 1858–65. 1 box	95–97
3. Miscellaneous. 1837–97. 1 box	97

7. Post-Civil War Presidents

ANDREW JOHNSON
Seventeenth President—National Union
1865–1869

Born in Raleigh, North Carolina, in 1808, Andrew Johnson lost his father, a laborer, when he was three years old. He was apprenticed to a tailor at 14, learned from a co-worker to read, and moved with his family to Greeneville, Tennessee, in 1826. In 1827, Johnson married 16 year old Eliza McCardle and opened his own tailor shop. His wife taught him to write and do simple arithmetic. He was elected to the village council when he was 19 and became mayor of Greeneville two years later. A supporter of Andrew Jackson, Johnson became known as a defender of the rights of the working man. He served in the Tennessee House of Representatives from 1835–37 and from 1839–41, and as a member of the Tennessee Senate from 1841–43. In 1843, he was elected to Congress and served for four terms, supporting the Polk administration on the Mexican War and later the Compromise of 1850. He became governor of Tennessee in 1853, and when he was elected U. S. Senator from Tennessee in 1857, he said: "I have reached the summit of my ambition."[1]

Tennessee proposed Johnson as a presidential candidate at the Democratic convention of 1860, but he withdrew and campaigned for John Breckenridge. He opposed southern secession; when Tennessee joined the Confederacy, he remained in Washington and was considered a traitor in the South. Lincoln appointed him military governor of Tennessee in 1862 and he proved to be an excellent and fair administrator. Tennessee was the only seceding state to outlaw slavery by its own action and be exempted from the Emancipation Proclamation.

In 1864, the National Union convention chose Johnson as Lincoln's running mate and he was sworn in as president after Lincoln's death. He did not expect the opposition of the Radical Republicans in Congress to his moderate approach to reconstruction. Neither side was willing to compromise and his conflict with Congress increased further when he issued a general amnesty, followed by several proclamations enabling southern states to re-establish their civil governments. In response, the Republican Congress enacted harsh reconstruction legislation and finally started impeachment procedures against Johnson. After months of tension, Johnson escaped conviction by one vote, but the deadlock between president and Congress continued until an embittered Johnson left Washington at the end of his term. Determined to prove that his actions as president had been right, he ran unsuccessfully for Congress in 1869 and

1872. He was finally elected to the U.S. Senate in 1874 and died of a stroke in July 1875, half a year after his return to Washington. His most notable achievements, beyond the re-admission of the seceded states, were the purchase of Alaska and his attempts to improve the civil service.

The Johnson Papers

As a man who had learned to read and write comparatively late in life, Andrew Johnson greatly valued the records of his career. Before the Civil War, he and his wife had carefully gathered and organized his books and papers in one room of his office in Greeneville, but few records of his early career survived the war. The office was used at various times by both sides as barracks, hospital, officers' residence, and den for camp followers. When he returned to Tennessee in 1862 as military governor, Johnson was headquartered in Nashville, while Greeneville, in East Tennessee, remained in rebel hands.

In 1864, Robert Johnson wrote to his father that it was "rumored at Knoxville that the rebels had taken possession of all our books, papers, etc at Greeneville."[2] Confederate Major Raphael J. Moses, on the staff of General James Longstreet, was using the Johnson library in Greenville as his headquarters in 1864. He reported seeing a big wooden box that was all nailed up, and that he thought might contain "some of the good old rye whiskey Old Andy was very fond of."[3] When a detail of soldiers broke open the box, they found to their disappointment nothing but old letters and private papers. Moses looked over the papers, kept 40 or 50, including some written to Mrs. Johnson and President Polk, and destroyed the rest. After the war, Moses returned the papers he had saved to President Johnson.

Johnson's concern for these lost materials is expressed in a letter he wrote to General Longstreet in June 1869, in which he complained that several trunks had been removed from a storehouse while the general was in command of the post in 1864. He stated: "These trunks contained many valuable articles of property as well as papers: such as deeds, bills of sale, mortgages, memoranda of matters of much importance to me, also a number of valuable letters many of them of a private character."[4] Apparently few of the early Johnson papers, except the ones taken and later returned by Major Moses, have survived.

After the end of his term in 1869, Johnson and his family returned to Greeneville, bringing with them papers from the White House years. These papers, the record of his stormy presidency, were carefully stored. After Johnson's death in 1875, Johnson's oldest daughter, Mrs. Martha Johnson Patterson, became the guardian of the papers and declined all requests to read or borrow them. The only exception was Laura Carter Holloway Langford, a Brooklyn writer and editor and an acquaintance of the family, who was given access to the papers in the 1890s to work on a Johnson biography. Around 1900, Langford again asked to work on the papers, many of which had at that time been loaned by Mrs. Patterson to David M. DeWitt, who was working on his book, *Impeachment and Trial of Andrew Johnson*.[5] DeWitt sent some of the papers to Mrs. Langford, who apparently did not return all of them. Before her death in 1901, Mrs.

Patterson gave access to some papers to Reverend James S. Jones, pastor at Greeneville, who was writing a biography entitled *Life of Andrew Johnson,*[6] and who also sent some papers to Langford which were not returned. After the death of Mrs. Patterson, all extant papers came into the possession of Andrew Johnson Patterson, the President's grandson.

In 1903, Worthington C. Ford, chief of the Manuscript Division of the Library of Congress, examined the Johnson papers, found them all "extraordinarily valuable,"[7] and recommended that they be purchased. In 1904, the collection was acquired by the Library. In subsequent years, minor additions were made, mainly from the Patterson family; one large addition of 1,500 pieces from the pre-presidential period was made in 1930. The Library holds a total of over 32,000 Johnson papers. A collection of letters, identified as materials given by Martha Patterson to Mrs. Langford, was purchased by the Henry E. Huntington Library in 1919. Records of Johnson's services as governor are in the Tennessee State Library. There are no other large collections of Johnson manuscripts.

The Johnson Papers in the Library of Congress

Series	*Reels*
1. General Correspondence. 1841–91.	1–39
2. Additional Correspondence. 1814–1900.	39–42
3. Letterbooks. 1864–69. 10 vols.	42–43
A. 1865–69. 6 vols.	
B. 1864–69. 4 vols.	
4. Indexes to Letters Received and Record Book.	
1862–69. 7 vols	44–45
A. 1865–69. 5 vols.	
B. 1862. 1 vol.	
C. 1862–63. 1 vol.	
5. Messages. 1862–69. 14 vols., 2 boxes	45–47
A. 11 vols.	
B. 1 vol.	
C. 1 vol.	
D. 1 vol.	
E. 2 Boxes	
6. Applications and Appointments. 1865–69. 10 vols.	48–49
A. 1865–69. 5 vols.	
B. 1865–69. 5 vols.	
7. Executive Documents. 1865–69. 5 vols.	49
A. 1865–68. 2 vols.	
B. 1865–69. 1 vol.	
C. 1865–67. 2 vols.	
8. Courts-Martial and Amnesty Records. 1864–69.	
5 vols.	49–50
A. 1865–69. 2 vols.	
B. Jan.-May 1864. 1 vol.	
C. 1865–69. 3 vols.	
9. Moore Diaries. 1866–71. 3 boxes	50–51
A. The Small Diary. July 8, 1866–Mar. 20, 1868.	
B. The Large Diary. Mar. 21, 1868–Jan. 24, 1871.	
C. A Diary consisting of a free longhand transcript.	
July 1866–Apr. 8, 1868.	
10. Financial Records. 1829–77. 2 vols.	51–52

11. Scrapbooks. Ca. 1861–75. 12 vols.	52–53
12. Lists. ca. 1858–92.	54
13. Newspaper Clippings. ca. 1868. 1 vol.	54
14. Essays. 1866. 1 vol.	54
15. Dolittle Letters. 1866. 1 vol.	54
16. Diplomatic List. 1 vol.	54
17. Military Documents. 1862–65. 2 boxes	54
18. Miscellaneous Documents. 1783–1932.	54–55
19. Calling Cards and Pictures. 1 folder.	55
20. Printed Matter. 1854–60.	55

ULYSSES S. GRANT
Eighteenth President—Republican
1869–1877

Grant's career proved that a superior general and leader of men in war can turn out to be a bad president. Born in Ohio in 1822, the son of a tanner and farmer, he worked on the farm. He had a less than average education, but was admitted to West Point where he graduated in 1843 as twenty-first in a class of 39. He participated as second lieutenant in the Mexican War and was promoted to captain for his bravery. Grant married in 1848, was assigned to military duty on the West Coast, began to drink heavily, and was forced to resign his commission in 1854. He failed as a farmer, failed in the real estate business, and moved his family in 1860 to Galena, Illinois, to work as a clerk in his brother's store.

In 1861, in response to Lincoln's call for volunteers, he became commander of an Illinois volunteer regiment. Success for Grant began with the capture of 20,000 Confederate prisoners at Fort Henry and Fort Donelson in 1862, and continued through the battles of Shiloh, Vicksburg, and Chattanooga, leading to his appointment to command all Union armies in 1864. In 1865 he led the Union forces to the capture of Richmond, and accepted Lee's surrender at Appomattox Court House. After the war, he served as secretary of war under President Johnson, was elected president in 1868 at age 46, and re-elected to a second term in 1872. He selected a rather incompetent cabinet, executed the Reconstruction Acts with uncompromising rapidity, failed to improve the civil service, saw Congress reject his plan to annex Santo Domingo as a refuge for freed slaves, and had two cabinet members resign to avoid impeachment. He admitted that it was his "fortune, or misfortune to be called to the office of Chief Executive without any previous political training."[8]

After leaving the presidency, Grant toured Europe where he was celebrated as the hero of the American war for freedom. Encouraged by this success, he tried to run again for the presidency in 1880. A deadlock between him and James G. Blaine at the Republican convention gave the nomination to James A. Garfield, a dark horse candidate. His bad luck continued when he lost all his savings in a bank failure in 1884. Destitute and seriously ill with throat cancer, he decided to write his memoirs for magazine serialization in order to provide for his family. His brilliant work was a popular success and, in spite of his illness, he courageously persisted in this task and finished his work a week before he died in July 1885. Mark Twain had the memoirs published in book form and Grant's family received a profit of half a million dollars.[9]

The Grant Papers

In his military career, Grant once received a reprimand from General Henry W. Hallek for failure to report promptly the fall of Fort Donelson. Grant's excuse was that he "was writing daily and sometimes two and three times a day."[10] He issued a general order on record keeping in which he stated: "The necessity of order and regularity about head-quarters, especially in keeping the records, makes it necessary to assign particular duties to each member of the staff."[11] However, he also wrote in his memoirs that he was "no clerk" and went on to say: "The only place I ever found in my life to put a paper so as to find it again was either a side coat pocket or the hands of a clerk more careful than myself."[12] Among papers he misplaced were a whole chapter of Adam Badeau's *Military History of U.S. Grant,*[13] the entire manuscript of John Russell Young's book *Around the World with General Grant,*[14] and an important letter of President Lincoln.

A close associate reported that when he met Grant in 1861 in Cairo, Illinois, he found that "Grant's office was substantially in his hat or his pockets . . . and the camp story was but slightly exaggerated which asserted that half his general orders were blowing about in the sand and dirt of the streets of Cairo."[15] Grant wrote about himself: "I have been very much employed in writing. I wrote my own orders, plans of battle, instructions and reports. As President I wrote every official document usual for a President to write."[16] Horace Porter, Grant's secretary, commented that Grant seldom dictated but wrote most of his documents in his own hand.

The Grant papers were used by Adam Badeau for his *Military History,* which was published between 1868 and 1881. The *Official Records of the War of the Rebellion*[17] made use of headquarter records compiled by Grant. The most intensive use of his papers was made by Grant himself when he wrote his *Personal Memoirs of U.S. Grant.* Badeau lived in Grant's house during the last year before Grant's death, and helped with the writing and editing of the *Memoirs,* but Grant maintained that the work was "the product of my own brain and hand."[18] Some editorial assistance and verifications were also contributed by his eldest son, Frederick D. Grant.

The Library of Congress began to collect Grant's papers in 1904. Worthington C. Ford, chief of the Manuscript Division, thought that there might be two letter books in the White House that he believed at the time to be "the sole relic of any Presidential papers."[19] In 1919, not two but four letter books were discovered and placed in the library by Major U.S. Grant III, the President's grandson. Major Grant and his mother also located the original manuscript of the *Personal Memoirs* and deposited it in the Library of Congress. In 1922, they deposited Grant's first inaugural speech and his reports about the battles of Vicksburg and

Chattanooga in the library. Grant papers in the Huntington Library were copied and sent to the Library of Congress in 1925. In 1953 and 1957, Major Grant presented the "Headquarters Reports" in 111 volumes, and in 1960 he gave the Library 300 of Grant's letters to his wife. Through other gifts of the family and some purchases, the Grant collection has grown to over 47,500 manuscripts, providing a very representative documentation of his life, except for his youth. There are also some Grant papers in the New York Historical Society Library.

Arrangement of the papers is difficult due to duplications; some of the military documents exist in as many six copies. The volumes of papers were compiled long after the events to which they related, resulting in mistakes in dating. How many essential documents are missing and where and how they got lost will probably never be ascertained. However, the remaining documents comprise the basic materials for one of the most controversial presidents.

The Grant Papers in the Library of Congress

Series	*Reels*
1. General Correspondence and Related Materials. 1844–1922. 15 vols.	
A. Letters Written by Grant to Julia B. Dent. 1844–83. 3 vols.	1
B. General Correspondence and Related Items. 1861–1922. 6 vols.	1–2
C. Copies of Grant Documents. 1849–86. 5 vols.	3
D. Copies of Grant's Correspondence. 1853–83. 1 vol.	3
2. Letterbooks. 1869–77. 5 vols.	4
3. Speeches, Reports, Messages. 1863–76. 4 vols.	4–5
4. Personal Memoirs. 1884–85. 10 vols.	5–6
5. Headquarters Records. 1861–69. 111 vols.	6–30
6. Miscellany. 1839–67. 3 vols.	
A. Military Records. 1861–67. 2 vols.	30
B. Photocopy of Grant's Account. 1839–43. 1 vol.	30
C. Miscellaneous Documents.	30
7. Scrapbooks. 1870–92. 15 vols.	30–32
8. Addenda.	Not filmed
9. Addenda.	Not filmed

JAMES A. GARFIELD
Twentieth President—Republican
1881

James Abraham Garfield, born in 1831 in Orange township, Ohio, and brought up in considerable poverty, was the last of the "log cabin" presidents. His father died when he was an infant, but his mother kept the family together. Garfield developed an early interest in reading and education and was determined to go to college. After working as a sailor and as an Ohio Canal tow boy, he was able to attend Hiram Eclectic Institute (later Hiram College) and cover his expenses by tutoring other students, including Lucretia Rudolph, who later became his wife. Garfield transferred to Williams College in Massachusetts, where he graduated in 1856. He returned to Hiram as a professor of Latin and Greek, and became president of the school a year later. He studied law and trained to be an evangelist lay preacher, which polished his oratorical skills.

Garfield was elected to the Ohio Senate in 1859. At the outbreak of the Civil War, he joined the Ohio Infantry Volunteers as a lieutenant colonel; he fought with great courage, rose to the rank of brigadier general, and was given a battlefield promotion to major general. He was elected to Congress while on active duty; upon President Lincoln's urging, he resigned from the army in 1863 to take his seat in the House of Representatives. He was re-elected eight times and served in the House for 17 years. Garfield sided with the Radical Republicans, voted for Andrew Johnson's impeachment, and was a member of the Electoral Commission named to decide the disputed Hayes-Tilden election in 1876. During the 1880 Republican convention he was nominated as a dark horse compromise candidate and won the presidential election by a narrow margin. His feelings against the South remained strong and he stated that he would only restore friendship with the South if "it shall be admitted, forever and forever more, that in the War for the Union, we were right and they were wrong."[20]

As president, he adopted as his domestic platform civil service reform and the strengthening of the executive powers of the presidency. In foreign policy he meant to assume a new direction in inter-American affairs and arranged for a Latin American conference to meet in Washington in 1882. The conference never took place because, on July 2, 1881, Garfield was shot by Charles J. Guiteau, a disgruntled, mentally disturbed office seeker. He lingered painfully for over two months, dying at the age of 50.

The Garfield Papers

Like John Adams, Garfield showed great concern for recording his experiences meticulously and kept everything he wrote. Both presidents loved and collected books, and organized and preserved their papers with care; both families continued this tradition. When Garfield visited the Adams family, he wrote to his wife on July 8, 1869: "Before I left the Adams House, I looked through a few of the manuscript journals and letters of John and John Q. Adams. Charles Francis is now at work preparing a mass of them for publication. Do you suppose Hal or Jim will ever care to look over your letters to me and mine to you?"[21] Both presidents' wives were close helpmates in their work and in the preservation of their papers. Mrs. Garfield continued the collection and upkeep of the President's records until her death in 1918.

Garfield started to collect his papers at an early age. In 1856, he assured his future wife that her letters are "all arranged in chronological order."[22] His diary contains frequent references to his papers, on many of which he had noted "to be preserved." While he served in Congress, the

Garfields meticulously kept their papers in their homes in Washington and Ohio. In 1876, the Garfields purchased a farm called Lawnfield, near Mentor, Ohio, and enlarged the house to have space for his office and library where he kept his books and papers. In contrast to presidents such as Grant and Coolidge, Garfield's rule as a public official was to answer every letter and to keep records of this correspondence. He employed two private secretaries and also obtained the help of some family members, particularly his son James R. Garfield. After the attack on the president, his wife requested from the newspapers that everything that had been written about her husband be sent to her. This material is preserved in scrapbooks entitled "Eighty Days," the period of the President's survival after the attack on his life.[23]

Joseph Stanley-Brown, Garfield's private secretary, continued as curator and indexer of the papers with the full support of Mrs. Garfield. His first task was to segregate, seal, and store the private papers in the vaults of the Treasury Department. His second task was to sort Mrs. Garfield's papers, which he did at his home in Washington. Burke A. Hinsdale used some of the papers when he edited *The Works of James Abraham Garfield*,[24] which included only speeches, addresses, and published papers and did not deal with Garfield's life. In 1885, after all the papers had been bound, they were shipped to the Garfield home in Mentor, where Mrs. Garfield added a fireproof and secure "Memorial Room" to the home. Over the years the family worked to add other papers to the collection.

In June 1903, Murat Halstead, a newspaper man, wrote to James R. Garfield, trying to interest the family in publishing the papers of the President; Garfield replied that the family had "very thoroughly considered the question of publication and have determined that nothing fragmentary should be done."[25] In July 1911, the family asked Professor Theodore Clarke Smith of Williams College to write the biography of the President, which was published under the title *Life and Letters of James Abraham Garfield*.[26] Professor Smith did his research partly at Mentor and partly at Williams College, where Harry Garfield, the President's son, was president.

Just as in the case of the voluminous Adams papers, the question of permanent storage and access to the collection became a family concern. Formal contacts with the Library of Congress were made for the first time in September 1922, when Charles Moore, head of the Manuscript Division, contacted James R. Garfield and got a noncommittal reply. In 1926, when the Smith biography was completed and all papers had been returned to the Mentor home, Harry Garfield suggested to his brother and sisters that the papers be placed in the Library of Congress, to which all agreed. However, James R. Garfield, who was very attached to his father's legacy, wrote on September 10, 1928, that "it will be with regret that I send this material away from Mentor."[27] He continued to find reasons for further delaying the shipment. The decision to separate papers that were purely personal, the loss of keys to the Memorial Room, and the death of Mrs. James R. Garfield in a car accident caused further delays. Finally, in December 1930, eight boxes of papers, 150 bound volumes of letters, and 10 indexes were sent to Washington. A second and third shipment followed shortly afterwards, but none of the personal and family papers, except the diaries, were included. In February 1931, J. Franklin Jameson, the director of the Manuscript Division, thanked Garfield for the family's generous gift, assuming that all extant papers had been received. However, in 1937, the Library discovered that a substantial collection of personal papers was still in the Memorial Room at Mentor.

In 1950, James R. Garfield died and the papers were left in the custody of his youngest brother, Abraham. In 1954, the Library of Congress received the letters of Harry A. Garfield and four years later those of James R. Garfield. In 1955 and 1956 additional papers were sent to the Library. In 1960, the surviving Garfield offspring cleared out the Memorial Room at Mentor and sent almost everything to the Library of Congress. The President's granddaughters, Ruth Feis and Lucrecia Comer, helped to sort and identify some of the family papers in the Manuscript Division. They also wrote two books, *Mollie Garfield in the White House* [28] and *Harry Garfield's First Forty Years; a Man of Action in a Troubled World.* [29] With these papers and books by and about the Garfields, the record of the President and his family is in fairly complete form in the Library of Congress, which holds approximately 77,000 documents. The Ohio Historical Society and the Rutherford B. Hayes Library have small collections of Garfield papers.

The Garfield Papers in the Library of Congress

Series	Reels
1. Diaries. 1848–81. 21 vols.	1–3
2. Family Correspondence. 1839–81 and Undated. 3 boxes	3–4
3. James A. Garfield–Lucretia R. Garfield Correspondence. 1853–81. 4 boxes	5–8
4. General Correspondence. 1852–82. 150 vols.	8–106
5. Recipients' Copies and Related Material. 1852–81. 5 boxes	106–108
6. Letterbooks and Outgoing Correspondence. 1868–81. 24 vols.	109–120
7. Additional Outgoing Correspondence. 1854–81. 3 boxes	121–122
8. Military Correspondence and Maps. 1861–81. 7 vols.	122–123
9. Executive Mansion Letter List. Mar. 7–Sept. 21, 1881. 6 vols.	124–125
10. Speeches, Articles, and Public Statements. 1850–81. 11 vols.	126–128
11. Notes and Memoranda. 1860–80. 22 vols.	129–133
12. Law Cases. 1866–77 9 vols.	133–136
13. College Notebooks. 1849–61 7 vols.	136–137
14. Financial Papers. 1853–81. 9 boxes	137–142
15. Scrapbooks. 1854–85. 40 vols., 24 boxes	142–147
16. Shorthand Notebooks and Notes. 1871–81. 80 Notebooks and Unbound Shorthand Notes.	148–163
17. Miscellany.	163–169
18. Memorials. (Oversize volumes)	170–173
19. Commissions. (Oversize volumes)	173
20. Bound Newspapers. 1881.	174–177

CHESTER A. ARTHUR
Twenty-first President—Republican
1881–1885

Chester Alan Arthur was born in 1830 in Fairfield, Vermont, the son of a Baptist clergyman and avid abolitionist. He attended various schools in New York, entered Union College in Schenectady at age 15, and graduated Phi Beta Kappa three years later. He was admitted to the bar in 1853. Arthur was active in Republican party politics and held several army positions during the Civil War. In 1871, he was appointed collector of the Port of New York by President Grant, a reward for his faithful work in the New York State Republican machine and his assistance in Grant's nomination and election. He held the position for eight years until President Rutherford B. Hayes, in his attempts to reform the civil service, removed Arthur from this lucrative position. At the 1880 Republican convention, Arthur was nominated as vice presidential running mate of James Garfield as a compromise candidate between two wings of the Republican party.

After Garfield's death, Arthur, who had never held an elective office, assumed the presidency. To everyone's surprise, he turned into a champion of civil service reform and supported the 1883 Pendelton Act which established the bipartisan Civil Service Commission. He signed the 1883 Tariff Act which revised trade protection downward; he also supported the first federal immigration laws and advocated federal support for education. Because he followed a middle of the road policy on most national issues, the Republicans did not renominate him and backed instead James G. Blaine, who was defeated by Grover Cleveland. The day before he left office in 1885, Arthur dedicated the George Washington Memorial. He returned to his law practice, but illness soon forced him to retire and he died on November 18, 1886.

The Arthur Papers

The Library of Congress purchased one letter of President Arthur in 1902. In 1910, Gaillard Hunt, the director of the Manuscript Division, started the search for the main body of Arthur's papers. In 1914, Hunt contacted Chester A. Arthur, Jr. concerning his father's papers. Six months later, on March 13, 1915, he received an answer stating: "The question of my father's papers is a very sore subject with me. These papers were supposed to be in certain chests which were stored in the cellar of 123 Lexington Avenue. After my father's death they were removed. Several years ago on making my residence in Colorado, I sent for these chests of papers and found in them nothing but customs house records of no particular value or importance. Where the papers they were supposed to contain have vanished, is a mystery."[30]

In 1918, the Library of Congress acquired on loan from Arthur H. Masten, a nephew of the President, a second Arthur document. A few years later Masten's heirs gave this manuscript to the Library of Congress. In 1924, Charles Moore, the acting director of the Manuscript Division, wrote a letter to the *New York Times* which resulted in the publication of an editorial plea for Arthur papers. Other inquiries were sent to people who had known and worked with Arthur. One response to this plea was the receipt of Arthur's will, supplied by the county clerk of New York City.

In 1925, Louise Reed Mitchell, the daughter of Arthur's secretary, wrote to the Library of Congress that she had inherited 50 Arthur manuscripts, which the Library of Congress bought from her. In 1938, Dr. Thomas P. Martin of the Manuscript Division contacted the President's grandson, Chester A. Arthur III, regarding his grandfather's papers. Arthur replied: "You may be sure that I am as interested as you are in having the Arthur papers finally come to rest in the Library of Congress . . . During his lifetime my father would never let anyone see the papers—not even me. When they finally came into my possession, I was amazed that there were so few. At my father's funeral I inquired of all the cousins there assembled, the nieces and nephews of my grandfather, as to what had happened to the bulk of the papers . . . The day before my grandfather died, he caused to be burned three large garbage cans, each at least four feet high, full of papers which I am sure would have thrown much light on history."[31]

As a result of this correspondence, the President's grandson deposited 90 of the more important documents in his possession in the Library of Congress. Twenty years later, these documents, together with another 470 documents which he had kept, were sold to the Library. A dozen letters written by President Arthur in the 1850s were given to the Library by the noted Detroit collector, Charles A. Feinberg. In 1959, J. Wilson Newman, the president of Dun & Bradstreet, presented some copies of the Arthur letters in the company files to the Library. Robert G. Dun had been a friend of the President for over a quarter century and had preserved the Arthur papers. Slowly, individual letters were added to the collection before the microfilm edition was produced in 1960, which covers 1,413 documents.

The New York State Library has 200 Arthur papers; there are also some in the New York Historical Society, the Boston Public Library, the Rutherford B. Hayes Library, and several other libraries. Other papers by, to, or about President Arthur are in 30 different Library of Congress manuscript collections.

The Arthur Papers in the Library of Congress

Series	Reels
1. General Correspondence and Related Manuscripts. 1843–1938. 4 boxes	1–3
2. Arthur-Dun Manuscripts. 1862–87. 1 box	3
3. Arthur Transcripts. 1872–1926. 1 box	3
4. Addenda.	1–7

GROVER CLEVELAND
Twenty-second and Twenty-fourth President—Democrat
1885–1889; 1893–1897

Born on March 18, 1837, in Caldwell, New Jersey, Cleveland was the son of a Presbyterian minister. When he was 14, his formal education ended, and he began to work in a grocery store and on a farm to help support his family. His father died when he was 16. In 1855, he obtained a job as a law clerk in Buffalo, studying law while working. He was admitted to the bar in 1859, began to practice law, and became interested in Democratic party politics. He served as assistant district attorney and sheriff of Erie County, and, in 1881, accepted the nomination to run as a reform candidate for mayor of Buffalo to clean up the corruption in the city government. In 1882, he was elected governor of New York.

During his successful governorship, Cleveland gained a reputation for honesty and incorruptability at a time of widespread political dishonesty. He was nominated for the presidency at the Democratic national convention in 1884 as "Cleveland the Good." A few days later, a Buffalo newspaper revealed that Cleveland, who was a bachelor, had fathered a son out of wedlock 11 years earlier.[32] The charge was true; Cleveland did not deny it and won the election by a narrow margin after a stormy campaign against James G. Blaine.

As president, Cleveland strongly supported civil service reform and vigorously fought against corrupt political practices. He vetoed all special interest legislation, running up a total of 300 vetoes during his first administration. He supported the rights of Indians, fought for lower tariffs, and signed the Interstate Commerce Act to regulate the railroads. In 1886, the 49 year old president married 21 year old Frances Folsom in the White House. The Clevelands had five children, one of whom was born in the White House during the second Cleveland administration.

The Democrats nominated Cleveland for a second term in 1888, but because Tammany Hall, New York's Democratic machine, refused to support him, he lost the election to Benjamin Harrison. Cleveland joined a New York law firm and attacked the high spending programs of the Republican administration. In 1892, he was nominated on the first ballot at the Democratic convention in spite of Tammany Hall opposition and won the election.

During his second term, Cleveland faced the economic panic of 1893. Labor unrest increased with rising unemployment; in 1894, Cleveland stopped Coxey's march of the unemployed on Washington and broke up the American Railway Union strike in Illinois. Cleveland became increasing unpopular and the Democrats nominated William Jennings Bryan for president in 1896. Cleveland refused to support Bryan on the free silver issue and was pleased with the election of McKinley. He retired to Princeton, New Jersey, where he kept active in University affairs. He died in 1908.

The Cleveland Papers

Cleveland was so fully absorbed in the events in which he participated that he was not especially concerned with preserving a written
record of his activities. He wrote to Richard Watson Gilder, a lifelong
friend and editor of *Century Magazine*: "I have been so prodded by
public duty for a number of years past that I have had no opportunity to
look after the preservation of anything that might be useful in writing
history. 'Things done are won, but joy's full soul lies in the doing' has
perforce been the motto over my mantel."[33] He wrote many of his letters
in longhand and often did not keep copies of them. He preferred to
conduct his business orally rather than by correspondence. He also frequently gave away copies of his papers to autograph collectors.

On the other hand, no other president, except Richard Nixon, ever
expressed such strong feelings about his right to the possession of his
papers. During an argument with the Senate in 1886, Grover Cleveland
refused to turn over certain papers on file in the office of his attorney
general and directed him to refuse compliance with the Senate's demand.
He made it plain that the Senate had no right to search his private papers:

> I regard the papers and documents addressed to me or intended for
> my use and action purely unofficial and private, not infrequently
> confidential, and having reference to the performance of a duty
> exclusively mine. I consider them in no proper sense as upon the files
> of the Department, but as deposited there for my convenience, re-
> maining still completely under my control. I suppose if I desired to
> take them into my custody I might do so with entire propriety, and if
> I saw fit to destroy them no one could complain. Their nature and
> character remain the same whether they are kept in the Executive
> Mansion or deposited in the Departments. There is no mysterious
> power of transmutation in departmental custody, nor is there magic
> in the undefined and sacred solemnity of Department files. The
> papers and documents which have been described derive no official
> character from any constitutional, statutory, or other requirement
> making them necessary to the performance of the official duty of the
> Executive.[34]

Since Cleveland did not show a great deal of interest in his presidential papers, it is not surprising that he paid even less attention to
documents of his pre-presidential public career. Some papers relating to
this period, as well as to his 11 years of retirement, were later found
among papers in the attic of his home in Princeton, New Jersey.

The papers from Cleveland's first administration were kept for him
by Daniel Scott Lamont, who served as his private secretary. Before
returning to Washington in 1893, Cleveland asked Lamont to pack the
papers for the return to the White House. However, after the President's
death, a large body of Cleveland papers was found in Lamont's country
house. The papers of the second administration were probably stored with
Henry T. Thurber, who was Cleveland's personal secretary at that time,
but they apparently did not survive.

In 1912, the Library of Congress asked Mrs. Cleveland's help in the
collection of her husband's papers. She referred the Library to John H.
Finley, to whom she had given papers in her possession for the prepara-

tion of Cleveland's biography. Finley made little progress with the biography and the papers in his care, consisting almost entirely of letters received by the President, arrived at the Library of Congress in 1915 in two large packing cases as a deposit of Mrs. Frances Folsom Cleveland who by then had become Mrs. Thomas J. Preston, Jr.[35]

Professor Robert McNutt McElroy of Princeton University succeeded Finley as the authorized biographer and received additional material from Mrs. Cleveland and from Finley. McElroy wrote in his biography of Cleveland:

> Mr. Cleveland, as have all presidents, left an enormous mass of manuscript material, but he left it in chaotic condition. The papers were packed into rough wooden boxes, without systematic arrangement, the important and the unimportant thrown together; and many of the most valuable manuscripts contain neither title, date, nor other indication of the purpose for which they were prepared. In most cases, except personal letters, the very authorship of the manuscript would be in doubt but for the fact that all are written in 'copper plate,' as he called his own neat but distressingly illegible handwriting. Practically every letter, message, proclamation, executive order, even the publicity notices and the successive copies of addresses often revised, are wholly in his own hand. He apparently made no attempt to keep his files complete, and frequently the only copy of an important document was given to some friend who wished a specimen of his handwriting. The forty or fifty thousand miscellaneous documents, mostly letters to the president, but including the final copies of many of his presidential messages which he brought from Washington at the end of his public life were stored in a wing of Colonel Lamont's country home at Millbrook, New York, and apparently forgotten. These, with a collection of thirty thousand manuscripts from the Library of Congress, and a smaller one from the attic of his Princeton home constitute the bulk of manuscript sources upon which this biography has been based.[36]

McElroy and Mrs. Preston also managed to collect approximately 1,500 letters from the President's friends. While most of the papers were still at Princeton, the Library of Congress received some 200 letters written by Cleveland to E.C. Benedict and smaller groups of letters he wrote to other friends. In 1923, McElroy completed his book. At Mrs. Preston's request, he turned all papers used for the book over to the Library as a gift. Additional small shipments arrived until 1925. The Library holds over 87,000 Cleveland manuscripts. The Detroit Public Library has 1,250 items primarily relating to the second administration. The Buffalo Historical Society, the New York Historical Society, Princeton University, and the Pierpont Morgan Library have smaller collections.

The Cleveland Papers in the Library of Congress

Series	Reels
1. Diaries. 1898-1905. 7 vols.	1
2. General Correspondence. 1846-1910. 366 vols.	1–100
3. Additional Correspondence. 1828–1945. 165 vols. numbered 367–531	100–145

4. Letter Press Copy Books. 1885–89. 30 vols. numbered 532–561	145–157
5. Speeches. 1883–1907. 2 boxes	157
6. Messages. 1885–97. 12 boxes	
A. Cleveland's Messages to Congress. 1885–89, 1893–97. 8 boxes	157–160
B. Transcripts by Senate and House Clerks of Communications from the President. 1885–88. 4 boxes	160–162
7. Cleveland Writings. 1884–1907. 1 box	162
8. Gilder Notes. ca. 1908–09. 1 box	162
9. Miscellany. ca. 1884–1907. 5 boxes	
A. Subject Index to Letters Received by Cleveland. 1 box	163
B. Card Index (Incomplete) of Cleveland's Correspondents. 1 box	163
C. Short Personal Accounts of Cleveland by Several Contemporaries.	163
D. Manuscripts by Frances F. Cleveland in French and German.	163
E. Personal and Household Bills. 1885–96. (Subseries C, D, and E in 1 box)	163–164
F. Writings by Others than Cleveland.	164
G. Calling Cards. Those with Messages Filmed.	164
H. Tickets to Events to which the Clevelands Were Invited.	Not filmed
I. Duplicates, Checks. A Checkbook, Memorabilia. (Subseries F, G, H, and I in 1 box)	Not filmed
10. Printed Matter. 20 containers.	Not filmed

BENJAMIN HARRISON
Twenty-third President—Republican
1889–1893

Born in 1833 at North Bend, Ohio, Benjamin Harrison came from a distinguished family; his great-grandfather was a signer of the Declaration of Independence and governor of Virginia; his grandfather was the ninth president of the United States. He graduated from Miami University in Oxford, Ohio, in 1852, married his college sweetheart Caroline Lavinia Scott, practiced law in Indianapolis, and became secretary of the Republican State Central Committee in 1858. During the Civil War he commanded the 70th Indiana Regiment of Volunteers. Harrison was short and was nicknamed "Little Ben" by his troops.

After the War, he returned to his law practice and became one of the leading political figures in Indiana. He ran for governor in 1876 but was defeated. In 1880, he led the Republican delegation of Indiana to the national convention where he supported the candidacy of Blaine, but in the end switched to Garfield and helped to decide the nomination. Harrison served in the U.S. Senate from 1881 to 1887, supporting various veterans' pension bills, increased tariffs, a larger navy, and civil service reforms.

During the 1888 Republican convention a deadlock between Sherman of Ohio and Graham of Indiana was resolved by Harrison's nomination because it was thought that he would be easily controlled by Congress. He defeated Cleveland by a narrow margin. During his administration, six new states were admitted, bringing the total to 44. The first Pan American conference met in Washington, establishing better relations among the nations of the Western Hemisphere. But the McKinley Tariff Act raised import duties to new highs and resulted in higher prices; with the slogan "Throw the rascals out," the Democrats won the midterm elections in 1890 and Harrison lost the 1892 presidential election to Grover Cleveland.[37]

In his retirement, Harrison lectured on law at Stanford University and wrote a book, *This Country of Ours,* which was published in 1897.[38] In 1896, he married Mary Scott Lord Dimmick, the 37 year old niece of his first wife, who had died in 1892. He successfully represented Venezuela before an international arbitration tribunal in 1899, and died in 1901 in Indianapolis.

The Harrison Papers

Benjamin Harrison aimed throughout his life to maintain a complete and accurate record of his activities and carefully preserved all documents. The second Mrs. Harrison was instrumental in having his papers kept intact so that his biography could be written. In 1910, when the Library of Congress inquired about the Harrison papers, it was learned that they were in the hands of John L. Griffiths, U.S. consul general in London, who was working on a Harrison biography. This was the first and only time that a collection of presidential papers traveled overseas.

In 1913, Griffiths died without having finished the biography, and the papers were stored in a London warehouse. A year later, they were returned to the United States and Mrs. Harrison asked Gaillard Hunt, the director of the Manuscript Division of the Library of Congress, to ask Ohio Senator Theodore E. Burton whether he would agree to write the Harrison biography. Burton refused due to the pressures of his office. Three months later, in March 1915, Mrs. Harrison made the first deposit of papers in the Library of Congress with the understanding that the papers could only be used with her approval. She continued to cooperate with the Library to organize the collection and to find a suitable biographer. In 1926, Albert T. Volwiler, a professor of history at the University of Pennsylvania, who had been Harrison's secretary, was permitted access to the papers by Mrs. Harrison to write her husband's biography. In 1933, the deposit of Harrison papers was converted into a gift.

Through Volwiler's efforts to provide materials for the biography, significant additions to the collection were made. These included 165 letters of the President to his first wife, deposited by Mary Harrison McKee; extracts from the diary of Elijah W. Halford, Harrison's White House secretary; letters of Louis T. Michener, Harrison's campaign manager; and many others. Volwiler also initiated the Tibbott transcription project. Frank E. Tibbott, Harrison's stenographer and private secretary, was employed by the Library of Congress "to transcribe his shorthand notebooks, those he had originally produced in his secretarial capacity and those made by stenographers who preceded him."[39] The letterbooks and records of the law firms the President had worked in were also located through Volwiler's efforts. By 1940 the Harrison papers were bound in 181 volumes and the remaining papers placed in about 100 manuscript boxes. The materials contained a substantial number of papers of President William Henry Harrison, which were made into a separate collection by the Library. The papers of Benjamin's father, Congressman John Scott Harrison, also became a separate collection. Volwiler did an outstanding job of collecting, organizing, and transcribing these papers over a period of two decades, but never produced a biography.

In 1945 the restriction on the use of the papers was lifted at Mrs. Harrison's request. Finally in 1948, the Reverend Harry J. Sievers, S.J. started to work on a biography which was published in three volumes between 1952 and 1968.[40] The Library of Congress collection amounts to approximately 70,000 documents. Some papers are in the Indiana State Library and the Rutherford B. Hayes Library.

The Harrison Papers in the Library of Congress

Series	*Reels*
1. General Correspondence and Related Materials. 1787–1912. 181 vols.	1–43
2. Additional Correspondence and Related Items. 1853–1909. 83 boxes	43–97
3. Letter Press Copy Book. 1880–92. 1 vol.	97–98
4. Telegrams. 1888–96. 5 vols.	98–99
5. Social. 1889–92. 2 vols. 1890–97. 3 boxes	99–100
6. Shorthand Notebooks. 1884–1901. 127 vols.	100–116
7. Records of Letters Received at the White House. 1889–93. 6 vols.	116–117
8. Speeches. 1878–1901. 6 boxes	117–121
9. Writings. 1895–97. 3 boxes	121–122
10. Legal Instruments. 1852–98. 1 box	122–123
11. Legal Cases and Firm Letter Press Copy Books. ca. 1855–1900. 7 boxes, 5 vols.	123–135
12. Financial. 1836–1900. 6 boxes, 17 vols.	135–140
13. Venezuela Boundary Dispute. 1895–99. 4 boxes	140–143
14. Miscellaneous Manuscripts. 1814–1901. 6 boxes	143–144
15. Volwiler Collection of Harrisoniana. 1850–1938. 1 box	145
16. Scrapbooks. 1853–1908. 53 vols.	145–151
17. Certificates, Memorials, and Printed Invitations. 4 boxes	Not filmed
18. Pamphlets. 3 boxes	Not filmed
19. Photographs and Drawings. 2 boxes, 1 volume	Not filmed
20. Miscellaneous Printed Matter. 9 boxes	Not filmed

8. Twentieth-Century Presidents

WILLIAM McKINLEY
Twenty-fifth President—Republican
1897–1901

William McKinley was born in 1843 in Niles, Ohio. After attending Allegheny College in Meadville, Pennsylvania, for one year, he taught in a country school, and enlisted in the Ohio Volunteer Infantry in 1861. He served in the Union army in the Civil War under Col. Rutherford B. Hayes, and left the service as major. McKinley then studied law in Albany, New York, was admitted to the bar in 1867, and began to practice in Canton, Ohio. He was elected Stark County prosecuting attorney in 1869. In 1871, he married Ida Saxton with whom he had two daughters who died in infancy. Mrs. McKinley was an invalid for much of her life.

In 1876, McKinley helped Hayes in his presidential campaign, and was elected U. S. representative from Ohio. He served in Congress from 1877 to 1891. McKinley made his reputation in Congress by his continuous support of high protective tariff rates. He became chairman of the Ways and Means Committee and was the author of the McKinley Tariff Act of 1890, which pushed tariffs to new highs. The high retail prices caused by this legislation produced a backlash at the polls, and many Republican congressmen, including McKinley, lost their seats. In 1891, he was elected governor of Ohio and served for two terms.

McKinley chaired the Republican national convention in 1892 and received a substantial number of votes, but could not defeat Benjamin Harrison. He was nominated in 1896 and won the election against William Jennings Bryan, his Democratic opponent. As president, McKinley used his long experience in Congress to influence passage of legislation he wanted and rarely had to use his veto power. Illinois Senator Shelby said of him: "We have never had a president who had more influence in Congress than Mr. McKinley."[1] In 1897, the higher tariffs he had requested were passed, and economic recovery began.

While McKinley tried to find a diplomatic solution to the growing tension between Cuba and Spain, the unexplained explosion of the battleship Maine created public and congressional pressure which resulted in the United States declaration of war against Spain in 1898. The Spanish-American War lasted less than four months. The Treaty of Paris recognized Cuba's independence and gave Puerto Rico, Guam, and the Philippines to the United States. The same year, the United States occupied Wake Island and annexed Hawaii. In 1900, the Boxer Rebellion in China was quelled with the help of U.S. Marines, and Congress acceded to McKinley's wishes to make gold the basis of the country's monetary system by passing the Gold Standard Act.

McKinley received unanimous nomination for a second term as president from the Republican convention in 1900, and won an impressive second victory over William Jennings Bryan. In the first few months of the second administration, McKinley went on a tour through the country; when his wife became ill in California, they returned to their home in Canton. On September 5, 1901, he went to Buffalo, New York, to speak at the Pan-American Exposition. In what turned out to be his last speech, McKinley called for closer trade relations and the end of protectionist policies, and predicted the growing significance of the United States in the world: "Isolation is no longer possible or desirable . . . . The period of exclusiveness is passed."[2] The next day he was shot by Leon F. Czolgosz, an anarchist who wanted to kill "a ruler." The president's senseless death plunged the nation into deep mourning.

The McKinley Papers

When McKinley prepared his will in 1897, he was concerned only with providing financial support for his wife, his mother and his two sisters, and left no directions about his papers. The executors of the President's estate were Supreme Court Associate Justice William R. Day and the President's personal secretary, George B. Cortelyou, who assumed the responsibility for most matters relating to McKinley's papers. Cortelyou planned to write a biography of McKinley, but his busy career after the President's death prevented him from doing so and he made the papers available to Charles S. Olcott, who wrote an official biography, *The Life of William McKinley* , published in two volumes in 1916.[3]

McKinley did not commit his plans, purposes, and thoughts routinely to paper; he preferred meeting people face to face and talking to them. Cortelyou said of McKinley: "Generally speaking, President McKinley did not write letters on important government matters. When occasion arose, members of Congress or others interested were asked to call at the White House, where the matter would be discussed."[4] The Library of Congress started to correspond with Cortelyou in 1905 concerning the McKinley papers. This correspondence continued for 30 years during which Cortelyou promised the papers to the Library, but delayed releasing them until his retirement in 1935, when he presented over 100,000 items to the Library. The papers were organized and bound, but Cortelyou exercised tight control over access to them until his death in 1940. His son, George B. Cortelyou, Jr., continued this control until 1954. During World War II, the papers were shipped for safekeeping to the University of Virginia in Charlottesville, along with other presidential papers. Between 1960–62, the papers were indexed and microfilmed, and became publicly available in 1963, 62 years after the President's death. In 1987, the Library held 131,000 items in its collection.

Most of the papers in the Library of Congress cover the period from 1896 to 1901; there are very few documents from McKinley's Civil War days, his private law practice, and his 14 years in Congress. He wrote few letters, and as a congressman he had neither office space nor staff until his last term, when the services of a stenographer were available to him to write the tariff bill. Like other congressmen, he discarded most of his files after the end of each session. There is no evidence of any willful removal or destruction.

The papers of McKinley's terms as governor and his Civil War diary are in the Ohio Historical Society; a small group of papers from his early years are at the Western Reserve Historical Society in Cleveland, and seven White House telegraphers' diaries are at the Hayes Library in Fremont, Ohio.

The McKinley Papers in the Library of Congress

Series	*Reels*
1. General Correspondence and Related Items. 1847–1902. 86 vols.	1–16
2. Letter Press Copy Books. 1894–1901. 99 vols.	16–57
3. Additional Correspondence and Related Items. 1879–1901. 55 boxes	57–81
4. Speeches. 1878–1901. 6 boxes	81–85
5. Messages. 1897–1900. 4 boxes	85–87
6. Record of Letters Received. 1897–1901. 7 vols.	87–90
7. Shorthand Notebooks and Notes. 1898–1901. 2 boxes	90–92
8. Guest List for Receptions at the White House. 1901. 1 vol.	92
9. Photographs. 1901. 1 vol.	92
10. Assassination Records. 1901. 3 vols.	92
11. Miscellaneous Manuscripts. ca. 1897–1901. 3 boxes	92–93
12. Scrapbooks. 1897–1901. 34 vols.	94–98
13. Newspaper Clippings. 1897–1901. 5 boxes	Not filmed
14. Printed Matter. 1897–1901. 10 boxes	Not filmed
15. Bound Volumes and Books. 4 boxes	Not filmed
16. Duplicates. 1897–1901. 8 boxes	Not filmed

THEODORE ROOSEVELT
Twenty-sixth President—Republican
1901–1909

Theodore Roosevelt, the second son of a wealthy merchant and banker, was born in New York City in 1858. He was a sickly child; to overcome his weakness he turned into an enthusiastic sports and physical fitness champion. He graduated from Harvard University in 1880, married Alice Hathaway Lee, and started to study law at Columbia University; being independently wealthy, he soon decided to shift his interests to writing and politics.

In 1882, Roosevelt's mother and his wife died on the same day. He served in the New York State legislature from 1882 to 1884. In 1886 he remarried and lost his race for mayor of New York City. He served on the Civil Service Commission from 1889 to 1895, was president of the New York City Board of Police from 1895 to 1897, and assistant secretary of the navy from 1897 to 1898. At the outbreak of the Spanish-American War, he became a lieutenant colonel in the volunteer cavalry regiment known as the Rough Riders, and returned home as a hero after the Battle of San Juan.

Upon his return in 1898, Roosevelt was elected governor of New York; in 1900, he was elected vice president on the Republican ticket with McKinley. When President McKinley was assassinated in 1901, Theodore Roosevelt was sworn in as the country's youngest president. He proceeded with a great deal of energy to carry out McKinley's policies, established the departments of Commerce and Labor, and succeeded in having the Supreme Court uphold the Sherman Anti-Trust Act, which made it possible to dissolve the railroad and banking monopolies. Roosevelt supported the enactment of the Pure Food Act and legislation providing for the inspection of stockyards and packing houses. His great interest in preservation of natural resources prompted him to organize the National Conservation Conference; 150 million acres were added to the national forests, and the number of national parks was increased during his administration.

In 1903, Roosevelt supported the revolution in Panama to free that country from Colombia; this made the building of the Panama Canal possible, which Roosevelt considered his greatest accomplishment. He also was able to settle the Alaskan boundaries with Canada and Great Britain. In 1904, the Republican party nominated him for president by acclamation and he won the election by a large margin. In 1905, he helped negotiate an end to the Russo-Japanese War through the Treaty of Portsmouth, which earned him the Nobel Peace Prize. In 1908, he used his influence to obtain the Republican nomination for William Howard Taft, who he felt would carry on his policies.

After his retirement from the presidency, Roosevelt, who was only 50, travelled widely in Africa and Europe. Dissatisfied with Taft's presidency, he ran against him in 1912 on the Progressive party ticket; this split the Republican vote and resulted in Wilson's election. During the campaign, Roosevelt was shot in the chest by an assassin in Milwaukee. He was seriously wounded, but recuperated quickly and embarked on a trip to Brazil. In 1916, he was again nominated for president by the Progressive party, but declined to run. He died suddenly on January 6, 1919, at his home in Oyster Bay, from an arterial blood clot. Roosevelt himself probably provided the best description of his effect on the presidency: "While President I have been President emphatically; I have used every ounce of power there was in the office . . . I have felt that in showing the strength of, or in giving strength to, the executive, I was establishing a precedent of value."[5]

The Roosevelt Papers

Long before he became president, Roosevelt had written several well-known historical books such as *The Naval War of 1812,*[6] the *Life of Thomas Hart Benton,*[7] and *The Winning of the West.*[8] In 1903, he issued an Executive Order that transferred the papers of George Washington, James Madison, Alexander Hamilton, Thomas Jefferson, James Monroe, and Benjamin Franklin, as well as the papers of the Continental Congress and some other documents from the Department of State to the Library of Congress.

Roosevelt was a personal friend of Herbert Putnam, the librarian of Congress, and invited him to make suggestions about the Library's functions, which he included in his first annual presidential message to Congress. During his unusually active life, Roosevelt remained interested in history and writing; after he left the White House, he worked on his autobiography,[9] and was elected president of the American Historical Association in 1912. It is not surprising that he was most concerned with the care and preservation of the papers he had taken to Sagamore Hill, his home in Oyster Bay, New York. On December 5, 1916, he wrote a letter to Herbert Putnam about his plans for the disposition of his "great mass of papers. They include, in immense numbers, copies of my letters and of letters to me while I was President; also letters from sovereigns, etc., etc. If I sent them to you, could they be catalogued and arranged, and permission be given to me, or any of my representatives, to examine them at any time, with a clear understanding that no one else was to see them until after my death?"[10]

The papers to be deposited in the Library of Congress had been stored in large and heavy boxes in a bank in Oyster Bay; the boxes were reinforced and shipped to Washington in January 1917. However, they were locked, and when Putnam asked Roosevelt for the keys, he answered: "The Lord only knows where the key is. Break the cases open and start to work on them!"[11] Additional papers were sent to the Library later.

In September 1918, Roosevelt wrote a letter to Putnam requesting that full access to the papers be given to his friend Joseph B. Bishop, who planned to write a two-volume biography of Roosevelt. After Roosevelt's death, Bishop, the President's literary executor, sent several shipments to the Library of Congress, containing letters from 1897 to 1918. Since Bishop found that there were considerable gaps in the correspondence, he returned to Oyster Bay in March 1919 and located four large cases of papers covering the years 1910 to 1912, which he also sent to the Library of Congress. In July 1919, Mrs. Roosevelt came across papers of the years 1911 and 1912, which she shipped to Washington. In October 1920, Bishop completed the biography and returned the papers with which he had worked to the Library. In the preface to his book, Bishop stated:

> At different stages of the work I went over with what I had written with the President and had the inestimable advantage of his suggestions, obtaining from him incidents and anecdotes which added immeasurably to the interest and historical value of the narrative, making it virtually his own . . . . While in a few instances, in order to maintain the continuity of the narrative, the present record overlaps the *Autobiography*, it really supplements and completes it, and the

two works together constitute authentically the Life and Letters of Theodore Roosevelt as designed by himself.[12]

In 1922, two years after Bishop's book appeared, Mrs. Roosevelt found in the garret of the house in Oyster Bay papers and documents dating from the time Roosevelt was governor of New York (1898–1900), including dozens of scrapbooks, with press clippings and letterbooks covering the entire period of his public life until he became president. These items were added to the Library's collection. During the following years, smaller additional contributions of papers were made by Mrs. Roosevelt. In 1958, Roosevelt's daughter, Mrs. Alice Roosevelt Longworth, sent her father's diaries from the years 1878 to 1884 to the Library; these covered, in part, his college career and his days as a rancher in the Dakotas.

The Library holds over 275,000 Roosevelt documents, making it one of the largest presidential collections. During his early career, Roosevelt was not systematic in retaining his incoming correspondence and, before the days of the typewriter, rarely made copies of his outgoing letters. The presidential papers were originally arranged in two series, comprising only about 25 percent of the documents; this is probably due to the executive staff weeding out routine and unimportant documents from the White House files. The post-presidential materials are far more voluminous.

The Theodore Roosevelt Memorial Association, an organization founded shortly after Roosevelt's death, provided funds for indexing and organizing the papers. Its executive director, Herman Hagedorn, helped to search for Roosevelt letters in private hands. He envisioned something in the nature of a presidential library at Sagamore Hill to which "historical students from all over the country will come for authoritative information about Theodore Roosevelt . . . in the place where Roosevelt lived for almost fifty years."[13] While this expectation was not realized, Sagamore Hill and the Roosevelt birthplace on East 20th Street in New York hold fine collections of Roosevelt memorabilia and manuscripts. Other important papers are at Harvard University.

The Roosevelt Papers in the Library of Congress

Series	Reels
1. Letters Received and Related Material. 1759–1919.	
77 vols., 385 boxes	1–308
A. Additional Letters Received and Fragments.	
1857–1919. 2 boxes	308–309
B. Letters from Royalty. 1904–14. 1 vol.	309
C. Undated Letters Received. 1901–19. In 2 period	
groups: 1901–19 1910–19	309–313
2. Letter Press Copy Books. 1897–1916. 109 vols.	313–362
3. Letters Sent. 1888–1919. 198 vols., 7 boxes	
A. Carbon Copies of Letters Sent. 1894–1919.	
198 vols.	363–412
B. Additional Copies of Letters Sent. 1888–1918.	
7 boxes.	412–415
4. Recipients' Copies. 1887–1918. 8 boxes	
A. Letters. 1887–1918. 5 boxes	415–416

    B. Roosevelt/John Hay Letters. 1897–1905. 1 box   416
    C. Undelivered Letters. 1898–1918. 2 boxes   416–417
  5. Speeches and Executive Orders. 1899-1918. 13 vols.,
    21 boxes
    A. Speeches and Executive Orders. 1899–1918.
      17 boxes   417–424
    B. White House Volumes. 1901–09. 13 vols.   424–426
    C. Published Speeches. 1901–17. 4 boxes   426–427
  6. Press Releases and Proclamations. 1901–09. 2 vols.   427–428
  7. Articles and Public Statements. 1886–1919. 2 boxes   428–429
  8. Personal Diaries. 1878–84. 7 vols.   429–430
  9. Desk Diaries. 1901–09. 10 vols.   430–431
10. Reception Books. 1901–09. 10 vols.   431–437
11. Letter Record Books. 1901–09. 8 vols.   437–438
12. Shorthand Notebooks. 55 vols.   439–446
13. Miscellany.
    A. Business Papers. 1901–19. 1 box   446
    B. A Brief Summary of the Administration of
      Theodore Roosevelt; Governor 1899–1900. 1 vol.   446
    C. The Immigrant in America. 1913. 1 vol.   446
    D. Progressive Party Minutes. 1912–16. 2 boxes   447–448
    E. Puerto Rico Journals. 1900–01. 2 vols.   448
    F. Cross References. 1901–09. 4 boxes   448–450
    G. Muster Rolls. 1st Regiment, U.S. Volunteer
      Cavalry, May-Sept., 1898. 1 box   450
    H. Miscellaneous Notes and Memoranda.
      1881–1920. 1 box   450
    I. Diplomas and Certificates. 1899–1931. 1 portfolio   451
    J. Clippings. 2 boxes   Not filmed
    K. Calling Cards. 1 box   452
    L. Photographs. 1 box   452
    M. Maps and Photostats. 1 box   452
    N. Printed Matter. 9 boxes   452
14. Additional Correspondence and Other Documents.
    1897–1903. 2 boxes   453
15. Scrapbooks. 1895–1909. 123 vols.   454–485
16. Addenda, 1760-1930. 2 containers.

WILLIAM HOWARD TAFT
Twenty-seventh President—Republican
1909–1913

William Howard Taft, the most outstanding jurist among presidents, served in the White House and was also Chief Justice of the Supreme Court. He was born in 1857 in Cincinnati, Ohio, the son of Alfonso Taft, a lawyer who served in the Grant administration as secretary of war, attorney general, and minister to Austria-Hungary and to Russia. After graduation from Yale, Taft attended the Cincinnati Law School, became a court reporter, earned his law degree, and was admitted to the bar in 1880. He became active in the Republican party and was appointed tax collector for the first district of Ohio by President Chester Arthur in

1882. In 1886, Taft married Helen Herron, the daughter of a law partner of President Rutherford B. Hayes.

In 1887, Taft was named to a vacancy on the Ohio Superior Court and the next year was elected to this seat for a five-year term. President Benjamin Harrison appointed him U.S. solicitor general in 1890; in 1892, he became judge of the Sixth Circuit Court of Appeals. He also was a professor and dean of the law department at the University of Cincinnati. President McKinley appointed Taft president of the U.S. Philippine Commission in 1900, and governor general of the Philippines in 1901. He turned down two Supreme Court appointments offered him by President Theodore Roosevelt, but in 1904 accepted the position of secretary of war in Roosevelt's cabinet. Taft supervised the early stages of the Panama Canal construction and served as provisional governor of Cuba. In 1908, President Roosevelt persuaded him to run as Republican candidate for president, which he did reluctantly. He won the election, but his presidency was not as successful as his earlier or later careers.

During his presidential term he was responsible for many anti-trust suits, reclaimed millions of acres of federal land from public sales, organized the Bureau of Mines in the Department of Interior, supported a tax on corporate earnings, extended the civil service merit system, advocated the establishment of a Children's Bureau in the Department of Commerce and Labor, and supported the passage of the 16th amendment which established the personal income tax. Taft's close relationship with Roosevelt cooled because they had completely opposite views of how to conduct the presidency. Roosevelt was an activist and Taft, a lawyer at heart, believed strongly that a president should only undertake actions defined by the Constitution or spelled out in acts of Congress. He is reported to have said: "I love judges, and I love courts. They are my ideals, that typify on earth what we shall meet hereafter in heaven under a just God."[14]

After his retirement as president, Taft enjoyed teaching law at Yale University. In 1918, he was appointed to the National War Labor Board by President Wilson. In 1921, President Harding nominated him for the Supreme Court, where he served as chief justice until 1930, a position he loved more than any other he had held. In 1925, he wrote: "The truth is, that in my present life I don't remember that I ever was President."[15] He resigned from the Supreme Court in February 1930 because of heart trouble, and died one month later in Washington.

The Taft Papers

President Taft was a systematic collector of his papers and showed great concern for the preservation of government records. In his Executive Order Number 1499 of March 1912, he directed the librarian of Congress to examine papers of the executive departments before their disposal to determine which of these papers are to be preserved for "historical interests."[16] Stressing the importance of the written word over oral expressions, Taft, speaking to the American Antiquarian Society in 1912, made the point that "the documentary form was an essential ingredient in establishing facts." He also mentioned at this occasion the need for a National Archives building, "not merely for preservation but also for classification and indexing in the interest of historical investigation."[17] At another occasion he pointed out that "The vast amount of correspondence that goes through the Executive office of the President, signed either by the President or his secretaries, does not become the property or record of the government, unless it goes on to the official files of the Department to which it may be addressed. The retiring President takes with him all of the correspondence, originals and copies, which he carried on during his administration."[18]

When leaving office in 1913, Taft asked Rudolph Forster, executive clerk of the White House, to send all his papers to his home in New Haven. He wanted his 30 boxes of law books and "boxes of files in the attic containing the letters written while Secretary of War up to the time I came to the White House on March 4, 1909, as also the boxes containing the letter press books."[19] In 1917, Forster sent a letter to Wendell W. Mischler, the President's secretary, that a collection of Taft papers had been discovered during a thorough housecleaning at the executive office. "These papers," Forster wrote "evidently were mixed in with a lot of our permanent records at the time the office was rebuilt in 1909."[20] These papers were also forwarded to New Haven.

In 1915, Gaillard Hunt asked Taft whether he would care to deposit his father's papers in the Library of Congress. No request was made at that time for the President's own papers, which would have been of greater historical significance. Taft answered that he needed time to put his father's papers in order. Four years later, Charles Moore, the acting chief of the Manuscript Division, made a direct appeal to Taft for his "public" papers. A week later Taft responded, expressing his concern that "I have in my correspondence a lot of truck which is good for nothing. I have thought that possibly there were experts who could run the papers through and make a digest of what I have."[21] The two men met and reached an agreement about the deposit of the papers in the Library of Congress. A week later, 34 boxes arrived at the Library along with an inventory prepared in 1913 by Rudolph Forster. After close examination of the papers it was noted that the letterbooks ended with the beginning of the Taft administration. Moore asked Taft whether he would be willing to deposit his presidential papers as well, and an additional 18 boxes were shipped from New Haven to Washington. The Roosevelt-Taft correspondence was hand-carried to the Library by Moore at Taft's request. Taft continued to deposit papers in the Library during the nine years he was on the Supreme Court.

In 1924, a publisher asked Mr. Mischler about the correspondence between Taft and Lord Bryce. Some of these papers were found in the Library of Congress, but a card index that had been included in the shipment of the Taft papers indicated that more Bryce-Taft letters existed. Mischler searched for these letters in the White House and found them. As a follow-up, Moore went to the White House on December 22, 1924, and found not only extensive office files from the Taft administration but also papers from the administrations of Presidents Wilson and Harding. These three collections of presidential files were found because the White House routinely divided all papers into two categories, the

"President's Personal File," which was turned over to him at the end of the term, and the "White House General File," which was considered to belong to the White House office rather than to the particular occupant. Moore concluded that it would not be feasible to go through the voluminous files to extract intermingled correspondence; to maintain the integrity of presidential collections and their historical value, all the files were sent to the Library.

In 1926, during the remodeling of Chief Justice Taft's residence on Wyoming Avenue in Washington, additional papers from his presidential years, letters from his grandparents, and letters he wrote to Mrs. Taft between 1913 and 1921 were discovered. Taft wrote to Moore about this find, concluding that he had decided not to send the letters of his father and grandfather because "as I glance at them I don't think they would have much interest in the collection of my letters."[22] Moore disagreed and urged Taft to reconsider. Taft sent some of his own correspondence to the Library before his death. The letters of his father and grandfather were finally deposited in the Library by the President's children, Robert A. Taft, Charles P. Taft, and Helen Taft Manning in 1933. Between 1930 and 1952 the family donated additional papers; all the materials were converted into a gift to the Library, amounting to over 500,000 items, one of the most complete presidential collections in existence. Some Taft materials are at Yale University, Princeton University, Western Reserve University, and the Ohio Historical Society.

The Taft Papers in the Library of Congress

Series	*Reels*
1. Family Correspondence and Related Items. 1805–1909. 3 boxes	1–22
2. William Howard Taft/Helen Herron Taft Correspondence. 1882–1929. 17 boxes	22–28
3. General Correspondence and Related Material. 1877–1930. 624 boxes	29–319
4. William Howard Taft/Theodore Roosevelt Correspondence. 1897–1918. 8 boxes	
A. 1897–1918. 6 boxes	319–322
B. 1907–09. 2 boxes	322
5. Executive Office Correspondence (Presidential Series, No. 1). 1909–10. 151 boxes	323–353
6. Executive Office Correspondence (Presidential Series, No. 2). 1910–13. 215 boxes	354–452
7. The President's Personal File (Presidential Series, No. 3). 1909–13. 17 boxes	452–461
8. Letterbooks. 1872–1921. 222 vols.	462–562
9. Speeches, Articles, and Messages. 1850–1929.	
A. 1901–20. 42 vols.	563–575
B. 1874–1917. 2 boxes	575–576
C. ca. 1874–1929. 33 boxes	576–593
D. 1850–75. 1 box	593
10. Professional Diaries. 1902–18. 43 vols.	593–609
11. Family Diaries and Miscellaneous Personal Volumes. 1835–1930. 30 vols.	608–610
12. Legal Papers of Alphonso Taft. 1784–1889. 3 boxes	610–611

13. Legal Papers of William Howard Taft. 1880–1929.
    7 boxes   611–616
14. Legal Notebooks. 1887–1900. 11 vols.   616–617
15. Miscellaneous Legal Manuscripts. 1881–1930.
    3 boxes   617–618
16. Law Lectures and Related Material. 1897–1921.
    7 boxes   618–623
17. Scrapbooks. 1879–1922. 25 vols.   623–626
18. Taft Family Financial Papers. 1880–1930. 46 boxes   626–635
19. Taft Family Financial Account Books and Related
    Material. 1831–1926. 39 vols.   636–637
20. Miscellaneous Correspondence and Related Material.
    1797–1941. 5 boxes   637–640
21. Special Correspondence. 1890–1909. 3 vols.   640
        Vol. 1. 1890–1908.
        Vol. 2. 1900–01.
        Vol. 3. 1909
22. Miscellaneous Addresses, Articles, and Related
    Material. 1807–1909. 2 boxes   641
23. Miscellaneous Reports and Minutes. 1905–29.
    3 boxes   641–643
24. Miscellaneous Messages. 1908–13. 10 boxes   643
25. Miscellany. 42 boxes   644–658
26. Diplomas, Certificates, Passports, Photographs,
    Cartoons, and Sketches. Oversize Material.
    15 containers   658
27. Addenda.

WOODROW WILSON
Twenty-eighth President—Democrat
1913–1921

Thomas Woodrow Wilson, son of a Presbyterian minister, was born in 1856 in Staunton, Virginia; during his youth, he and his family moved to different pastorates in Augusta, Georgia; Columbia, South Carolina; and Charlotte, North Carolina. In 1879, he graduated from the College of New Jersey (now Princeton University), attended the University of Virginia Law School from 1879 to 1881, and, for a short time, practiced law in Atlanta, Georgia. In 1883, he entered the graduate school of Johns Hopkins University, where he received a Ph.D. He married Ellen Louise Axson in 1885 and turned to an academic career, teaching history and politics at Bryn Mawr and Wesleyan University. In 1890, he was appointed professor of jurisprudence and politics at Princeton University. A popular lecturer and an indefatigable researcher, Wilson published widely, including his monumental *History of the American People.*[23] In 1902, he became president of Princeton University and won a national reputation through his writings on political questions of the time.

In 1910, Wilson was elected governor of New Jersey. Election reform, regulation of utilities, women and child labor regulations, workman's compensation, and employer liability were passed by the legislature during his administration. Nominated for president at the 1912 Democratic convention, Wilson won a three-way race against Roosevelt and Taft with 42 percent of the popular vote, but a much higher electoral vote, carrying 40 of the 48 states.

Wilson was the first president since John Adams to address joint sessions of Congress, and the first ever to hold regular press conferences. He had a strong impact on Congress, his active influence resulting in establishment of lower tariffs, passage of a graduated federal income tax and the Federal Reserve Act, and creation of the Federal Trade Commission. His interest in political and historical research was instrumental in 1914 in obtaining appropriations for strengthening the legislative reference services of the Library of Congress. He also pushed through Congress legislation prohibiting child labor, limiting railroad workers to an eight-hour day, and establishing federal farm loans. After Mrs. Wilson's death in 1914, he met Edith Bolling Galt, an attractive Washington widow, whom he married in December 1915.

When the war in Europe started in 1914, Wilson issued a Neutrality Proclamation that was violated repeatedly by both the Germans and the Allies. The overriding issue of the 1916 election was war, with Theodore Roosevelt demanding immediate intervention. The Democratic slogan "he kept us out of war" and Wilson's legislative record narrowly won him re-election to a second term over Republican Charles Evans Hughes.[24] Wilson continued his efforts to end the war in Europe, but without success. In February 1917, he protested against Germany's sinking of neutral ships in the Atlantic; he announced the breaking off of diplomatic relations with Germany to a joint session of Congress while expressing his continuing hope for peace. However, by April it became clear that war could no longer be avoided and Wilson asked Congress for a declaration of war. After the Allies' victory in November 1918, Wilson's "Fourteen Points" became the basis for the Paris Peace Conference, and led to a commitment to the formation of the League of Nations being incorporated into the Treaty of Versailles. The treaty was rejected by the Senate and Wilson, putting all political considerations aside, toured the country to raise popular support for his stand. The intensity of his approach did not appeal to a nation trying to return to normal after the trauma of war. In October 1919, a stroke incapacitated Wilson. He remained under the constant care of his wife, his physician, and his personal secretary, and never fully recovered. At the end of his term, he moved to his home on S Street in Washington; he passed away on February 3, 1924.

The Wilson Papers

The first contact of the Library of Congress to obtain the Wilson papers was made by Charles Moore in October 1920. The President's secretary, Joseph P. Tumulty, replied that, for the time being, the President preferred to keep his papers in his own possession. Wilson wrote to Moore in April 1922: "I have no doubt there could be no safer or more honorable custodian than the Library of Congress. But I am not willing yet to make any such disposition of my papers. I think it best to leave the matter for my last will and testament."[25]

During the active and productive part of his life, Wilson did not collect his papers with care, and paid little attention to their preservation. After his stroke, the President's wife controlled his activities and guarded his papers with an intensity that kept most associates at a distance. Three weeks after Wilson's death, Charles Moore contacted Mrs. Wilson about the disposition of the papers. She answered a few days later: "You may rest assured that I will give consideration to the suggestions which you make."[26] Three months later, on May 30, 1924, she wrote to Herbert Putnam, the librarian of Congress: "I feel very strongly that the Library of Congress is the place for this entire collection, and I am writing you frankly—feeling you will deal with me as openly in your response." She went on to say that she had learned from her correspondence with Moore that the Library of Congress staff would go over the papers and decide on the importance of the various documents. "Would it be possible," she asked, "for this decision to rest with me?"[27]

When Charles Moore went to the White House in December 1922 to search for missing Taft papers, he reported to Mrs. Wilson that he had also found "some seventy boxes from the Wilson Administration. Ostensibly they were the official files, as distinguished from the President's Personal Files, which are taken away at the close of a President's term. The officials at the President's Office would be glad to deliver all of the files to any other Government agency, like the Library of Congress, in order to be rid of them. It is annoying to be asked for papers pertaining to a previous administration."[28] While negotiations between the Library and Mrs. Wilson continued, she was anxious to choose a biographer and to complete the records of her husband's presidency. She started to solicit materials from friends and relatives and collected a substantial number of documents between 1924 and the 1950s. In 1925, she selected Ray Stannard Baker of Amherst, Massachussetts, Wilson's long-time friend and associate, as the authorized Wilson biographer and sent all available papers to him. The Wilson-Baker collaboration had its beginnings with Baker's service as director of the Press Bureau of the American Commission to Negotiate Peace in Paris. Baker had asked Wilson's approval to search through the presidential papers in preparation of a book about the Peace Conference, *Woodrow Wilson and World Settlement*, which was published in 1922.[29] Baker wrote later: "I shall not forget that day in January 1921 when I went up with the president to his study on the second floor of the White House. One of the men accompanied us carrying the shiny steel cabinet box which I had so often seen on the desk of his study in Paris. He had kept his important documents in it and I recalled just how he shut and locked it every night. I then learned that there was not only the trunkful of Paris documents to which the President had referred . . . but three trunkfuls, besides the steel cabinet, and a precious smaller box which Wilson had kept in a bank vault."[30]

In 1929, J. Franklin Jameson suggested that the papers be sent to the Library as Baker finished successive portions of the biography. Mrs. Wilson responded by stating five conditions under which she would consider placing the Wilson papers into the Library of Congress:

(1) The papers will be delivered as Baker is finished with their use.

(2) The papers will be sealed and can't be broken unless she gives the permission.

(3) If she gives permission for access to the papers, it has to be requested from her during her lifetime; after her death the control passes to the Library of Congress.

(4) If she leaves no details about the disposition of the papers, they pass on January 1, 1935 to the Library of Congress.

(5) In case she decides to remove the papers from the Library of Congress, she is free to do so.

She requested that this agreement be kept confidential.[31]

The Wilson papers that were under Baker's care for 17 years were only once in danger; a fire broke out in his Amherst home during the winter of 1927, but no losses occurred. By 1937, Baker had completed eight volumes of the biography, but his health forced him to stop with the text at the conclusion of the 1918 Armistice. The biography was published under the title *Woodrow Wilson: Life and Letters.*[32]

The papers were shipped to the Library in 1939 and a press announcement about the transfer of the papers to the Library was authorized by Mrs. Wilson. Ten months later, in July 1940, the papers were declared open to the public under the conditions that Mrs. Wilson had to approve the user and the purpose of the access to the papers. In addition, notes taken by the user had to be approved by Katherine E. Brand, the special custodian of the papers, who had been selected by Mrs. Wilson, or by the chief of the Manuscript Division. Eventually these rules were somewhat simplified, particularly for properly accredited representatives of a government department or agency.

In 1946, Mrs. Wilson gave Woodrow Wilson's personal library of 9,000 volumes to the Library of Congress, to be housed in a special room adjacent to the Rare Books Division. The Woodrow Wilson Room was formally dedicated on January 8, 1949, with Mrs. Wilson in attendance.[33] In 1958, the most intensive study of the Wilson papers was begun for the preparation of *The Papers of Woodrow Wilson,*[34] a project that had the full support of Mrs. Wilson. Edited by Arthur S. Link, John W. Davidson, and David W. Hirst, the work was published by Princeton University Press in 40 volumes between 1966 and 1986.

Until her death in 1961, Mrs. Wilson continued to contribute papers to the collection in the Library, and also maintained complete control over it. Once, when the Library received a package containing the correspondence between Wilson and his first wife, starting two years before their marriage and continuing until Ellen Axson Wilson's death, and also including some correspondence with their three daughters, Mrs. Wilson insisted that these papers be withdrawn. She sent them to Mrs. Eleanor Wilson McAdoo, the President's youngest daughter, who eventually presented this collection to the Firestone Library at Princeton University.

The Woodrow Wilson collection in the Library of Congress consists of approximately 300,000 items. Besides the papers at Princeton University, there are substantial collections at Columbia University and the University of Virginia, and some materials at other locations.

The Wilson Papers in the Library of Congress

Series	*Reels*
1. Diaries and Diary Material. 1876–1924. 54 vols., 8 boxes	1–3
2. Family and General Correspondence. 1850–1924. 227 boxes	3–131
3. Letterbooks. 1913–21. 62 vols.	132–159
4. Executive Office File. 1913–21. 510 boxes	160–383
5. Peace Conference Correspondence and Documents. 1914–21. 112 boxes	
A. Policy Documents. 1914–19. 3 boxes	383–384
B. Peace Conference Correspondence. 1918–20. 54 boxes	385–415
C. Wilson/House Correspondence. Oct. 16–Dec. 9, 1918. 2 boxes	415
D. Unofficial Correspondence. 1918–19. 42 boxes	416–443
E-K. Additional Letters and Documents. 11 boxes	443–448
6. Peace Conference Documents. 1918–21. 44 boxes	
A. Minutes of Executive Bodies. 1918–20. 14 boxes	448–456
B. British War Cabinet Papers. Mar. 13–June 26, 1919. 1 box	456
C. Peace Conference Commissions Records. 1919–20. 2 boxes	457–458
D. Austrian Treaty. 1919. 1 box	458–459
E. German Treaty. 1919–20. 3 boxes	459–461
F. Chinese Delegation. 1919. 1 box	461
G. Maps and Reports. 1 box	461–462
H. Maps and Reports with Appendices.	462
I. Maps. 1 box	462
J. ANCP Bulletins. Economic, Political, and Military Reports. 1918–21. 9 boxes	462–467
K. Executive Departments. Weekly Reports. Jan. 27– June 16, 1919. 2 boxes	467–468
L. War Department. Weekly Reports.	468
M. Central Powers Reports. State Department. 1917–18	468
N. Intelligence Summaries. 1918–20. 3 boxes	468–470
O. See P.	
P. Intelligence Reports. Cables. 1918–21. 3 boxes	470–472
Q. Treaty Proofs. 1919. 1 box	473
7. Speeches, Writings, and Academic Material. 1875–1923. 53 boxes	
A. Speeches. 1882–1923. 17 boxes	473–479
B. Messages to Congress. 1913–21. 3 boxes	479–480
C. Books. 1885–1908. 16 boxes	480–487
D. Academic Material. 1873–1912. 13 boxes	487–493
E. Essays and Articles. 1875–1923. 3 boxes	493–494
F. Swem Transcripts. 1913–19. 1 box	494–495
8. Financial Material. 1864–1927. 21 boxes	
A. Account Books.	495
B. Miscellaneous Financial Letters.	495
C. Insurance Policies.	496
D. Dickinson Trust Company Letters.	496
E. Grant Squires Company Letters.	496
F. Bills and Receipts.	496–502

G. Harris & Company and Harris–Forbes & Company Letters.	502
H. Investments.	502
I. Taxes.	
J. Taxes.	502
K. Checkbook Stubs.	
L. Canceled Checks.	
9. Scrapbooks. 1873–1944. 18 vols., 22 boxes	503–520
10. Social Records. 1875–1924. 5 vols., 8 boxes	521–523
11. Woodrow, Axson, and Wilson Family Material. 1835–94. 3 boxes	523–524
12. Miscellaneous Documents. 1826–1928.	524–528
13. Oversize Material. 1879–1931.	528–531
14. Supplement. Recipients' Copies of Letters with some Photocopies of Originals and Collected Wilson Materials. 1880–1946. 2 vols., 17 boxes	531–536
15. Writings About Wilson. 1897–1961. 3 boxes	536–538
16. Princeton Miscellany. 2 boxes	538
17. Miscellaneous Printed Matter. 9 boxes	538–539
18. Photographs. ca. 1875–1923. 5 boxes	539
19. Miscellaneous Shorthand. 1 box	540

CALVIN COOLIDGE
Thirtieth President—Republican
1923–1929

Calvin Coolidge was born in 1872 in Plymouth, Vermont, the son of a village storekeeper. He graduated *cum laude* from Amherst College in 1895, worked as a law clerk in Northampton, Massachussetts, and, in 1897, was admitted to the bar and opened a law office. He entered Republican politics in 1899 as a councilman, married Grace Anna Goodhue in 1905, and served as mayor of Northampton and member and president of the state senate. In 1916, Coolidge was elected lieutenant governor of Massachussetts, became governor in 1919, and was chosen as the vice presidential running mate of Warren Gamaliel Harding in 1920.

In 1923, Harding died in California. Coolidge was visiting in Vermont at the time and was notified in the middle of the night that he was president. His father, who was a notary public, administered the oath of office, and Coolidge went back to bed. Some years later, as Charles Hopkinson was painting his portrait, he asked the President what his first thought was when he heard that Harding had died. Without a change in expression, Coolidge answered: "I thought I could swing it."[35]

After the many scandals of the Harding administration, Coolidge managed to restore dignity to the office of the president. He retained Harding's cabinet and promised the country to maintain the status quo, but had to accept the resignation of the secretary of the navy and of the attorney general because of the scandals with which they were involved. His political genius, as Walter Lippmann pointed out in 1926, "was his talent for effectively doing nothing."[36] Coolidge advocated reduction of taxes and limited aid to farmers; he vetoed bills granting increases for veteran's pensions. His basic philosophy was: "The business of America is business." [37] In foreign policy, he stood for isolation.

Coolidge was re-elected in 1924, but the coalition of Democrats and progressive Republicans in Congress made his life difficult during the second term. In 1928, true to his famous laconic style, he handed a ten-word statement to reporters: "I do not choose to run for president in 1928." [38] After his retirement, he returned to Northampton and wrote his autobiography.[39] With the proceeds, he bought a large mansion, "The Beeches." In spite of urging from Republican friends, he refused to participate in politics. He died unexpectedly of a heart attack in 1933.

The Coolidge Papers

When President Coolidge left the White House he left about 170,000 documents behind. After a 1929 correspondence with Franklin Jameson from the Manuscript Division, the papers were deposited in the Library of Congress, and their use was permitted, provided that Coolidge, or, after his death, Mrs. Coolidge, approved the request. In 1953 the papers were given to the Library; since 1957, when Mrs. Coolidge died, access to the papers has not been restricted. The papers left in the White House were mostly from people who wrote to him for various reasons, and carbon copies of his routine replies. There are only a small number of letters from people who had served in the government or had important positions. In 1933, Edward T. Clark, Coolidge's private secretary during his vice presidential and presidential years, wrote to Harry E. Ross, the President's last secretary, that "Mr. Coolidge's desire was to destroy everything in the so-called personal files and there would have been nothing preserved if I had not taken some things out on my own responsibility." [40] In another letter, he commented that the destruction of the papers would not "involve the loss which you might at first imagine because as President, Mr. Coolidge did not follow the practice of other presidents in trying to explain his administration through letters to friends." [41] A few years later, Mrs. Coolidge also told St. George Sioussat of the Manuscript Division that the President had destroyed all his personal papers. Coolidge's motive for doing this may be best explained by quoting his statement: "I have never been hurt by what I have not said." [42]

Claude M. Fuess, who wrote Coolidge's biography after the President's death, reported that Mrs. Coolidge generously permitted him to examine a large number of letters written by Coolidge to his father and stepmother from his schoolboy days until his death.[43] William Allen White, who wrote *A Puritan in Babylon: The Story of Calvin Coolidge,* recalled spending several days with the President in 1924, and wrote: "What I wanted was to get his slant on things, his point of view, the light that glowed in the inner chambers of his heart. He kept it hooded." [44]

The Library of Congress has almost 180,000 items in the Coolidge collection. Materials relating to Coolidge can also be found in the Edward T. Clark papers and other contemporary collections in the Library. A substantial number of Coolidge documents relating to his pre-presidential years are in the Calvin Coolidge Memorial Room of the Forbes Library in Northampton, Massachusetts.

The Coolidge Papers in the Library of Congress

Series	Reels
1. Executive Office Correspondence. 1923–29.	
283 boxes	1–188
2. Additional Correspondence. 1921–29. 1 box	188
3. Reception Lists. 1925–27. 3 vols.	188–190

PART III

Presidential Papers in Historical Societies and Special Libraries

9. Historical Societies

JOHN ADAMS
Second President—Federalist
1797–1801

Born in 1735 in Braintree, now Quincy, Massachusetts, John Adams was a fifth generation American. His father was a farmer and part-time shoemaker who had graduated from Harvard College and believed in education. John Adams graduated from Harvard in 1755, taught school for a year and decided to study law. In 1758, he was admitted to the bar and began to practice law in Braintree. He married Abigail Smith in 1764 and raised three sons and two daughters with her. Adams was drawn into the revolutionary camp by the British Stamp Act and, in 1765, wrote a protest for the community of Braintree that was adopted by other Massachusetts towns. In 1766, the Adamses moved to Boston.

In 1768, Adams' defense of John Hancock, who had been accused of smuggling by the British customs officials, made him well known throughout the colonies. His most famous case was the defense of the British soldiers charged with murder during the Boston massacre of 1770; this case created a great deal of antagonism toward him by Boston patriots, but at the same time won him respect for his sense of fairness. He was absent from Boston during the Boston Tea Party in December 1773, but he noted in his diary: "This destruction of the tea is so bold, so daring, so firm, so intrepid and inflexible and it must have so important consequences . . . that I can't but consider it as an epoch of history."[1]

Adams participated in the Continental Congresses as delegate from Massachusetts from 1774 to 1777, and chaired 25 of the 90 congressional committees. In order to unite the quibbling delegates of North and South, he nominated George Washington to be commander-in-chief of the Continental Army. When Congress elected him to a committee to write the Declaration of Independence, Adams let Thomas Jefferson take the lead because: "I had a great opinion of the elegance of his pen, and none at all of my own."[2] However, during the debates on the Declaration of Independence, Adams spoke, as Jefferson later described it: " . . . with a power of thought and an expression that moved us from our seats."[3] During his last year in Congress Adams presented a resolution to establish a United States flag with 13 red and white stripes and a union of 13 white stars in a blue field.

Between 1778 and 1788, Adams served in diplomatic missions to France, England, and the Netherlands; his posts included that of America's first minister to the Court of St. James. In 1779, he returned briefly to Boston and wrote the major part of a new constitution for Massachusetts. He went back to Europe to participate in negotiations with the British that resulted in a peace treaty ending the Revolutionary War. Upon his return to the United States, he served two terms as vice president under George Washington. He was bored by this office, which he described as "the most insignificant office that ever the invention of man contrived . . . it is not quite adapted to my character—I mean it is too inactive and mechanical."[4]

In 1796, Adams was elected president by a narrow margin with 71 votes against Jefferson's 68. When he assumed the presidency, he took over Washington's cabinet without change; this gave Alexander Hamilton the opportunity to manipulate the Federalists from behind the scenes. To complicate matters further, Thomas Jefferson, the head of the Democratic-Republicans, was vice president. After the death of George Washington, Adams appointed his own cabinet. In 1798 and 1799, he spent a great deal of effort to defuse the growing tension with France. A peace agreement with France gave Adams the satisfaction that his efforts to avoid war had been successful. Internal party conflicts damaged his re-election chances, and Jefferson won the election of 1800 with 73 electoral votes to Adams' 65.

The last few months of Adams' administration were conducted from Washington, the new capital, and the Adamses lived in the still unfinished White House. They retired to Quincy, Massachusetts, and Adams lived to see his son, John Quincy, become president in 1825. He died on July 4, 1826, a few hours after Thomas Jefferson had passed away.

JOHN QUINCY ADAMS
Sixth President—National Republican
1825–1829

John Quincy Adams, the oldest of three sons, was born in 1767, almost next door to the birthplace of his father in Braintree (now Quincy), Massachusetts. He described himself as "a man of reserve, cold, austere and forbidding manners: my political adversaries say, a gloomy misanthrope, and my personal enemies, an unsocial savage."[5] His appearance hid a brilliant man with an unusually objective power of observation which he displayed in his diaries. He started to write letters and copied some for his father at an early age.

Partly by coincidence, and partly due to his training, education, and extensive travels, John Quincy had one of the most varied careers of any president. From age 12 to age 20, he served as his father's secretary in Paris, The Hague, and other capitals in Europe; he knew French sufficiently well to serve as French interpreter during the first United States mission to Russia.

In 1785, he returned to the United States, graduated from Harvard College in 1787, and became a journalist. In 1790, he was admitted to the bar and began to practice law in Boston. At the age of 27, he was appointed by George Washington as minister to the Netherlands and served as minister to Prussia under his father's administration. He married Louisa Catherine Johnson in 1797. Returning to Boston in 1801, Adams resumed his law practice, failed to win election to the U.S. House of Representatives, and was appointed to the Massachusetts state senate. In 1802, he won election to the U.S. Senate, where he served from 1803 to 1808, when he broke with the Federalists and resigned from the Senate. Madison, a Democratic-Republican, appointed him first U.S. minister to Russia in 1809; from 1815 to 1817 he was U.S. minister to England; he served as secretary of state in the Monroe administration from 1817 to 1825, assisting in the formulation of the Monroe Doctrine.

In the election of 1824, none of the four candidates received a clear majority. The election then went to the House of Representatives which, according the Constitution, was to choose the president from the top three candidates. The fourth candidate, Henry Clay, threw his support to Adams who became president. Adams made many innovative proposals, such as development of a highway and canal system, the establishment of a national university in Washington, and the financing of scientific expeditions, all of which fell on deaf ears in Congress. He was defeated for re-election by Andrew Jackson and returned to his home in Massachusetts, bitterly disappointed. He noted: "The sun of my political life sets in the deepest gloom. But that of my country shines unclouded."[6]

Adams had barely started to inspect some of his father's and his own papers, considering how to organize and store them, when he was invited to consider running for office. Much to his pleasure and satisfaction, he was elected to Congress in 1830. He remained in Congress for the next 18 years, an office he found more rewarding than any he had held during his illustrious career. He fought persistently against slavery and for the advancement of science and technology. He sponsored the establishment of the Smithsonian Institution and of a federal astronomical observatory. In February 1848, he suffered a stroke on the floor of the House of Representatives and died two days later.

THE ADAMS FAMILY PAPERS IN THE MASSACHUSETTS HISTORICAL SOCIETY

A few of the Adams family records go back to 1639. The beginnings of the diaries of John Adams have been traced to June 1753 when he was a student at Harvard College. He made few entries during the next two years, but in 1755 an earthquake impressed him sufficiently to start his record keeping on a more regular basis and to continue it practically throughout life. Few of his notes, papers, diaries, and letters have been lost, except those which he discarded in his youth, much to his later regret. Besides keeping his diary, he also kept "Letter Books" to preserve his correspondence, and recorded his financial status in "Books of Receipts and Expenses." To assure that this trait stay in the family, John Adams wrote in 1815 to his two oldest grandsons, George Washington Adams, age 14, and John Adams II, age 11:

> I wish you to have each a Pencil Book, always in your Pockett, by which you minute on the Spot any remarkable thing you may see or hear. A pocket Inkhorn, any cheap Thing of the kind, and a Sheet or two of paper, ought always to be about you. A Journal, a Diary is indispensible. Without a minute Diary, your Travels, will be no better than the flights of the Birds through the Air. They will leave no trace behind them. Whatever you write preserve. I have burned Bushells of my Silly notes, in fitts of Impatience and humiliation, which I would now give anything to recover.[7]

John Quincy Adams acquired the habit of record keeping at the age of 12 and practiced it even more assiduously than his father. What makes the papers of John and John Quincy Adams so interesting is that both men displayed, as Lyman H. Butterfield observed, "a kind of genius for being in interesting places at interesting moments,"[8] and that they also had the discipline to record the events they witnessed and participated in during the day, often working late into the night. Both Adamses managed to have their papers shipped from place to place in the United States, from the United States to Europe and back, and to never lose any of them.

The Old House in Quincy

In 1787, before John and Abigail Adams returned from their last foreign assignment in England, they purchased a house in what is now Quincy, Massachusetts. They managed to squeeze most of their possessions, mementos, books, and ever growing number of papers into this building by enlarging it several times. They and their family referred to it as "The Old House." John Adams used an area on the second floor as his storage, work, and bedroom space. He preferred to do his writing and recording in this comfortable room, crammed with books that are preserved to this day. There he used his manuscripts to prepare his autobiography and to write regular letters about his diplomatic and presidential years to the *Boston Patriot*, a newspaper of very limited circulation. Some of these letters were reprinted in *Correspondence of the Late President Adams. Originally Published in the Boston Patriot in a Series of Letters*, and included in *The Works of John Adams*,[9] edited by Charles Francis Adams.[10]

Two months after Abigail's death in 1818, John wrote to John Quincy that he was "deeply immersed in researches ... after old Papers, Trunks, Boxes, Desks, Drawers, locked up for thirty Years ... broken open because the Keys are lost. Every Scrap shall be found and preserved for your Affliction . . . The huge Pile of family Letters will make you Alternately laugh and cry, fret and fume, stamp and scold, as they do me."[11] Nine months after he wrote this letter, John Adams signed his will and a separate deed by which he left to John Quincy all his papers, letters, journals, and account books and described how they were arranged and stored.

John Quincy Adams, who kept his diaries even more thoroughly than his father, sent very detailed dispatches from the embassies to the Department of State in Washington while serving with John Adams in Paris and The Hague, and later when he was stationed in Berlin, St. Petersburg, Ghent, Paris, and London. His writing was precise, but rarely showed emotions and was always without humor. Occasionally, indications of pessimism crept into his diaries regarding the chores of keeping accurate records. He noted on March 25, 1844, that his efforts to keep his entries up to date were "like a race of a man with a wooden leg after a horse," and yet he continued his work even though complaining that he could have accomplished more had he not spent so much time on this work, resulting in "a multiplication of books to no end and without end."[12]

In 1824, John Quincy visited the family graves at Quincy and noted in his diary: "Four generations, of whom very little more is known, than is recorded upon these stones. There are three succeeding generations of us now living. Pass another century, and we shall all be mouldering in the same dust."[13] When he returned from Washington to Massachusetts in 1829 to what he thought would be permanent retirement, John Quincy began to give serious consideration to the preservation of his and his father's papers. He thought of building a new house with a library facility or a fireproof office. He also began working on a memoir of his father, researching the chronicles of early New England to the arrival of the first Adamses about 1640. However, when he was asked to run for Congress from his district, he eagerly returned to public life and remained there until the day of his death. The memoir had gotten only as far as 1770 and was dropped, though he returned to it occasionally during the next decade. It constitutes the preliminary genealogical sketch and the first two chapters of "The Life of John Adams" in the *Works of John Adams, Second President of the United States.*[14] Meanwhile, he accumulated quantities of papers and correspondence and would not throw any of them away because he did not have time to sort the worthless from the valuable. He noted in his diary of December 9, 1842, that he had "no chests and boxes and bureaus and drawers sufficient in numbers and capacity to contain these documents."[15]

John Quincy's only living son, Charles Francis, was scholarly inclined and interested in history and in the preservation of the family's records. In January 1847, a year before he passed away, John Quincy signed a will in which he bequeathed to Charles Francis "my library of books, my manuscript books and papers and those of my father." He recommended to his son that he "cause a building to be erected, made fireproof, in which to keep said library, books, documents and manuscripts safe." He added the hope that "as long as possible the books and manuscripts be kept together as a single collection and in the possession of the family."[16]

The Stone Library

Charles Francis continued the family practice of keeping records, starting in his teens; he added editorial skill to the family thoroughness and was anxious to carry out his father's wishes regarding the preservation of the family papers. In the 1830s, he collected his grandfather's and grandmother's letters, which he published in 1840 as *The Letters of Mrs. Adams*.[17] However, he had to delay his plans to build a fireproof library according to his father's wishes until after he returned from his post as minister to London, where he served from 1861 to 1868 and from where he brought back more papers, adding to the mass of Adams documents that had accumulated for a century and a quarter. In 1869, he hired the well-known architect Edward C. Cabot and selected with him a site for a library on the property next to the "Old House." During the fall of 1870 the "Stone Library" was completed, and Charles Francis proceeded to move the family papers into this facility. He was interrupted by another government assignment which took him to Geneva, Switzerland, between 1871 and 1872, but he spent his later years working on the family records in the library, and edited *The Works of John Adams, Second President of the United States: With a Life of the Author*,[18] and *Memoirs of John Quincy Adams, Comprising Portions of his Diary from 1795 to 1848.*[19]

Charles Francis shared with his father the feelings of doubt regarding the usefulness of keeping such detailed records and confided in his diary in 1876 that "it occurs to me whether all my labor will prove of any use. The continuation of families is so uncertain and the changes of habitation so much depend on the growth of the neighborhood that it is idle to expect permanency. This is the only large house left from the early part of the last century."[20] Charles Francis died in 1886 and left all the papers, manuscripts, and books "to such of my four sons as may survive me, and the survivors and survivors of them . . . to be kept together in the Stone Library as long as any of my male descendents bearing the family name shall continue to reside upon the said mansion house estate."[21]

The Adams Family Trust and the Massachusetts Historical Society

Charles Francis' four sons, John Quincy II, Charles Francis II, Henry, and Brooks, were aware of their responsibility as custodians of a unique treasure of historical records, but were not sure what to do about it. John Quincy II died in 1894. As historians in their own rights, Charles Francis II and Brooks were not anxious to dispose of the papers; however, they also did not take any action to edit them or to prepare them for publication. Both of them agreed that it was useful to have the family papers close at hand and decided to leave things as they were.

In 1902, the three surviving sons of Charles Francis, and Charles Francis III, the son of John Quincy II, agreed that to assure the preservation of the large number of documents it would be advantageous to deposit them at the Massachusetts Historical Society in Boston for safekeeping. John's and John Quincy's papers were deposited at that time; the papers of the third generation were not deposited until later because

Charles Francis II was using them for his work on his father's life and writings, *Charles Francis Adams.*[22] In 1905, the four Adamses reached the decision to establish the Adams Manuscript Trust of which they were the trustees; the Trust would serve as a way station until further action could be taken concerning the eventual organization and publication of the papers. The Trust consisted of the three Adams homes (the home of John's father, the birthplace of John, and the "Old House") as well as the Stone Library, with all their furnishings and contents, including the Adams papers already located in the Massachusetts Historical Society. The trustees of the Adams Manuscript Trust were charged to care for the properties for the next 50 years, appoint their successors, and dispose of the items in their trust "with a view to their public or family interest and significance."[23] The trustees could sell or pass on to others parts of or all the properties of the trust. In the case of the manuscripts, the trustees had the privilege of destroying any offending parts.

Charles Francis III, the president of the Trust, wanted to see use made of the papers as long as the family was in charge of controlling this use. He became president of the Massachusetts Historical Society in 1908 and induced Worthington Chauncey Ford to leave the Library of Congress and to come to Boston to serve as editor of the Society and consultant to the Adams Manuscript Trust. Ford suggested a 12-volume edition of the John Quincy Adams papers, but by 1917 only seven volumes of the *Writings of John Quincy Adams*[24] had appeared, covering selectively the years 1779 to 1823. After the death of Charles Francis II in 1915, Henry in 1918, and Brooks in 1927, the publications program came to a halt. The family's opinion was that everything that ought to be published had been published and the papers were protected from access by anyone, including the officers and staff of the Massachusetts Historical Society where they were stored. The responsibility for the Trust remained with Charles Francis III, who died in 1954.

In 1940, the Trust disposed of the two old Adams homes by deeding them to the city of Quincy, Massachusetts. The Old House and the Stone Library were given to the United States government in 1946; all the properties are now under the care of the U.S. Park Service. The only property remaining in the hands of the trustees was the family archives in the Adams Room of the Massachusetts Historical Society.

Fortunately for American history, two members of the sixth Adams generation, Thomas Boylston Adams and John Quincy Adams IV, joined the trustees of the Adams Manuscript Trust in the 1950s and invited a distinguished group of scholars to advise them on what to do with the papers. The result of the deliberations was the recommendation to microfilm all 300,000 documents of the Adams family, going back to 1639, with the purpose of offering these sets to major research libraries. In 1954, Harvard University Press agreed to prepare under the imprint of the Belknap Press a comprehensive publication of the Adams papers; Time, Inc. offered to furnish editorial funds to the Society in return for the right to serialize selections from the edited copy. To effect this enterprise the Adams trustees transferred "all letters, letterbooks, documents of public and private nature as well as diaries belonging to the said trust and now located on the premises of the Massachusetts Historical

Society" to the Society, which assumed the obligation to carry out the agreements made by the Trust in 1954 and 1955.[25] *The Adams Papers* are being published in four series by the Belknap Press:

- Series I. Diaries
- Series II. Adams Family Correspondence
- Series III. General Correspondence and Other Papers of the Adams Statesmen
- Series IV. Adams Family Portraits.

As of 1988, 32 volumes have been published in the four series. The Massachusetts Historical Society estimates that the project will be completed in approximately 40 years.

The Microfilms of the Adams Papers

Series	*Reels*
John Adams	
I. Diaries.	
Nov. 18, 1755–July 5, 1771	1
Dec. 16, 1772–Aug. 1804	2
1755–72	3
II. Letterbook.	89–124
May 26, 1776–Feb. 20, 1825	
Journal of European Bank Drafts 1785–88	
Miscellany Autobiography.	180
Miscellany.	181–196
July 1781–July 23, 1826	
Abigail Adams	
Miscellany	197–198
June 20, 1784–Nov. 1818	
John Quincy Adams	
I. Diaries.	
Nov. 12, 1779–Dec. 31, 1779	4
Jan. 1780–Jan. 31, 1780	5
July 25, 1780–Sept. 30, 1780	6
June 9, 1781–Aug. 27, 1781	7
Jan. 27, 1782–Nov. 23, 1782	8
Dec. 31, 1782–Feb. 26, 1783	9
Aug. 6, 1783–Sept. 22, 1783	10
II. Diaries and Almanacs.	4–48
Nov. 12, 1779–Aug. 10, 1846	
III. Diaries and Miscellaneous Papers.	49–52
Rubbish I–IV. June 1829–Feb. 1848	
IV. Letterbooks.	125–155
Aug. 1781–Feb. 4, 1848	
V. Miscellany.	199–263
1782–March 1849	

MILLARD FILLMORE
Thirteenth President—Whig
1850–1853

Born in 1800 in Cayuga County, in the Finger Lakes area of New York, Millard Fillmore was the son of a poor frontier farmer. He received only a primary education, was apprenticed to a cloth maker at the age of 14, and worked for a short time in a local store. At 18, he fell in love with Abigail Powers, a school teacher who tutored him. Encouraged by her to seek a better life, he taught school and began to read law, at first with a county judge, and later in Buffalo. In 1823, he was admitted to the bar of New York, married Abigail in 1826, and built a home in East Aurora where he started to practice law. He became interested in politics, moved to Buffalo, and served in the New York State Legislature from 1829 to 1831.

Fillmore served in the U.S. Congress from 1833 to 1835, and from 1837 to 1843. While in Congress, he became chairman of the Ways and Means Committee, where he perfected his skills as a compromiser and assumed the leadership of the anti-slavery movement of his party. In 1844, he tried unsuccessfully to be nominated for vice president on the Whig ticket, and failed in his attempt to become governor of New York. In 1847, he was elected state comptroller and the following year was chosen as vice president on the Whig ticket with Zachary Taylor; the Whigs won the election and carried New York. When Taylor died in July 1850, Fillmore was sworn in as president.

Since he did not share most of his predecessor's views, Fillmore accepted the resignations of all cabinet members and signed the 1850 Compromise Act. This act admitted California to the Union as a free state, settled the boundary dispute between Texas and New Mexico, and established New Mexico and Utah as territories. The residents of each territory could decide whether to accept slavery in their state constitutions. The act prohibited the slave trade, but not slavery, in the District of Columbia, and included a strengthened Fugitive Slave Law that made federal officials responsible for recovering fugitive slaves. The compromise split the northern and southern segments of the Whigs, and caused northern abolitionists to become more militant.

During the 1852 Whig convention, the party refused to back Fillmore for a second term because he had signed the Compromise of 1850; they nominated General Winfield Scott, who was defeated by Democrat Franklin Pierce. In 1853, Fillmore's wife and daughter passed away, and he retired to Buffalo where he resumed his law practice. In 1856, he accepted the presidential nomination of the remnants of the Whig party and the American party, also called the Know Nothings, but finished behind Democrat James Buchanan and Republican John C. Fremont. In 1858, Fillmore married a wealthy widow. He died in 1874.

THE FILLMORE PAPERS IN THE BUFFALO HISTORICAL SOCIETY

When Millard Fillmore died, he left a will that made no reference to his papers. Millard Powers Fillmore, his only son, never married, and died in 1889. He left a will in which he requested that his executors "burn or otherwise effectively destroy all correspondence or letters to or from my father, mother, sister, or me."[26] This sentence could be interpreted to mean that the executors should destroy only the correspondence of President Fillmore with members of his family, or that all his correspondence should be destroyed.

Whatever the son's intent, it seems unlikely that President Fillmore meant to have his papers destroyed. During his White House years, his papers were carefully kept and systematically arranged; incoming letters were placed into letterbooks. When he retired to Buffalo in 1853, he had his papers shipped there. In 1862, he accepted the position of president of the Buffalo Historical Society and donated the last letter he had received from Daniel Webster to the Society. When Fillmore was visited by his friend, James Grant Wilson, and showed him through his house in Buffalo, he told him: "In these cases can be found very important letters and documents . . . which will enable the future historian or biographer to prepare an authentic account of that period in our country's history."[27] This certainly makes it appear that he meant to have his papers preserved to help with the writing of an account of his presidency. As a lawyer he had always shown great concern for books, historical documents, and his own papers. As president, he approved funds for repair of the damage caused by fire in the Library of Congress in 1852, for replacement of the destroyed books, and for a temporary room for the Library's use. His concern for the preservation of historic materials was also illustrated in his third annual message to Congress, in December 1852, when he warned that

> the building appropriated to the State Department is not fireproof;
> that there is reason to think there are defects in its construction, and
> that the archives of the government in charge of the Department,
> with the precious collections of the manuscript papers of Washington,
> Jefferson, Hamilton, Madison and Monroe, are exposed to destruc-
> tion by fire.[28]

In spite of this, it was generally believed that Powers Fillmore's instructions were actually carried out and that Fillmore's presidential papers were destroyed by his son's executors. The Buffalo Historical Society set out to find as many Fillmore papers from various sources as possible and, in 1899, arranged a meeting under the title "An Hour with President Fillmore and His Friends" which was well attended and produced some interesting reminiscences. Mrs. S.G. Haven, the widow of Fillmore's law partner, made the announcement at that meeting that many letters which her husband had received from the President, particularly during the formation of his cabinet, were carefully preserved for more than four decades, but finally destroyed because "they were of too personal and confidential a nature to be subjected to the risk of ever falling into other hands."[29]

In 1903, Frank H. Severance, the secretary of the Buffalo Historical Society, visited Washington to collect some materials for the Society. Severance had started a nationwide effort to locate and collect Fillmore papers; he obtained papers from the Manuscript Division of the Library of Congress and the files of executive departments in Washington. He was very successful in getting access to records in the departments, with the exception of the War Department, which had a general restriction against public access. In 1907, Severance published *The Millard Fillmore Papers*,[30] a two-volume edition of letters and papers written by Fillmore. Letters written to Fillmore were not included in this collection.

The most important discovery of Fillmore papers was made in 1908 at the home of Charles D. Marshall, a Buffalo attorney, who was the last surviving executor of the Powers Fillmore estate. After Marshall's death, 44 volumes of letterbooks were found which contained more than 8,400 letters written to Fillmore between 1849 and 1853. This find was brought to the Society by Mrs. Hazel Koerner, Marshall's adopted daughter and the administrator of his estate. Severance announced this discovery in the *New York Times* and the *Buffalo Illustrated Times* in January 1909, inviting scholars to make use of these materials. The Society also owns several scrapbooks and a few letters presented by Fillmore himself or his second wife. Over the years, additional items have been acquired, most notably the Niederlander Gift Collection of Fillmore manuscripts presented in 1966.

About 550 books from President Fillmore's personal library were given to the Buffalo Historical Society by him and by his second wife. Some of the books owned by Fillmore are in the Buffalo and Erie County Public Library. The Historical Society also owns a collection of paintings and photographs of the President's family.

The Fillmore Papers at Oswego, New York

In 1966, another collection of Fillmore papers was discovered through a series of coincidences that started with the death of Miss Lillian A. Wells of Traverse City, Michigan. The College of Oswego, New York, was bequeathed her real estate property in New Haven, New York, not far from Oswego. The house had been the family home of C. Sidney Shepard, a cousin of Miss Wells, who died in 1934 and left her the property. The Shepards were related to the Marshall family who had stored some of their belongings in the Shepard home. When the College representatives examined the contents of the house, they found a collection of papers covering Fillmore's life from young manhood to his death, except for the period of his presidency from 1849 to 1853. The collection at Oswego also contains one official item of the presidential period, the "Register of Letters Received, President of the United States."[31]

The Microfilm Edition of the Fillmore Papers

The microfilm edition of 68 reels of the Fillmore papers, which was completed in 1975, was funded by a grant from the National Archives Historical Publications Committee to the Buffalo Historical Society. Copies of the papers at Oswego were interfiled with the papers in the Historical Society collection and Fillmore documents copied from the collections of over 100 institutional repositories, private collectors, the House and Senate records in the National Archives, and more than 20 manuscript collections in the Library of Congress. This effort was in effect the reconstruction of a presidential archive because of the dispersion of the originals. The papers in the microfilm collection cover Fillmore's pre-presidential, presidential, and post-presidential periods.

Series	*Reels*
1. General Correspondence and Related Materials: Family, Political, Professional. 1809–74.	1–54
2. Index to Letters Received, Vice President and President of the United States. 1849–53.	55
3. Register of Letters Received, President of the United States. 1850–53.	56
4. Register of Nominations	56
5. Documents in the National Archives	
Subseries A: House of Representatives.	
23rd Congress, 1833–35	57
25th Congress, 1837–39	57
26th Congress, 1839–41	57–58
27th Congress, 1841–43	59–61
Subseries B: U.S. Senate.	
31st Congress, 1849–51	62–63
32nd Congress, 1851–53	64–65
6-17. Presscopy Book, Copies of Business and Personal Correspondence, Letterbooks, Real Estate, Memoranda, Financial Statements, Catalog of Millard Fillmore's Library, Index to Presidential Messages, Miscellany.	66
18. Scrapbooks.	67
19. Miscellaneous.	68

JAMES BUCHANAN
Fifteenth President—Democrat
1857–1861

James Buchanan, the eldest of 11 children of an Irish immigrant store owner and farmer, was born in a log cabin near Mercersburg, Pennsylvania, on April 23, 1791. In 1796, when the family's fortunes improved, they moved into town where Buchanan attended a local elementary school and an academy. He entered Dickinson College in Carlisle, Pennsylvania, and graduated in 1809. Buchanan read law at Lancas-

ter, Pennsylvania, was admitted to the bar in 1812, and started a successful legal career. During the War of 1812, he volunteered his services and
participated in the defense of Baltimore.

From 1814 to 1816, Buchanan served a term in the lower house of
Pennsylvania as a Federalist; he returned to his law practice between
1816 and 1821. In 1818, he became engaged to Ann Coleman, the
daughter of a wealthy family. She broke the engagement and shortly
thereafter committed suicide. Buchanan wrote: "I feel that happiness has
fled from me forever."[32] Buchanan never married. His niece, Harriet Lane
Johnston, was brought up by him, lived with him for many years, and
acted as his hostess in the White House. In 1821, Buchanan was elected
to the U.S. House of Representatives, where he served for 10 years. He
became a strong supporter of Andrew Jackson and switched to the
Democrats in 1828. In 1832, Jackson appointed Buchanan minister to
Russia, where he negotiated the first trade treaty between the two countries. He returned to the U.S. in 1834 and was elected to the Senate,
where he remained for 11 years, serving under Presidents Jackson, Van
Buren, Harrison, and Tyler. He became chairman of the Foreign Relations Committee, and declined appointments as attorney general and
Supreme Court justice.

In 1844, Buchanan ran unsuccessfully for the Democratic presidential
nomination. He supported nominee James Polk in the presidential campaign and was rewarded with the appointment of secretary of state,
serving from 1845 to 1847. In 1848 and 1852, he again ran for the
presidency but was defeated both times. Under President Pierce, Buchanan served as minister to Great Britain. By 1856, Buchanan had given
up hope of becoming president; he admitted to a friend "my aspirations
for the presidency all died four years ago,"[33] but a coalition of southern
senators persuaded him to run again. He won the election against John C.
Fremont, the Republican candidate, and Know-Nothing and Whig candidate Millard Fillmore, because he was considered a supporter of slave
state interests, who was also acceptable to the North. Buchanan aimed to
be even handed and selected a cabinet representing both sides of the
growing controversy. However, he favored the Dred Scott decision of the
Supreme Court, and antagonized the North by sponsoring the admission
of Kansas to the Union, with or without slavery; this inflamed Congress
and, by 1858, produced a political paralysis. Tension was further increased by John Brown's raid on the federal ordinance depot at Harpers
Ferry, which convinced many southerners that secession was their only
means of protecting themselves from northern abolitionists.

During the last months of his presidency, Buchanan worked unsuccessfully to reach compromises with the secessionists. He warned of an
"impending open war by the North to abolish slavery in the South" and
called without success for amendments to the Constitution to compromise
the issues. He wanted to postpone fighting until he was out of office, so
that the onus of civil war would fall on the Republicans.[34] While Buchanan made progress in foreign relations during his presidency, this was
overshadowed by the nation's drift toward civil war. At the end of his
term, he turned the government over to Abraham Lincoln with the words:
"If you are as happy in entering the White House as I shall feel on

returning to Wheatland, you are a happy man indeed."[35] Buchanan died at Wheatland, his home near Lancaster, in 1868.

THE BUCHANAN PAPERS IN THE HISTORICAL SOCIETY OF PENNSYLVANIA

Buchanan was an unimaginative but methodical man who filed his papers with regularity and care, and kept meticulous accounts. He was concerned with his legacy and said a day before his death: "History will vindicate my memory."[36] One could assume that, as a successful lawyer, he would have prepared a clear, well thought-out will to dispose of his property and assets, including his papers. Actually, his will contained provisions that left ownership of his papers in doubt and resulted in pilfering, disorganization, partial destruction, exposure to fire, and several lawsuits for custody of the papers, from the time of his death until the deposit of the remaining papers in the Pennsylvania Historical Society, nearly 30 years later.

The will was written in Buchanan's own hand in 1866; three codicils were added in 1867, which created considerable problems for the disposal of the estate. His executors were his brother, the Reverend Edward Y. Buchanan, and his friend, Hiram B. Swarr. They were pitted against Buchanan's favorite niece, Harriet, who had married Henry E. Johnston, a Baltimore banker, shortly before the will was drawn. The executors were directed to hold the principal of Harriet's share of the estate in trust for her as long as her husband lived; Buchanan also willed that the real estate and household furnishings be sold, which shocked Harriet who considered Wheatland her home. In the codicil of a later date, Buchanan bequeathed Wheatland to Harriet but ordered his executors to charge $12,000 for it, to be deducted from her share of his estate. Harriet blamed her uncle Edward Buchanan for these confusing provisions.

The president's papers are referred to in the second codicil as follows:

> I hereby direct my Executors to place all the papers, correspondence and private and public documents connected with my public life in the hands of my friend, William B. Reed, having shown to me in my retirement great kindness and in whom I have entire confidence to enable him to prepare such a biographical work [as] I desire. With this view I direct my Executors to pay to the order of William B. Reed such sums not to exceed one thousand dollars, as may be necessary in his opinion to secure the proper publication of such biographical work . . . . As some compensation for the work which Mr. Reed has undertaken to perform, I give and bequeath to his wife the sum of five thousand dollars . . . said amount to be paid to her on the completion of the work.[37]

The will did not mention the ownership or the final disposition and care of the papers. In the two months after Buchanan's death, Edward and his daughter, Annie, "went through the papers at Wheatland, mixed them up somewhat, removed some, apparently destroyed some, and seemed to be planning to take them all from the house."[38] Harriet, who belatedly learned about these plans, was determined to keep the papers intact for their political and monetary value as well as for the President's vindication, while Edward attempted to maintain exclusive control over the papers. As a result of these disagreements, several lawsuits developed. Harriet took her own correspondence with the President to her home. Other papers were put at the disposal of hired biographers, first Reed and then Judge John Cadwalader, neither of whom completed the task. Finally, George Ticknor Curtis became the temporary custodian of the papers and completed his two-volume biography in 1883.[39] Buchanan's diplomatic correspondence was compiled by John Bassett Moore in a two-volume publication.[40]

In 1884, Harriet sold Wheatland and the papers were stored in a New York warehouse where a fire destroyed part of the collection. In 1895, Edward Buchanan died. Annie, his daughter, agreed with her cousin, Harriet, that the papers should be deposited in a suitable facility. Between 1895 and 1897, the Buchanan papers were taken from the New York warehouse and deposited in the Historical Society of Pennsylvania. Hiram Swarr, the other executor of the President's will, had kept some papers that had not been given to the biographers. After his death, this collection of about 1,000 documents was given to the Buchanan Foundation and is deposited in the Lancaster County Historical Society.

Dickinson College, where Buchanan was a student, owns several hundred letters of the President. Smaller collections are located in the Franklin and Marshall College Library, the Princeton University Library, the Pierpont Morgan and Rutherford B. Hayes Libraries, the New York Historical Society, and the Pennsylvania Historical and Museum Commission. About 90 percent of the extant Buchanan papers are available in the Historical Society of Pennsylvania, either in the original or as copies, and are included in its microfilm edition, produced in 1974.

The Microfilm Edition of the Buchanan Papers in the Historical Society of Pennsylvania

Series	Reels
I. Incoming Correspondence. 1815–67.	1–45
II. Outgoing Correspondence, Speeches, Notes, Memoranda, etc. 1811–55.	46–53
III. Third Party Correspondence, 1856 Democratic National Convention, and Miscellaneous. 1787–1893.	54–56
IV. Drafts and Manuscripts of Books of Buchanan and his Biographers.	57
V. Manuscripts and Printed Materials.	58
VI. Business Papers. 1831–67.	59
VII. Legal Papers and Indexes.	60

The Buchanan and Harriet Lane Johnston Papers in the Library of Congress

The Library of Congress Manuscript Division holds approximately 1,200 items relating to Buchanan, which are divided into three series. Series 1, the James Buchanan Papers, covers the years 1825 to 1868; most of them relate to the period prior to the election of 1856. They consist chiefly of correspondence, but include notes, drafts of remarks made in the House of Representatives, Department of State commissions and transmittals to foreign service officers, land patents, petitions, a presidential message to Congress, and clippings. Topics discussed include Democratic politics in Pennsylvania and the nation, negotiations with Mexico, the Delaware Canal, the Oregon question, the blockade of Mexico, Democratic presidential possibilities, the 1852 Democratic convention, and the anti-Buchanan attacks in the *New York Herald*.[41]

Series 2 comprises the correspondence between Harriet Lane Johnston and the President. This collection was discovered among Harriet's possessions some years after her death in 1909, by her cousin, May S. Kennedy, who gave it to the Library of Congress in 1918. The Harriet Lane Johnston papers cover the years 1846 to 1878; most of the letters were written between 1855 and 1866. Harriet's correspondence deals with ladies fashions, social affairs, romantic ventures, some letters to her husband, Henry Elliott Johnston, and letters concerning the selection of a biographer for President Buchanan and financial support for this work.

Series 3 consists of a special documents file, 1826–61, of selected Buchanan materials, the originals of which are in other repositories, and of typed transcripts. Series 1 and 2 are available in microfilm. Between 1962 and 1972, the National Historical Publications Commission conducted a search for letters of, from, and about Buchanan, which were added to the Library of Congress collection; copies were given to the Historical Society of Pennsylvania.

The Microfilm Edition of the Buchanan and Harriet Lane Johnston Papers in the Library of Congress

Series	*Reels*
1. James Buchanan Papers. 1825–68 and undated.	1–2
2. Harriet Lane Johnston (his niece). 1846–47 and undated.	3–4
3. Special Documents File 1826–61 and undated.	Not filmed
1,200 items	1.6 linear ft.

WARREN G. HARDING
Twenty-ninth President—Republican
1921–1923

Warren Gamaliel Harding was born in 1865 on a farm in Blooming Grove Township in north central Ohio. His father, a teacher, farmer, and practitioner of homeopathic medicine, moved his family in 1870 to Caledonia, Ohio. In 1882, Harding graduated from Ohio Central College and joined his parents who had moved to Marion, Ohio. He taught school for a short time and then became a reporter at the *Democratic Mirror*, a weekly local paper. By 1884, he was co-owner and publisher of the Marion *Star* and soon branched out into other businesses. In 1891, he married Florence Kling DeWolfe, the daughter of one of the richest men in Marion and five years older than Harding. She was a divorcee and the real driving power in the success of the *Star* and her husband's career. He joined the Republican party, served in the Ohio State Senate from 1900 to 1904, and was lieutenant governor of Ohio from 1904 to 1906. In 1909, he won the Republican nomination for governor, but was defeated in the election. Harding's manager in that campaign was Harry M. Daugherty, a small town lawyer.

At the Republican convention of 1912, Harding was chosen to give the nominating speech for President Taft, who was defeated in the election. In 1914, Harry Daugherty and Mrs. Harding urged him to run for the U.S. Senate and, with some reluctance, he agreed and won the election. He served in the Senate from 1915 to 1921; his record in Congress was undistinguished, but he was politically astute, took care not to make enemies in either party, and voted for prohibition and for women's suffrage, though he was personally opposed to both issues. Under the management of Harry Daugherty, he was elected chairman of the Republican convention of 1916 where he gave the keynote address. While he loyally supported President Wilson's efforts to win the war, he opposed America's participation in the League of Nations after the war and supported a "return to normalcy."

In 1920, the Republican convention reached an impasse in the nominating process. The inner circle of politicians who considered Harding as a compromise candidate asked him "whether there is anything that might be brought against you that would embarrass the party, any impediment that may disqualify you or make you inexpedient, either as a candidate or as a president." There were rumors that he had been carrying on several affairs, one of them with Carrie Phillips, the wife of a Marion department store owner, the other with Nan Britton, a young woman who later claimed that her daughter was Harding's child. Harding is reported to have answered: "nothing; no obstacles."[42] He was nominated and won the election with over 60 percent of the popular vote.

Harding's cabinet included such distinguished members as Herbert Hoover, Andrew Mellon, and Charles Evans Hughes. Harry Daugherty, who had masterminded Harding's political career, became attorney general, and Albert B. Fall, a colleague from the Senate and the friend of Western oilmen who had contributed heavily to the campaign, became secretary of the interior. During Harding's two and one half years in office he ended wartime economic controls, cut taxes, and brought the Bureau of the Budget and the Veterans Bureau into existence. In 1921, in spite of his opposition to the League of Nations, he convened a disarmament conference that outlawed the use of poison gas and guaranteed China's independence. Late in 1922, Harding became aware of corruption and scandals in his administration. He set out on a speaking trip across the country in June 1923, a deeply worried man. He died of a heart attack in San Francisco on August 2, 1923, before the Teapot Dome and other scandals, which involved Albert Fall, Daugherty, and others of his political cronies, came to light.[43]

THE HARDING PAPERS IN THE OHIO HISTORICAL SOCIETY

From the beginning of his career, Harding gave a great deal of thought to the collection and organization of his papers. When he left Marion in 1915 for Washington, he kept the files of his personal and business papers in the offices of the *Star*. He authorized George B. Christian, Jr., the son of a close personal friend, to work on the preservation of his Senate papers and later on his 1920 campaign correspondence. After Harding was elected to the presidency, Christian was appointed secretary to the President and the papers were moved from Marion to his home in Washington. Christian was put in charge of the executive and the private office of the President; this gave him control over all incoming mail, which was filed either in the official file or the private file. Christian followed the case filing system that was in operation in the White House from the Taft to the Eisenhower administrations.[44]

After Harding's death, his papers had to be moved quickly from the White House to make space for Calvin Coolidge, the incoming president. Mrs. Harding asked Christian to pack all the files from the executive office and ship them to Marion. Christian packed approximately 100 cubic feet of official file materials, keeping them in exact file order, but instead of sending them to Ohio, he stored them in the White House basement. Mrs. Harding moved the papers in the President's private file to the Washington estate of Edward and Evalyn Walsh McLean. With the help of her secretary, Laura Harlan, and Major Ora M. Baldinger, Harding's military aide, she carefully went through the files for the next few weeks, burning some of the papers. She moved to Marion in September 1923 and had the papers sent to the offices of the *Star*, where she continued to go through and destroy many of them until October, when she became too ill to continue with this project. Her aim was to remove any materials from the files that might have proven detrimental to her husband's memory. These may have included items relating to the political and personal scandals that surfaced after the President's death. How much and what was removed will never be known. According to Major Baldinger, the destruction may have resulted in the removal of "as much or more than half of the materials available to her."[45]

In January 1924, Mrs. Harding recuperated sufficiently to return to Washington for a visit. When Charles Moore of the Manuscript Division of the Library of Congress inquired about the Harding papers, she told him that she had burned all of them. Publisher Charles N. Doubleday also called on Mrs. Harding to ask about the papers and was told that they had been destroyed because she "was afraid some of it would be misconstrued and would harm his memory."[46] Mrs. Harding died in November 1924, and left her husband's papers to the Harding Memorial Association, which had been founded shortly before her death by close associates and friends. Alfred Donithen, a longtime friend of the President and the secretary of the Association, let it be known after the widow's death that some of the Harding papers had not been burned. He reopened negotiations with Doubleday to prepare a selection from the private and personal files, to be edited by Judson C. Welliver, a former secretary of the President. Some months later, Doubleday, Page & Company sent one of their editors to Marion; the editors made approximately 5,000 typed copies of various papers. George Christian, the guardian of the papers, who had not been consulted about the publishing project, enlisted the support of Harry Daugherty, Harding's attorney general, in whose department congressional investigations had uncovered evidence of fraud, in opposing the publication plans. In the fall of 1925, the Association held a meeting and concurred with Christian and Daugherty to keep the papers closed to the public until 1975.

In 1925, Charles Moore visited Marion several times to persuade Association officials to give the papers to the Library of Congress. He was not successful and tried to enlist public support to force the Association to act. On Christmas morning 1925, the *New York Times* carried an article under the title "Harding Papers Burned by Widow," claiming that the Association refused to turn over copies of letters that had been burned or letters that had escaped destruction. In August 1925, Daugherty further reduced the remaining Harding papers when he burned a group of records of the Midland National Bank, the Daugherty family institution in Washington Court House, Ohio. Daugherty, who was under grand jury investigation, claimed that his motives were "loyalty to the memory of the president," and not a desire to protect himself. This gave credance to the gossip of the day that Harding had kept secret accounts in the Midland National Bank to cover his stock market speculations and the financing of his love affairs.[47]

During 1924, while searching for papers of President Taft in the White House, Charles Moore found not only the papers he was looking for, but also extensive collections of papers of Presidents Wilson and Harding. The Harding papers were turned over to George Christian. In July 1929, workmen found the official Harding papers that Christian had stored in the White House basement contrary to Mrs. Harding's wishes in 39 letter file cases. They were turned over to the Library of Congress. J. Franklin Jameson, Chief of the Manuscript Division, hoped to be able to keep them, but when he informed the Association of the discovery, the trustees insisted that the papers be shipped to Marion where they were stored in the law office of Hoke Donithen, secretary of the Association. After the scandals associated with the Harding administration, the Association had lost much of its national membership. The culmination of its activities came in 1931 when the Harding Memorial, an elaborate structure in quasi-Greek style, where President and Mrs. Harding are buried, was dedicated by Herbert Hoover.

In 1932, Jameson, as stubborn a collector of presidential papers for the Library as anyone, paid a visit to Marion. He was shocked to see that the official Harding papers were kept on wooden shelving in a building that was not fireproof, and that additional papers, the ones that had survived the burnings, were stored in Mrs. Harding's bank in Marion. He attempted to convince individual members of the Association to deposit the papers in the Library of Congress. Donithen agreed in principle, but thought that it would be difficult to bring about formal action by the trustees to accomplish this transfer.

In 1934, Jameson almost succeeded. He reached an agreement with the Association that the papers would be placed in the Library as a "revokable deposit" and that scholars could see them only with permission of the Association's executive committee until 1943, 20 years after Harding's death. Before the plan could be implemented, Donithen died, and the papers remained in Marion. In the fall of 1934, George Christian decided to turn over Harding's senatorial correspondence and the papers from the 1920 campaign in his possession to the Library of Congress. These papers, which were stored in seven large and three small wooden boxes and 18 letter file cases, remained with Jameson until May 1935 when, much to his disappointment, they had to be turned over to the Association on the trustees' insistence.

Christian died in 1951 and donated the last of the Harding papers in his possession directly to the Association. In 1958, nine Harding letters were found in the Calvin Coolidge collection in the Library of Congress and were turned over to the Association. In 1961, Daniel Reed, who worked at that time in the Manuscript Division of the Library, again tried to bring the Harding papers to Washington, and spent a day with Dr. Carl Sawyer, the son of Harding's surgeon general, who at that time was the president of the Harding Memorial Association. Dr. Sawyer was working on arranging the Harding papers and hinted that the Association might soon turn them over to the Library. Around that time, the Ohio Historical Society began to collect papers of Harding's contemporaries and actively sought to acquire the Harding papers. After long discussions, in October 1963, the papers were officially donated to the Ohio Historical Society, but the the wording of the gift agreement was ambiguous; while the Society assumed that it had acquired title to the entire collection, the Association released only the presidential letters. The senatorial papers and Harding's political, personal, and business files for the period from 1895 to 1914 were held back and taken to the Sawyer Sanatorium where they were further analyzed by the Association before being shipped to Columbus in small batches.[48]

In late October 1963, Francis Russell, who was working on his Harding biography, *The Shadow of Blooming Grove: Warren G. Harding in His Times,*[49] came to Marion to do some research. He interviewed Don Williamson, a lawyer who had been the guardian of Carrie Phillips, Harding's close friend between 1909 and 1920, who had died destitute in a nursing home in 1960. Williamson had found a box full of letters from Harding to Phillips among her possessions and told Russell that he "felt—rightly or wrongly—if I turned them over to the Harding Memorial Association they'd go up in smoke . . . I didn't know what else to do, so I just kept them in a safe place."[50] Russell examined the box containing about 100 letters, made some notes, and told Williamson that the papers should be turned over to the Ohio Historical Society. Both men notified Kenneth Duckett, the Society's curator, who accepted the letters. Russell had assumed that he would be able to work with them because he had found them, but Duckett told him that he could not allow him to use them before they were opened to the general public. Duckett was afraid that if the Association "should get wind of what was in the letters and that he had them, they might hold up the parts of the main Harding papers they hadn't sent yet."[51] Duckett microfilmed the letters to insure their safety, but did not disclose their existence until after the official opening of the Harding papers in the Ohio Historical Society in April 1964.

When the board of trustees of the Society was told that a large collection of intimate letters from Harding to another man's wife were in the possession of the Society, several of the trustees wanted to destroy the letters at once. When lawyers pointed out that the Society had a legal duty to preserve historical materials in its custody, and that an outsider had already read them and taken some notes, Fred J. Milligan, the president of the Society, ordered the letters to be impounded in the vault of the Ohio National Bank. Later, a judge decided that Williamson had no legal rights to the letters and therefore could not give them to the Society; they were turned over to the Phillips heirs. The microfilm of the papers was sent to *American Heritage* in New York where it was kept unopened in a bank vault. Harding's heirs subsequently sued Russell, Duckett, *American Heritage,* and the McGraw-Hill Company, which had agreed to publish Russell's book, to prevent them from making any use of the papers.[52] The editors of *American Heritage*, in publishing Kenneth Duckett's and Francis Russell's accounts about the discovery of the papers stated: " . . . these letters must be preserved. As part of the record of the Presidency they ought to be placed in a reputable library and, in good time, be available to serious scholars of American history."[53] The suit was settled out of court and the letters were turned over to the Harding heirs who deposited a collection of 185 items covering the period from 1908 to 1923 in the Library of Congress. This collection will remain closed until 2014.

Harding's correspondence with Carrie Phillips is historically important because he expressed in his letters far more than his amorous emotions; he poured out his observations about political contacts, his experiences and ambitions, thoughts and hopes, which were a commentary on his life and a substitute for the diary he never wrote. As Francis Russell noted:

> If I had not managed to uncover the Phillips letters, I am convinced that others less interested in history than in local decorum would soon have gotten them and that the letters would have disappeared forever . . . . Now, after all the varied legal twistings and turnings, they will, I hope, eventually be made available to scholars . . . . One cannot properly understand Harding in his time without consulting the Phillips letters. These hundred or so letters are more significant

for Warren G. Harding the man than the hundreds of boxes of documents now in the official Harding Collection at Columbus.[54]

In 1968, 45 years after Harding's death, the Ohio Historical Society received a grant from the National Historical Publications Commission to prepare a microfilm edition of the Harding papers and seven related collections of correspondence. Since 1970, this collection has been available to the public. The Ohio Historical Society also operates the Harding historic site in Marion, consisting of the Harding home and the Harding Memorial.

The Harding Microfilm Collection

Series	Rolls
I. Marion Papers, 1888–1920.	1–19
a) Business Matters	
b) Personal and Political Correspondence	
c) Shorthand Notebooks	
II. Senatorial Papers, 1915–21	20–27
a) Personal and Political	
b) Constituent Correspondence	
c) Shorthand Notebooks	
III. Presidential Election Papers, 1918–21.	28–129
a) Preconvention and Convention	
b) Campaign	
c) Pre-Inaugural	
IV. Presidential Papers, 1921–23.	130–237
a) Executive Office Correspondence	
b) Private Office Correspondence	
c) Miscellaneous File (Household Bills, Invitations, Resolutions)	
V. Speeches, 1899–1923	238–240
VI. Harding Papers Acquired Independently of the Harding Memorial Association	241
VII. Genealogical Data (undated)	241
Written by Wilbur Judd, a cousin of the President; incomplete, never published	
VIII. Florence Kling Harding Papers, 1916–26	242–247
Nonpolitical, social correspondence	
IX. Charles E. and Carl W. Sawyer Papers, 1916–42	248
Relationship of the Surgeon General to President and Mrs. Harding and his role in the Administration	
X. Harding Memorial Association Papers, 1923–65	248
XI. George B. Christian, Sr. Papers, 1918–24	249
XII. George B. Christian, Jr. Papers, 1928–33	249–250
XIII. Papers of Kathleen Lawler, Cyril Clements, Hoke Donithen, and others	251–263

10. Special Libraries

RUTHERFORD B. HAYES
Nineteenth President—Republican
1877–1881

Rutherford Birchard Hayes was born in Delaware, Ohio, on October 4, 1822, three months after the death of his father, a successful merchant who left his family well provided for. His uncle, Sardis Birchard, became his guardian and saw to it that he had a good education. Hayes graduated from Kenyon College in 1842 and studied law at Harvard University. He was a serious young man who kept an extensive and perceptive diary for many years and, besides law, read a great deal of philosophy, history, and the classics of literature. In 1845, he began to practice law, first in Fremont and then in Cincinnati, Ohio. In 1852, he married Lucy Ware Webb with whom he raised a large family. He was city solicitor of Cincinnati from 1858 to 1861.

During the Civil War, Hayes assisted in organizing the 23rd Ohio Volunteers and was commissioned a major. He distinguished himself on the battlefield and his admirers at home nominated him for Congress in 1864. When they urged him to campaign, he answered: "Thanks. I have other business just now. Any man who would leave the army at this time to electioneer for Congress ought to be scalped."[1] He resigned from the service as Brevet Major General to take his seat in the United States House of Representatives in December 1865. During his short service in Congress, his most important contribution was the chairmanship of the Joint Committee on the Library, which was instrumental in enlarging the Library of Congress's holdings of Americana through the purchase of the Peter Force collection. (See Chapter 1).

In 1868, Hayes became governor of Ohio and served two terms. He again ran for Congress in 1872, but lost the election and thought that his public career had come to an end. He moved to Spiegel Grove near Fremont, Ohio, the estate of his uncle, which he inherited a year later. However, in 1876, he was elected governor and nominated for the presidency at the Republican convention. Samuel J. Tilden, the Democratic candidate, won the popular vote at the election, but the Republicans challenged the election results in four states, claiming that all the electoral votes of these states would give Hayes a victory margin of one vote. Two days before the inauguration, a congressional commission decided by a partisan vote of eight to seven in favor of Hayes. The Republicans smoothed out the conflict by promising the Democrats federal patronage, a cabinet post, and the withdrawal of federal troops from the South; Hayes also let it be known that he would serve only one term.

During the first two years of his administration, the Democrats controlled the House of Representatives, and during the last two years the Senate as well, preventing Hayes from passing any meaningful legislation. An economic depression, which had started under the Grant administration, worsened; railway workers went on strike and federal troops had to restore order in four states. Indian fighting broke out in the West. Hayes tried to establish new standards of official integrity after eight years of corruption in Washington and substituted nonpartisan civil service examinations for political patronage. Among the many office holders he fired was Chester Arthur, at that time the collector of the Port of New York. After Hayes left the White House, he spent 12 years in retirement at Spiegel Grove, during which he devoted himself to humanitarian causes, especially educational opportunities for southern blacks. He worked on his papers and his library, and accepted many speaking engagements. He died in January 1893 at Spiegel Grove.

THE RUTHERFORD B. HAYES PRESIDENTIAL CENTER

Hayes was a lifelong collector of historical documents and books, a great friend and supporter of libraries, and truly interested in the organization and preservation of his own library, papers, and memorabilia. When governor of Ohio, he saw to it that the Ohio State Library obtained significant documents of the state's history.[2] As a personal friend of Ainsworth Rand Spofford, the librarian of Congress, he was most supportive of the Library's programs and mentioned in his first annual message to Congress the need for a fireproof building to house its collections. Hayes biographer, Harry Barnard, writes: "From the time he was a boy he saved almost all letters written to him, and his sons collected many that he wrote, especially to his mother, his sister and his uncle. He also kept a diary from youth, and it was from it and his letters, as well as letters of his family, that I was able to reconstruct his personal life."[3]

When Hayes moved to Spiegel Grove in 1873, he immediately added a room to the house to accommodate his personal library and the library of his uncle, Sardis Birchard. He wrote in 1874: "I am given to antiquarian and genealogical pursuits. An old family letter is a delight to my eyes. I can prowl in the old trunks of letters by the day with undiminished zest."[4] After he retired from the presidency, he made extensive alterations and additions to the house, converting it into an elegant Victorian mansion; the library was enlarged to include about 6,000 volumes of an Americana collection he had bought from Robert Clarke, a bookseller in Cincinnati. Hayes wrote in his diary on May 3, 1881: "My library is approaching completion. I must begin to catalogue my books."[5] He worked on the organization of his own official and private papers and memorabilia and noted in his diary on March 30, 1892 "that a history of my administration, containing good portraits and sketches of Lucy and myself, may be written and I place the materials where they will be found together."[6] At the time of his death, the library contained over 10,000 volumes.

The President's son, Col. Webb C. Hayes, who inherited the 25-acre Spiegel Grove estate, offered it to the State of Ohio as a public park in memory of his parents. In the announcement to donate Spiegel Grove, the Ohio State Archaeological and Historical Society commented: ". . . this offer of the family is unusual 'for its liberality and most worthy of commendation for the filial desire it expresses to perpetuate the memorial to loved and honored parents."[7] The property was deeded to the state in 1910 with the following provisions:

> . . . the Ohio State Archaeological and Historical Society should se-
> cure the erection upon that part of Spiegel Grove heretofore conveyed
> to the State of Ohio for a State Park, a suitable fireproof building, on
> the site reserved opposite the Jefferson Street entrance, for the pur-
> pose of preserving and forever keeping in Spiegel Grove all papers,
> books and manuscripts left by the said Rutherford B. Hayes. . . which
> building shall be in the form of a Branch Reference Library and
> Museum of the Ohio State Archaeological and Historical Society, and
> the construction and decoration of the said building shall be in the
> nature of a memorial also to the soldiers, sailors, and pioneers of
> Sandusky County; and suitable memorial tablets, busts and decora-
> tions indicative of the historical events and patriotic citizenship of
> Sandusky County shall be placed in and on said building, and said
> building shall forever remain open to the public under proper rules
> and regulations to be hereafter made by said Society.[8]

The Ohio legislature appropriated $50,000 for the Hayes Memorial, of which $40,000 was used toward the library building and $10,000 for paving the streets surrounding Spiegel Grove. Impressive entrances to the grounds, through gateways bordered with massive walls of granite boulders, were constructed by Col. Hayes. Two of these gateways "are between immense cannons inscribed, to the memory of the French and British Explorers, and the Soldiers of the War of 1812 who passed over the Harrison Trail; and to the soldiers of Sandusky County who served in the War with Mexico and the War for the Union. The bodies of President and Mrs. Hayes were transferred to a beautiful knoll in the Grove, together with the modest monument which President Hayes had erected before his death."[9] In addition, Col. Hayes provided about $100,000 in cash for the upkeep of the memorial which is considered "the prototype of the presidential library concept adopted by the federal government."[10]

Ground was broken for the Rutherford B. Hayes Library and Museum in 1912, and the building was dedicated on May 30, 1916. An annex, which doubled the library space, was paid for by Col. Hayes and dedicated in 1922, the centennial of President Hayes' birth. Further additions have been made since. The Library is administered by the Ohio Historical Society and the Rutherford B. Hayes and Lucy Webb Hayes Foundation and has its own board of governors. The Hayes family continued to occupy the mansion until 1966 when the home and the tombs were opened to the public. The Rutherford B. Hayes Presidential Center also includes the Dillon house, a neighbor's home, which has been converted into a museum annex and guest house for visiting scholars. The museum contains many memorabilia of the Hayes period. The various buildings are filled with the furniture of the family, their carriage, and many contemporary artifacts.

While Hayes' presidency made a very limited impact on the nation's history, his and his family's influence on the preservation of presidential papers is significant. Franklin D. Roosevelt never visited Spiegel Grove, but he used the Hayes Memorial Library to some extent as a model for the establishment of his own library and museum in Hyde Park. However, Roosevelt, rather than his heirs, donated the papers and property to the public, and selected the National Archives rather than the state as the supporting agency. In a letter to Webb C. Hayes II, written on October 21, 1937, Roosevelt stated: "I think it is particularly fitting that this comprehensive collection should include, besides President Hayes' own library, his correspondence and other papers associated with his public life—a veritable gold mine for historical scholars."[11]

Materials in the Hayes Memorial Library

The Hayes Memorial Library, an Ohio sandstone structure of over 54,000 square feet, contains Hayes' personal library of over 10,000 volumes. The library has evolved into a research center for the study of nineteenth-century American history; it holds over 70,000 volumes and continues to acquire American historical materials about the "Gilded Age" in the United States, defined as the period between 1865 and 1916, with emphasis on the Civil War and Reconstruction periods; the Spanish-American War; civil service, prison, and monetary reforms; and social and local history. Several special collections include the papers, books, manuscripts, and first editions of William Dean Howells, noted American author and former editor of the *Atlantic Monthly*, and many local history materials. The library also acquires copies of the government records created by the Hayes administration.[12]

The manuscript collection of over 1 million items includes 164 linear feet of Rutherford B. Hayes papers, from the period 1835 to 1893. The collection consists of 34 volumes of diaries, dating to 1834, messages and speeches, and 300 volumes of letterbooks, scrapbooks, and newsclippings. There is an in-depth card index to the Hayes papers, which have also been microfilmed. Other manuscript collections include the papers of Lucy Webb Hayes, the Hayes children, other family members, and individuals associated with the federal government during the Hayes administration. There are 750 pieces of White House correspondence of presidents who preceeded Hayes between 1860 and 1875, and other presidential letters. The library also has a collection of 75,000 photographs and publishes a quarterly newsletter *The Statesman*, the semi-annual *Hayes Historical Journal*, and sponsors occasional lectures and film showings.

The Hayes Family Papers

1. Rutherford B. Hayes Papers, 1835–93
2. Lucy Webb Hayes Papers, 1841–90
3. Richard Austin Hayes Papers, 1862–1926
4. Webb Cook Hayes Papers, 1886–1934
5. Frances Hayes Papers, 1878–1950
6. Scott Russell Hayes Papers, 1873–1929
7. William King Ropers Papers, 1830–1922

HERBERT HOOVER
Thirty-first President—Republican
1929–1933

Herbert Clark Hoover was born in 1874 in West Branch, Iowa. He lost his father at the age of six and his mother three years later. He and his two siblings were distributed among their Quaker relatives. Herbert was sent to his aunt in Newberg, Oregon, where his uncle, one of the founders of Newberg College, a Quaker secondary school, saw to it that he received a good education. He left school at 15 and worked in a real estate office in Salem, Oregon, where he attended a small business college. Through office contacts, he heard about the opportunities for engineers and decided to enter the newly founded Engineering School at Stanford where he worked his way through college with summer jobs at the Arkansas Geological Survey and the United States Survey.

Hoover graduated in 1895, but since there were no engineering jobs in sight, he went to work as a miner for a year. He finally found a position writing evaluations of mining fields for a San Francisco consulting firm. A year later, his big chance came when he was sent to Australia to prepare a report on the prospects of a gold mine; while there, he was employed as a gold mine manager by a British company. He was very successful, became part owner of a mine, and, in 1899, accepted the position of chief engineer of China's Bureau of Mines. However, he first returned to the United States to marry his college sweetheart, Lou Henry. In 1900, during the Boxer Rebellion in Tientsin, China, he helped defend the foreign quarters by taking charge of the construction of barricades and organizing the food and water supply. In 1901, he went to London as partner of a British engineering firm with worldwide responsibilities; he remained with this firm for seven years before founding his own firm and becoming a millionaire. During his spare time he wrote a textbook on mining, *Principles of Mining,*[13] and translated a Latin classic on mining.

At the outbreak of World War I, Hoover changed his career to public service activities, for which he accepted no compensation; he did outstanding work as chairman of a relief commission in Belgium. In 1917, Woodrow Wilson appointed him U.S. food administrator and in 1918 chairman of the Allied Food Council, which provided millions of tons of food to starving Europe. Warren Harding offered him the position of secretary of the interior, but Hoover preferred to head the Department of

Commerce, a position he also held during the Coolidge administration. As secretary of commerce, he eliminated child labor, improved child health, reduced the working day in the United States from 12 to 8 hours, and developed dams, flood control facilities, and various hydroelectric projects.

At the 1928 Republican convention, Hoover was nominated for president on the first ballot, even though Coolidge refused to endorse him. During the campaign against Democrat Alfred Smith, Hoover promised to continue prosperity and to enforce prohibition. Because Smith was a Catholic, Hoover's sweeping victory is generally explained by the strong anti-Catholic feelings among southern Democrats. He won the election by 444 to 87 electoral votes. Hoover's plans for a reform movement collapsed with the October 1929 stock market crash and the Great Depression that followed. His programs for public works and reduction of income taxes did not stem the sweeping tide of unemployment. His opposition to direct federal relief to the unemployed undermined his position; the Bonus Act, which provided help for veterans, was passed over his veto. In the 1930 elections, the Republicans lost their majority in the House and had their Senate majority reduced to one. Hoover was criticized in 1932 for his dispersal of the "Bonus Army" of unemployed veterans who marched on Washington demanding additional compensation for their wartime service. In 1932, Franklin D. Roosevelt won a landslide victory over Hoover, 472 to 59 electoral votes. Hoover was one of the most energetic and activist presidents, but his "continued commitment to the concept of voluntarism, his fiscal conservatism, and his limited view of the role of government doomed his policies to failure; he left office a frustrated and thoroughly discredited man."[14]

In his retirement, Hoover moved to Palo Alto, California, where he continued his writing and speaking career, and worked on the organization of his library at Stanford University. He wrote his memoirs[15] and published *The Ordeal of Woodrow Wilson.*[16] From 1946 to 1949, he assisted the Truman administration as chairman of the Famine Emergency Commission to prevent starvation in Europe, and as chairman of the Commission on Organization of the Executive Branch of the federal government, known as the Hoover Commission. President Eisenhower appointed him to head a commission on reorganization of the federal government between 1953 and 1955, which subordinated the National Archives to the General Services Administration.

Hoover's presidency may have been the least successful of his many outstanding careers, which included mining engineer, independent businessman, speaker and author, exceptional public servant, and world famous humanitarian. It remains puzzling that he seemed to have a deeper compassion for the starving millions of Europe than for the economically distressed of his own country. He died in 1964 at age 90, and was buried near his birthplace in West Branch, Iowa, where his presidential library is located.

THE HOOVER INSTITUTION AND LIBRARY ON WAR, REVOLUTION AND PEACE

The papers of Herbert Hoover are the only presidential records to be deposited in two libraries established by a president himself: the Hoover Institution Library on War, Revolution and Peace on the campus of Stanford University in California, and the Herbert Hoover Presidential Library in West Branch, Iowa.

During one of his frequent Atlantic crossings when chairman of the Commission for Relief in Belgium, Hoover was reading a book by Andrew D. White that discussed the problems of collecting contemporary documents years after the events to which they referred had taken place. Such items disappeared quickly and were dispersed beyond retrieval.[17] Hoover realized that his position gave him virtually unlimited access to many of the belligerents and that he had the unique opportunity to collect records concerning the war in areas that had been invaded by German armies. In 1917, when Hoover became administrator of the United States Food Administration, his scope of activities expanded and he decided to enlarge his collection of materials beyond areas under the control of the Allied governments. Between 1918 and 1919, Hoover served also as alternating chairman of the Interallied Food Council, which directed his interests toward the amelioration of hunger and disease. As Hoover collected more and more papers, he realized that he would need help to cover a larger area than he could reach himself. He consulted with Ray Lyman Wilbur, the president of Stanford University, who put him in touch with Ephraim D. Adams, a professor in the history department. Financed by Hoover, Adams organized a volunteer group of young scholars in Europe who joined Hoover's collecting efforts after their release from military service. Due to the connections of Hoover with government agencies in central, eastern, and western Europe and in Russia, the Hoover Collection expanded rapidly with the support of friendly governments.

In 1919, Hoover started to deposit materials in a special collection at Stanford University, named the Hoover War Collection, which grew into a special library, the Hoover War Library. The scope of this Hoover War Library's collection expanded from Europe and the United States to all continents and its concerns grew from war activities to mandates, plebiscites, the League of Nations, the formation of new governments, and the changes from democracy to fascism. The library developed into the Hoover Institution and Library on War, Revolution and Peace, which at first shared its space with the main library of Stanford University. After the end of the Hoover presidency, his presidential and other federal records were added to the library's holdings. A separate building, the Hoover Tower, was built to accommodate the volume of materials and was dedicated in 1941. After World War II, the Far East region attracted increased American research interests; to house this rapidly expanding collection, the Lou Henry Hoover building, memorializing the President's wife, was added in 1967. The third building, the Herbert Hoover Federal Memorial, partly funded by Stanford University and partly by Congress, was dedicated in July 1978.

When Hoover decided to establish a presidential library in accordance with the provisions of the Presidential Libraries Act of 1955, he offered all his public service career papers and related documents to the government. These papers were withdrawn from Stanford in 1962 and transferred to the Hoover Presidential Library in Iowa. The papers he and his assistants had collected about the impact of war, revolution, and peace and some related documents remained at the Hoover Institution and are stored in its archives. The Institution had by then been expanded into one of the country's major national centers for documentation and research about problems of political, economic, and social change in the twentieth century.

The Hoover Institution grew far beyond Hoover's original aims. As its prospectus indicates, it is an independent institution within the frame of Stanford University. While the University moved from a conservative Republican to a more moderate middle-of-the-road political position, the Hoover Institution's conservative stance and independence have been emphasized and maintained since 1960 by W. Glenn Campbell, who was appointed director upon Hoover's recommendation. The Institution's research programs have received increased national attention as a conservative think tank. The director reports to the president of Stanford University and through him to its board. A 65-member board of overseers from across the nation makes recommendations regarding overall policy and helps maintain interest in the Institution. The Institution is funded from three sources: an annual university contribution; income from endowments; and voluntary contributions. It has a research staff consisting of economists, historians, political scientists, and sociologists. During the last 65 years well over 300 books have been published under its auspices, dealing with bibliographic, policy, and basic research studies. Visiting scholars using the facilities of the Hoover Institution have produced several times that number of volumes under the imprint of other publishing houses.

The budget reached close to $13 million in 1986, of which 27 percent was paid by the University; the Institution's endowment exceeds $100 million. Campbell claims that "Reaganomics" was born at the Hoover Institution. While there are resemblances between the Hoover Institution and the John F. Kennedy School of Government at Harvard, the Wilson School for Public and International Affairs at Princeton, and the Lyndon B. Johnson School at the University of Texas, the Hoover Institution does not hold regular courses and does not award academic degrees.

The Hoover Papers

The Herbert Hoover Collection in the Hoover Institution Archives covers the years from 1895 to 1976 and consists of about 278,000 items stored in 366 boxes on about 185 linear feet of shelving. The division of the Hoover papers between Stanford and the Hoover Presidential Library in West Branch is not clear cut; many items relating to the President's public service can be found both at Stanford and at the Hoover Library, in either original or copied form.

Important parts of the papers at Stanford include originals of some of Hoover's correspondence while secretary of commerce (boxes 11–12), reports of General Douglas MacArthur and other documentation of the Washington Bonus March in 1932 (boxes 23–24), and materials on the presidential campaigns of 1928 and 1932 (boxes 74–77). The correspondence between Herbert Hoover and Woodrow Wilson reveals major policies of the relief and conservation programs directed by Hoover during World War I (boxes 6–9). A series of addresses, letters, magazine articles, and press statements, and a detailed calendar identifying the items in this series is maintained in the archives reading room; the Hoover Library has a duplicate set of this series, together with a subject card index. A second series of Hoover speeches and writings and some original drafts of manuscripts and published books includes memoranda on the Paris Peace Conference and relief work in Europe. The subject file includes materials on the Commission for Relief in Belgium (boxes 329–330), the American Relief Administration in Hungary and Russia (boxes 326–327), the Jewish Joint Distribution Committee (box 336), the 1937 Roosevelt attempt to pack the Supreme Court (box 344), and Hoover's position on U.S. involvement in World War II (box 355).[18]

Audiovisual materials include motion picture films relating to World War I and relief work, presidential campaigns, Hoover's presidency, the reorganization of the federal government, and his funeral and memorial services. There are full length films and newsreels covering the years between 1916 and 1949, with emphasis on the 1920s. There are over 3,300 photographs of Herbert Hoover and his family and friends. The Herbert Hoover Oral History Collection contains transcripts of interviews with 315 people who knew Hoover. There are also records of about 30 organizations in which Hoover played an active part, and approximately 150 collections of papers of his friends and associates.

Besides the materials listed below, the Herbert Hoover Archives also contain a photograph collection, a collection of Hoover memorabilia (1917–86), microfilms (1923–63), motion pictures (1916–64), phonograph recordings (1938–66), and phono tapes (1931–64).

Materials in the Hoover Institution Archives

Files	*Boxes*
Biographical File (1895–1971)	1–5
Hoover Wilson Correspondence (1914–20)	6–9
Commerce Department File (1914–66)	10–16
Presidential File (1920–71)	17–91
Addresses, Letters, Magazine Articles, and Press Statements (1898–1960)	92–148
Speeches and Writings (1897–1964)	149–218
Writings about Herbert Hoover (1915–76)	219–229
Clippings, Press Summaries, Press Releases (1897–1969)	230–295
Editorial Analyses (1928–33)	296–312
Correspondence (1917–64)	313–326
Subject File (1900–64)	326–355
Card File to Subject File	356–366

Part IV

Presidential Libraries Administered by the National Archives

11. The Franklin D. Roosevelt Library and Museum in Hyde Park, New York

FRANKLIN D. ROOSEVELT
Thirty-second President—Democrat
1933–1945

Franklin Delano Roosevelt was born in 1882 in Hyde Park, New York, at Springwood, a large Hudson River estate; he was the second son of James Roosevelt, a financier and railroad executive, and the only child of his second wife, Sara Delano. Franklin was educated by private tutors, traveled widely in Europe, spoke French and German, and attended Groton Preparatory School from 1896 to 1900. He graduated from Harvard in 1903 with specialization in history and government, stayed at Harvard for one year of postgraduate study, and attended Columbia University Law School. He passed the bar examination in 1907 and worked in a prestigious law firm in New York City for the next three years. In 1909, he attended the Democratic state convention and was elected to the State Senate where he served from 1910 to 1912. During the 1912 presidential race, Roosevelt campaigned for Woodrow Wilson; he resigned from the State Senate in 1913 to serve as Wilson's assistant secretary of the navy, a post he held throughout World War I.

In 1920, the Democratic convention chose James Cox for president and Franklin D. Roosevelt for vice president; the ticket was defeated by Harding and Coolidge by a landslide of 60.4 percent of the popular vote. In 1921, Roosevelt entered a New York law firm, but was stricken with poliomyelitis during a summer vacation. His legs were permanently paralyzed, but he learned to move about with the help of braces, crutches, and a wheelchair, and was able to resume his legal career in 1924. At the 1924 Democratic convention, Roosevelt put Alfred Smith in nomination; Smith did not become the presidential candidate, but Roosevelt's nominating speech drew national attention. In 1928, he nominated Smith again. Smith became the Democratic candidate but was defeated by Herbert Hoover; Roosevelt, however, was elected governor of New York and served from 1929 to 1932.

Roosevelt defeated Herbert Hoover in the 1932 presidential election with a sweeping victory of 472 to 59 electoral votes. In his campaign, he attacked irresponsible business interests, advocated unemployment compensation, tariff reductions, repeal of prohibition, and the protection of American industry. When Roosevelt took office on March 4, 1933, the Great Depression had worsened, while bank and business closures and unemployment skyrocketed. Trying to reverse this trend, he spoke to the nation these famous words: "Let me assert my firm belief that the only thing we have to fear is fear itself—nameless, unreasoning, unjustified terror which paralyzes needed efforts to convert retreat into advance."[1]

On March 6, Roosevelt called a national bank holiday, closing all the banks in the United States until they could be inspected for their soundness; he gave his first radio "fireside chat" on March 12, reassuring the nation about the bank holiday. The next day, the sound banks were permitted to reopen. He called for a special session of Congress on March 9, and, in the next 100 days, an unprecedented amount of "New Deal" legislation was enacted, including the Agricultural Adjustment Act (AAA), the National Industrial Recovery Act (NIRA), the Home Owners Loan Corporation (HOLC), the Civilian Conservation Corps (CCC), and the Tennessee Valley Authority (TVA). Roosevelt took the country off the gold standard in order to preserve gold reserves; the Federal Emergency Relief Administration was set up to make direct grants to states for relief to the unemployed. At the end of the congressional session in June, the President wrote: "I am certain that this special session of Congress will go down in the history of our country as one which, more than any other, boldly seized the opportunity to right great wrongs, to restore clearer thinking and more honest practices . . . and to set our feet on the upward path."[2]

During the next few years, Roosevelt led Congress in developing new federal agencies such as the Public Works Administration, the National Youth Administration, the Rural Electrification Administration, the Federal Housing Administration, the Federal Communications Commission, and the Securities and Exchange Commission. At his urging, Congress passed Social Security legislation in 1935. Roosevelt was re-elected to a second term in 1936, defeating Republican Alfred M. Landon by a landslide.

The Supreme Court of the United States declared some of the New Deal legislation unconstitutional and Roosevelt, trying to make the Court more liberal, proposed legislation requiring mandatory retirement of the justices by age 70. Congress opposed this move to "pack the Supreme Court," but the Court rendered a number of more liberal decisions, upholding the social security laws and the right of states to fix a minimum wage. In foreign relations, Roosevelt effected a major change of policy by giving diplomatic recognition to the Soviet Union and encouraging "Good Neighbor" relationships with Latin American countries, The expansion of Hitler's Germany in Europe, of Mussolini's Italy in Africa, and the Japanese in Asia led to the outbreak of World War II in 1939. In spite of a strong isolationist movement at home, Roosevelt initiated rearmament and caused Congress to revise the neutrality laws in 1939, making it possible for the United States to sell supplies to friendly nations fighting the Axis powers, though he continued an official policy of neutrality.

Roosevelt was renominated for a precedent breaking third term by the Democrats in 1940, and won the election against Wendell L. Willkie. After the overthrow of France and the Battle of Britain, he initiated a lend-lease program for military assistance to Great Britain, Free France, China, and the Soviet Union. On December 7, 1941, Japan launched its surprise attack on Pearl Harbor and the United States declared war on the Axis powers. Roosevelt mobilized the country, coordinated the U.S. war effort with the Allies, initiated the concepts for unconditional surrender, and helped with the creation of the United Nations. In April 1945, shortly before victory was achieved, he died of a cerebral hemorrhage in Warm Springs, Georgia.

Roosevelt left the most detailed instructions for his own funeral, written eight years before his death. These instructions called for very simple services, "no Lying in State anywhere . . . interment where the sundial stands in the garden (in Hyde Park) . . . a casket of absolute simplicity . . . a plain white marble monument, no carving or decoration."[3] Ironically, this document was located in the safe of his bedroom in the White House a few days after the funeral. However, the funeral was very much as he had requested it because his family knew how he wanted to be buried.

Franklin D. Roosevelt had an enormous impact on history. His concern and compassion for the poor, the unemployed, the sick, the old, and the destitute contributed to his greatness. In several polls conducted by Arthur M. Schlesinger, Sr. of Harvard University, experts in history and political science were asked to rate presidential greatness; Roosevelt was rated third, after Lincoln and Washington.[4] Throughout his political career he was able to focus on a specific goal and, despite great obstacles, adhere to that goal with determination until he accomplished it.

THE PLANNING OF THE FRANKLIN D. ROOSEVELT LIBRARY

Among Roosevelt's many important national and international goals was the establishment of his place in American history by creating a

> repository for manuscripts, correspondence, books, reports, etc., etc., relating to this (the New Deal) period of our national history. There is much material which will be available in scattered form . . . throughout libraries and private collections in the United States. For example, my own papers should, under the old method, be divided among the Navy Department, the Library of Congress, the New York State Historical Division in Albany, the New York City Historical Society, Harvard University, and various members of my family . . . . If anything is done in the way of assembling a fairly complete collection in

one place, the effort should start now, but it should have the sanctions of scholars.[5]

In spite of worldwide turmoil and the extraordinary stresses of the last years of his presidency, Roosevelt accomplished his goal by establishing the Franklin D. Roosevelt Library in Hyde Park, New York. This library initiated the concept of the preservation of presidential records and memorabilia in a presidential library and museum administered by the National Archives. Without doubt, Roosevelt was motivated to create this library by vanity, with which he was abundantly endowed, as much as by a sense of history.

Roosevelt would, said historian Samuel Eliot Morison, "have gone down in history as a great collector even if he had done nothing else."[6] He was an enthusiastic stamp collector and owned over 1,200,000 stamps, though few rare or very valuable ones. On the day of his death, he discussed with Postmaster General Walker the purchase of the first issue of the stamp commemorating the United Nations Conference in San Francisco. He also collected Christmas cards, Dutch tiles, historical manuscripts, naval prints and paintings, ship models, and books. While a junior at Harvard, he was appointed librarian of the "Hasty Pudding Club," and, having a small fund to purchase books at his disposal, sought the advice of William Chase, a famous Boston book dealer, who told him that the first principle of collecting is never to destroy anything. He scrupulously followed this advice throughout his life, much to the despair of his family and staff. Eleanor Roosevelt mentions that on their honeymoon "Franklin bought books, books, everywhere we went."[7] At the time of his death his personal library had grown to about 15,000 volumes.

The idea of preserving his various collections in a depository at Hyde Park had occurred to Roosevelt as early as 1934 when he mentioned to a neighbor: "We can have a fireproof building in Hyde Park in which historical documents can be safely kept."[8] Hyde Park appealed to him as the site for his library because of his family's long association with the place. Claes Martenszen Roosevelt came to New Amsterdam in 1644; his grandson Jacob married a young lady in Dutchess County, New York; James Roosevelt, a grandson of Jacob, acquired some land in 1818 in the town of Hyde Park. Later descendants added to this original purchase and expanded their holdings well beyond the original Roosevelt purchase of 500 acres. It is on this plot of land where the President was born in an old, reconditioned colonial home. He was for many years a member of the Dutchess County Historical Society and served as its local Hyde Park historian.

It is reasonably certain that Roosevelt never considered depositing his papers in the Library of Congress but, in August 1935, he told U.S. Archivist Connor that he thought his papers should be deposited in the National Archives Building. By the fall of 1937, however, the White House contacted some architects concerning a document depository at Hyde Park; the President had made sketches for a library building which would retain the flavor of the old Dutch colonial style used in New York before 1800. One of the architects, Henry J. Toombs from Warm Springs, Georgia, commenting on the sketches, summarized the features of this style as: "1. Extreme simplicity of the exterior (and interior). 2. Small and few windows and large wall surfaces. 3. Rather steep pitched roofs. 4. Simple porches could be used as they were introduced before 1800." He estimated that the building would cost between $275,000 and $300,000.[9]

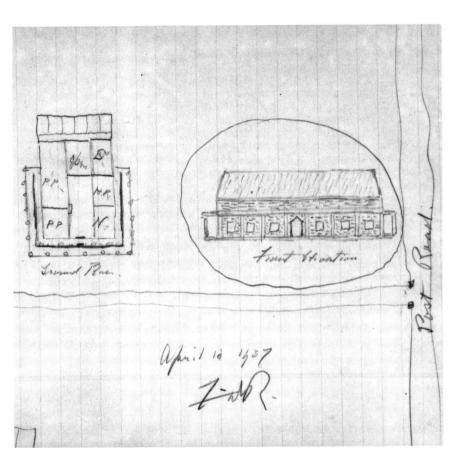

On April 12, 1937, eight years to the day before his death, FDR drew this sketch of the proposed Roosevelt Library at Hyde Park. Photo courtesy of the Franklin D. Roosevelt Library.

In his reply to Toombs, the President went into great detail about the number of potential visitors, which he estimated would be as many as 3,000 a day in the summer months.

That is an appalling number of sightseers to handle, and these visitors would have to go in and pass through the rooms and exhibition halls and out again on regular tour. That makes me think that what we call a reading room would not be a reading room at all for students but rather a very carefully designed living room which would contain portraits, several of my favorite paintings and perhaps a thousand of my favorite books—the room to be kept as a liveable sitting room and visitors to pass in one door and out another through an isle formed by stanchions and ropes. This room, incidentally, I could use myself in the work of preparing the collections during hours when the public was not admitted. Before you and I die we will have revived Hudson River Dutch—a real feather in the cap of a Georgia secessionist.[10]

By 1938, Roosevelt had definitely decided on Hyde Park as the site for his library. Responding to the suggestion of a Roosevelt repository in Warm Springs, Georgia, he wrote:

The creation of a center devoted to the history of this period must have the support of the fraternity of historians. The average of them say at first thought that such a collection should be placed in the Library of Congress—or in Harvard University or Columbia University or some other institution of learning or existing historical society. When I point out to them that in any such general organization, public or private, such a collection would be a tail on the dog, and that my idea is to have the whole thing in a place by itself, most of them are agreeing that I am perhaps right and that they would, therefore, go along with the idea. Then comes the second point . . . . Such a collection must be of very easy access to students and historians—as well as to the general public. Hyde Park fits into this picture because it is only two hours from New York City, because students and historians can live comfortably in Poughkeepsie and because far more people pass over the New York–Albany Post Road directly than pass over any other road in the nation . . . . Warm Springs is altogether too inaccessible . . . .[11]

In July 1938, Roosevelt invited Robert Connor and Frank C. Walker to lunch and told them about his plans for his papers. He specifically ruled out at that time both the Library of Congress and the National Archives as depositories. He thought the Library was "dilatory in arranging papers" and that the Archives were inappropriate because much of his material related to matters other than the federal government. He also felt that in case of war there was too much danger that some of the holdings of the two institutions would be destroyed. He proposed Hyde Park as the site for the construction of a depository to be financed by private subscriptions. He would donate the building, papers, and collections as well as some land to the government. This newly created institution would be under the control of the archivist of the United States. Roosevelt asked Walker to head the subscription campaign. Thus the foundations for the Roosevelt library were in effect laid at this meeting.[12]

To solicit support for his project from the academic and cultural world, Roosevelt invited 18 distinguished American scholars, educators, and public opinion makers to a luncheon at the White House on December 10, 1938, to obtain their advice regarding his plans "to set up for the first time in this country what might be called a source material collection relating to a specific period in our history."[13] In the memorandum attached to the invitation, the President outlined the record of his papers, going back to 1910, a period of 28 years of public service. Included would be many documents not connected with his service in the federal government, his collections about the American navy and the Hudson River area, books, pamphlets, pictures and other memorabilia, and materials contributed by others, all of which would be available to scholars in one definite locality. He planned to vest title to the building and all materials in the United States Government and place it under the primary responsibility of the archivist of the United States under the supervision of a committee of historians working in cooperation with the archivist and the librarian of Congress. During his lifetime, he hoped to continue to live at Hyde Park and to give assistance to the maintenance of the collection.

At the press conference held after the luncheon, Roosevelt stressed that the facility would be financed by private funds and that Frank Walker would handle fund-raising. The royalties from his *Public Papers,*[14] edited by Judge Rosenman, and from other of his writings would be contributed to the building fund. He also expressed the hope that members of his administration would donate their papers relevant to the New Deal for deposit. In the question and answer period following the announcement, the fate and availability of other presidential papers were discussed; Lincoln's, Theodore Roosevelt's, and John and John Quincy Adams' papers were still closed to the public. Professor Morison announced that the participants of the meeting were "one hundred per cent favorable to the president's proposal" and went on to say that

> lamentable mistakes have been made in the past in disposing of and dealing with presidential papers. The presidents have sometimes passed their declining years in trying to rearrange them, with unfortunate results because the order of documents has been entirely spoiled. And their widows have given them away as souvenirs and children have played with them and the rats have eaten them up. After a lapse of years, sometimes two or three generations, they were turned over to the Library of Congress . . . . But it is an unsatisfactory system because, in the meantime, a great many of the papers have been disposed of . . . and the historian does not know where to turn to find the information he wants . . . President Roosevelt has proposed, for the first time, to keep all of his files intact . . . and to place them immediately under the administration of the National Archives so that . . . they will be under public control and will not be subject to dilapidation or destruction or anything else. The whole thing will come down in its entirety to the historians of the future.[15]

After the December 10 meeting, Connor and Morison established an executive committee of scholars; Connor had hoped to have Morison serve as chairman, but this offer was not accepted because Morison had plans to spend the next half year abroad. The two agreed to recommend Waldo Gifford Leland as chairman of the executive committee. Leland was executive secretary of the American Council of Learned Societies and a distinguished historian. Roosevelt accepted this nomination, even though he knew that Leland was a Republican. On December 12, 1938, Robert Connor informed Leland "that the President hoped he would agree to be chairman of a small 'Executive Committee', to plan the construction and organization of the proposed depository."[16] Leland was not sure he approved of the idea because he thought that the Library of Congress, being good enough for Washington, Jefferson, and Jackson, should be good enough for Franklin D. Roosevelt. In the end he yielded to Connor; Roosevelt appointed him chairman of the executive committee and announced that the group would meet on December 17, the very next Saturday, by which time the other members had also been appointed: Randolph G. Adams, librarian of the University of Michigan; Dean Helen Taft Manning, Bryn Mawr; Charles E. Clark, Yale University Law School; and Stuart A. Rice, chairman of the Central Statistical Board.

The speed with which the President advanced his plans, the details which concerned him, and the time he devoted to the development of his library are amazing. Julian P. Boyd, who had attended the December 10 conference, wrote to Roosevelt on December 12 that he was deeply impressed by his plan to maintain his complete collection and not eliminate "unimportant documents . . . a distinct departure from the regrettable practices of former Presidents . . . . Indeed, aside from the many inherent values in your plan, it has this additional one: it cannot help but create a noteworthy precedent for future Presidents and it cannot help but elevate scholarship to a new position of dignity."[17] Boyd also referred to the technological changes taking place in communications, and suggested that phonographic recordings of speeches and films of presidential activities be included in the archival materials and that the library be equipped with a microfilm camera. On December 15, he received a one and a half page answer in which Roosevelt assured Boyd that Archivist Connor was collecting newsreels and recordings going back to the 1920s.

At the December 17 meeting, the executive committee agreed that its functions would be advisory and that it would have no responsibility for raising funds; that it would need expert advice about the design and construction of the library building as well as the legislation to be drafted regarding the acceptance of the gifts of the collections, land, and building, and to provide for their administration by the National Archives; and that the name of the depository should be the Franklin D. Roosevelt Library. At lunch at the White House, the committee was joined by the President and by Judge Rosenman, Frank C. Walker, and Vice President Garner. In response to questions from chairman Leland, the President described in some detail his own collections, explained his thoughts about the appearance of the building, and expressed his hope for space to display a vast number of miscellaneous objects. He only agreed reluctantly to the name of "Franklin D. Roosevelt Library" because he did not want it to appear that the library was a personal memorial.

In order to translate the deliberations of the executive committee meeting into action, Connor asked Fred W. Shipman, chief of the Archives Division of the State Department, to study the size of the collection of the Roosevelt papers and books. W.L.G. Joerg, an Archives employee, and L.V. Coleman, of the American Association of Museums, were asked to survey the over-sized materials and museum objects. Coleman located 400 pictures, 37 ship models, and a large quantity of smaller items and memorabilia, which he estimated would require 3,000 square feet to display. On December 19, Connor asked the Department of the Treasury for the services of architect Louis A. Simon to prepare plans for the library, and the Department of Justice to prepare a draft of the legislation for its incorporation. This draft was in Leland's hands by December 21 and was filed with the State of New York the following day. In addition to the executive committee, a national advisory committee of 30 members was established to represent professional concerns and provide encouragement and general support; it was headed by Basil O'Connor, Roosevelt's former law partner. A ways and means committee of 63 members was formed to provide financial backing for the library's construction and related expenses.

The Franklin D. Roosevelt Library was incorporated as the operating agency in charge of the building's construction. The first trustees of this corporation were Samuel Eliot Morison, Randolph Adams, W.G. Leland, Frank Walker, and Basil O'Connor. The certificate of incorporation was filed on December 22, 1938, in order to construct and equip the building, landscape the grounds, solicit funds, accept gifts, transfer property to the United States, and prepare the necessary legislation for the permanent upkeep and maintenance of the facility. By December 27, 1938, the reports on the surveys of source materials were completed, and Louis Simon presented the first architectural drawings to Roosevelt, Connor, and Leland on January 5, 1939.

Leland and Connor agreed with the President that Mrs. Roosevelt's papers would also be given to the library. The President repeated his hope that his cabinet members and other political associates would deposit their papers, and Connor was authorized to send appropriate invitations to the cabinet for this purpose. The decision was made to store the papers in buckram-covered fiber boxes designed by FDR. (Unfortunately, these boxes had to be replaced in the 1980s because the acid content of the cardboard had started to affect the documents.) When the point was made that too much space might be allocated to the museum functions of the library, Roosevelt commented: "Well, you know, if people have to pay a quarter to get into the library, they will want to see something interesting inside."[18]

THE FRANKLIN D. ROOSEVELT LIBRARY AND MUSEUM

Eleanor Roosevelt, in her personal recollections of Hyde Park, wrote:

> I think Franklin realized that the historic library, the house, and the peaceful resting place behind the hedge, with flowers blooming around it, would perhaps mean something to the people of the United States. They would understand the rest and peace and strength which he had gained here and perhaps learn to come, and go away with some sense of healing and courage themselves. If this place served this purpose, it will fulfill, I think, the desire which was nearest my husband's heart when he gave the place to the government.[19]

The official fundraising campaign for the library was started on February 4, 1939, during a meeting at the Carlton Hotel in Washington where the President spoke and Louis Simon showed the sketches of the library plans. Roosevelt hoped that the fund would be made up largely of small contributions. The campaign was very successful, and within a short time some 28,000 people had donated $400,000 for the construction of the library.

On March 6, 1939, Judge Rosenman presented the draft of a document to inform Congress of the gift the President intended to make to the nation, and draft legislation to implement such a gift. The proposed legislation had originally been prepared by the Department of Justice, then revised by Connor, the executive committee, and the President. The legislation surfaced on April 19 as a joint resolution in the Senate and the House. The resolution passed the Senate the next day, but ran into difficulties in the House and was not approved until July 18. The legislation dealt with both the library and the residence, created a board of trustees, and provided for the upkeep of the library, and the preservation of the historical materials by the United States Government.

On May 22, New York Governor Herbert H. Lehman informed the President that he had just signed the bill permitting "one F.D.R. of Hyde Park, Dutchess County, N.Y." to build a library at Hyde Park.[20] Roosevelt planned to deed the Hyde Park property to the United States in a ceremony to be held on July 24, 1939. Just before the ceremony, it was discovered that part of the land to be deeded actually belonged to the President's mother, who was on a vacation in Europe and had not left a power of attorney for the transfer of the property. Therefore, the President could not actually sign the required deed and the archivist could not accept it, although Roosevelt and Connor went through the motions of signing empty pages for the press. Sara Delano Roosevelt shortly thereafter signed the proper papers in Paris, and Archivist Connor countersigned the acceptance on August 11. The building contract was let on September 5 to the firm of John McShain. Groundbreaking started on September 14 and on November 19 the cornerstone was laid by the President and Archibald MacLeish, the new librarian of Congress. The basic construction of the library was finished in the summer of 1940 and the building was turned over to the government on July 4, less than 19 months after Roosevelt had publicly announced the plans for his library. It had been stipulated that on the death of the President and his mother, the entire Hyde Park Estate would be deeded to the United States, with the provision that Mrs. Roosevelt would continue to use the estate until her death. Springwood, the house in which the President was born and lived with his mother and his family, and Val-Kill, Eleanor Roosevelt's retreat a few miles away, are now National Historic Sites administered by the United States Park Service.

Recruitment for a director of the library started in 1939. Connor and Leland assumed that it was up to them to find a suitable candidate and asked the executive and national advisory committees for nominations. During the middle of January 1940, applications for the directorship of the library arrived. In March, Connor was told that no appointments to the library staff were to be made without consultation with the President. Connor felt that the position should be given to a professional archivist. Roosevelt wanted to consider Samuel Eliot Morison; Henry Pringle, the biographer of President Taft; and Harry Hopkins, his secretary of commerce and close personal advisor. Frank Monaghan, the biographer of John Jay, was suggested by Connor, who, after several unsuccessful meetings, expressed his frustration in his journal: "I don't envy the man who takes over the job of administering the FDR Library unless he is able to conform to the ideas—I may say the queer ideas of FDR—about how it ought to be administered."[21]

On April 10, at another meeting of the President with Connor, Archibald MacLeish, and Justice Felix Frankfurter, there was some agreement that a historian might be a good candidate. Roosevelt again mentioned Hopkins, but no decision was reached. On June 27, when Connor and the President discussed details of the ceremonies to turn the library over to the government on Independence Day, Connor recommended Fred W. Shipman for the library directorship. Roosevelt met and liked Shipman and he was appointed on July 1, 1940.

By June 1941, the building housing the library and museum, standing on a 16-acre plot of the Hyde Park estate, was completed, the grounds landscaped, and many of the museum objects installed. The library was formally dedicated and the museum section was opened to the public. The building, in keeping with Roosevelt's original plans, is a low, unassuming structure inspired by old Hudson Valley farmhouses, and is faced with native field stone. Two wings, dedicated to Eleanor Roosevelt, were added to the original structure in 1972. One wing contains enlarged research facilities; the other contains an exhibition gallery devoted to Mrs. Roosevelt's life and career, an auditorium, and a special exhibits area.

RESEARCH MATERIALS IN THE FDR LIBRARY

President Roosevelt began shipping White House files to the Roosevelt Library in August 1940. In the year between Shipman's appointment and the official opening of the library, he and his staff had started to sort and arrange the documents. The new approach to the preservation of presidential papers was explained by Shipman: "This is the first time in our history that a president has deliberately placed the papers of his office in the custody of the nation .... The task of caring for the President's papers has now grown too big for any family to handle. The Hayes Library at Fremont, Ohio, contains approximately 120,000 pieces of typewritten paper. Where Mr. Hoover received 600 letters a day, President Roosevelt receives 6,000. From 1933 to 1938 over 6,000,000 documents had accumulated in the White House."[22]

Additional accessions were received throughout Roosevelt's presidency. After his death, the remainder of the Central Files were received from his estate in December 1947. Security classified material in the President's Secretary's File and the Map Room Papers were transferred to the library from the National Archives in November 1951. Concerning his personal papers, the President sent a memorandum to the director of the library on July 16, 1943, explaining that he intended to go through his personal and confidential files to decide which of his papers should be retained by his family, which should be restricted for a limited period, and which should never be made accessible to the public. He also indicated that if prevented from making the decisions they should be made by a committee to consist of Judge Samuel Rosenman, Harry Hopkins, and his secretary, Grace Tully. This task was completed and the papers added to the library's holdings in March 1951.

During 1941, 743 linear feet of documents were labelled and shelved. By 1942, uniform procedures for the inventorying, arranging, labelling, and shelving of materials, and the assigning of files titles were adopted.

Inventories for 844 linear feet of documents were completed, and central control for the assignment of titles was established. The need for an understanding of the functioning of the White House offices became apparent after the first shipments of papers arrived. Fred Shipman undertook a study of these offices which was published as "Report on the White House Executive Office" by the FDR Library in 1945. Shipman knew that the tasks he faced and the solutions he found would be precedent setting and that the need for arranging and clearly describing materials for easy retrieval would become even more imperative as time went on.

When the United States entered World War II, Shipman left Hyde Park for wartime assignments. His assistant, Edgar B. Nixon, became acting director. A skeleton staff made little progress in the arrangement of the papers and the production of finding aids, and wartime traveling restrictions limited visitors to the library. The opening of the research section and the search room was delayed until May 1946. In 1948, historian Herman Kahn, who had joined the newly established National Archives in 1936, was named director of the library; under his efficient administration, the library became the excellent reference resource it is today. He actively solicited the personal papers of President Roosevelt's associates, was able to open 85 percent of the President's papers within five years of his death, and began a program of documentary publications.

The library's search room compares to the reference room of any larger library, but personal registration and a description of the purpose of the visit are required for use. Basic information resources such as bibliographies, dictionaries, encyclopedias, current serials, and selected books and vertical file materials on the Presidency, the New Deal, World War II, and books by and about the Roosevelts are shelved in the search room. Manuscripts and other books must be requested and are delivered from the stacks. The search room is staffed at all times by an archivist who assists researchers in identifying and locating requested materials. Finding aids, which are detailed guides to the individual documents, are used to locate the documents which are filed in folders arranged by subject and date. The folders are placed in numbered boxes arranged by various collections. The preparation of finding aids is used in historical societies and archives throughout the United States; the need to prepare them for presidential papers on a large scale originated in the FDR Library. The presidential library archival staff reviews and classifies each individual document, prepares finding aids, and answers letters and personal requests concerning detailed information about presidential actions. The pattern established in the FDR Library was adapted with slight modifications by all other presidential libraries.

Part of the text of Shipman's "Report" was incorporated in the introduction to the finding aids used by archivists and researchers in the FDR Library. While some of the content is specific to the Roosevelt administration, the report provides an overview of the White House filing system that has basically remained through subsequent administrations; these introductions, somewhat abbreviated, are reproduced in Appendix 4.

A White House Map Room was established in January 1942 under the supervision of the President's naval aide as a military information center and communication office for the President. The files of the Map Room grew very rapidly and on the death of President Roosevelt in April 1945 there were seven filing cabinets in the Map Room filled to capacity. Included in the Map Room Papers are wartime messages sent and received by the President, as well as much of the President's correspondence with the secretary of war, the secretary of the navy, and the joint chiefs of staff. The Map Room was the link between the President and the White House when he was away from Washington. Messages for the President were encoded in the Map Room and sent to him by army or navy circuits. The President's replies, returning through the same military channels, were decoded in the Map Room. These message files for the periods when President Roosevelt was in Casablanca, Quebec, Cairo, Teheran, and Yalta constitute a very valuable addition to the sparse records of the President's participation in international conferences with Churchill, Chiang Kai-shek, and Stalin. There are also a number of "Special Subject" folders on military and diplomatic topics in which the President was vitally interested and about which he sent a great many messages. All available army, navy, joint chiefs of staff, and State Department documents, whether directly related to the President's messages or not, were placed in the Special Subject folders. This type of file was begun in early August 1943 in preparation for the President's conference with Prime Minister Churchill in Quebec, and two of the first Special Subject folders related to the bombing of Rome and Anglo-American relations with the French National Committee. These folders were found so useful that the practice of filing the President's personal messages with military and diplomatic papers on selected topics in special folders continued until his death.

Another group of Map Room papers comprises messages, reports, maps, and official publications of the War and Navy Departments. These were sent to the White House where they were studied by the officers in the Map Room, who posted the information contained in them on maps and charts and summarized it in writing or orally for the President, Harry Hopkins, Admiral Leahy, and the military and naval aides.

By 1985, very few documents in the FDR Library remained closed because of donor restrictions or security classification. The library staff is continuously reviewing closed materials with a view to opening as many as possible. The materials in the library are being used extensively for research and documentation on the Roosevelt presidency, which includes many prize-winning books. Lists of publications based in part on research in the Franklin D. Roosevelt Library are available from the library on request.

The holdings of the library are summarized below by type of material, based on the lists published in *Historical Materials in the Franklin D. Roosevelt Library* [23] and on personal communications with the staff.

Manuscripts

The Papers of Franklin D. and Anna Eleanor Roosevelt

Files	*Linear Feet*
New York Senator (1910–13)	14
Assistant Secretary of the navy (1913–20)	53
Vice Presidential Candidate (1920)	11
Papers (1920–28)	3
Campaign (1924)	18
Campaign (1928)	11
Governor of New York (1929–32)	72
White House Files (1933–45)	
Alphabetical	68
Official	1174
Presidential Personal	608
Secretary's File	130
Press Conferences	15
Map Room (1941–45)	81
Personal Papers	114
Papers of Anna Eleanor Roosevelt	1107

Donated Papers and Records

	Linear Feet/ Microfilm Reels
195 collections	4309/452

Federal Government Records

	Linear Feet/ Microfilm Reels
16 collections	359/3

Oral History Interview Transcripts

FDR Collection

This collection contains 15 items, of which the most noteworthy are 233 pages of interviews with Samuel I. Rosenman, counsel to Governor Roosevelt and special counsel to President Roosevelt and justice of the New York Supreme Court; and 133 pages with Rexford G. Tugwell, assistant to the President, undersecretary of agriculture, and governor of Puerto Rico.

Eleanor Roosevelt Collection

This collection has 68 items. Among these are interviews with children, grandchildren, and friends of the family and associates of both Roosevelts.

The Printed Materials Collection

The library has 45,000 volumes, including Roosevelt's personal library of 15,000 volumes. The collection is particularly strong in the following subject fields:

- Dutch immigration and settlement in America
- Hudson Valley and Dutchess County history
- The Roosevelt family
- History of the U.S. Navy

The library also has a large collection of periodicals, government publications, dissertations, and pamphlets. It tries to keep up to date with books and articles dealing with the Roosevelt administration, the New Deal era, and key people of the Roosevelt administration, with topics the President stressed in his own collection efforts, within the confines of the budget.

The Audiovisual Collection

Still Pictures

This collection is divided into four main files: the Franklin D. and Eleanor Roosevelt Files, the General Subject File, and the Album File. The collection covers the period from 1870 to the Present and contains 132,000 items. The Franklin and Eleanor Roosevelt Files are arranged chronologically, usually composed of 5″ by 8″ index cards with 4″ by 5″ contact prints attached. Descriptive information is included on the index card. The original prints have been retired for preservation, except for those of poor quality.

The General Subject File is subdivided into three categories: People, Places, and Subjects. A folder list of the General Subject File is available. All files contain photographs taken by family members (including FDR), other private individuals, professional and commercial photographers, or news services and government agencies. Some of the photographs date back to the period of the daguerreotype.

The library has some 20 color photographs of FDR, including a picture taken in June 1944 by the photographer of the King of Sweden, and several taken at the Yalta Conference in 1945. There are approximately 300 color photographs of Eleanor Roosevelt. The library also has a collection of color transparencies of exhibits, historical naval paintings, and other objects.

Motion Pictures

The collection consists of films donated by the Roosevelts, their estate, other members of the family, and various individuals and organizations. It covers the period 1912 to 1980 and contains 680 reels of 85,000 feet of 16mm film. Recently the library has begun receiving videocassette tapes of television programs about the Roosevelts. Most of the films are black and white; approximately 15 percent are color. All 35mm nitrate films have been converted to 16mm safety stock. Eighty-five reels of original color film have been placed in the cold storage vault of the John F. Kennedy Library.

Franklin D. Roosevelt Films. The core of the collection of films on Roosevelt consists of newsreels tracing his activities from the 1932 presidential campaign to his death. They also contain some footage taken while he was assistant secretary of the navy, governor of New York, and vice presidential candidate in 1920. The navy Department filmed the President's wartime inspection trips and overseas conferences, 1940–45, including those at Cairo, Teheran, and Yalta. The Signal Corps covered the 1943 Casablanca Conference. Amateur films in the library's collection provide informal glimpses of the President. The collection also includes commercial motion pictures and television documentaries, news programs, and movies.

Eleanor Roosevelt Films. These films cover Eleanor Roosevelt's career from the 1932 campaign until her death in November 1962. They include appearances with FDR and their children during the 1920 campaign. The newsreels focus on President Roosevelt, but also contain footage of Eleanor involved in her own activities, including her trips to Puerto Rico, the Virgin Islands, Great Britain in 1942, and the Pacific Islands in 1943. Her post-1945 activities include a portion of an address to the United Nations; speeches before the AFL-CIO meeting in December 1955 and the Democratic national convention in August 1956; and appearances on television discussion and interview programs.

General Subjects. The remainder of the motion picture collection covers personalities, institutions, places, social conditions, and events of the Roosevelt era. Films include "Lest We Forget" (1944) and "Pursuit of Happiness" (1956), produced for the Democratic National Committee; "Youth Visits Our Nation's Capitol" (1939) and "Training Women for War Production," produced by the National Youth Administration; "Glimpses of the Workers Education Program in Florida," produced by the Works Progress Administration; and "The 1940 Census," produced by the Department of Commerce. Major events of World War II are covered in "Countdown to World War II"; films from the "Why We Fight" series, including "Prelude to War: The Nazi Strike" and "The Battle of Britain"; and in "The Negro Soldier" and "Washington in Wartime."

Recorded Speeches and Other Statements of Franklin D. Roosevelt 1920–45

This collection contains 314 speeches and statements of Franklin D. Roosevelt. The core of the collection consists of 238 disc-recorded speeches presented to President Roosevelt by radio networks and other sources. Also included is a series of unique recordings made in the President's office between August 23 and November 8, 1940, using an acetate recording material and an experimental machine made by the Radio Corporation of America. These recordings consist of 14 presidential press conferences, and conversations between President Roosevelt and visitors to his office.

THE MUSEUM AREA

The desire to collect objects and preserve them never slackened in Roosevelt, busy and preoccupied as he was with matters of world-shaking importance. Visiting the troops in Africa during the height of World War II in 1943, he spotted a rusty horseshoe in the sand and instructed an aide to have it sent to the library in Hyde Park. He was pleased to accept Richard Connell's silk hat for the collection, because Connell, the only Democrat elected from Dutchess County since 1870, ran for Congress at the same time Roosevelt first ran for the State Senate. He submitted a piece of bone from a deer, found on a road in Hyde Park, because he thought that the Indians had tried to fashion it into an arrow head or a needle, and he sent lengthy memoranda to Shipman detailing various items he had received as presents.[24]

As visitors enter the museum area, they face the desk and chair used by Roosevelt in the Oval Office during his presidency. Grouped around the desk are exhibit cases illustrating the "Powers of the Presidency": Party Chief; Chief Executive; Head of State; and Commander in Chief.

The display, "The Presidential Years," illustrates important aspects of the Roosevelt presidency: The First Hundred Days; the Great Depression; Social Security Legislation; Banking and Wall Street; and the WPA and PWA.

A number of separate displays cover the Second World War; these include his message to Congress of December 8, 1941, calling for a declaration of war on Japan, and the famous letter from Albert Einstein that led to the development of the atomic bomb.

For many visitors the most memorable room in the building is the President's study. He furnished this room for himself; whenever he visited Hyde Park he worked there on his papers and books. Because of the pressures of the times, he was able to use it only occasionally between 1941 and 1945, but he was looking forward to working there after he retired from office. The room has large windows, a reproduction of George Washington's desk, a fireplace decorated with old Dutch tiles relating to marine life that were collected by the President, and book cases holding special editions and rare books from his collection. His homemade wheelchair also stands in the room. On the wall is a painting of the destroyer *Dyer,* which Roosevelt used to inspect U.S. naval forces when he was assistant secretary of the navy. A large portrait of his mother stands on an easel.

A gallery with pictures and mementos of FDR's childhood and youth exhibits photographs of his wedding and his pre-presidential career. A large Dutch family bible, printed in Holland in 1686, on which Roosevelt took every oath of office since he became governor of New York, is on display. There are mementos from the campaigns and elections. One case reminds the viewer of Roosevelt's handicap, displaying his cane, crutch, and a device used to pick up items from the floor.

Throughout the museum are portraits of FDR, Eleanor, his mother, and his children. An oil painting shows the Castle of Clervaux, the ancestral home of the Delano family in Luxembourg. A substantial number of gifts received from foreign governments is on exhibit: rugs from

Iran, bejewelled daggers for the Middle East, and wood carvings from Africa. There are also many interesting gifts from American admirers. The china used in the White House is shown, as well as such personal belongings of the President as watches, pins, medals, cigarette cases, and cigarette holders. The Naval Exhibition Room contains selections from Roosevelt's large collection of ship models and naval paintings and prints. The gallery in the basement displays the manually operated car, donated by the Ford Motor Company, which Roosevelt used to drive visitors around the estate. There is also the display of his collection of Dutchess County carriages, sleighs, and iceboats.

The Eleanor Roosevelt gallery shows her life as wife and mother, her career as the President's eyes and ears, and her work as U.S. delegate to the United Nations, especially her efforts to achieve the adoption of the U.N. Declaration of Human Rights. At the entrance to the gallery stands a Steuben glass sculpture of her hands, which was inspired by the words of Adlai Stevenson: "She would rather light a candle than curse the darkness, and her glow has warmed the world."[25]

THE FRANKLIN AND ELEANOR ROOSEVELT INSTITUTE

In his State of the Union message in January 1941, Roosevelt described his concept of the four basic human freedoms: freedom of speech, freedom of worship, freedom from want, and freedom from fear. These four freedoms became an integral part of the United Nations Universal Declaration of Human Rights, which came into existence through Eleanor Roosevelt's efforts as U.S. delegate to the United Nations.

The Franklin and Eleanor Roosevelt Institute is the result of the 1987 merger of the organizations created by President and Mrs. Roosevelt and their friends to build the presidential library at Hyde Park and to perpetuate the ideals of the four freedoms: the Eleanor Roosevelt Institute, and the Franklin D. Roosevelt Four Freedoms Foundation. The library's director, William R. Emerson, serves as coordinator of the Roosevelt Institute's programs, which include:

The Franklin Delano Roosevelt Library and Museum. Its activities include making grants to scholars, historians, and students of the Roosevelt era (request application forms from the director of the Franklin D. Roosevelt Library); acquiring historical materials; holding annual conferences, seminars, and colloquia; publishing the newsletter *A View from Hyde Park;* and developing a curriculum to assist public schools in teaching the history of the Roosevelt era.

The Universal Declaration of Human Rights Trust. It sponsors experimental high school and youth employment programs that deal with social and educational problems, and is promoting the 40th anniversary of the Declaration of Human Rights.

The Roosevelt Study Center in The Netherlands. It maintains a major research center for European scholars and students of American history, and promotes the teaching of American history in Europe.

The Franklin Roosevelt Four Freedom Awards. Five medals commemorating Franklin Roosevelt's four freedoms have been awarded annually since 1982, President Roosevelt's centenary year. They are awarded alternately in Hyde Park to Americans and in The Netherlands province of Zeeland, the Roosevelts' ancestral home, to international figures whose lives have given meaning to the four freedoms.

Memorials to Franklin and Eleanor Roosevelt. Organizes efforts to establish memorials for FDR and Eleanor Roosevelt in Washington and New York.

The FDR Library and Museum, its research program, and the multifaceted programs of the Franklin and Eleanor Institute have not only served the purpose of keeping the President's legacy intact for posterity, but have also provided a model that has been followed, with some adaptations and variations, by all successive presidents.

12. The Harry S. Truman Library in Independence, Missouri

HARRY S. TRUMAN
Thirty-third President—Democrat
1945–1953

Born on May 8, 1884, in Lamar, Missouri, Harry S. Truman, the son of a farmer and mule trader, grew up in Independence, Missouri where he attended public schools. He was an avid reader throughout his life, in part because his poor eyesight kept him out of games and sports. He was especially interested in history and stated in his *Memoirs* that "the one great external influence which, more than anything else, nourished and sustained my interest in government and public service was the endless reading of history which I began as a boy and which I have kept up ever since."[1] His involvement with politics began at the age of 16 when he served as a page at the Democratic national convention of 1900 in Kansas City. After graduating from high school, he worked at various clerical jobs until 1906, when his parents asked him to move to Grandview, now a suburb of Kansas City, to help run the family's 600-acre farm. After his father died in 1914, he also took over his job as road overseer, became postmaster of Grandview, and began to attend meetings of the Democratic Political Club in Kansas City. When the United States entered the First World War in 1917, he joined the National Guard as a lieutenant, and transferred a few months later to the regular army. He served in France until the end of the war, and was mustered out as major in May 1919. On his return to Independence, he married his former classmate, Elizabeth "Bess" Wallace, and operated for the next three years a man's clothing store, which ended in failure. In 1922, he entered active Democratic party politics on a full-time basis. He was elected judge of Jackson County with the help of his army friends and of Kansas City political boss T.J. (Tom) Pendergast. During the two years he served in that position, he attended law school at night, but did not earn a law degree. In 1926, he became presiding judge of Jackson County, a position he held for eight years, giving him wide administrative and political experience.

In 1934, Truman was elected to the U.S. Senate. In Washington, he became a consistent supporter of New Deal legislation; however, his generally moderate approach earned him the respect of many conservative Democrats. He gained considerable attention as chairman of a sub-committee of the Interstate Commerce Committee which investigated railroad financing. Re-elected in 1940, he became nationally prominent with his investigations of wartime profiteering. His work in the Senate was characterized by his evenhanded performance, complete impartiality, and impeccable honesty. When Roosevelt looked for a running mate in 1944 to replace Henry Wallace, Truman's conservatism and his good relations in the Senate served him well. Robert Hannigan, the Democratic National Committee chairman, helped to win Truman the nomination for vice president on the second ballot. During the first few months of his fourth term, Roosevelt travelled a great deal and Truman spent comparatively little time with him.

Less than three months after he took office, on April 12, 1945, Truman was informed by Mrs. Roosevelt of the President's death. He said that he felt "like the moon, the stars and all the planets had fallen on me."[2] His first decision as president was to give his full support to the United Nations, which had its first planning meeting two weeks later. Less than a month later, on May 8, 1945, Germany surrendered. In June, the United Nations Charter was signed in San Francisco, and Truman prepared for his meeting with Churchill and Stalin at the Potsdam Conference, where the occupation of Germany was agreed on and an ultimatum for the surrender of Japan was drafted. Shortly thereafter, Truman made the historic decision to drop the first atomic bomb on Hiroshima and, a few days later, the second one on Nagasaki. On August 14, 1945, Japan surrendered.

In his "Fair Deal" proposals to Congress, Truman expanded Social Security, worked toward full employment, and endorsed the Fair Employment Practices Act, public housing, and slum clearance. Due to the difficult transition from a war to a peace time economy, labor unrest broke out in 1946, culminating in the railroad and coal miner strikes, which he settled by taking over the railroads and the mines. On the international scene, he opposed Soviet expansionist moves in Greece and Turkey by enunciating what became the "Truman Doctrine," stating that "It must be the policy of the United States to support free people who are resisting attempted subjugation by armed minorities or outside pressures."[3] Congress approved the Truman Doctrine by implementing the Marshall Plan of 1948. The Soviet response to the Marshall Plan was the blockade of Berlin; the United States supplied the city with food and fuel through the Berlin airlift for almost a year, until the Soviets stopped the blockade.

At home, Truman requested from Congress a 10-point civil rights program that antagonized the southern states and resulted in the formation of the Dixiecrat party. In 1948, with his popularity at a low ebb, Truman won a stunning national victory in the election over Republican Thomas Dewey, Dixiecrat Strom Thurmond, and Progressive Henry Wallace. In his inaugural address, Truman announced his "Point Four Program," the first major step to improve underdeveloped Third World countries. This program and the North Atlantic Treaty Organization were ratified by Congress in April 1949. Communist expansion swallowed China in 1949, when Chiang Kai-shek fled to Formosa where he established the government of Nationalist China. In June 1950, communist North Korea invaded South Korea; the United Nations Security Council denounced this action and called on U.N. members to aid South Korea. Truman ordered U.S. forces into action and the fighting lasted more than three years; eventually, Chinese forces entered the conflict and ultimately the 38th parallel was recognized as the dividing line between the two Koreas.

Truman decided in the spring of 1952 not to seek re-election, and in 1953 returned to his home in Independence, Missouri, where he spent the next 20 years as an elder statesman, writing books, including his *Memoirs*, giving speeches, and using the facilities of the Harry S. Truman Library. He died on December 26, 1972. Winston Churchill said that Truman "more than any other man, has saved Western Civilization."[4]

THE ESTABLISHMENT OF THE TRUMAN LIBRARY

Few presidents were more concerned with history and more interested in the preservation of presidential papers than Harry Truman. He was aware of their dispersion by his predecessors and said: "The papers of our Presidents are among the most valuable source materials of our history. They ought to be preserved. More than that, they ought to be used . . . . The papers of Presidents of the United States are important because of the unique character and importance of the Presidential office."[5]

He gave his personal support to the provisions of the Federal Property and Administrative Services Act of 1949, and the Federal Records Act of 1950, which authorized the National Archives to accept, store, and care for the papers of present and future presidents. In July 1950, Truman's friends formed a nonprofit corporation in Missouri to collect funds to obtain a site and to construct a building to house the Truman papers. Following the Roosevelt model, the President consulted a committee of historians about functional details concerning his library and made contacts with two architectural firms to prepare designs for such a building.

Before leaving the White House in January 1953, Truman wrote a letter to GSA Administrator Jess Larson, in which he expressed his desire that his personal papers be preserved and ultimately made available for historical research. He proposed that

> as a preliminary step towards such a disposition, to offer my personal papers for deposit in the National Archives, pursuant to the provisions of section 507(e) of the Federal Records Act of 1950 . . . I propose to retain all of these in my personal possession when I leave office, and to move them to a secure place of storage under guard in Kansas City, Missouri. There I intend to review them and prepare them for ultimate deposit . . . . I am requesting you to designate two or three experienced archivists to work with me on this project. I expect to be consulted regarding the particular individuals to be assigned to the work. [6]

Larson assigned two archivists to assist Truman in the task of arranging, classifying, indexing, and packing the papers in preparation for ultimate deposit.

The original library corporation was reorganized as the Harry S. Truman Library, Inc., and its Board of Governors and Executive Committee were enlarged in 1953. Basil O'Connor became president of the corporation and Truman selected David D. Lloyd, his former administrative assistant, as executive director. The fund-raising, coordinated by Lloyd, got under way with a goal of $1,750,000, and resulted in the contributions by 17,000 individuals and organizations, actually oversubscribing the stated goal. Originally, Truman planned to have the building constructed on his farm in Grandview, several miles outside of Independence, and to donate 40 acres of land for this purpose. Before a decision was reached, other sites were proposed. The board of curators of the University of Missouri at Columbia, 125 miles east of Kansas City, invited the President to locate his library on a site in the center of the campus. The board of trustees of the University of Kansas City offered a site on their campus, located in the southern part of the city. Mayor Robert C. Weatherford, Jr., of Independence, Truman's lifelong friend, tried to convince him of the advantages of locating the library in Independence, close to his home, on land that would be donated by the city. In 1954, at the Jackson Day Democratic luncheon, Truman mentioned to Weatherford: "I've got a decision to make in two weeks where I am going to put this Library. I'd like to put it on the farm out at Grandview, but the utility installation's going to be so expensive I can't do that. The people in Kansas City want it over there, but there's so many of them that have fought me over the years that I don't want it there. The University of Missouri wants it and that's too far away; I couldn't find time to go to it nor be there." In response, the mayor said, "Well Mr. President, why don't you put it here in Independence." Truman replied: "I would like to have it here. This is where Margaret was born, it's been my home, it's where I grew up." Weatherford asked the President to give him "a couple of weeks and see what we can develop," to which the President replied, "I'll just leave it up to you, Bob."[7]

The final decision to locate the library in Independence was made in July 1954 at a meeting of the Harry S. Truman Library, Inc. After a study of available areas, which was conducted without publicity to counteract possible land speculation, a site of 13½ acres adjoining Slover Park, about five blocks north of the Truman home, was chosen to be donated by the city for the construction of the Truman Library. In order to make the library grounds easily accessible, the Highway Department constructed an underpass and two access roads which cost over $500,000. The building was completed in September 1957.

On August 12, 1955, President Eisenhower signed the Presidential Libraries Act as an amendment to the Federal Property and Administrative Services Act of 1949, which provided for the acceptance and maintenance of presidential libraries under the same general terms as for the Franklin D. Roosevelt Library. Eighteen months later, in February 1957, Truman offered his papers and mementos to Franklin G. Floete, the administrator of General Services, under the provisions of the act. Simultaneously, Basil O'Connor, president of the of the Harry S. Truman Library, Inc., deeded the land and building to the government.

The actual transfer of the deed occurred on July 6, 1957, when the library was dedicated and accepted as part of the National Archives system. Chief Justice Earl Warren made the dedicatory address in which he remembered the history of Independence and the contributions of Truman to his time.

> The Truman era is already recognized as one of the most momentous periods in the history of our country and of the world. . . . Complicated events crowded upon one another giving Mr. Truman little or no time to sit, ponder and mull over historical precedents. . . . His response was always action . . . . The best evidence of the magnitude of the office he held, of the considerations basic to his decisions, of the methods he adopted to meet new and pressing problems will be found in the Truman papers housed in this library. Without them the world would never fully understand his courage and stamina in responding in the vigorous and effective way he did to crises such as few other executives ever had to face.[8]

Among other speakers were Sam Rayburn, Speaker of the House of Representatives; Joseph W. Martin, minority leader of the U.S. House of Representatives; Lyndon B. Johnson, majority leader of the U.S. Senate; and William F. Knowland, minority leader of the U.S. Senate.

The museum opened in September 1957; the archives facility was opened to researchers in May 1959. About the same time, the Harry S. Truman Institute for National and International Affairs was founded to assist in the guidance of the library's program activities to raise funds, and to issue grant fellowships. David D. Lloyd, the director of the Truman library, served also as the director of the Institute, keeping both functions in close cooperation.

THE HARRY S. TRUMAN LIBRARY BUILDING

Surrounded by an extensive park and located on its highest elevation, the two-story Harry S. Truman Library was constructed in the form of the letter "J" and covered 70,000 square feet; the original plans for the building were done by the Shreveport architectural firm of Neild and Somdal, in cooperation with Kansas City architects Gentry and Voskamp. Truman had a structure in the style of the Jackson County court house in Independence in mind, which is Georgian Colonial, reminiscent of Independence Hall in Philadelphia, and had been designed by Neild. Since Neild died before the library plans were completed, Gentry and Voskamp finalized the drawings. They favored a more contemporary design and Truman, who did not like modern art, saw in the building's style "at least a taint of the evil genius of Frank Lloyd Wright. 'It's got too much of that fellow in it to suit me,' he said,"[9] but overall he was very pleased with his library. Both he and his trustees wanted the library to be not a monument to a single president but a celebration of the American presidency as an institution.

The building is covered by yellowish Indiana sandstone over reinforced concrete. Its main entrance is decorated by six 22-foot columns, which provide a quiet dignity without towering over the landscape or the visitors. The original building was constructed at a cost of $1.5 million by the Harry S. Truman Library, Inc., though the actual value was considerably greater as many services and materials were contributed.[10] The government added an extension to the building in 1968 at a cost of $312,000, and completed a major 24,000 square foot addition costing more than $2.5 million in 1980. This addition changed the building into the shape of the letter "O" and created a court that holds the tomb of the President and his wife.

The entrance hall is decorated by a large mural; behind the mural is an auditorium, seating 250 visitors. The museum exhibits start on the right side of the mural; the areas on the left are reserved for the research room, staff offices, and storage space for documents. At the end of the staff offices is Truman's simple personal office, which he used almost daily, including Saturday mornings, though with decreasing frequency during the last few years of his life. Several offices were occupied by his personal staff. The basement has additional staff work rooms and offices, a photographic laboratory, storage areas, and heating and air conditioning equipment.

RESEARCH MATERIALS IN THE HARRY S. TRUMAN LIBRARY

Most of the White House files and Truman's Senate papers were donated to the library in 1957. Between 1974 and 1983, the library obtained papers from the White House years that Truman considered confidential and preferred to keep separate, and the papers of his pre-presidential and post-presidential careers. In addition, the library acquired close to 400 sets of papers of members of the Truman administration and people associated with the President. The library has over 13 million items in the manuscript collection, covering 6,700 linear feet; 2,800 of these comprise the papers of Harry S. Truman. The following tabulations are based on *Historical Materials in the Harry S. Truman Library*[11] and on interviews with the library staff.

Manuscripts

The Papers of Harry S. Truman

Files	Linear Feet
Presiding Judge of Jackson County, Missouri (1926–34)	2
Senatorial and Vice Presidential (1934–45)	124
Other	2
White House Central Files (1945–53)	2784
WHCF cross-reference file	292
White House Files	
Secretary's File	136
Map Room File (1945)	1
Bill File (Bureau of the Budget Reports on Pending Legislation)	56
Misc. Historical Documents (1862–1972)	6
Office of Social Correspondence	91

Official Reporter Files	17
Press Releases and Subject File	11
Social Office Files	42
Fiscal and Accounting Files	25
Other	18
Post-Presidential (1953–73)	372

Donated Papers and Records

Linear Feet/ Microfilm Reels

358 collections   2689/101

Federal Government Records

Linear Feet/ Microfilm Reels

50 collections   343/32

Oral History Interview Transcripts

The oral interviews were started in 1961 to fill gaps in the written records, particularly in the areas of the President's pre-senatorial career, U.S. foreign policy (1945–52), and the White House staff. Nearly 400 interviews were held adding up to over 42,000 typed pages.

The Microfilm Collection

The library has a collection of microfilms of historical source materials held by other depositories or individuals; materials include selected U.S. government records and newspapers from the Truman era. In addition, it has microfilms of the papers of the presidents that are stored in the Library of Congress, and of the Adams papers.

The Printed Materials Collection

The library contained in 1987 close to 45,000 volumes and a large number of serials, dissertations, and periodical articles. The policy of the library is to acquire printed and audiovisual materials relating to the Truman era and to the President and his public career, as well as items of reference value to the research visitors and the staff of archivists and curators of the museum.

Truman's personal library of 7,000 volumes, many of which were gifts to him while he was president, strongly emphasizes history, but also covers poetry, novels, economic and political tracts, cookbooks, and Bibles; many of the volumes are dedicated by their authors to the President.

The Audiovisual Collection

The library's audiovisual holdings include 75,000 still pictures covering Truman's career, and photographs of his family, personal friends, and political associates. The motion picture collection of approximately 375 items comes from newsreel, television, and commercial sources, and from private donors. There is also a collection of sound recordings of Truman's speeches and informal remarks, and some videotapes.

THE MUSEUM AREA

The large mural in the entrance hall is by Kansas City painter Thomas Hart Benton, entitled "Independence and the Opening of the West." It illustrates a segment of the history of President Truman's hometown, and was dedicated in April 1961. There is a reproduction of the White House Oval Office as it existed during Truman's administration; the description is narrated by the President. Photographs, selected documents, and detailed inscriptions provide a vivid story of his family and youth; jobs as a young man; military service during the First World War; courtship and marriage; co-ownership of a haberdashery; and his government services in Missouri and as senator, vice president, and seven years as president. The exhibit on the presidency is divided by functions: Chief Executive, Legislative Planner, Head of Party, Commander-in-Chief, and Director of Foreign Policy. Displays include the ending of World War II, the atomic bomb, the creation of the United Nations, the Truman Doctrine, the Marshall Plan, the 1948 "Whistlestop" Campaign, price supports, full employment, the Taft-Hartley Act, the Farewell Address, his role as elder statesman, and the Truman funeral.

Featured among the many ceremonial gifts from foreign heads of state are a huge carpet presented by the Shah of Iran, a long, beautifully carved mahogany table and chairs from the Philippines, and vases from Japan. Noteworthy among the paintings is the Eisenhower portrait, painted by Thomas E. Stephens, which was purchased on Truman's request because he wanted the library to have a portrait of the man who was president of the United States. An extensive collection of presidential campaign memorabilia from the 1820s to the 1970s is displayed. There are several pianos used by Truman, two Bibles from the swearing-in ceremonies, the table used during the Japanese surrender protocols on the battleship U.S.S. *Missouri,* and the table on which the United Nations Charter was signed. Other items on display include two cars used by the President and a large collection of cartoons of the Truman presidency. A separate exhibit area displays the life of Bess Truman, illustrated by pictures and mementos.

A valuable U.S. coin collection, donated by Truman's Treasury Secretary John W. Snyder, and a rare collection of daggers and swords contributed by the king and crown prince of Saudi Arabia, were stolen from the building. The coin collection has been only partly replaced by collectors from all over the country; the swords were never replaced. These thefts resulted in the installation of a very sophisticated alarm system. The museum collection has about 21,000 objects and shows rotating temporary exhibits. Visitors have the opportunity throughout the day to view at frequent intervals several films about the Truman presidency and the Truman Library. The Medicare Bill was signed in the Truman Library by President Johnson.

THE HARRY S. TRUMAN LIBRARY INSTITUTE

This private, nonprofit corporation was formed in 1957 to assist the library in its mission of becoming a national center for study and research in the fields of history and political science. It was originally funded by Mr. Truman's honoraria for lecture appearances. Additional funds are received as gifts and bequests and through annual contributions to the Honorary Fellows program.

The purpose of the Truman Institute is to encourage study and research in the historical materials collected in the Harry S. Truman Library, to promote the acquisition of research materials regarding the Truman period, and to provide financial assistance to scholars and researchers. It also issues a newsletter, fosters cooperation with historical and academic institutions, and supports publications related to the work of the library. Its overall aim is to encourage public understanding of the nature and functions of the government of the United States. Every two years, it awards the David D. Lloyd Prize for the best book published during the preceding biennium that deals with the Truman period. It also sponsors conferences that focus on various aspects of the Truman administration, and special research projects of particular interest to the Harry S. Truman Library. The Truman Institute awards small grants to individuals studying the Truman administration and senior research fellowships to individuals working on book length publications.

13. The Herbert Hoover Library and Museum in West Branch, Iowa

THE ESTABLISHMENT OF THE HOOVER LIBRARY AND MUSEUM

In 1935, two years after President Hoover left the White House, his sons acquired the cottage in which their father was born and lived until age nine, and had it restored to its original state. In 1939, West Branch citizens organized the Hoover Birthplace Society, which opened the Hoover cottage to the public and acquired some land nearby. In 1954, the Herbert Hoover Birthplace Foundation was incorporated as a private Iowa corporation, to preserve the President's birthplace, promote the principles for which he stood, and preserve some memorabilia of his administration. Both of these institutions cooperated in the reconstruction of the blacksmith shop of Hoover's father.

In the late 1950s, the organizations merged as the Hoover Birthplace Foundation, Inc., and financed the construction of a Herbert Hoover Library-Museum in the 28-acre Hoover Park. In December 1960, when the building was still under construction, the Foundation offered the land and the building to the federal government for the purpose of creating a presidential archival depository in accordance with the provisions of the Presidential Libraries Act of 1955, which included former living presidents. On the same day, Hoover offered all papers of his public service career and related documents to the government under the same provisions, with the exception of the "war and peace" documents, which were to be retained at the Hoover Institution at Stanford University, where all his papers had been previously deposited. Congress authorized acceptance of the gifts in March 1962.

Hoover assisted in the selection of the library's site on a bank of the Wapinonoc Creek, across from his birthplace. When engineers determined that the site of his choice had been a riverbed in prehistoric times, and that the ground might not support the modern structure, Hoover insisted that no changes be made, because "nothing in my lifetime is to be higher than my birthplace."[1] The engineers found ways to anchor the building solidly in the ground with cement-filled steel pilings. Hoover also insisted on a local limestone for the outer facing of his buildings.

On August 10, 1962, the Herbert Hoover Library was dedicated, with former Presidents Hoover and Truman and Vice President Lyndon B. Johnson in attendance. Hoover gave an address in which he said:

> When members of Congress created these Presidential Libraries, they did a great public service. They made available for research the

records of vital periods in American history. Within them are the thrilling records of supreme action by the American people, their devotion and sacrifice to their ideals. Santayana rightly said: 'Those who do not remember the past are condemned to relive it.' These institutions are the repositories of such experience—hot off the griddle. In these records there are, no doubt, unfavorable remarks made by our political opponents, as well as expressions of appreciation and affection by our friends.[2]

Interestingly, he gave Congress credit for the creation of the presidential library system and did not even mention Presidents Roosevelt, Truman, and Eisenhower, without whose initiatives Hoover would not have been able to establish his own presidential library.

In 1964, the Hoover Birthplace Foundation deeded the property to the government, including the library, the Hoover birthplace cottage, the reconstructed blacksmith shop, the Hoover grave site, the first school in West Branch, and the Friends Meeting House. The General Services Administration transferred the grounds and buildings, except the library, to the Department of the Interior in 1971; the site is administered by the National Park Service as the Herbert Hoover National Historic Site. The Herbert Hoover Library and Museum remains under the jurisdiction of the National Archives. The original library and museum buildings cost about $2 million, contributed by the Foundation, which changed its name to the Hoover Presidential Library Association in 1972. Two additions to the Hoover Library building were made in 1970–71 and in 1973–74 by the government, at a cost of over $1 million.

RESEARCH MATERIALS IN THE HOOVER LIBRARY

In addition to the documents from Stanford, the library received in 1962 the papers and possessions of the President from his last residence at the Waldorf Astoria Towers in New York City. It has been said that Hoover actually welcomed the opportunity to take some of his materials out of Stanford. He had the feeling that his alma mater could no longer be entirely trusted because it had moved politically from a conservative Republican to a more moderate middle-of-the-road position.

The Hoover papers at West Branch number about 3.2 million pages and occupy almost 2,500 feet of shelf space. Copies of most of the major documents relating to World War I relief and reconstruction work, which are deposited at Stanford, are available at the Presidential library in West Branch. The library holds the personal papers of more than 90 individuals, including Hoover's cabinet members, Republican officials, family members, associates, members of Congress, politicians, and friends, as well as the papers of associations and organizations. The Hoover papers were opened to the public in 1966, two years after the President's death. Less than one percent of the deeded collections are under restrictions imposed by the donors and there are only a few security restricted materials. The privately funded oral history program, established in 1966, resulted in 319 interviews.

The holdings have been made accessible through finding aids, of which the registers are the most complete. Container lists are somewhat less detailed, but provide box-by-box and folder-by-folder organization of collections. Indexed materials are organized in bound volumes. Finding aids for the oral history transcripts consist of an individual index for each interview and a composite card index for the entire oral history collection. The following tabulations are based on *Historical Materials in the Herbert Hoover Presidential Library.*[3]

Manuscripts

The Papers of Herbert Hoover

Files	*Linear Feet*
Pre-Commerce Period (1895–1921)	78
Secretary of Commerce Period (1921–28)	385
Campaign and Transition Period (1928–29)	100
White House Files (1929–33)	
Cabinet Office	32
Subject File	155
Secretary's File	264
States File	11
Foreign Affairs	23
Individual Name Files	17
Other	106
Post-Presidential (1933–64)	
General Correspondence	131
Individual Correspondence	142
Subject File	196
Commissions on Organization of the Executive Branch of the Government (1947–49; 1953–55)	51

Donated Papers and Records

	Linear Feet
97 collections	2428

Federal Government Records

	Linear Feet
7 collections	66

Special Collections

Files	*Linear Feet*
Agricola Collection (1908–61)	7
Appointment Calendar (1901–64)	12
Articles, Addresses, and Public Statements (1892–1964)	260
Book Manuscript Material	46
Clipping File (1920–64)	214
Genealogy (1750–1964)	8

Hoover Scrapbooks (1866–1966)   1
Misrepresentations File (1917–61)   8
Reprint File (1853–   )   122

The Microfilm and Microfiche Collections

The library has a microfilm collection of historical materials held by other depositories or individuals. These include selected documents from 21 collections relating to Hoover; American and foreign newspapers covering the Hoover period; a collection of reels from the Department of State and the Department of Labor; selected papers supplementing the holdings of the Hoover Library, such as some papers of Presidents Harding and Coolidge, the Franklin D. Roosevelt-Winston Churchill messages, and related materials of Roosevelt and Churchill; and dissertations and theses that drew on the resources of the library.

Oral History Transcripts

The oral history transcripts supplement the written documents. Many of the interviewees are already represented at the Hoover Library through their papers, others are not. Significant interviewees include Joel T. Boone, Vice Admiral, U.S. Navy, physician of the President; Thomas E. Dewey; Dwight D. Eisenhower; James E. Farley, Chairman of the Democratic National Committee; Lyndon B. Johnson; Rose Fitzgerald Kennedy, whose husband, Joseph P. Kennedy, was a member of the Hoover Commission in 1947–49; and Ohio Senator Robert A. Taft.

Audiovisual Materials

The collection of photographs numbers close to 30,000 still pictures of Hoover, his family and boyhood, and other activities from his student days to his funeral. A photo card catalog provides quick access to the materials. The motion picture collection has over 150,000 feet of 16mm movies consisting of professional films and family home movies. The collection of sound recording has 14 hours of videotape, 227 hours of audiotape, and 70 audio discs. The recordings cover 65 Hoover addresses.

Printed Materials

The library has a collection of over 24,000 books, relating primarily to Hoover's life; new items are added as they appear. There is an extensive collection of periodical materials by or about Hoover, reference materials, theses and dissertations, and bound copies of the *London Times,* the *New York Times,* and the *West Branch Times.* Many of the books written by, belonging to, or dedicated to Hoover are stored in the library.

THE MUSEUM AREA

The Hoover Museum is part of the building that houses the library, and was dedicated on August 10, 1962, the 88th birthday of the President. The original building was 27,000 square feet; two additions were made in 1970–71 and 1973–74. The original part of the building is now almost completely taken up by the museum, while the additions form the main part of the library and its storage facilities. There is also a large auditorium where movies are frequently shown and conferences conducted.

Many of the more than 4,000 museum items are on display. The Hoover museum is arranged in the same manner as the Hoover papers: the "Early Years"; his activities as a mining engineer; his World War I relief activities; the years as secretary of commerce; the presidency, grouped around a replica of the Oval Office; and his post-presidential years. In the center of the main display area is an exhibit dedicated to the first lady and a space for special exhibits. Also on display are the many books and articles Hoover wrote, along with exhibits of federal activities he initiated, such as the Federal Bureau of Investigation, the Federal Power Commission, and the Reconstruction Finance Corporation. As in all presidential museums under the care of the Archives, there are displays of gifts the President received and some of the furniture he used in the Oval Office.

The Hoover Library and Museum provides a great variety of exhibits and public programs about Mr. Hoover's life. Films are shown at regular intervals during visiting hours. The Herbert Hoover Presidential Library Association, Inc. helps to support the library as a center for independent research. It offers annual research grants, ranging from $1,000 to $10,000 to scholars engaged in research dealing with the ideals and personal philosophy of Herbert Hoover, and with the Hoover era. It also sponsors conferences dealing with topics related to Hoover's concerns and interests, and helps to acquire necessary furnishings for the library. The Association commissioned the writing and publication of a Hoover biography; the first volume, *The Life of Herbert Hoover: The Engineer, 1874–1914,* written by George H. Nash, appeared in 1983.[4]

14. The Dwight D. Eisenhower Library in Abilene, Kansas

DWIGHT D. EISENHOWER
Thirty-fourth President—Republican
1953–1961

Dwight David Eisenhower was born in Denison, Texas, on October 14, 1890, and moved at the age of two with his parents to Abilene, Kansas, which he considered his home town. His father worked in a creamery and later in a gas plant. The family belonged to the River Brethren, a Protestant sect that abhorred violence, and the children were brought up in a strict, old-fashioned atmosphere. Dwight, the third of six boys, graduated from high school in 1909. The Eisenhower family could not afford to send him to college and he decided after a year of working in the creamery to apply for admission to West Point, where he graduated in 1915 as a second lieutenant. In 1916, he married Mamie Doud while stationed at Fort Sam Houston, Texas. He served at a tank training school in Pennsylvania, and in the Panama Canal Zone. In 1926, he was assigned to the Command and General Staff School in Leavenworth, Kansas, where he graduated first in a class of 275. As a result, he was appointed to the Army War College in Washington. His next assignment was with the American Battle Monuments Commission, which was under the command of General John Pershing. This assignment brought him also into contact with Col. George C. Marshall, who later helped him in his career during the Second World War. In the following years he was assigned to the staff of the assistant secretary of war as aide to Chief of Staff Douglas MacArthur. In 1934, he moved with MacArthur to the Philippines, where he stayed until 1938; in 1941, he was promoted to colonel and assigned as chief of staff of the Third Army stationed in San Antonio, Texas.

After the Japanese attack on Pearl Harbor, Chief of Staff General Marshall appointed him chief of the Operations Division of the War Department's General Staff, with the rank of major general; he developed plans for opening a "second front" in France and became commanding general of the European Theater of Operations. Eisenhower commanded the Allied landing in French North Africa in November 1942, and the invasions of Sicily and Italy in the summer of 1943. In December of the same year, President Roosevelt appointed him supreme commander, Allied Expeditionary Force, with the rank of full general. He planned and executed the Allied landings in Normandy in June 1944, which led to Germany's unconditional surrender in May 1945.

President Truman appointed Eisenhower chief of staff of the U.S. Army, a position he held until 1948 when he retired from military service to accept the presidency of Columbia University. During that period he wrote his personal account of World War II, *Crusade in Europe.*[1] Both Republicans and Democrats encouraged him to run for president of the United States, but he rejected all offers. When Leonard V. Finder, the publisher of the *Manchester Union-Leader* wrote him that a slate of delegates pledged to him would be entered in the 1948 New Hampshire primary, he responded: "Politics is a profession; a serious, complicated and, in its true sense, a noble one. In the American scene I see no dearth of men fitted by training, talent and integrity for national leadership. On the other hand, nothing in the international or domestic situation especially qualifies for the most important office in the world a man whose adult years have been spent in the country's military forces. At least this is true in my case."[2] In 1950, he accepted President Truman's appointment as supreme commander of NATO.

Eisenhower had never voted in national elections. When he was again approached about his availability as presidential candidate by both parties in 1952, he finally and reluctantly agreed to run as a Republican. New York Governor Thomas E. Dewey, who had been the 1944 and 1948 Republican presidential candidate, threw his support to Eisenhower, which led to his nomination. Eisenhower's war record, administrative competence, and promise during the election campaign to visit Korea to bring hostilities to a conclusion, gave him an electoral victory of 442 to 89 over Democrat Adlai E. Stevenson.

Eisenhower came into office a political novice, but gradually developed into a rather sophisticated politician. He was a liberal in international affairs and political relations, but a middle-of-the road conservative in domestic affairs and economics.[3] With his "Modern Republicanism" or "Dynamic Conservatism," as he called it, he supported development of the interstate highway system, and approved expansion of Social Security and an increase of the national minimum wage. In 1954, the Supreme Court, headed by middle-of-the-road Eisenhower appointee Earl Warren, ruled that compulsory segregation in public schools was unconstitutional. In 1957, Eisenhower sent federal troops to Little Rock, Arkansas, to protect black students when the first high school was integrated there. The Republican party as a whole did not adopt Eisenhower's liberal-conservative approach and lost control of Congress in 1954; Congress remained Democratic during both Eisenhower administrations, but the President worked well with liberal Democrats and won re-election in 1956 by an even wider margin than in 1952.

While successful at home, Eisenhower failed to reduce increasing tensions with the Soviet Union. He called on the United Nations to plan for peaceful uses of atomic energy, which resulted in the creation of the International Atomic Energy Commission. Just before the 1956 election, the USSR invaded Hungary, which had tried to free itself from Soviet domination and had appealed to the United States for help. A few days later, France, Great Britain, and Israel invaded Egypt to re-establish international control over the Suez Canal; the Eisenhower administration joined the Soviet Union in condemning this action and arranging a cease-fire. In 1957, Congress approved the "Eisenhower Doctrine," which authorized the President to use armed force to aid nations "requesting assistance against armed aggression from any country controlled by international communism."[4] As a result, the U.S. sent marines to Lebanon in 1958 to support its independence, and protected Chinese Nationalist ships against the threatened invasion of Formosa by Communist China. In 1959 Fidel Castro invaded Cuba and established a close cooperation with the Soviets. Eisenhower tried to ease tensions between the United States and the USSR by meeting with Premier Krushchev, but hopes for improved understanding were dashed when the Soviets shot down a U-2 plane and Eisenhower refused to apologize for the spy flights.

Eisenhower had three major medical emergencies during his presidency, but was always able to return to his duties. In his farewell address, he expressed his concern about not having sufficiently succeeded in "making progress with world wide disarmament and in reducing the bitterness of the East-West struggle." He also warned about the growing influence of America's expanding "military-industrial complex."[5] After the end of the second administration, the Eisenhowers retired to their farm in Gettysburg, Pennsylvania, which was the first permanent home they ever had. Eisenhower enjoyed the farm, remained active as an elder statesman, and worked on his memoirs, *The White House Years.*[6] He died of congestive heart failure on March 28, 1969, and was buried in Abilene, Kansas.

THE EISENHOWER CENTER IN ABILENE, KANSAS

Abilene is a small town on the grassy plains of Kansas, roughly midway between Kansas City and Denver. It was settled in the 1850s, and the Eisenhowers moved there in 1890. After General Eisenhower accepted the unconditional surrender of Germany in May 1945, his friends and admirers felt that the preservation of his home would be an appropriate reminder of his accomplishments. Under the leadership of Charles M. Harger, editor of the *Abilene Reflector-Chronicle* and an old friend of the family, and Albert Reed, a New York artist, the Eisenhower Foundation was established to honor Eisenhower's wartime service and the United States Armed Forces. In 1946, after the death of Ida Stover Eisenhower, the general's mother, her sons gave the home to the Eisenhower Foundation. The simple frame structure had been occupied by the family from 1898 until 1946, and was opened to the public in 1947.

The Foundation then began to raise money for a museum. Aiming to gain a national image in its fund-raising campaign, its executive committee decided to conduct the campaign without respect to race, creed, color, or politics, and "to invite the following to accept membership on this committee: a Catholic Bishop, a prominent Jewish person, a prominent Negro, a prominent woman in the State and heads of state organizations, such as the American Legion, Veterans of Foreign Wars, Daughters of the American Revolution, teacher's associations."[7] The museum was built next to the home in 1952, dedicated and first expanded in 1954; it was renovated and enlarged a second time in 1971. On November 11, 1954, during the dedication of the museum, Eisenhower said: "Tremendous satisfaction comes from knowing that your neighbors and your old friends. . . have been so helpful to you during your life—indeed, let me remark, there is present today a gentleman who way back in 1910, 44 years ago, was one of those who worked so hard to allow me to embark on a military career; I should like to take advantage of this digression to thank personally Mr. Harger for all he did for me in those days."[8]

In 1954, the Foundation began to plan the construction of the library to contain the Eisenhower papers. In March 1954, Eisenhower wrote Emmett S. Graham, the secretary of the Foundation:

> In order to fulfill the Trustees' purpose of constructing the library, and providing for management of it under the supervision of the Archivist of the United States, it will be necessary to develop detailed arrangements with appropriate Federal officials . . . and authorization by Congress will be requisite. I appreciate the desire of the Trustees, before proceeding further, to have now a definite indication that the proposal meet with my approval. . . . It does, for it seems to me the most desirable method for preserving papers closely associated with the history of our Nation and insuring that successive categories of them will become available for study at appropriate intervals.[9]

A 1954 memo from the National Archives states:

> Arrangements for ultimate deposit of Presidential papers ought to be made at the earliest possible time and certainly before the President leaves office. . . early determination is desirable to allow completion of construction prior to end of term. . . a timely decision provides the greatest insurance against later dispersal, loss, misuse, or destruction of the papers. . . . The Abilene Foundation has plans under way for constructing a library in the hope that the President's papers will be entrusted to it under an arrangement with the National Archives, whereby the latter would be responsible for supervision and management . . . . Congressional approval would be necessary for making a connection with the National Archives. Congress did so approve the Hyde Park arrangement, but has still to act on the Truman proposal if and when the library is built.[10]

In 1955, passage of the Presidential Libraries Act opened the way for the development of the library. Through cooperation of members of the Eisenhower Foundation with the governor and the Kansas legislature, the Eisenhower Presidential Library Commission, co-chaired by Governor George Docking and former Kansas Senator Harry Darby, was established to raise funds for the project. The funds came from thousands of contributors across the country; the campaign was a bipartisan effort, personally supported by retired President Harry S. Truman. In 1957, the State of Kansas appropriated $275,000 for the acquisition of the land adjacent to and south of the museum upon which the library would be built, and the state architect, in cooperation with the General Services Administration, began to make preliminary plans for the building. With individual contributions and additional Kansas state appropriations, expenditures for the library building amounted to about $3 million.

The groundbreaking ceremonies took place on October 14, 1959, the President's 69th birthday. In April 1960, the Eisenhower Presidential Library Commission offered the land and building to the government. At the same time, the President offered his papers and other documentary materials to the government, conditioned upon the government's acceptance of the building and land, and its agreement to maintain the property permanently as a presidential archival depository. During the hearings before the Government Activities Subcommittee of the Committee of Government Operations, Chairman Jack Brooks summarized the subcommittee's bipartisan support by stating on April 28, 1960, "Posterity will reap rich benefits from the treasury of presidential information this library will contain. What a wonderful thing it would be if libraries such as this had been established all the way back down the long line of our Presidents immediately upon expiration of their terms of office."[11]

Early in 1961, the Eisenhower papers were moved directly from the White House to Kansas. The first professional archivists arrived at the library building in February 1961. The small staff had to sort and arrange about 11 million pages of manuscripts, as well as photographs and recordings. Fifteen months later, on May 1, 1962, the library was dedicated, with Vice President Lyndon B. Johnson representing the Kennedy administration.

Funds were also raised to construct a nondenominational chapel, "The Place of Meditation," on the Eisenhower Center grounds, as the final resting place for President and Mrs. Eisenhower. The Eisenhower's first-born son, Doud Dwight, who died in infancy and was originally buried in the Doud family plot in Denver, was also interred there. In 1965, Eisenhower wrote to William E. Robinson, a personal friend, vice chairman of the fund-raising committee, and president of Coca-Cola, Inc.: "I was most appreciative of my friends' refusal to employ me in any fashion on the firing line of fund raising. The only work I have ever done in this was to write personal notes of thanks to friends and a few others who have helped the construction of the Meditation Chapel. As soon as I left the Presidency, Mamie and I made an immediate contribution. . . to help in building the Chapel."[12] From 1962 to 1966, the Eisenhower Center operated on a two-track system that put the library under the jurisdiction of the National Archives, while the Eisenhower Home and Museum continued under the Foundation. In 1966, when Dr. John A. Wickman was appointed director of the Eisenhower Library, the Eisenhower Museum and Home, and the Meditation Chapel were deeded to the government, and the four existing buildings came under the management of the National Archives. An addition to the museum was constructed by the government in 1971; the Visitors' Center, containing a sales desk and a large auditorium, was added in 1975.

The library and museum buildings are constructed of native limestone. The two simple modern buildings face each other on a large and impressive mall. The walls of the lobby and corridors of the library are made of bookmatched Loredo Chiaro marble from Italy and the floors in the public areas are Roman travertine trimmed with French marble. In addition to a reading room for researchers, and storage areas for documents, books, and audiovisual materials, the building has a well equipped photographic laboratory, a 165 seat auditorium, areas for exhibits, and work rooms for the staff.

RESEARCH MATERIALS IN THE EISENHOWER LIBRARY

In November 1960, shortly before the end of the second Eisenhower term, a one-page memorandum from Wilton B. Persons, assistant to the President, gave the White House staff guidelines on how to deal with office files at the end of the administration. Purely personal correspondence, books, pamphlets, and periodicals were considered personal property to be taken away by the individual. All records and copies of records having to do with the official business of the office, all diaries recording activities incident to the office, and all documents pertaining to government business were considered property of the President and were to be turned over for transmission to the Eisenhower Library.[13]

The manuscript collection of the Eisenhower Library consists of 19.5 million pages of documents relating to all activities of Eisenhower's military, political, and educational careers. The collection also includes the papers of the first lady and their son, and those of the President's commissions and committees, related private organizations, and of many of his associates and friends. The following tabulations and descriptions are based on *Historical Materials in the Dwight D. Eisenhower Library*[14] and on interviews with the library staff.

Manuscripts

The Papers of Dwight D. Eisenhower

Files	Linear Feet
Pre-Presidential (1916–52)	138
White House Central Files (1953–61)	3,241
WHCF Official (766,000 pages)	
WHCF General (1,050,000 pages)	
WHCF Presidential Personal (790,000 pages)	
WHCF Confidential (100,000 pages)	
WHCF Pre-Inaugural (20,000 pages)	
WHCF Alphabetical (3,000,000 pages)	
Other (800,000 pages)	
Ann Whitman File (Papers as President 1953–61)	135
White House Office Records	
Budget and Accounting	30
Official Reporter	24
Press Secretary	10
National Security Council Staff/Affairs	179
Social Office Records	342
Daily Appointments	13
Other	332
Personal	24
Post-Presidential (1961–69)	935

Donated Papers and Records

	Linear Feet/ Microfilm Reels
274 collections	3213/65

Federal Government Records

	Linear Feet/ Microfilm Reels
28 collections	414/3

U.S. Military Records

	Linear Feet/ Microfilm Reels
23 collections	1137/631

The papers as president of the United States, in the Ann Whitman File, constitute the richest historical collection in the Dwight D. Eisenhower Library. These are the President's office files, maintained during his administration by Ann Whitman, his personal secretary. The documents in this collection, totalling approximately 274,000 pages, include correspondence and memoranda of conversations with heads of state, government officials, friends, and associates, as well as correspondence, memoranda, agenda, press releases, and reports and other materials documenting the foreign and domestic policies of the Eisenhower administration, the political activities of the President and his associates, and the President's personal affairs.

At the close of the Eisenhower administration, these materials were shipped to Gettysburg, Pennsylvania, where Eisenhower used them in preparing his presidential memoirs, *The White House Years.* Following Eisenhower's death in 1969, the papers were transferred to the Eisenhower Library. Six series, constituting approximately 50 percent of the collection, were made available for research in May 1975; by March 1983, the 12 remaining series in the collection had been processed and opened to scholars, although portions remain closed in keeping with donor restrictions or government regulations.

One series, the National Security Council (NSC) series, has only been partially processed; small portions have been declassified and are now available for research. A rudimentary finding aid has been prepared in order to facilitate mandatory review requests for classified documents in this series. The NSC series consists primarily of NSC records of actions and summaries of NSC discussions. Most other types of NSC-related materials are contained in the records of the Office of the Special Assistant for National Security Affairs, a body of records which are part of the library's holding but which are not included in Dwight D. Eisenhower's papers as president.

Finding aids have been prepared for each series. These vary considerably in size and detail. Some consist of unannotated container (folder title) lists; but the container lists for most of the series have extensive annotations indicating the subjects documented by the folder. Several of the finding aids also have scope and content notes which give an overview of the series.

The White House Central Files, 1953–61, comprise the largest collection in the library, totalling approximately 6 million pages. All of the major foreign and domestic issues and policies associated with the Eisenhower administration, as well as the political events of the period, are documented by the Central Files. By 1987, approximately 2 million pages of the Central Files had been processed. Available for research at this time are the Confidential File (CF), the Official File (OF), 80 percent of the General File (GF), and 50 percent of the President's Personal File (PPF). The unprocessed portions of the General File and the President's Personal File largely pertain to subjects of marginal historical value, such as message requests from organizations, public requests for photographs, birthday congratulations, and invitations.

The Microfilm Collection

This collection consists of 21 items containing sets of papers and documents deposited in locations outside the Eisenhower Library and microfilmed to complement the resources of the library. Twelve of these collections relate to military units; most of the originals are deposited in the Modern Military Records Division of the National Archives.

Oral History Transcripts

Based on interviews with close associates, friends, and staff of Eisenhower, this project was started by the Oral History Office of Columbia University. Since 1966 the Eisenhower Library has continued it in combination with its collection of manuscripts. During the last 20 years, the interviews have been conducted by the library's staff. The collection consists of over 500 transcripts; among well-known interviewees are Sherman Adams, President Eisenhower's chief of staff; Joseph Alsop, news correspondent; Ezra Taft Benson, secretary of agriculture; Charles Bohlen, U.S. ambassador to the Soviet Union; Robert Bolton, acting director of the Eisenhower Library 1961–63; and Wilbur Cohen, secretary of health, education and welfare during the Johnson administration. President Eisenhower gave four interviews, one of which was still closed in 1987; Generals Jacob L. Devers and James M. Gavin gave interviews, as did Andrew Goodpaster, Eisenhower's staff secretary from 1954–61, and Barry Goldwater, U.S. Senator from Arizona and Republican presidential candidate. James C. Hagerty, the President's secretary, provided one of the longest interviews—572 printed pages. The interview of James R. Killian, the President's science advisor, and the 881-page interview with Clifford Roberts, a close personal friend of the President, are closed to the public.

The Printed Materials Collection

The library book collection contains approximately 24,000 titles relating primarily to the period of Eisenhower's life. There are approximately 23,000 items from periodicals in the vertical files, and a large number of microfilmed dissertations and theses. In 1981, the library published *Dwight D. Eisenhower: A Select Bibliography of Periodical and Dissertation Literature.*[15]

The Audiovisual Collection

This collection covers the period 1944 to the late 1960s and consists of over 202,000 still photographs, over 500 16mm motion picture films, 75 35mm motion picture films, five 8mm motion picture films, and over 2,100 audio discs and tapes. The materials have been received from private individuals, organizations, and government agencies. Six hundred thousand feet of original and 365,000 feet of duplicate motion picture film primarily cover the presidential years; most of this film was given to the President by the Columbia Broadcasting System. Among the documentaries is the film version of Eisenhower's book, "Crusade in Europe," which is shown regularly at the Visitor's Center.

THE EISENHOWER MUSEUM

The museum's 30,000 square feet are used for the display and storage of over 25,000 items. As one enters the lobby, one is attracted by a mural presenting sketches of various military events of the Second World War in Europe. Having shared the experience of wading ashore on the Normandy beaches and entering into abandoned small French towns, the mural, while not great art, made an unforgettable impression on this author. The exhibits illustrate in pictures, paintings, displays, documents, and objects the President's careers as military, academic, and political leader. The exhibits are mostly permanent with the exception of a few areas set aside for temporary displays, such as an exhibit of quilts made by the President's mother.

The Introductory Gallery provides pictures of the Eisenhower family and documents of the President's life through high school. The Early Military Career Gallery and the World War II Area display uniforms, photographs, paintings, and memorabilia relating to West Point and the many military posts at which Eisenhower served at home and abroad, including the four years spent in the Philippines on General MacArthur's staff. The General's career as commander of the European Theater of Operations from the invasion of Normandy to V-E day is depicted, including Eisenhower's first handwritten report noting the end of the war: "The mission of this Allied Force was fulfilled at 3.00 a.m., local time, May 7, 1945. Eisenhower." The Military Hall exhibits a collection of small arms and military service flags, military vehicles, and weapons used during World War II, including the General's staff car. There is an exhibit of the awards, medals, and orders given to Eisenhower during and after the war.

The White House Years display documents of the President's Korean trip, and the replaying of TV press conferences gives immediacy that no other medium could accomplish. Several of the paintings that hung in the Oval Office are also on display. A collection of campaign objects consisting of posters, clothing, buttons, and other items, reminds the viewer of Eisenhower's two presidential campaigns. There is a replica of his post-presidential office, which was located on the campus of Gettysburg College. The Gifts to the President Gallery exhibits gifts from American admirers and foreign dignitaries. Great care has been used to preserve a wide array of the first lady's gowns and jewelry, and items used by the Eisenhowers throughout life, many of them from their retirement home in Gettysburg. These items are exhibited in the Mamie Doud Eisenhower Gallery. An extensive collection of political cartoons gives a lighter touch to the exhibits.

THE EDUCATIONAL PROGRAMS AT THE LIBRARY

The Eisenhower Foundation, from the very beginning, stressed the importance of the Eisenhower Center as a major research and educational resource. The Foundation publishes a quarterly newsletter *Overview*, which highlights events in Eisenhower's life and in military history. In 1966, a conference program to inform the public and the academic community of the resources available in the library was begun. Conferences on museum work were held in 1968 and 1969. Also in 1969, a conference on Western history was given that developed into a continuing biennial arrangement. The same year a two-day conference on the 25th anniversary of D-Day was held; the papers from this conference were published in 1970 as *D-Day: Normandy Invasion in Retrospect*, by the University of Kansas Foundation Press.[16]

15. The John F. Kennedy Library in Boston, Massachusetts

JOHN F. KENNEDY
Thirty-fifth President—Democrat
1961–1963

John Fitzgerald Kennedy was born on May 29, 1917, in Brookline, Massachusetts, the second of nine children of Joseph and Rose Kennedy. The son of wealthy parents and the grandson of a mayor of Boston, he was educated in private schools and graduated from Harvard University in 1940 with honors in economics and political science. His thesis, dealing with French and British appeasement of Germany prior to World War II, was published under the title *Why England Slept,*[1] and became a bestseller. He briefly attended the graduate business school at Stanford University and tried to enlist in the army in 1941, but was rejected because of a back injury that plagued him throughout his life. Strenuous exercise allowed him to pass his Navy physical examination, and he was assigned to PT boat training. He received a commission as lieutenant (j.g.) and was given command of a torpedo boat in the South Pacific. Attacked by a Japanese destroyer, he and his crew clung for days to their wrecked boat and were eventually rescued by natives. After months of painful back operations and malaria attacks, he was discharged from the service in 1945.

As reporter for the Hearst papers, Kennedy covered the United Nations organizational meeting in San Francisco and then worked for a while as a reporter in England. In 1946, he decided to enter politics and campaigned for the Democratic nomination to Congress from Boston's eleventh district. His family assisted him with unparalleled enthusiasm and unlimited funds. Kennedy won the primary election against nine contenders and easily defeated his Republican opponent in November. He was re-elected to the House in 1948 and 1950; in 1952, he was elected to the U.S. Senate. The following year he married Jacqueline Lee Bouvier. While recovering from back surgery in 1954, he wrote *Profiles in Courage,*[2] a bestseller and Pulitzer Prize winner.

Despite his very conservative father, Congressman Kennedy supported most of Truman's "Fair Deal" policies, and introduced bills for slum clearance, housing, and federal aid for public and private education. In foreign policy, he was less supportive of Truman, criticizing the loss of China to the Communists, the reduction of U.S. forces in Europe during the Korean War, and the large amounts spent on foreign aid. Regarding the two major issues of the time, McCarthyism and the Communist threat, he never came to grips with the first issue, but lined up with others in Congress against Soviet expansion, accusing Eisenhower of allowing a missile gap by ignoring accelerated Soviet production of intercontinental missiles.

Kennedy placed Adlai Stevenson in nomination at the Democratic convention in 1956 and made an effort to win the vice presidential nomination, but was defeated by Tennessee Senator Estes Kefauver. He was re-elected to the Senate in 1958 and spent the next two years, assisted again by his family and friends, seeking the presidential nomination. He defeated first his major Democratic challenger, Senator Hubert Humphrey, and then his Republican opponent, Vice President Richard Nixon. In four television debates with Nixon, he clearly established his agenda, including the expansion of civil rights legislation and an enlarged social security program, while Nixon was forced to defend the Eisenhower record. It was the first time that the American electorate was able to see and hear both candidates face to face on television. Kennedy's youth, speaking ability, and charisma were all in his favor and helped him to win the election by the very narrow margin of 118,550 votes. At the age of 43, he became the youngest elected president, the first one born in the twentieth century, and the first Catholic president.

Kennedy had a way with words. Those who stood in the freezing cold of his inaugural will remember especially these:

> Let the word go forth from this time and place to friend and foe alike, that the torch has been passed to a new generation of Americans, born in this century, tempered by war, disciplined by hard and bitter peace, proud of our ancient heritage, and unwilling to witness or permit the slow undoing of those human rights to which this nation has always been committed. . . . Let every nation know, whether it wishes us well or ill, that we shall pay any price, bear any burden, meet any hardship, support any friend, oppose any foe to assure the survival and the success of liberty. . . . And so, my fellow Americans, ask not what your country can do for you; ask what you can do for your country.[3]

After his victory, Kennedy assembled a young staff under a banner of new ideas, hopes, and challenges called the "New Frontier." He recommended the establishment of the Peace Corps to bring American know-how to Third World countries, and the Alliance for Progress, a foreign aid program for Latin America. Few presidents had created a more enthusiastic and innovative staff; few had more candidly expressed ideas or conveyed such a feeling of youth or the need for change.

Kennedy's biggest challenge was his support of the invasion of Cuban exiles on April 17, 1961, to unseat Fidel Castro. The landing at the Bay of Pigs ended in disaster; Kennedy took full responsibility, although Eisenhower and the CIA had planned the coup prior to his becoming president. "Victory has a hundred fathers," he wrily observed, "but defeat is an orphan."[4] In April 1961, when the Soviet Union sent the first astronaut into space, Kennedy promised that America would land on the moon within the next decade, which promise was redeemed during the Nixon administration.

Relations with the Soviet Union continued to deteriorate in spite of a Kennedy-Khrushchev summit in Vienna, and the Communists erected the Berlin Wall in August 1961 to prevent the escape of East Berliners to the West. Kennedy called the wall "the most obvious and vivid demonstration of the failures of the Communist system."[5] Fidel Castro aligned Cuba with the Soviet Union and Red China; in October 1962, when aerial photographs showed that Soviet missiles capable of launching nuclear attacks on the U.S. or other Latin American countries had been installed in Cuba, Kennedy responded with a blockade of Cuba and the request that the Soviets dismantle the base and remove the missiles. When Khrushchev complied, the threat of war was averted. Within a short time, the Soviet Union started again to test nuclear weapons in the atmosphere in spite of the unofficial understanding with Eisenhower to end such tests. Kennedy was forced to resume U.S. testing, but initiated at the same time talks with the Soviets that led to the signing in 1963 of a treaty banning nuclear tests in the earth's atmosphere.

In spite of his personal popularity, the domestic policies of the Kennedy administration had mixed success. At the end of the first session of the 88th Congress, only 37 of Kennedy's 405 legislative requests had passed.[6] The minimum hourly wage was raised somewhat, tariffs were lowered, and defense spending was increased. However, Kennedy's requests for improved civil rights measures, increased federal aid for education, and medical care for the aged were stalled by a Congress with a large contingent of conservatives on both sides of the aisle. The drive to uphold the civil rights of black citizens to ride on buses, to integrate public schools, and to enroll in public universities continued. Federal troops were sent to Montgomery, Alabama, and the University of Mississippi to assure these rights. On November 22, 1963, while on a speaking tour in Dallas, Texas, Kennedy was assassinated by Lee Harvey Oswald, a former marine and confessed Communist. The details of the assassination are still not clear and may never be known, because Oswald was murdered two days later in jail by a Dallas night club owner. Kennedy did not have enough time in office to provide the country with a full record on which to judge his performance, but "he brought to all sectors of the American public a new feeling that they were wanted, that there was a place in America for them—regardless of religion or race."[7]

THE ESTABLISHMENT OF THE JOHN F. KENNEDY LIBRARY

John F. Kennedy was the first president under whose administration the provisions of the Presidential Library Act of 1955 were in effect. On December 19, 1960, U.S. Archivist Wayne C. Grover offered the president-elect the services of the Archives to securely store his pre-presidential papers and related materials such as "books, audiovisual materials, and personal mementoes which are not scheduled for transfer to the White House." He enclosed a copy of the Presidential Libraries Act and two articles "setting forth the background, purposes, and advantages of such institutions to the President, the Government, and the world of scholarship." He assured him that if he decided to leave these papers and mementos in the care of the Archives, it would not obligate him towards their ultimate disposition.[8] Within a week of the inauguration, Kennedy's pre-presidential papers were transferred to the National Archives.

Very early in the administration, the question of a library location was brought up by the White House. Even before the inauguration, Nathan M. Pusey, the president of Harvard University, and Paul H. Buck, librarian of Harvard College, had agreed that Harvard would be the appropriate place to locate the Kennedy papers.[9] Buck described the project to Arthur Schlesinger, Jr. in February 1961:

> The prospect of Harvard acquiring the President's papers is indeed exciting. . . . However, much would be involved. We should have a new building, close to the Widener Library. . . . Money would have to be raised to build and to maintain it. (This should not be difficult. Certainly the friends of Eisenhower, Hoover, and Truman came through readily and liberally to build their libraries) . . . . The first step is to inform Pusey of the possibility and of its proportions, and then get clearance from the Corporation to proceed. It is not too early to begin. I have an appointment in early March with Pusey to discuss the matter.[10]

In March, Pusey wrote to the President:

> Although it is yet perhaps too early in your administration, I venture to raise with you at this time the question of eventual disposition of your presidential, political and personal papers and those of others in your administration. I do this not only to express the hope that you may think of Cambridge as an unusually appropriate place, but also to tell you of the University's earnest interest and eagerness to have them deposited in close proximity to the Harvard University Library. . . . It seems unusually advantageous to the scholarly world to have your archives located in the Boston-Cambridge area, which is already a focal point for scholarship regarding the Adams family and that of Theodore Roosevelt. There will, of course, be many questions to be settled concerning the precise location, the financing, and the staffing of a Kennedy Library, but I am sure they are not insurmountable. . . . I have the warm endorsement of the Corporation and others here in presenting this idea for your consideration.[11]

In May, Kennedy answered: "While I have made no final decision about the eventual disposition of my papers, I am much attracted by the thought of a repository established in association with Harvard and I would welcome the opportunity for further discussion of this idea with you."[12]

In June 1961, when Pusey visited him in Washington, Kennedy mentioned that he was also thinking about other places for the library, such as Hyannis Port or Palm Beach, but in December 1961, the White House announced that President Kennedy would build his presidential library, consisting of a museum and archives, in Cambridge, Massachusetts. General Services Administrator Bernard Boutin recalled that

> President Kennedy had an immense interest in these libraries because he had such a great interest in history and high regard for the office of President. He planned his library almost from the day of election. Shortly after the Inauguration he started to talk to us about what he visualized his library would be. He sent a memorandum to the heads of all agencies telling them to preserve all of their records so that they

would be available for study at the library in perpetuity by students of history. . . . He visualized his library as. . . a place where he would work after he left the Presidency. He had a great love for Harvard University.[13]

On Pusey's suggestion, Kennedy asked his special assistants, Theodore Sorenson and Arthur Schlesinger, Jr., and representatives of the National Archives to work with Pusey's representatives on plans for the library. Schlesinger remained the coordinator of these efforts even after the President's death. In order to acquire as complete a collection of records of the Kennedy years as possible, Schlesinger sent letters to cabinet officers and heads of agencies to deposit their personal files in the library at the close of the administration. He asked them to include personal notes, appointment books, pictures, press releases, articles, and books and pamphlets written about or by them.[14] Meetings were held by the Archivist to inform the representatives of the heads of the major departments and agencies about plans for the JFK Library, to encourage the heads of these agencies to deposit their papers and related materials in the library, and to begin to assemble microfilm or other copies of selected official reports.

In 1963, Grover and Boutin went to Massachusetts and selected three or four sites for the President to inspect. The President personally selected the location for his library only about two months prior to the assassination. This was going to be the location of his office as well as the library of his presidency; he wanted it linked to Harvard because he planned to teach after his retirement from the presidency. The chosen site was a 12-acre area on the Charles River, just outside Harvard Square, occupied by the Metropolitan Boston Transit Authority (MBTA) repair and storage yards. When he found out that the MBTA had no intention of giving up the site, he agreed to a two-acre location in Brighton near the Harvard Business School. A few days later this selection was formalized and Harvard agreed to donate the land.

Pusey recalled that "the situation changed sharply after the assassination because all the people close to him felt that to have just another presidential library would not be adequate. We all wanted a more unique memorial for him in connection with his presidential library. Very early the idea arose of adding some kind of educational institution."[15] On December 5, 1963, the President John F. Kennedy Memorial Library was incorporated, with Robert F. Kennedy as president. The Library Corporation raised a total of $18 million from an estimated 30 million people from all over the world, and selected architect I. M. Pei to design the building. Hopes were high that the building could be completed within two to three years.[16]

Late in December 1963, Herman Kahn, the assistant archivist for presidential libraries; Richard Neustadt, an outstanding Harvard historian; and Senator Edward Kennedy presented detailed plans for the Kennedy Memorial and Library to Schlesinger. Richard Neustadt suggested that the Kennedy-Fitzgerald saga in American life and politics would make a good theme for the museum, and that educational ventures addressed to the general public should be planned as part of the museum. He also suggested that an institute for advanced study, patterned on the model of the "Think Tanks" at Stanford and Princeton Universities, and/or an institute of politics in which practicing politicians would teach and inspire young people to devote their lives to elective public service be incorporated in the library plans.[17] Edward Kennedy stressed that first priority should be given to the memorial itself: ". . .an impressive and beautiful building rising from the banks of the Charles, with a series of visual and aural displays that will make it one of the outstanding attractions of New England."[18]

The only site in Cambridge that could possibly accommodate the Kennedy library and memorial, as its goals were envisioned at that time, was the MBTA car barn because the area near the Business School was too small. In 1965, the Commonwealth of Massachusetts purchased the major portion of the land from the MBTA and turned it over to the federal government for the library; the Library Corporation bought the remaining portion for the proposed institute of politics. In 1966, Harvard announced the creation of the John Fitzgerald Kennedy School of Government, comprising all schools of government and political science plus the Library Institute of Politics, all to be eventually situated on the library site.

However, the MBTA was unable to find an alternate site for its car barn until 1970, when an agreement was reached with the Pennsylvania Central Railroad to move the facility to the Dover Yards in Boston. The site was finally cleared in 1973 and architectural plans for the library were announced. In the meantime, residents in the nearby communities began to oppose the plans on account of traffic problems that would be created by museum visitors. Suggestions were made to locate the archives in Cambridge but to move the museum elsewhere. Considerable controversy centered on whether the memorial should be structured with the museum for the general public dominating, or whether it should be primarily a center for research and scholarship serving the intellectual community. The National Archives strongly resisted the idea of separating the museum and the archives because the kind of program it had planned could not be implemented under these conditions. Because a negative environmental impact study prepared for the General Services Administration would have opened the way for lengthy litigation, the Library Corporation announced in February 1975 that it would abandon its plans to build the library and museum in Cambridge.

As soon as the announcement was made, numerous offers for library sites were made, eventually reaching 175; by November 1975, the Corporation had evaluated all of them and decided on locating the library on the Boston campus of the University of Massachusetts. The Commonwealth of Massachusetts took back the Cambridge land and donated 12 acres at the tip of Columbia Point on Dorchester Bay, an area that has developed into a Boston landmark as the site of the University of Massachusetts-Boston, the Massachusetts Archives, and the Kennedy Library. The recent history of Columbia Point was less distinguished; it had been a prison camp, a garbage dump, and finally a crime-ridden public housing project. Dorchester was first settled in 1630 by Puritan settlers. It was eventually absorbed by Boston and became a prosperous Irish-American neighborhood. The Fitzgerald family had a house in the

Ashmont section of Dorchester where the President's mother grew up. The spectacular view of downtown Boston and the sea particularly appealed to Jacqueline Kennedy Onassis, and to Senator Edward Kennedy, who said at the ground breaking ceremonies in 1977: "Jack's library and this site were made for each other."[19]

THE KENNEDY LIBRARY BUILDING

The library building, which was dedicated and opened to the public in October 1979, is the result of architect I.M. Pei's fifth design. It is a stunning structure of white concrete and black glass that rises 110 feet into the sky, standing on a bluff at the water's edge; while it rises from the Dorchester Bay rather than the banks of the Charles River, it does fulfill Edward Kennedy's plans for a memorial that is "one of the outstanding attractions of New England and . . . serves as a vivid reminder of John F. Kennedy and his career to present generations and those to come."[20] At first glance it appears as a combination of three geometric shapes: a dark square, the pavilion; a stark white triangle, the archives structure; and a white circle, the two theaters. The building area is 115,000 square feet; the ticketing and information lobby on the entrance level opens into the theater area. A 30-minute film, "John F. Kennedy, 1917–1963," produced by Charles Guggenheim, is shown at 20-minute intervals in the two auditoriums. The theaters exit into the extensive museum area on the lower level, beautifully designed by Chermayeff and Geismar Associates. The exhibits terminate on the bottom of the 10-story, $70'' \times 70''$ pavilion, made of darkened glass. There are no exhibits in the pavilion, just the view of Boston, the sea and the sky, and a huge American flag hanging above. Outside the pavilion, almost casually set on the ground as if heading out to sea, is JFK's sailboat "Victura," possibly reminding visitors of an interrupted voyage into the future. The archives, reading room, and administrative offices are located in the tower, with windows looking out at the pavilion and the panorama beyond its window walls. The building is set in a beautifully landscaped park with a walkway that follows the shoreline.

RESEARCH MATERIALS IN THE KENNEDY LIBRARY

The Kennedy presidency was the first in which, from the beginning, the National Archives staff was actively engaged in the arrangement, preparation, and preservation of the Presidential records in cooperation with the White House staff. During 1962, the staff began to arrange John Kennedy's pre-presidential papers. Bibliographies of the papers, and of articles, books, and statements relating to the President, his associates, and his administration were compiled. A collection of gifts to the President was packaged and indexed, and the papers were boxed in labelled archives containers and shelf lists were prepared. The same treatment was given the records of the Democratic National Committee, which date chiefly from 1952–60. A file of the names and biographical data of associates of the President, in and out of government, was developed and maintained, to be used in soliciting papers for the library.[21]

President Kennedy's papers and related historical materials form the core of the holdings of the Kennedy Library. They were donated to the government in February 1965 by Jacqueline, Robert, and Edward Kennedy, the trustees of the President's estate. In 1966, the National Archives moved the materials for the library to the Federal Records Center in Waltham, Massachusetts, to be stored there until the construction and opening of the building. The records and objects were cataloged. The oral history program, which started in 1964 with a Carnegie grant at Columbia University as a volunteer effort, was taken over by the professional staff. As the building of the library was postponed from year to year, the Waltham operation grew and the Kennedy Library was actually established in these temporary quarters in October 1969, where it remained for 10 years, until the Columbia Point building was ready for occupancy. The first papers and oral histories were opened for research use in 1970. In 1971, Dan H. Fenn, a Boston native and graduate of Harvard College, who was a staff assistant to President Kennedy from 1961 to 1963, a member of the United States Tariff Commission, and a teacher at Harvard Business School, became director of the library.

In addition to some 11 million John F. Kennedy documents, the manuscript collection includes 180 donated document collections from Kennedy associates. The Robert F. Kennedy materials form the second largest collection in the library, consisting of 2 million pages of documents, an oral history project focusing on his life and career, still photographs, motion pictures, and sound recording and museum objects. The papers of author Ernest Hemingway, 40,000 pages of manuscripts, 1,100 letters, and scrapbooks and photographs, were deposited in the library by special arrangement between the widows of the two men, Jacqueline Kennedy and Mary Hemingway. Some portions of the manuscript collections and the oral history interviews are still closed due to security and personal donor restrictions. The library does not permit access to collections that have not yet been processed by the library staff. The following tabulations and descriptions are based on *Historical Materials in the John Fitzgerald Kennedy Library* [22] and interviews with the library archivists.

Manuscripts

The Papers of John F. Kennedy

Files	Linear Feet/ Microfilm Reels
House of Representatives (1947–52)	39
Campaign (1946–58)	10
Senatorial (1953–60)	321
Campaign (1960)	55
Transition	5
White House Central Files (1961–63)	
WHCF Subject	440
WHCF Name	1247

WHCF Chronological File	8
WHCF Security Classified	30
White House Files	
Social Files	491
Office Files	73
Staff Files	559
Bureau of the Budget Bill Report	15
National Security Files	153
Other Presidential Files	438
Personal Papers	20/5
Papers of the Post-Assassination Period (1963–74)	1570

Donated Papers and Records

	Linear Feet/ Microfilm Reels
180 collections	7887/439

Federal Government Records

	Linear Feet/ Microfilm Reels
53 collections	261/1971

Oral History Interviews

The collection totals more than 1,100 interviews with government officials, Kennedy family members and friends, artists, journalists, educators, diplomats, and others whose recollections of events are likely to be of interest to researchers who use the Kennedy Library. The interviews with Robert F. Kennedy cover over 1,000 pages, portions of which are closed. The interviews are available on tape and as transcriptions. There are detailed indexes to the transcriptions. Researchers using the oral history collection are encouraged to donate a copy of resulting books, articles, or dissertations to make the library's printed materials collection as comprehensive as possible.

Printed Materials

The printed materials collection is a special library of published and unpublished materials relating to mid-twentieth-century American history, politics, and government, centering on the life and career of President Kennedy. It contains some 15,000 books, theses, dissertations, government publications, periodicals, clippings, and microform materials and serves as the foremost bibliographic center for Kennedy studies. The books are cataloged by a special adaptation of the Library of Congress catalog system, and are shelved in the research room. A detailed dictionary card catalog and a number of reading lists are available to researchers. New acquisitions on topics of interest to the library are made continuously; categories of materials include all known works, including translations and foreign editions, of John F. Kennedy's works; books by and about the members of the Kennedy family; studies of the Kennedy administration and of the presidency; selected writings of Kennedy associates; materials relating to significant topics of the period; and works based on research done in the Kennedy Library. Special collections include the White House Gift Collection, selected candidates for the Robert F. Kennedy book awards, the Arthur Price Collection of Kennedy literature, and the Seymour Harris Collection on economics. Except for basic standard reference works, no effort is made to acquire general works on the presidency or other materials easily available in libraries in the Boston area.

Audiovisual Materials

The audiovisual archives document the life and career of John F. and Robert F. Kennedy, other family members, and their friends and associates. The photographs, films, and sound recordings come from items generated by White House personnel during the Kennedy administration and from contributions of government agencies, newspapers, private organizations, and individuals. There are almost 150,000 photographs, from 1863 to the present, 30,000 of which were made by White House photographers. Over 6 million feet of motion picture film, primarily donated by the major television networks, government organizations, and White House photographers, cover Kennedy's career and official functions. Over 4,500 sound recordings include all presidential addresses and remarks, and songs, poetry, and music written in memory of Kennedy. A collection of 500 cartoons, most of them presented to Kennedy during his life time, highlight issues of his career and his family and relate to national, international, and local Boston politics.

THE MUSEUM AREA

The museum has nine distinct theme areas, moving the visitor, at his or her pace, from entrance to exit. In the center of the exhibit is the President's desk as it appeared in the Oval Office. Among the very personal mementos are a glass sculpture with the etching of PT-109, a gift of the PT boat veterans he commanded during World War II, and the coconut shell on which he carved the SOS message when he and his crew were stranded on an island. The desk is surrounded by a window wall that explains in pictures and documents the President's major functions.

The exhibits tour starts with mementos, documents, and photographs that describe Kennedy's formative years, from his ancestry to his experiences during the Second World War. The next area is dedicated to displays of his congressional career, beginning with the 1946 campaign, proceeding through his service in the House and the Senate, and concluding with the 1960 presidential campaign. The Kennedy administration is represented as a time line coordinated with displays that highlight major events of these years, such as the Bay of Pigs, the Berlin visit, the Cuban missile crisis, the Nuclear Test Ban Treaty, civil rights, the Peace Corps, the space program, and economic policies. "The President and the Press" is a videotape of excerpts from press conferences, shown in a small alcove. The President's personal interests, his family life, and the special atmosphere of the Kennedy White House are portrayed in a series of pictures, books, documents, and mementos. The audio track in this area plays a concert of cellist Pablo Casals, recorded live in the White House. The exhibit, "A Day in the Life of the President," uses slides to show the busy presidential schedule during a randomly picked day, September 25, 1962. Two areas of the museum are dedicated to Robert F. Kennedy. One portrays his youth, early career, service as attorney general and senator, and his bid for the 1968 presidential nomination. The other, an alcove showing the film "RFK Remembered," captures some of the milestones of his life. The exhibit area exits into the vast space of the pavilion, conceived by Architect I.M. Pei as "a place where people could think about what they had seen, and let those thoughts soar."[23]

THE EDUCATIONAL PROGRAMS AT THE LIBRARY

The original plans for the Kennedy Library had envisioned a facility on the Harvard University campus where the Institute of Politics would be integrated with the library and museum. However, Harvard established the Institute as part of the John Fitzgerald Kennedy Institute of Government in 1966, long before the library was built; it has remained independent of the library. Its aim is to increase the understanding and cooperation between the scholarly community and the political world, thereby encouraging young people of ability to participate in active public life. It accomplishes these aims through the Program of Faculty Studies, which sponsors efforts of Harvard faculty members to identify major issues of public policy or government operations; the Program for Institute Fellows, which brings a select group of fellows to Cambridge to pursue their own studies; and the Program for Students, which makes it possible for students to pursue their interest in practical politics, the political process, and public policy.

The John F. Kennedy Library Foundation is a private, nonprofit educational organization that raises funds and actively supports the library's archival and educational programs. Research grants are awarded to help defray living and travel costs incurred while doing research at the library. Grants and prizes are also awarded for the improvement of teaching American politics. Individuals from area colleges and universities are recruited as archival interns to assist in a variety of archival processing projects. There is also an active volunteer program to assist the staff in the performance of various museum and archival functions, including acting as guides for group visits, especially museum visits by school classes. Every year since 1979, approximately 30 academic conferences, special conferences, colloquia, public forums, and lectures have been held. The Foundation also publishes the quarterly *John F. Kennedy Library Newsletter*. Fund-raising efforts are very active; besides extensive direct-mail appeals, fund-raisers include such spectacular events as the elegant dinner held at Senator Edward Kennedy's McLean, Virginia, home in 1985, which was attended by President and Mrs. Ronald Reagan. The Reagans were invited by the Kennedy children, who were spearheading a drive to raise an $8 million endowment for the library.[24] The John F.

Kennedy Library and Museum, the Foundation, the Institute of Politics, and the Kennedy family are doing an excellent job to convey JFK's strong convictions about the significance of records of the past for a comprehension of the present, as expressed in his statement of January 19, 1963: "Documents are the primary sources of history; they are the means by which later generations draw close to historical events and enter into the thoughts, fears, and hopes of the past."[25]

16. The Lyndon B. Johnson Library in Austin, Texas

LYNDON B. JOHNSON
Thirty-sixth President—Democrat
1963–1969

Lyndon Baines Johnson was born on a ranch in the hill country of Texas in 1908, the oldest of five children of a tenant farmer. Both his parents had at times been teachers. Politics was a family tradition; his father and both grandfathers had served in the Texas legislature. At the age of five, Lyndon moved with his family to Johnson City, which was named for his grandfather. He was a good student and graduated from high school at the age of 15. After working at odd jobs for a few years, he enrolled and worked his way through Southwest State Teachers College, graduating in 1930.

In 1932, after briefly teaching public speaking at Sam Houston High, he was invited by U.S. Congressman Richard Kleberg to come to Washington as his secretary. This gave Johnson the opportunity to learn how Congress works and started his political career. In 1934, on a trip to Texas, he met Claudia "Lady Bird" Taylor and married her after an ardent two-week courtship. He became friendly with Congressman Sam Rayburn who persuaded President Roosevelt to appoint Johnson as director of the National Youth Administration in Texas, becoming, at 26, the youngest NYA state administrator. When a congressional vacancy occurred in his district, he campaigned with the support of many NYA "graduates" and won the election by such a landslide that Roosevelt invited him on a train ride, which gave Johnson considerable political exposure, an unusual opportunity for a new congressman. He served in the House from 1937 to 1948, with two interruptions. In April 1941, he ran for an unexpected Senate vacancy, but was defeated. After the bombing of Pearl Harbor, he was among the first in Congress to volunteer for active duty; as a lieutenant commander in the Naval Reserve, he saw military action in the Pacific. He returned in July 1942 when Roosevelt recalled all members of Congress from active duty.

In Congress, Johnson was a supporter of rural electrification, slum clearance, and public housing. He was an active member of the Naval Affairs Committee and was unopposed for re-election in 1938, 1940, and 1942. In 1948, he ran again for the U.S. Senate and won. He held the position of Democratic party whip from 1951 to 1953, and of Senate majority leader from 1955 to 1960. His Senate leadership during the

Eisenhower administration is remembered as generally supportive and even-handed, with Johnson frequently giving the President more support than the Republicans did. His most notable successes during that period were the adoption of the Civil Rights Acts in 1957 and 1960, and the advancement of the space program. His candidacy for the 1960 presidential election started only shortly prior to the national convention; on the first ballot Johnson trailed Kennedy by 409 votes to 806. When Kennedy asked him to be the vice presidential candidate, he accepted and was nominated by acclamation.

As vice president, Johnson was very active as chairman of the National Aeronautics and Space Council, the President's Committee on Equal Employment Opportunities, and the Peace Corps Advisory Council; he was a regular member of the cabinet and the National Security Council. In addition, he toured many parts of the globe as Kennedy's goodwill ambassador in the Middle East, Africa, the Far East, South Asia, and Latin America. His visit to India was the most successful of his many trips, but it became widely known that he was not too happy as vice president and missed the limelight and challenges he had enjoyed as the Senate's majority leader.

On November 22, 1963, after the assassination of President Kennedy, Johnson was sworn in as president on the plane that took him from Dallas back to Washington. He was the eighth vice president to enter the White House on the death of his predecessor. Known and feared by many as a forceful personality, he showed a great deal of tact in the transition period and retained, at first, the Kennedy cabinet. He continued the policies initiated by Roosevelt and Kennedy and, with his exceptional political skills, was able to convince Congress to pass his "Great Society" programs: a massive attack on poverty and unemployment, a sweeping civil rights act, and a large tax cut. In the election of 1964, he defeated Senator Barry Goldwater of Arizona, his Republican opponent, by 15 million votes, the biggest presidential victory up to that time.

During the second Johnson administration, Congress passed a multibillion dollar federal aid to education program and expanded the Social Security Act to cover medical care for the elderly and handicapped. In 1966, the Department of Housing and Urban Development and in 1967, the Department of Transportation were established. When a revolt started in the Dominican Republic in 1965, Johnson sent 20,000 troops there to assure free elections. This intervention had the approval of the Organization of American States and was very successful. The Johnson foreign policy, however, faced increasing problems in Vietnam, where U.S. military advisors and supplies had been sent under Eisenhower and Kennedy to help the South Vietnamese against Communist infiltration from North Vietnam. In 1964, two American destroyers were allegedly attacked by torpedo boats in the Gulf of Tonkin. On Johnson's request, Congress passed the "Tonkin Resolution" giving him the authority to prevent further aggression. He ordered the bombing of North Vietnam and by 1968 over one half million U.S. soldiers were fighting in the war. This situation created great resentment and student unrest at home, as the Vietnamese refused negotiations and the war dragged on.

The legislation Johnson sponsored to help the poor did not stop major riots from breaking out in many black ghettos in the large cities; in 1968 Martin Luther King's assassination caused additional riots and unrest. With increasing problems at home and abroad, Johnson announced in March 1968 that he would not seek another term. After his retirement in 1969, he spent his remaining years at his ranch near Johnson City; he entertained many visitors, engaged in cattle raising, had an active schedule of lectures and seminars, and spent a good deal of time in his office in the Lyndon B. Johnson presidential library in Austin. He had originally planned to use his papers to write his memoirs, but, being a man of action rather than contemplation, he really never settled down to the task. "They'll get me anyhow, no matter how hard I try. . . . No matter what I say in this book the critics will pull it apart. . . I might as well give up and put my energies in the one thing they cannot take away from me—and that is my ranch."[1] Rather than working on the memoirs, he completed *The Vantage Point: Perspectives of the Presidency 1963–1969.*[2] He enjoyed his retirement but he "agonized over reports in the papers about the course of the war in Vietnam and the fate of the Great Society. . . On January 20, 1973, Nixon was inaugurated for a second term. The next day, a cease-fire was announced in Vietnam. . . and a new Nixon plan was announced for the dismantling of the Great Society programs. The following day, on January 22, 1973, Lyndon Johnson had a fatal heart attack."[3]

THE ESTABLISHMENT OF THE LBJ LIBRARY

Johnson's mother was sure that her son was destined for greatness and preserved many mementos of his childhood, youth, and career, including his school papers and his letters; she suggested in 1958 that these items be preserved in an appropriate facility. In reply, Johnson mentioned to her the idea of establishing a museum in Johnson City to hold the many papers collected in 22 years of public service as director of the Texas NYA, congressman, and senator.[4] A paperwork management program was established in his office to identify, organize, and analyze his records so that they would be ready for deposit in a library or archive at some future date. In 1959, the trustees of the University of Texas expressed their desire to obtain and establish an archive for the Johnson papers. In July 1961, when Johnson was vice president, librarian of Congress L. Quincy Mumford asked him to deposit his papers in the Library of Congress, to which he replied that he felt honored but was not ready to make decisions concerning his papers. In 1962, Southwest Texas State University in San Marcos, his alma mater, requested that he consider depositing his papers there.

When Johnson became president in November 1963, he was too pre-occupied with the establishment of his administration and the 1964 election to decide where to deposit his papers. However, after the 1965 inauguration, the Johnsons began to give serious thought to the establishment of his presidential library. He was a man of action and did not have time or patience for details, but he and Mrs. Johnson asked Horace Busby, the President's special assistant, speech writer, and longtime associate, to review and summarize various concepts of presidential libraries. Busby gathered information on the other presidential libraries, on presidential papers stored in the Library of Congress, and on existing legislation concerning the establishment and maintenance of archival depositories. He described the Truman Library's thrust to "be more toward a memorial to Harry S. Truman than a contribution for history of the future . . . oriented more to the level of library visitors than library users."[5] The Eisenhower Library was also conceived in the "memorial and museum mold," while an Eisenhower Center at Columbia University might have been a contribution to the advancement of causes with which the general was identified. In contrast, he felt that the Kennedy Library would become a center for serious study of the presidency, which would "incorporate the entire archival project into a continuing, permanent program of scholarly research, lectureship, teaching and authorship which will assure the relevance of the materials in the depository to the world of one hundred years hence or more."[6] From then on, Busby, Press Secretary and Special Assistant George Reedy, and especially Mrs. Johnson were involved in the planning and implementation of the LBJ Library. Busby favored the campus of the University of Texas as a site, and suggested the establishment of a "School of Public Affairs" with endowed chairs and projects related to the "War on Poverty" and other Johnson efforts.

W. W. Heath, chairman of the Board of Regents of the University of Texas, along with Chancellor Harry Ransom and Regent Frank C. Erwin, Jr., strongly urged the President to have his library be the first to be built on a university campus. On August 6, 1965, Heath sent a letter of intent from the University of Texas, proposing:

> . . . to provide, at its expense, an appropriate site of 14 acres within the principal academic environs of the University at Austin, to be utilized as the site of a Presidential archival depository which will be known as the Lyndon Baines Johnson Library; to design, construct, furnish and equip a building to be located on such site . . . of not less than 100,000 square feet of space to be dedicated to use as a Presidential archival depository for the housing and display of Presidential papers and other historical materials relating to and contemporary with your life and works. . . to confer with the Administrator of General Services or his designee concerning site selection, design, construction, furnishing, and equipping the Library including its museum aspects.[7]

The proposal stressed the point that the University was expanding its teaching capabilities in history, government, economics, and public administration and that the library, as a national research institution, would be a valuable resource to faculty and students. Upon completion, it would be turned over to the United States for its use in perpetuity, and would be administered, operated, protected, maintained, and staffed by and at the expense of the United States. A graduate school of public affairs would be created in conjunction with the library and the University's large, accessible, urban campus in Austin would be the most desirable site for the library's aims.

Three days later, the President accepted the offer with a letter to Heath in which he said: "As you know, I am deeply committed to the preservation and safeguarding of our historical and cultural resources and have made an effort to preserve the papers of my own public career since 1937. . . . The fine public spirit and magnificent generosity that have prompted the University of Texas to make this unexampled offer of a site and structure on its campus for use as a Presidential Library should earn it the respect of the entire nation. . . . It is with heartfelt gratitude, therefore, that I accept your proposal and join with you in this undertaking."[8] The offer was indeed generous because it eliminated the need to raise funds for the library. According to Alfred Steinberg's biography *Sam Johnson's Boy*, "a Johnson associate who had graduated from and taught at the University confided, 'Frank Erwin. . .owed Lyndon a big favor. When Lyndon was majority leader and Frank was the lawyer for the gigantic Elgin-Butler Brick Company, Lyndon put through a nutty amendment to the tax laws so that the depletion- allowance break was extended to clay products. So Erwin let him move now to turn the University of Texas into an LBJ University, even though Lyndon hadn't even gone there.' "[9]

On August 13, 1965, Johnson offered his papers and other historical materials to the United States for deposit in a presidential archival depository. The offer was accepted by the Administrator of General Services on August 17, and on August 19, Representative Jack Brooks of Texas introduced a resolution in Congress that authorized the GSA to enter into an agreement with the University of Texas for the Johnson presidential depository without transfer of deed. On the same day, Senator John McClellan of Arkansas introduced a companion resolution in the Senate. These resolutions passed the House on August 31, and the Senate on September 1. On September 6, the President approved the resolution which became Public Law 89-169. This was, and has remained, the fastest action on record regarding the establishment of a presidential library. On September 10, the President was heard saying to some people in his office, "I want to have the greatest library ever in the world."[10]

On October 8, 1965, the University of Texas and the GSA entered into an agreement implementing the congressional authority to use, as the Johnson Library, land, buildings, and equipment made available by the University. Less than two months later it was announced that the architectural firms of Skidmore, Owings and Merrill, with Gordon Bunshaft as partner in charge, and Brooks, Barr, Graeber, and White, with R. Max Brooks as partner in charge, had been appointed to design, plan, and supervise the construction of the library. The establishment of the Lyndon Baines Johnson School of Public Service was announced in January 1966, to be located in a building next to the LBJ Library. Mrs. Johnson worked closely with the architects on the plans of what was to become a major research center on campus. Gordon Bunshaft recalled that the first time he was able to show the President a model and some drawings of the library, Johnson said: "Mr. Bunshaft, I only have five minutes." He stayed about 15 and Bunshaft could not really explain the plans to him. After he left, Mrs. Johnson remarked, "Well, we'll have to do a lot of thinking and talking about this." Yet, three days later, the President approved the design.[11] Construction was begun in September 1967.

THE JOHNSON LIBRARY COMPLEX BUILDINGS

The Lyndon Baines Johnson Library and Museum, and the Sid Richardson Hall, which houses the Lyndon B. Johnson School of Public Affairs, the Institute of Latin American Studies, and the Texas and Latin American collections of the University, are located on a 30-acre site on a high knoll on the eastern edge of the University of Texas campus in Austin. The two buildings are separated by a large plaza with three fountains. The Johnson Library and Museum building is an imposing, monolithic, windowless, eight-story structure of beige travertine marble which, in some ways, is reminiscent of a contemporary version of the National Archives building in Washington. It contains almost 150,000 square feet of floor space. In architect Gordon Bunshaft's mind the building communicates Lyndon Johnson's personality. "I thought the president was a really virile man," Bunshaft commented, "a strong man with nothing sweet or sentimental about him . . . . I think this building is kind of powerful, and he's kind of a powerful guy. There's nothing delicate about him."[12]

The Sid Richardson Hall, named for the late Texas businessman, Sid W. Richardson of Fort Worth, is a low contemporary structure of precast concrete with a special surface of exposed aggregate that harmonizes with the marble of the library building. It has three units; the North unit, directly opposite the library, houses the offices, classrooms, and library of the Lyndon B. Johnson School of Public Affairs. Construction costs of the two buildings came to approximately $18 million.

The library was dedicated on May 22, 1971. Four thousand guests from around the world, including President Richard M. Nixon and Vice President Spiro Agnew, attended the nationally televised ceremony. The University of Texas, while retaining title to the building, dedicated the library to the United States in perpetuity to be operated by the National Archives. In his remarks, Johnson spoke about the School of Public Affairs offering training for careers in public service to make the library a center for learning about the government, similar to the concept of the John F. Kennedy Library and the Kennedy School of Government. He said:

> The Library records reflect the Nation for forty years—from the 30s to the 60s. They picture a sweep of history beginning with the depression and ending with the most prosperous era we have ever known. They record a drive for change and social reform unparalleled in its energy and scope—and a World War unmatched in its destruction. . . They cover the time when liberty was challenged in Europe and Latin America and Asia—and record America's response to those challenges. It is all here: the story of our time—with the bark off. A president sees things from a unique perspective. . . . In my book, to be published this fall, I explain: "I have not written these chapters to say, 'This is how it was,' but to say, 'This is how I saw it from my vantage point.' " This Library does not say, "This is how I saw it," but, "This is how the documents show it was."[13]

President Nixon accepted the library for the United States and expressed the nation's indebtedness for this gift to President Johnson and the

University. Noting that the replica of the Oval Office in the library may prove to be the most exciting and popular room for visitors, he said:

> Sitting in the Oval Office in Washington the other day, I found myself reflecting on its shape—on the fact that it is built as an oval, without corners, and with walls that might be said to have no sides or an infinite number of sides—and on the fact that there is a certain parallel with the shape of that office and the Presidency itself. For the President cannot approach a question from one side or the other; on each issue that comes to the Oval Office there normally are an infinite number of sides and of competing considerations to be resolved or chosen among.[14]

The Lyndon B. Johnson Library, according to Johnson's wishes, and unlike other presidential libraries, does not charge admission fees to visitors. When the Library opened, Johnson repeatedly said that he wanted more people to come to it than had come to any other presidential library in the country. He pleaded with his staff to open the doors early in the morning and keep them open late at night. Asked to supply daily attendance figures, knowing that Johnson would be angry at them if the figures were low, the staff tended, gradually at first and then more regularly, to escalate the body count.[15] However, as a matter of fact, the number of museum visitors to the Johnson Library has far exceeded the number of visitors to any of the other libraries throughout the years. (See Appendix 1).

RESEARCH MATERIALS IN THE LYNDON B. JOHNSON LIBRARY

In September 1965, as soon as Congress had passed legislation authorizing the acceptance of a Lyndon B. Johnson Library by the federal government, an acquisition program was instituted on the suggestions of Dorothy Territo, who acted as archivist on the White House staff. She noted that "studies of earlier Presidential Libraries show that the most fruitful and productive period for acquisitions has been the period when the President was in the White House."[16] Based on the example of John F. Kennedy, who had sought early in his administration to obtain materials from cabinet members and agency heads for deposit in his presidential library, she suggested that the President invite members of his cabinet and heads of government agencies to deposit their papers in the Johnson Library, and to provide copies of official records of each agency, as well as pictures, publications, press releases, and other pertinent historical materials that "will show the important ideas, actions, policies and programs of the Johnson administration."[17] Also upon her suggestion, a Library Acquisitions Committee, chaired by Mrs. Johnson, was formed.

The intensive solicitation program yielded excellent results, and Johnson wrote to GSA Administrator Lawson Knott: "The marked success of this activity, which was carried out by the National Archives, leads me to believe that it should be established as a permanent activity of that Agency, so that henceforth all Presidential libraries will have the benefit of this enrichment of their collections. To that end I wish a continuing program of this character.[18]

By 1967, over 150 persons had actually donated or promised to contribute their papers; several microfilm cameras were in operation in government agencies filming selected records; the "Profile of Poverty" exhibit, which the Office of Economic Opportunity had assembled and toured around the country, was acquired for the museum; copies of 52 books about President Johnson and the Johnson administration that had been published abroad since November 1963 were acquired with the help of the United States Information Agency; the University of Texas Library had started to develop an exhaustive Lyndon Baines Johnson bibliography; and plans for an oral history program were made. The University of Texas offered rare documents going back to Fernando Cortez, Thomas Jefferson, and Napoleon Bonaparte. The books of Carl Sandburg and the papers of pioneer cardiologist Michael E. DeBakey were sent to the President. The small building where LBJ attended elementary school was offered to the library. This building was eventually moved to the grounds of the LBJ Ranch, as was a restoration of the house where LBJ was born. The Office of Presidential Libraries of the National Archives obtained a full collection of congressional documents, as well as other pertinent publications of the Government Printing Office and the Hearings of Senate and House committees for the period 1937–64. By April 1968, about 800,000 pages of documents of various agencies had been microfilmed; these were estimated by the GSA Administrator to represent 25 percent of the total. The U.S. Information Agency supplied films of major trips and events of the President.[19]

The extensive microfilming of departmental records was attacked on the Senate floor by Senator John J. Williams, Republican of Delaware, as a waste of the taxpayers' money. In response to this attack Johnson wrote to the GSA Administrator: "It is my wish that there be no delay on the copying of Government records for my Library and that the copying of selected records be completed as near January 20, 1969, as is possible. I have emphasized the urgency and priority of this project in recent meetings with the Cabinet and Under Secretaries. . . . I am urging every official concerned to cooperate wholeheartedly with the GSA, so that we do not lose a day in completing this important project." He added in his own handwriting: "Please give me bi-monthly reports to me [sic] on progress and thanks much."[20]

In May 1968, Johnson asked Joe B. Frantz, a history professor at the University of Texas, to head a team of historians to interview as many as possible of the associates and opponents made by Johnson in the third of a century since he came to Washington. Frantz wrote to Frank Erwin about that meeting: "We suspect that this project will take about three years and, and will give the Lyndon B. Johnson Presidential Library one of the most significant oral history holdings in the world. We should have at least 1,000 interviewees, and Lord knows how many thousands of pages of original memoirs."[21] Accusations about the Johnson administration's "rewriting of history" surfaced in many newspapers, and the magnitude of the planned oral history project added to the criticism. As a result, the oral history project was set up as a privately funded, independent project of the University of Texas and the Lyndon B. Johnson Foundation.

After Johnson's announcement on March 31, 1968, that he would not seek re-election, he became personally more and more interested in the development of the library. He "began to speak excitedly of his plans for his library and his school at the University of Texas and set up a schedule of seminars and lectures for the following years. . . . Hundreds of thousands of file folders had been shipped to Austin to be sorted through for the library and the work on the memoirs."[22] He also increasingly involved special assistants Joseph Califano and Ernest Goldstein in library problems.

By December 1968, the library's director and key professional staff members had been appointed. The library headquarters were moved to the Federal Office Building and Federal Courthouse in Austin, to be used as the staging area for the library. An inventory of the pre-presidential and presidential papers was prepared to control their shipment and shelving. Plans were made to establish a pilot project for the computerized listing and indexing of unrestricted archival and audiovisual materials. In 1988, these plans had not yet been implemented, though the initial steps had been taken by PRESNET. (See Chapter 3.)

The following tabulations and descriptions are based on *Historical Materials in the Lyndon B. Johnson Library,*[23] and interviews with the library archivists.

Manuscripts

During the Johnson administration, most nonclassified correspondence and memoranda were sent to Central Files; no separate office file was maintained. The National Security Files were the working files of the President and his two successive special assistants for National Security Affairs, McGeorge Bundy and Walt W. Rostow. Most of the documents in the National Security Files are classified and require authorization for declassification.

The Papers of Lyndon B. Johnson

Files	Linear Feet/ Microfilm Reels
House of Representatives (1937–49)	132
Senatorial (1949–61)	825
Vice-Presidential (1961–63)	146
White House Central Files (1963–69)	
WHCF Subject	1368
WHCF Name	2065
WHCF Chronological	22
WHCF Confidential	76
WHCF Oversize Attachments	290
WHCF Storage	
White House Office	573/62
White House Aides	565
Miscellaneous	1195
President's Staff Files	1103
National Security Files	411 feet, 109 vols.
Statements of Lyndon B. Johnson	81

White House Social Files	499
Appointment Files, Administrative Histories, Scrapbooks	
Post-Presidential (1969–73)	708

Donated Papers and Records

	Linear Feet/ Microfilm Reels
285 collections of personal and organizational papers	3516/84 12 items, 26 vols., 82 tapes

Federal Government Records

	Linear Feet/ Microfilm Reels
54 collections	1351/3310

Oral History Interviews

Interviews with over 1,000 people have been conducted since 1968. The oral history project is expected to continue until 1989. As of the end of 1987, there were over 2,200 hours of interviews recorded (51,000 transcribed pages), considerably more than in any other presidential library. An interview of 250 pages with Secretary of State Dean Rusk will remain restricted until 1990. Other extensive interviews are with Clark Clifford, secretary of defense; William P. Bundy, assistant secretary of defense; and Harry McPherson and Larry Temple, special counsels to the President.

Printed Materials

The printed materials collection consists of approximately 15,000 titles of published and unpublished materials dealing with Lyndon B. Johnson and his family, his career, his presidency and the presidency in general, selected items on twentieth-century U.S. history, and a small reference collection. The library continues to acquire materials on the Johnson era. A large vertical file of journal articles and current subscriptions to some periodicals, primarily historical, is maintained.

Audiovisual Materials

The audiovisual archives contain more than 600,000 still pictures; 500,000 of these are from the White House collection and over 60,000 from other government agencies. The pre-presidential collection contains 8,600 negatives and prints, including early family and ancestral photographs. There are 800,000 feet of motion picture films, most of them supplied by television networks and government agencies. Also included are Democratic National Committee campaign advertisements, films from foreign governments, films given to President Johnson by various individuals and organizations, and an expanding collection of films produced by, or commissioned for, the LBJ Library. More than 12,000 hours of videotape and 13,000 hours of audio tapes and discs capture presidential addresses and speeches, congressional briefings, the television and radio coverage of conventions and campaigns, and various activities of government agencies, departments, and commissions. An expanding LBJ Library tape series covers special events sponsored by the library, including the appearance of guest speakers and symposia, beginning in May 1971.

THE MUSEUM AREAS

In her *White House Diary,* Lady Bird Johnson mentioned that on February 12, 1965, she had a meeting "with Clark Clifford and Bill Heath on that phantom that I want to clothe with flesh—the Lyndon B. Johnson Library."[24] During the year, she visited the existing presidential libraries, and shaped the Lyndon B. Johnson Library and Museum as a reflection of these visits. She wrote in September:

> Some things I began to see with new eyes—the presidential papers themselves, gray, anonymous, box after box, identically bound, hidden from the world on shelves behind locked doors, awaiting the very few scholars who come—the public comes in thousands and the scholars in trickles. Some more dramatic use ought to be made of these papers, I thought. They could be secure behind glass but some use could be made of color. . . . In my opinion there should be a melding of both library and museum, a melding from which they would both profit and both become more alive, more vividly used as an instrument to record and remember history. I think it would be useful to have the library where the traffic is, where the scholars are, where students come on a university campus, and not so far off the beaten track, even though there were sentimental reasons for placement of these Presidential libraries.[25]

These thoughts resulted in the dramatic display of thousands of document boxes bound in red buckram, each bearing a gold presidential seal, stored four stories high behind glass walls, overlooking the great hall of the Johnson Library and Museum on the second floor of the building, thus integrating the archives with the museum exhibits. This is the most impressive view of presidential records anywhere. The entrance to the building is on the first floor which has a reception desk staffed by volunteers, and an orientation theater showing a 20-minute audiovisual presentation as an introduction to the exhibits in which items selected from over 35,000 museum objects convey the essence of LBJ's life and career. "The Early Years" and "Family Album" illustrate Johnson's family background and youth, and show the Johnson daughters and their families. "Road to the Presidency" traces LBJ's career from his service in the House to his inauguration as president. Also on this floor, there is a display of America's foray into space, a short video presentation of LBJ's humor, a selection from the gifts given to the President by leaders of other countries, and an exhibit on foreign affairs, highlighting Vietnam, the Six-Day War in the Middle East, and the summit meeting with Soviet Party Secretary Kosygin at Glassboro.

From the first floor, a large open staircase leads to the great hall. On the landing, an exhibit explains the contents of the red manuscript boxes. Below the boxes is a large metal relief mural showing LBJ with Franklin Roosevelt, Harry Truman, Dwight D. Eisenhower, and John F. Kennedy, and a black pylon with selected statements from LBJ's speeches. Other exhibits in the great hall feature "The Great Society," describing the major social programs of the Johnson administration; a collection of American political memorabilia from George Washington to the present; more gifts from around the world; and "America's Handiwork," gifts from across the nation to the President of the United States. The First Lady Theater shows the life and work of Lady Bird Johnson and a film about her. A five-minute video presentation, "The Johnson Style," shows how LBJ worked. The Hall of American History features temporary exhibits that change every few months. Behind the rows of document boxes are five floors of archives stacks that are not accessible to visitors and researchers.

The museum exhibits are continued on the eighth floor, which contains a seven-eighth scale replica of the Oval Office used by LBJ; large color transparencies of some of the public and private rooms in the White House; an elegant reception and meeting room in which some of LBJ's books, sculptures, and paintings are displayed; and the office the President used when he was working in the library. The offices of the library and museum staff, and the reading room for researchers are also on this floor. The basement of the building houses a 1,000-seat auditorium, a lecture room that accommodates 250 people, service facilities, and storage and work areas.

THE EDUCATIONAL PROGRAMS AT THE LIBRARY

In October 1968, George E. Reedy sent a memo to the President suggesting a symposium program for the library. He developed this idea while attending a symposium at the Truman Library. "Because museums and archives have a somewhat dusty and dead past connotation, such programs tie the past to the contemporary. . .and could become a major activity of your library. . .this project would rise or fall upon the type of discussion. If truly contentious people of opposing points of view were invited, it would be a success."[26] This advice was taken, and the symposia at the LBJ Library started with "Educating a Nation: The Changing American Commitment" in January 1972, and have continued to be held very successfully once or twice a year, dealing with topics of interest to LBJ. The April 1985 symposium was a 20-year critique of the Great Society. A distinguished lecturers series started with British Prime Minister Harold Wilson in the spring of 1971 and has continued throughout the years, featuring speakers such as Averell Harriman, Henry Kissinger, Dean Rusk, John Kenneth Galbraith, and many others.

While the University of Texas funded the building of the library, and the federal government maintains it, the Lyndon B. Johnson Foundation, a nonprofit, charitable, and educational corporation, generally supports many of the library's activities through its Friends of the LBJ Library division. The Friends fund the lecture, symposia, oral history, and publication programs. The films on LBJ and Lady Bird Johnson shown in the library auditorium were financed through the Foundation, as are numerous special exhibits, the publication of exhibit catalogs, a newsletter, *Among Friends of LBJ*, which appears three times a year, and other publications about the library. A number of symposia have been published in book form in cooperation with the LBJ School of Public Affairs. The Foundation also finances a grants-in-aid program for scholars who conduct research in the library, and maintains an active volunteer program; volunteers act as docents, staff the reception and sales desks, and provide assistance to the library staff. In December 1977, "A National Tribute to Lady Bird Johnson," held at the library, culminated a drive to establish a permanent endowment for the Friends. The response was greater than expected and this made it possible to maintain free admission to the library, the lectures, and the seminars.

The LBJ Ranch, now the Lyndon B. Johnson Ranch and National Historical Park, operated by the National Park Service, is located 66 miles from Austin, and 14 miles from Johnson City, the President's boyhood home. The ranch house itself will not be open to the public as long as Mrs. Johnson is alive, but visitors can tour the rest of the ranch property, the reconstructed birthplace and the elementary school on the ranch, and the boyhood home in Johnson City. The property continues to be operated as an active cattle ranch; the proceeds are used to finance the expenses for the touring service.

17. The Gerald R. Ford Library in Ann Arbor, Michigan and the Gerald R. Ford Museum in Grand Rapids, Michigan

GERALD R. FORD
Thirty-eighth President—Republican
1974–1977

Gerald Rudolph Ford was born as Leslie Lynch King on July 14, 1913, in Omaha, Nebraska. After her divorce from Leslie King in 1915, his mother, Dorothy Gardner King, returned to Grand Rapids, Michigan, her home town. There she met and married Gerald Rudolph Ford, a successful paint factory owner, who adopted her son and renamed him Gerald Rudolph Ford, Jr. He grew up with three half brothers, and won an athletic scholarship to the University of Michigan, where he made a name for himself in football. After graduation, he received several offers to play professional football, which he declined, to become assistant football and boxing coach at Yale University. On the suggestion of his stepfather, he applied for admission to Yale Law School, was accepted, and continued to work as a coach until his graduation in 1941.

Returning to Grand Rapids, Ford entered into a law partnership with Philip Buchen. Shortly after Pearl Harbor, he volunteered for service in the navy, and was commissioned as ensign in April 1942. On his request, he was assigned to sea duty, was almost washed overboard during stormy weather, took part in 10 sea battles, and advanced to the position of lieutenant commander. After his return to Grand Rapids in December 1945, he started a private law practice. In 1948, he ran for Congress and won the Republican primary in a district that had never sent a Democrat to Congress. Before going to Washington, Ford married Betty Bloomer Warren. He served continuously in the House from 1949 to 1973, winning every election by at least 60 percent. In his second term, he became a member of the House Appropriations Committee, where he developed an expertise in military expenditures. In 1952, he passed up an opportunity to run for the Senate in favor of acquiring more House seniority, hoping to eventually become Speaker of the House, a goal he never reached. However, he was elected chairman of the House Republican Caucus in 1963. President Johnson appointed him to the Warren Commission which investigated the assassination of President Kennedy. After the Commission completed its report, Ford and Jack Stiles, an old college friend and his first campaign manager, wrote a book, *Portrait of the Assassin.*[1]

Ford became House Republican minority leader in 1965. He considered himself "a moderate in domestic affairs, a conservative in fiscal affairs, and a dyed-in-the-wool internationalist in foreign affairs."[2] He voted against the Medicare program, the War on Poverty, and increased aid to education, and advocated the impeachment of Supreme Court Justice William O. Douglas, which was never acted upon. Throughout his career in the House, he maintained cordial relations with members on both sides of the aisle. His ambition was still to become Speaker of the House, and, at a 1969 Gridiron Club dinner, he said: "I am not at all interested in the Vice Presidency. I love the House of Representatives, despite the long, irregular hours. Sometimes though, when it's late and I'm tired and hungry—on that long drive home to Alexandria—as I go past 1600 Pennsylvania Avenue, I do seem to hear a little voice saying: 'If you lived here, you'd be home now.' "[3]

After a quarter century of service as a congressman, Ford's fate took a sudden turn in 1973, when Vice President Spiro Agnew was convicted of income tax violations and forced to resign from office. The 25th amendment to the Constitution, which gives the president the authority to appoint a vice president with the consent of Congress, was used for the first time when President Nixon, burdened by the Watergate and Agnew scandals, had to nominate someone who would be accepted by the public and could quickly be confirmed by Congress. Carl Albert, the Democratic Speaker of the House, claimed that he was the first to suggest to Nixon that he should nominate Ford.[4] Ford's personal charm, integrity, and party loyalty stood him in good stead. The Senate confirmed him as vice president with a vote of 92 to 3 on November 27, and the House with a vote of 387 to 35 on December 6, 1973. During the next few months, Ford was in a difficult position. The Watergate problems had deepened, but as vice president he had to continue to exhibit loyalty to President Nixon; at the same time he also had to maintain his own credibility as it became more and more obvious that he might soon succeed Nixon. On August 1, 1974, Alexander Haig, the President's chief of staff, told Ford that there was new evidence against the President which might tip the balance for impeachment and asked him whether he was prepared to assume the presidency. On August 5, the tape was released which showed that Nixon had ordered the Watergate coverup long before he had publicly admitted it. On August 8, Nixon asked Ford to come to the Oval Office and informed him that he planned to resign. On August 9, Gerald Ford became the first U.S. president by appointment rather than by election.

Ford's inaugural address instantly endeared him to a disturbed nation:

> The oath that I have taken is the same oath that was taken by George Washington and by every President under the Constitution. But I assume the presidency under extraordinary circumstances never before experienced by Americans. This is an hour of history that troubles our minds and hurts our hearts . . . . I am acutely aware that you have not elected me as your President by your ballots, and so I ask you to confirm me as your President with your prayers . . . . If

you have not chosen me by secret ballot, neither have I gained office by any secret promises. I have not campaigned either for the Presidency or the Vice Presidency. I have not subscribed to any partisan platform . . . . I have not sought this enormous responsibility, but I will not shirk it. Those who nominated and confirmed me as Vice President were my friends and are my friends. They were of both parties, elected by all the people and acting under the Constitution in their name. It is only fitting then that I should pledge to them and to you that I will be the President of all the people . . . . As we bind up our internal wounds of Watergate, more painful and more poisonous than those of foreign wars, let us restore the golden rule to our political process, and let brotherly love purge our hearts of suspicion and of hate.[5]

On August 20, 1974, Ford nominated Nelson Aldrich Rockefeller as vice president; after lengthy congressional hearings, Rockefeller was confirmed on December 19, 1974. During his first month in office, Ford enjoyed great popularity, but on September 8 he stunned the nation with the announcement that he had granted Nixon a "full, free and absolute pardon," which amounted to a guarantee that Nixon could not be convicted for any Watergate related activities and that he would receive the same privileges as other retired presidents, including staff allowances and Secret Service protection. When Ford was asked during his confirmation hearings for the vice presidency in 1973 about a possible pardon for President Nixon, he had replied, "I do not think the public would stand for that."[6] The White House was deluged by protests against the pardon, and members of Congress of both parties were disturbed because they had not been consulted in advance. The Senate quickly passed a resolution that the President should not pardon anyone else connected with the Watergate scandals before they had been tried. A few days later, Ford announced a conditional amnesty for draft dodgers and deserters during the Vietnam War, but this action did little to revive his popularity. He assured Congress and the public that his actions had been taken in an honest effort to heal the wounds and that there had been no "deal" between him and Nixon. In the fall elections, the Democrats increased their majorities in both Houses, but not by the landslide proportions predicted by political analysts.

When Ford assumed the presidency, the nation faced serious economic problems brought about by increasing inflation. Ford instituted "a policy of government by veto . . . . He vetoed seventy-two acts passed by Congress in a little over two years. It had taken Nixon nearly six years to veto forty-two bills . . . . More than four fifth of Ford's vetoes were sustained."[7] On the international scene, Ford visited South Korea and affirmed U.S. support for its independence. He participated in a summit meeting with Soviet leader Brezhnev where an agreement was reached to limit the production and deployment of nuclear weapons; on the same trip he also visited Japan. He managed to prevent another Middle East war by having Israel and Egypt agree to an interim truce settlement.

In 1976, Ford won the Presidential nomination of his party over Ronald Reagan, but lost the national election to Jimmy Carter, who said in his inaugural speech: "For myself and for our nation, I want to thank my predecessor for all he has done to heal our land."[8] Before Spiro

Agnew's resignation, when Ford was minority leader in the House, his plans for retirement were "to practice law three days a week in Grand Rapids, play golf the other four, and take a vacation in the winter."[9] But after he retired from the presidency in 1977, Ford and his wife moved to southern California where the climate is better for Mrs. Ford's arthritis, and golf courses are plentiful. He manages a very busy retirement career from an office in Rancho Mirage. He enjoys good health, gives many lectures, and participates in various television appearances; he contributes to many programs of his library in Grand Rapids and is on the board of directors of several large corporations.

THE ESTABLISHMENT OF THE GERALD R. FORD LIBRARY AND MUSEUM

Gerald Ford's congressional papers from 1949 to 1963, with very few exceptions, were not preserved. Due to a small office and lack of space, Ford and his staff regularly and systematically eliminated the papers every two years to make room for the materials from the new Congress. In 1957, Dr. Robert M. Warner, the director of the Michigan Historical Collections (MHC), contacted Congressman Ford, not for his own papers, but for assistance in tracking down papers of several important Michiganders. The MHC was initiated in 1935 by Dr. Lewis G. Vander Velde, a history professor at the University of Michigan, who felt that the existing Michigan historical records required a more permanent home. In 1938 the regents of the University accepted the MHC as a separate research institution and provided space for it. In 1973, private donations funded the construction on campus of a separate building, the Bentley Historical Library, to house the MHC and its over 40 million manuscripts, 500,000 photographs, and 2,500 reels of film.

By 1964, Congressman Ford, who had become one of the more important and influential congressmen, was on the MHC list of outstanding Michiganders to be approached about depositing their papers. Mrs. Ruth Bordin, a staff member of the MHC, visited him in Washington and invited him to place his papers in the Collection. "He had never before given the matter a thought . . . . he was a little taken aback—he did not yet see himself as 'history' . . . . Until we suggested that he save his papers, he thought no one would ever be interested in the papers of the congressman from Michigan's Fifth District."[10] As the result of this meeting, Ford agreed to donate his papers to the University under the condition that they remain closed for a period of five years after which the subject of opening them would be reconsidered. Starting with the 1963 papers, every two years all congressional records of Gerald Ford were routinely shipped to the MHC; in addition, separate deposits were made of papers relating to special activities such as Ford's participation in the Warren Commission. All his papers were briefly inventoried and placed into the Willow Run storage facility of the Bentley Library, because it had been agreed in November 1969 that the Ford files would remain closed until January 1980. "The situation suddenly and dramatically changed on October 12, 1973 when Gerald Ford was nominated to succeed Spiro Agnew as Vice President . . . . Our reaction was one of surprise and excitement, coupled also with the realization that we now had a much greater archival responsibility and that the Ford papers [would be more] safely housed in our new building but were still in storage at our warehouse."[11] The Ford papers were immediately removed from storage and shipped to the Bentley Library, a fire-proof, modern, and secure depository. The University permitted the MHC to employ an additional full-time professional staff member for three years to survey the existing Ford papers, arrange and describe them for easy access, and put them into acid-free folders for better preservation.

Since no Michigander had ever occupied the White House, Grand Rapids, Ford's home town, and his alma mater in Ann Arbor were anxious to do everything possible to honor their famous citizen and have the presidential library located in their community. The regents of the University of Michigan, at a meeting on September 20, 1974, discussed the possibility of establishing a Ford presidential library in Ann Arbor. Shortly thereafter, Dr. Robert W. Fleming, president of the University of Michigan, asked Ford to deposit his presidential papers at the University. When asked about his papers at a press conference, President Ford said: "I have no desire personally to retain whatever papers come out of my administration. I made a decision some years ago to turn over all of my congressional papers to the University of Michigan archives." He did not indicate whether he preferred to deposit his presidential papers at the University or in a separate presidential library.[12] The reason for this was that the question of ownership of presidential papers was at that time under deliberation by several courts and the Archive's Public Documents Commission in the aftermath of the Watergate scandals.

At that time Grand Rapids was in the process of revitalizing its downtown area and many local people felt that a Ford facility would gain national attention and increase the city's tourist traffic. The Public Library Board let it be known that it considered itself the logical agency to oversee such a project. The Grand Rapids Public Museum had made plans for a Ford exhibit to open in January 1976, and had made arrangements to get memorabilia stored at the Bentley Library in Ann Arbor. The State of Michigan Historical Division was concerned with the preservation of an old house on Union Street in which the Ford family had lived between 1922 and 1929. This residence was close to the site of the new Grand Rapids Public Library.

In July 1975, Thomas Ford, the President's half brother, wrote a letter to Philip Buchen in which he addressed the problems and controversies that had arisen regarding the Ford papers and memorabilia:

> Regrettably Jerry was not raised in either a log cabin or the abundance of Hyde Park. The old house at 649 Union is simply not large enough to accommodate even a reasonable number of visitors if it were renovated . . . . No civic association wants it without an appropriation to refurbish it . . . [but] if it goes back on the market it might be bought by a private individual who would fix it up and charge admission to 'the only' Jerry Ford Museum . . . . I fully agree that all Jerry's papers are best served by being held in Ann Arbor. His mementos and such physical items he wants to donate belong in Grand Rapids. I am told there is some push and shove now between the University of Michigan, the Grand Rapids Museum and the

National Archives regarding these items . . . . I really believe Jerry should give consideration to a flat all out statement where he says once and for all that all his papers will be donated to the University of Michigan. At the same time he will, over a period of time donate his mementos and certain possessions to any organization now formed or which might be formed in Grand Rapids to permanently make them available for display.[13]

In his answer, Buchen pointed out that " . . . we are somewhat handicapped in developing a firm course of action until after Congress deals anew with the question of presidential papers and historical materials . . . . In the meantime, any assistance you can give toward keeping the citizens of Grand Rapids at peace with the University of Michigan will be much appreciated."[14] At the same time, the Gerald R. Ford Commemorative Committee was formed with the approval of Mayor Parks of Grand Rapids, and Carl H. Morgenstern, the chairman of the Committee, notified Ford that "the Committee is definitely interested in having the memorabilia accumulated during your public life come to Grand Rapids and that a suitable arrangement to house and display them would be made."[15] In an interview with Maury de Jonge of the *Grand Rapids Press*, Ford said:

> A long time ago I made a commitment to the University of Michigan for all my Congressional papers. I followed that with a pretty firm commitment for my Vice Presidential papers to the University of Michigan. We have made no decision yet on the Presidential papers. Arguments can be made that all of the papers ought to be in one place, so there would be a continuity of availability. Now, on the other hand, there are a great many mementos and other things that I am not sure have to go to the Library at the U of M, that can be set up and properly displayed in Grand Rapids. I was just at the dedication of Senator Dirksen's Research Center. This showed me that you can have a great many photographs, mementos, and things of that sort that can be properly displayed that do not necessarily relate to letters, documents and things of that sort. So there is a possibility, as far as I am concerned, of letting the University have the documents, on the one hand, but having Grand Rapids have a lot of other things that are interesting and would be, I think, perhaps better displayed in Grand Rapids, than at Ann Arbor.[16]

Philip Buchen, replying to Carl H. Morgenstern, stated that the conflict between the University of Michigan and Grand Rapids "can be resolved by providing all documents to the University and to designate the Grand Rapids Museum as recipient of the memorabilia."[17] The Grand Rapids Art Museum was moving into the renovated former Federal Building as part of the downtown reconstruction development, and, at first, plans were made to use the existing Art Museum building to display Ford's memorabilia. However these plans were abandoned in favor of erecting a new Gerald R. Ford Museum.

On December 13, 1976, President Ford deeded his papers and other historic materials going back to the beginning of his career to the United States Government, providing that:

> . . . the papers and related archival materials be housed in a Gerald Ford Library to be built at the University of Michigan in Ann Arbor,

and that the memorabilia be exhibited in a museum to be situated in or nearby his home town of Grand Rapids. Under the terms of the offer, the Federal Government will receive the papers and other materials and is to administer the twin facilities, but the library building is to be constructed and owned by the University of Michigan, and a suitable building is to be provided for the museum by an appropriate organization—possibly the Gerald R. Ford Commemorative Committee.[18]

James B. Rhoads, Archivist of the United States, accepted the papers and agreed to the proposed plans for the government; University of Michigan President Fleming accepted the University's role in the arrangement. President Ford had become the first U.S. president to make an outright gift of his presidential materials to the nation while still in office.

In 1977, a national fund-raising drive seeking to raise $5 to $6 million for the two buildings was begun. At the time of the Ford Library dedication in 1981, nearly $12 million had been raised.

THE GERALD R. FORD LIBRARY

On July 31, 1978, an agreement was signed between the University of Michigan and the National Archives to "utilize as a presidential archival depository land, buildings, and equipment of the University of Michigan as a part of the National Archives System."[19] On December 15, 1978, the University awarded $3.48 million in building contracts, and on January 15, 1979, ground-breaking ceremonies were held in the presence of President Ford. The cornerstone was laid on June 19, 1979. The Ford Library was designed by the architectural firm of Jickling, Lyman and Powell Associates of Birmingham, Michigan, as were the Bentley Library in Ann Arbor and the Gerald R. Ford Museum in Grand Rapids. The designs show the influence of the architectural concepts of Frank Lloyd Wright, who aimed to fit a building into its natural surroundings, rather than to dominate them. As a result of this approach, the two-story brick and bronze glass building is a low lying structure; its exterior fits well to its neighbor, the Bentley Library.

The interior of the building is partly covered by oak paneling; the building design permits natural light into most of the public and work areas. The first floor has a large inviting entrance hall used for exhibits of historic documents and/or related artifacts, and also accommodates a small, but very attractive office for Mr. Ford, and various meeting rooms for visiting groups, panel meetings, or seminars. The building cost almost $4.3 million; it contains about 40,000 square feet and has a small garden with benches in the back. The building was dedicated on April 27, 1981, in the presence of Michigan's Governor William G. Milliken; Gerald P. Carmen, the GSA Administrator, who represented President Reagan; and a comparatively small group of invited guests. A much more elaborate dedication was planned for the Museum in Grand Rapids in September. In his library dedication address, Ford commented: "I can say that in thirty months in the White House our stewardship did a lot of good. We solved our biggest problem and turned things around from the way they were on August 9, 1974." Referring to his library as "a superb facility," he said that "we want it to be a living facility that gives on a daily basis. We have a foundation to provide seminars, lectures and study groups to use the past and build the future."[20] In July, the pre- presidential papers were opened to the public; the first presidential documents were made accessible for research in early 1982 and almost all the others, with the exception of some classified or restricted files, have been opened since.

RESEARCH MATERIALS IN THE GERALD R. FORD LIBRARY

On February 5, 1974, when Ford was vice president, he and William Casselman, his legal counsel, met with Dr. Warner to discuss in some detail the future of his papers. It was decided to continue the shipment of the papers to the University of Michigan, and to separate the congressional and vice presidential files. Dr. Warner suggested that a record be kept of Ford's phone calls and important meetings. On May 2, 1974, when Ford came to Ann Arbor to deliver a commencement address, he visited the Bentley Library and had some discussions about the arrangement of his papers and their description in finding aids. Materials such as his scrapbooks were added, tracing some events back to the beginning of his political career.

General Services Administrator Arthur Sampson wrote to the President in December 1974 that he "was concerned that there are certain archival activities that were interrupted at the time of President Nixon's resignation which have not yet been reinstituted. These activities are important for the preservation of an adequate record of the Ford Administration."[21] In December 1976, when President Ford donated his congressional, vice presidential, and presidential papers to the United States Government, National Archives personnel took physical custody of the materials. On January 20, 1977, approximately 8,500 cubic feet of President Ford's papers were shipped to Ann Arbor and stored temporarily in a remodeled warehouse leased from the University and paid for by the National Archives. The vice presidential files start with President Ford's nomination, end with his assuming the presidency, and include his confirmation hearings. There are comparatively few items relating to his transition to the presidency. In September 1977, all Ford pre-presidential papers and materials that had previously been sent to the Michigan Historical Collection were transferred to the Gerald R. Ford Presidential Materials Project. From time to time since then, Ford has donated various personal and post-presidential materials. In 1987, the document collection amounted to over 17½ million pages.

The White House Central Files (WHCF) contain some unclassified or confidential defense and foreign policy materials. The White House Staff Files, kept by staff members in their offices in addition to their use of the WHCF, are arranged by offices, and thereunder by the individual or unit that created them. Many staff members did not keep separate files or their files were taken over by their successors. The National Security Adviser files are an example: Henry Kissinger was concurrently secretary of state and national security advisor until 1975, when Brent Scowcroft succeeded him in the latter post; Scowcroft's files include materials inherited from Kissinger as well as his own and various working files of the NSC staff.

Historical materials relating to President Ford's public and private career have been donated to the library. These include papers of Mrs. Ford and of many presidential assistants and counselors, the largest of which are the papers of Arthur Burns, chairman of the Federal Reserve Board from 1970–78; Edward Hutchinson, congressman from Michigan; and Ron Nessen, press secretary to the President.

The Gerald Ford Library served as the operational test site for PRESNET, the automated manuscript processing and reference system for presidential libraries and many of the collection data are online. (See Chapter 3). The following tabulations and descriptions are based on *Historical Materials in the Gerald R. Ford Library,*[22] and interviews with the library director and staff.

Manuscripts

The Papers of Gerald R. Ford

Files	Linear Feet
Congressional (1948–73)	921
Vice Presidential (1973–74)	106
White House Central (WHCF) (1974–77)	
WHCF Subject	970
WHCF Name	1420
WHCF Chronological File	31
WHCF Bulk Mail	285
WHCF Social Office	337
WHCF Reference Unit Computer Print-Outs (log of outgoing White House correspondence)	70
White House Staff (1974–77)	
Congressional Relations Office	87
Counsel to the President's Office	212
Counselors to the President	114
Domestic Affairs Assistant/Domestic Council Staff	302
Economic Affairs Assistant/Economic Policy Board	139
National Security Advisor/National Security Council Staff	253
Press Secretary's Office	185
White House Operations Office (Office of the Chief of Staff)	18
Other (operations support, scheduling, personnel, public liaison, editorial, staff and cabinet secretaries, first lady's staff)	1170
Miscellaneous Presidential (1974–77)	93
Personal and Post-Presidential (1913–present)	259
Scrapbooks (1929–present)	19 feet, 71 vols.

Donated Papers and Records (1945–present)

	Linear Feet/ Microfilm Reels
37 collections	1492/25 13 vols.

Federal Government Records (1959–1977)

	Linear *Feet*
4 collections	169

Oral Histories

In comparison to other presidential oral history projects, the Ford Library collection is very small, consisting of 173 pages of transcripts, representing eight hours of interviews conducted in 1980 with seven longtime Ford associates. All the interviews focus on early social and political experiences in Grand Rapids. The interview with Philip Buchen, for example, only concerns his early friendship with Ford, their entry into law partnership in 1941, and Ford's 1948 campaign for Congress.

Audiovisual Materials

Since audiovisual materials have shown such rapid growth during the last half century, each new library has greater quantities and types of media in color and sound than the previous incumbent's collection. The Ford materials were provided by Ford associates in government and politics, by government agencies and private individuals, and mostly relate to the Ford presidency. There are some 283,000 still photographs. The Naval Photographic Center and navy film crews provided some 710,000 feet of motion picture films. The White House Communications Agency supplied audio and videotape from the vice presidential days. There are 2,600 audio tapes and 765 videotapes of speeches, press conferences, and daily news reports from the TV networks. Many of these materials are available in reprints. There are also prints of a large number of scrapbook photographs. The Ford Congressional Collection has 4,800 photographs and negatives from Ford's 25 years in Congress. Separate finding aids for most audiovisual materials are available. The Ford Library has a very advanced audiovisual department with a skilled and experienced staff.

Printed Materials

The printed materials collection has nearly 9,000 volumes of information sources, reference works, and biographical materials about the American presidency, with emphasis on President Ford. The collection of federal government publications has a very complete set of congressional hearings, reports, agency annual reports, and other selected items from the President's years in Congress. There is a vertical file with news clippings, articles, and pamphlets. The serials holdings show a complete set of microfilm copies of the *New York Times* (1973–77), *New York Times Index* (1965–82), *Grand Rapids Press (1948–60),* and some other national news magazines. The Gerald R. Ford congressional publications, covering 1949–73, occupy over 200 linear feet.

THE GERALD R. FORD MUSEUM

The Ford Museum, unlike other presidential museums, is not a facility for the storage and study of presidential documents, but exclusively a museum. It is located on six acres of land on the west bank of the Grand River in Grand Rapids. Its construction was paid for by contributions from all over the country, solicited through the efforts of the Gerald R. Ford Commemorative Committee. An attractive public park and a pedestrian bridge integrate the site with the downtown redevelopment center on the east bank, where the city's new office buildings, hotels, museums, and shopping areas are located. The stunningly contemporary building is designed as a right-angled triangle; the longest side of the triangle faces the river and has a huge glass wall that mirrors the park, the river, and the city on the other side. Its two stories cover over 40,000 square feet of floor space; construction costs were $7 million.

The Museum dedication on September 18, 1981, was part of a week-long "Celebration on the Grand" of the "born again" Grand Rapids downtown, marking the opening of the Ford Museum, the Grand Rapids Art Center, the Grand Center convention-symphony hall, and the Amway Grand Plaza Hotel. The guest list included President Reagan, Vice President Bush, Prime Minister Pierre Trudeau of Canada, Governor William G. Milliken of Michigan, U.S. Senators Edward Kennedy and Howard Baker, Secretary of Defense Caspar Weinberger, and former Ford administration members Henry Kissinger, Allan Greenspan, and Ron Nessen. Comedian Bob Hope taped a television special for the occasion in DeVos Hall.

The building, its contents, and activities reflect Ford's sensibility and sincerity. The ground floor has an open area used for large meetings and exhibits. There is an auditorium where visitors can see the movie "Gerald R. Ford: The Presidency Restored." On the second floor are a gallery, mini-theaters, and staff offices. The permanent exhibits illustrate the life of the President, covering his youth, his years in Congress, and his presidency through pictures, films, mounted displays, and sound track explanations. There is a full-size replica of the Ford White House Oval Office. Part of a World War II surplus quonset hut that served as campaign headquarters in Ford's first congressional race is on display. An almost life-size photograph of Ford by Michigan artist David B. LaClaire was commissioned by the Ford Presidential Museum Commemorative Committee as part of the official opening of the museum and hangs on the second floor gallery wall. One of the exhibits is an exciting 12 ½ minute reprise of the 1976 Bicentennial, composed of hundreds of color slides. Other exhibits deal with the confrontation with Cambodia, the resignation of President Nixon, and Mrs. Ford's role as first lady. Gifts from foreign dignitaries and from Americans are also shown. In front of the Museum is a statue by artist Judson Nelson, called "Man in Space"; the Gerald R. Ford Foundation commissioned the work because President Ford wanted a statue to demonstrate his support for the space program.

Changing exhibits either relate directly to the Ford presidency, or deal with contemporary topics and with the presidency in general; they are often produced in cooperation with or are exchange exhibits from other presidential libraries. They are frequently presented in conjunction with conferences or symposia, such as the exhibit on presidential humor or on presidential photographs. The exhibits program is challenging, imaginative, attractive, and educational without overwhelming its visitors. Some of the older presidential libraries could improve their image by using the style of the Ford Museum. Tours of the museum are conducted by volunteer docents.

LIBRARY AND MUSEUM ACTIVITIES

The Gerald R. Ford Foundation supports the activities of the Ford Library in Ann Arbor and the Ford Museum in Grand Rapids. Both facilities conduct conferences, seminars, and symposia. In 1983, the first in a series of presidential library conferences on the public and public policy was held in Ann Arbor, cosponsored by the Ford Library and the Domestic Policy Association, with former Presidents Ford and Carter participating. The year before, Mr. Ford moderated a debate on the press and the presidency, with the press secretaries of Presidents Ford, Carter, and Reagan participating. In 1984, the Foundation sponsored the two-day forum *Modern First Ladies: Private Lives and Public Duties*, organized by Betty Ford. Other conferences brought together scholars, politicians, and journalists to discuss presidential primaries; "Humor and the Presidency" featured the country's outstanding cartoonists and their work. Several meetings were held to highlight "The Presidency and the Constitution," in conjunction with the Constitution's Bicentennial. In 1984, President Ford chaired a conference on the Middle East that President Carter had arranged at Emory University. Through their libraries, Presidents Ford and Carter sponsored a symposium on weapons technologies and American-Soviet relations at the University of Michigan's Rackham Auditorium. The cooperation of these former presidents contributes nationally to an understanding of many aspects of the presidency.

The Foundation also supports the construction of museum exhibits, sponsors the volunteer programs, and offers research grants of up to $2,000 for studies that make use of the Ford Library resources. Young researchers are particularly encouraged to focus their work on the public life of the President. A quarterly *Gerald R. Ford Foundation Newsletter* is published by the Foundation.

18. The Jimmy Carter Center in Atlanta, Georgia

JIMMY CARTER
Thirty-ninth President—Democrat
1977–1981

James Earl Carter was born in 1924 in Archery, near Plains, Georgia, the oldest in a family of four. His father was a farmer and storekeeper, his mother, a registered nurse. He was baptized at the age of 11, and considered himself thereafter a born-again Christian. After graduation from high school he spent one year at Georgia Southwestern College and, in 1942, entered the Georgia Institute of Technology as a naval ROTC student. In 1943, he was admitted to the U.S. Naval Academy in Annapolis where he graduated in 1946 among the top 10 percent of his class. After graduation, he married Rosalynn Smith with whom he raised four children. He served in the navy from 1946–53. In 1950, Carter applied for a navy program that was developing the first atomic submarines under the command of Admiral Hyman Rickover. Carter said of Rickover that he "demanded from me a standard of performance and a depth of commitment that I never realized before that I could achieve. I think that second to my own father, Admiral Rickover had more effect on my life than any other man."[1]

After his father's death in 1953, Carter resigned from the navy and took over the family's peanut plantation and agricultural supply business. He became interested in local politics, and served on the county board of education, the library and hospital boards, and the Georgia Planning Board. He became a Georgia state senator in 1963 and ran for the governorship in 1966, but was defeated by segregationist Lester Maddox. In 1970, after careful preparation and extended campaigning, he won the election for governor and served from 1971–75. During his stewardship, he reorganized the state government, switched to "zero base budgeting," and instituted savings that resulted in a multi-million dollar surplus. In his inaugural address he said: "The time for racial discrimination is over . . . . No poor, rural, weak, or black person should ever have to bear the additional burden of being deprived of the opportunity of an education, a job, or simple justice."[2] When he took over as governor, only three blacks held appointive state jobs; under his administration, this number increased to 53 and the overall number of black state employees increased by 40 percent. Before leaving office, he hung the portrait of Martin Luther King in the State Capitol.

In December 1974, Carter announced that he planned to run for president. His campaign announcement was not taken seriously because he was practically unknown outside Georgia and no Southerner had been elected president since James K. Polk in 1844. Carter campaigned steadily throughout 1975, and, in early 1976, won the Iowa precinct caucuses and a plurality of votes in the New Hampshire state primary, giving credibility to his statement that "a progressive Southerner can win in the North."[3] During the Democratic national convention in July 1976, he won the nomination on the first ballot and chose Senator Walter F. Mondale of Minnesota as his running mate. Carter won the election with 50.02 percent of the popular vote.

At his inauguration on January 20, 1977, he broke precedent by giving his name as "Jimmy Carter" rather than the more formal James Earl Carter, and by wearing a business suit instead of the traditional cutaway. After his inaugural address, he stepped out of his limousine and walked with his family down the parade route on Pennsylvania Avenue to the White House. Carter recalls that "People along the parade route, when they saw that we were walking, began to cheer and to weep, and it was an emotional experience for us as well."[4] However, many others disapproved of this change in style. Throughout his presidency, he continued his efforts to avoid pomposity and to bring the presidency closer to the people. On his first day in office, he issued a pardon to about 10,000 draft evaders, and gave over 430,000 less than honorably discharged veterans the opportunity to have their status reviewed.

Early in his administration, Carter started to reorganize the government, beginning with the White House staff, which he cut by 28 percent. He then reformed the Civil Service, placing more emphasis on job performance and less on length of service. While this reform had various advantages, it also politicized the Civil Service System by making it easier for new administrations to replace older employees. His presidential appointments included a larger percentage of women and blacks than had previously been employed in high federal positions. He established two new departments, the Department of Energy in 1977, and the Department of Education in 1979, by bringing related agencies together and combining some functions without adding new staff. The remaining functions of the Department of Health, Education and Welfare were consolidated in the Department of Health and Human Services. To stimulate the economy, Carter initiated legislation reducing income taxes in 1977 and 1978 and sponsored measures to deregulate the airlines, trucking, and railroad industries.

Among Carter's first appointments was that of his close personal friend, banker Bertram Lance, as director of the Office of Management and Budget. Lance came under investigation for illegal banking practices and allegations of writing large overdrafts on his personal checking accounts. He insisted on his innocence, but resigned in the fall of 1977; although he was eventually acquitted of all charges, the Bert Lance affair tarnished Carter's image of maintaining high ethical standards. The appointment of black Georgia politician Andrew Young as UN Ambassador, while successful in establishing good relations with Third World African leaders, also became an embarrassment to Carter due to Young's often undiplomatic disagreements with official positions of the State Department. In 1979, Young was forced to resign.

Even though both houses of Congress were controlled by the Democrats throughout his administration, Carter found it increasingly difficult to get his legislative proposals approved. He fought with Congress for several years over his energy conservation, military defense, and environmental protection programs. At the end of the administration, Congress approved the Energy Security Act and passed conservation and environmental protection legislation that he had sponsored. House Speaker Tip O'Neill said of President Carter: "When it came to understanding the issues of the day, Jimmy Carter was the smartest public official I've ever known. The range and extent of his knowledge was astounding . . . . His mind was exceptionally well developed, and it was open, too. He was willing to listen and to learn. With one exception. When it came to the politics of Washington, D.C., he never really understood how the system worked and . . . he didn't want to learn about it, either."[5] The reasons for Carter's cool relations with Congress may be explained by the fact that he won his elections without the help of Congress, and many senators and congressmen felt that they had won their offices without the help of Carter's campaign. Looking back on his presidency, Carter said his "biggest misjudgement" was the lack of coordination between his administration and Congress and his "overoptimism about the speed with which Congress could act on controversial matters."[6]

In foreign affairs, Carter was most concerned with the recognition of human rights in other countries, for which he did not get much international support, even from close allies. West German Chancellor Helmut Schmidt characterized Carter as an evangelist who developed foreign policy "from a pulpit."[7] In his attempt to improve relations with Cuba, an exchange of diplomatic representatives below the rank of ambassador was accomplished in 1979. When Cubans were allowed to leave, Carter stated that the United States would welcome them; however, he never expected the flood of people that arrived in Florida by boat as soon as the announcement was made. Among the 125,000 Cuban refugees were several thousand criminals whom Castro had released from prison under the condition that they would leave the country. Carter established full diplomatic relations with China in 1979, concluding the process of normalization of relations started by President Nixon in 1971. In 1977, he signed the Panama Canal treaty, which will relinquish the Canal and the Canal Zone to Panama in 1999. Carter's most outstanding foreign policy success was the Camp David Agreements that resulted from his negotiations with Egypt's President Anwar Sadat and Israel's Prime Minister Menachim Begin and that established the first peace treaty between Israel and an Arab country.

In June 1979, Carter reached an agreement on a new strategic arms limitation treaty (SALT II) with the Soviet Union at a summit meeting in Vienna. However, the Senate did not ratify the treaty in 1979; when the Soviet Union invaded Afghanistan in 1980, Carter asked the Senate to set aside further actions regarding SALT II, cancelled U.S. participation in the Olympic Games in Moscow, and stopped the sales of grain and high technology items to the Soviets. In January 1979, the Iranian revolt against the regime of Shah Mohammed Reza Pahlevi led by Ayatollah Khomeini, the Shiite leader who lived in exile in France, forced the Shah to leave. Khomeini returned to Iran and took control of the government. When the Carter administration permitted the Shah to come to New York for cancer treatments in October 1979, there were violent demonstrations in Teheran against the United States and the Carter administration. Revolutionary guards broke into the American embassy, took staff members prisoner, and threatened to kill them unless the Shah and his fortune were returned to Iran. Economic retaliation by the U.S. against Iran and a military rescue attempt failed. Diplomatic negotiations to release the hostages continued. Agreement was finally reached, but the Iranians procrastinated over minor details so that the American embassy staff remained prisoners in Iran throughout 1980 and Carter's re-election campaign. Carter lost all but six states in the November elections to Ronald Reagan. The Iran hostages were released on the day Reagan assumed the presidency.

The failure of Carter's presidency can be explained in various ways. Arthur Schlesinger wrote that Carter did not understand that an effective president must meet two indispensable requirements: "to point the republic in one or an other direction" and "to explain to the electorate why the direction the President proposes is right for the nation."[8] Speaker Tip O'Neill, in summarizing the Carter presidency, wrote that "Carter was a victim of bad luck and bad timing. It wasn't his fault that oil prices tripled and wrecked our economy, or that a band of Iranians seized our hostages and held them for over a year. The critics howled but nobody came up with a better plan than his—other than bombing Teheran which would have killed them all. Eventually, thanks to Carter's patience and persistence, the hostages made it home alive . . . without breaking any laws and without selling arms to the Ayatollah."[9]

President Carter moved back to Georgia after the election. He wrote his memoirs, *Keeping Faith*,[10] based on the 5,000-page diary of unedited notes that he had dictated nearly every day of his term. He continues his quest for solutions to global problems of deep concern to him, such as human rights, the environment, arms control, education, health, and international conflict resolution. In seeking solutions to these problems, he works closely with the Carter Center of Emory University and the foundations at the Carter Presidential Center in Atlanta.

THE ESTABLISHMENT OF THE CARTER PRESIDENTIAL CENTER

When Jimmy Carter assumed the presidency, the Supreme Court had ruled on the Nixon case, expressly holding the seizure of the Nixon papers to be a *class of one*, thereby clarifying the legal status of the Carter presidential records as his own property and leaving him the option of what to do with them. Early in his administration, he indicated to the U.S. archivist his intention "to donate his papers to the government and to build a Presidential Library."[11] The Carter administration was instrumental in the formulation and passage of the Presidential Records and Materials Act of 1978, which ended the private ownership of presidential records. Although this act did not go into effect until January 20,

1981, when the Reagan presidency began, Carter essentially abided by it. The act creates two categories of materials:

Presidential Records—documents created by a president or his staff in the course of carrying out the constitutional and legal duties of the office of president, which from the moment of creation, are the property of the United States government; presidential records will be closed for a period of five years to allow archivists time to process them, and the president may place certain restrictions on them for twelve years, after which time they will be controlled by rules applicable to all government documents.

Presidential Papers—documents created in the political and personal roles the president performs which, as in the past, the president owns and may dispose of at his pleasure and may choose to donate to the government, subject to donor restrictions as in the past.[12]

The Carter White House and the National Archives cooperated from the very beginning on plans for the arrangement and storage of the papers and the building of a library. A White House liaison office, designated as the Presidential Papers Staff, was established by the Archives and located in the Old Executive Office Building. This introduced for the first time in American history a systematic, archivally oriented approach to the handling of presidential papers and correspondence while the president was still in office. Procedures were developed which preserved the essential papers of the administration and disposed of the insignificant millions of pages like identical postcards generated by "mail in" campaigns, which had been accumulated by previous administrations only to be later disposed of after costly moves and storage. The essential files were maintained according to a system that would facilitate their move to a presidential library.

The Presidential Papers Staff consulted with White House staff as to what to preserve; was responsible for the upkeep of the President's daily diary; collected materials that would later be useful for processing and providing reference services at his presidential library; was instrumental in organizing and storing copies of White House staff papers relating to their official duties; conducted oral history interviews with members of the Carter family and exit interviews with staff members; solicited papers from the same two groups; maintained finding aids for materials to go into archival storage; collected publications about the President and his family; and started to work on interim storage and eventual transfer of materials. Another first under the Carter administration was the computerization of the subject file, and plans to control the flow of paper in the White House by computer. Unfortunately, this system was not fully implemented by 1981, and only a small part of the Carter materials were covered.

The President's Library Advisory Group, consisting of Hugh Carter, the President's cousin and special assistant for administration, and attorneys Robert Lipshutz and Michael Cardozo, were most involved in the planning of the Carter Library, though at times other high-level assistants were drawn into the process. In August 1977, the group suggested to the President, who readily agreed, that he express in writing his intention to donate, at the conclusion of his administration, his presidential papers to the nation for preservation and availability to the public in a Carter Presidential Library.[13]

In March 1978, Carter sent a note to the GSA Administrator that it was his intention to deposit his papers and historical materials in the Archives, and that he intended to work with the archivist in planning a presidential archival depository. During 1979, the citizens of Plains, Georgia, urged Carter to establish his library in his home town. He replied: "I look forward to returning back home for good, and . . . you can be sure that when the time comes for a decision on the Library site, I will give every possible consideration to the area where I held my first public office."[14] The cities of Atlanta, Athens, and Macon, and Emory University and the Georgia Institute of Technology also showed interest in being selected as the site for the Carter Library. After Carter's defeat in the 1980 presidential election, Hugh Carter requested authorization from the President to contact the communities that wanted to be considered for library locations, to establish a non-profit organization to handle the fund raising, to select trustees for this organization, to nominate a treasurer and finance chairman, and to meet with the President and first lady to discuss further details. Eventually, a site in the Great Park area near downtown Atlanta, owned by the State of Georgia, was selected. In October 1982, President Carter announced his plans for the Carter Center, which was to contain the Presidential library, the Carter Center of Emory University, and the foundations concerned with his global interests.

> As one of the younger former presidents in history, I expect to lead an active life of service in the future. . . . .Since my early days as a member of a county school board I have been interested in education, and will now have the opportunity to realize a longstanding ambition by teaching part-time as a professor at Emory University in Atlanta. . . . I will always have a deep interest in some of the major subjects that demanded my attention in the White House. . . . I have worked out a means by which the remaining years of my active life can be most productive. Dr. James T. Laney, President of Emory University, and the leadership of that institution have formed a partnership with me for embarking on a unique project—as exciting and challenging as any career I have had before.[15]

The Carter Presidential Center, Inc., was incorporated in the State of Georgia to raise funds for the project. Jimmy and Rosalynn Carter and many members of the Carter family were involved in the fund-raising and planning process. Over $25 million were raised; half of these contributions came from Georgia, led by the $5 million gift from Robert Woodruff of Coca Cola; the rest came from all over the United States and the world. The Atlanta architectural firm Jova, Daniels, Busby, in cooperation with Lawton, Umemura, Yamamoto of Hawaii, was selected to design the Center, and groundbreaking ceremonies took place in September 1984.

THE CARTER PRESIDENTIAL CENTER BUILDINGS

The Carter Presidential Center is located on Copenhill, a historic Civil War site where General Sherman maintained his headquarters during the Battle of Atlanta in 1864 and witnessed the city's great fire. The 30-acre site on one of the city's highest elevations, east of downtown, provides a beautiful view of the city. Christopher Hemmeter, a Hawaiian real estate developer and a friend of Jimmy Carter, provided the first plans for the complex of four modern circular buildings, carved into the cutaway of the sloping, beautifully landscaped hillside, with two man-made lakes and a Japanese garden. Highway access to the Great Park area had been disputed by neighborhood groups and the Georgia Department of Transportation for more than 10 years. Visitors still approach the Center through narrow old residential streets. The buildings provide about 130,000 square feet of space. The Jimmy Carter Library and Museum, the largest of the four buildings in the complex, occupies 70,000 square feet and is owned and operated by the National Archives. About 40,000 square feet are underground and are used for document storage. A long gallery connects the library with the other three buildings, which house the Carter Center of Emory University, Jimmy Carter's office and sleeping quarters, executive offices, Global 2000, and the Carter-Menil Human Rights Foundation.

The Center was dedicated on October 1, 1986, in the presence of President and Mrs. Reagan and about 5,000 well-wishers. President Reagan called the Carter Center a monument to those who had fought racial discrimination and a "celebration of the South—the new South that Jimmy Carter helped to build." He credited Carter with doing much to free the Americans held hostage in Iran and with "achieving a breakthrough for peace in the Middle East." Carter replied that he had never heard a tribute that was "more gracious and more generous and more thoughtful." Carter said that he wanted the Center not to be a tribute to him and his family but a place where people can learn history from the unique perspective of the presidency. Warren Christopher, Carter's deputy secretary of state, described the Center as "not just archives, but a dynamic center of action. . .devoted not to the past status but to present works. . . .Its purpose is not to aggrandize or to justify but to contribute."[16] The museum was opened to the public the day after the dedication and the library's research room opened in January 1987.

RESEARCH MATERIALS IN THE CARTER LIBRARY

On January 20, 1981, the day Reagan took his oath of office, a convoy of 19 trailer trucks left Washington for Atlanta, carrying the last presidential papers to leave the White House as the personal property of a president, transferred to the government under his own deed of gift. The materials were stored and processed by the Carter Library staff in the temporary repository at the old Atlanta Post Office Annex. The 22,056 cubic feet of materials consisted of 7,303 cubic feet of files from the White House; 12,803 cubic feet of materials from the National Archives Building, including presidential gifts and 1,000 cubic feet of audio- and videotapes and films; 1,200 cubic feet of GPO publications from the Washington National Records Center; and 250 and 500 cubic feet of unspecified material from, respectively, the Anacostia Facility of the White House Post Office and the Carter/Mondale Campaign Headquarters.

As of March 1988, no detailed account of historical materials in the Jimmy Carter Library was available. The following information is based on interviews and statistics provided by the Carter Library and Office of Presidential Libraries staff.

Manuscripts

Twenty-seven million Carter papers were shipped to Atlanta from the White House. At the opening of the research room in 1987, more than 6 million pages were available for research, including the White House name and subject files; significant parts of the files of the Domestic Policy Staff, The Office of Administration, the Press Office, and the Communications Office; and correspondence between President Carter and high White House officials. Among the library's documents are the original records of the Camp David Accords, the SALT II Treaty, and the Panama Canal Treaty.

Other Materials

The library holds approximately 1.5 million still pictures, 1.1 million feet of motion picture film, 1,400 hours of videotape, and 2,000 hours of audiotape recordings in various stages of processing for research use. There are 148 hours of oral interviews, a collection of about 1,400 books, and some 40,000 museum objects.

THE CARTER MUSEUM

The main entrance to the Carter Center is on the ground floor, leading past the entry gardens and fountains into the lobby which leads on one side to the cafeteria and the three other buildings, and on the other side through a long exhibit gallery to the Carter Library and Museum building. There are two orientation theaters off the lobby, each seating 250 people, in which movies about the presidency are shown. A separate entrance leads to the research area and offices of the library on the floor above. The museum aims to attract people from all walks of life and age groups and to provide them opportunities to understand presidential policy dynamics as seen and practiced by Jimmy Carter.

Arranged against the gallery wall leading to the library building are displays of Carter's early life in Plains, his career in the navy, and as governor of Georgia. This section of pictures, documents, and text is brief, compared to similar exhibits in other presidential libraries, partly because of Jimmy Carter's innate modesty, and partly because the family did not collect many significant mementos. One display, "Partner to the President," is dedicated to Rosalynn Smith Carter.

The exhibits stress opportunities for children and adults to access information about the history of the presidency in general and the Carter years in particular through multi-media sound and light displays created by Design and Production, Inc. of Lorton, Virginia. They allow the visitor, in a sense, to walk through brief periods of history with the President. In the center of the main circular exhibits hall is the "Town Meeting" area where seats are located so that people can relax and listen to the videotaped comments of President Carter on topics of the viewers' choice. Other major displays include large color photographs, recordings, and interactive video displays that cover the race to the White House, new relations with Panama, peace in the Middle East, strengthening ties with China, confronting the nuclear threat, the hostage crisis in Iran, and protecting the future.

There is an exhibit on twentieth-century presidents. The first temporary exhibit in the museum featured Eleanor Roosevelt's life. The full-size replica of the Oval Office during the Carter years is described by Carter himself. The display of memorabilia and presidential presents from the U.S. and abroad are held to a minimum. Prominently featured are a few sentences of Jimmy Carter's farewell address to the nation: "America did not invent human rights. Human rights invented America. . .the love of liberty is the common blood that flows in our American veins."

OTHER PARTS OF THE CARTER CENTER

After leaving the White House, Jimmy Carter felt an obligation to use the knowledge, influence, and experience he gained in office to continue his search for solutions to problems affecting the nation and the world, among them hunger, health, the declining state of the environment, abuses of human rights, international conflicts, and arms control. The Carter Center of Emory University, created in 1982, is housed at the Carter Presidential Center and combines the public policy agenda of President Carter and of Emory University. It appoints research fellows to develop national and international policy programs through research, consultation, inquiry, and public forums. Specific programs have been developed on such topics as Middle East Peace (1983); U.S. Health Policy (1984); Arms Control and International Security (1985); Latin American Debt Crisis (1986); and Global Health (1986). President Gerald Ford and other American and foreign leaders have been involved as participants and consultants. The Center has an executive director and its core budget is provided by Emory University.

Global 2000, Inc. was inspired by the 1980 report to President Carter that aimed to mobilize international cooperation regarding the environment and its relationship to poverty, injustice, and social conflicts that have led to economic instability and constitute a serious threat to peace. President Carter, as chairman, administers Global 2000 with the assistance of two major sponsors, Japanese philanthropist Ryoichi Sasakawa, and international banker Agha Hasan Abedi, who together provided $3 million a year for five years for projects in areas of food production increase, soil erosion reduction, water supply improvement, and the preservation of wilderness areas, wetlands, and forest. Food self-sufficiency programs are being developed in the Sudan, Tanzania, Zambia, and Ghana. Health programs in several Asian, African, and Latin American countries are in the planning stages.

The Carter-Menil Human Rights Foundation was established by Dominique de Menil, a native of Houston, Texas, who is a prominent critic of human rights violations, and by President Carter, to promote continued efforts on behalf of human rights. Mrs. de Menil is president and Jimmy Carter chairman of the Foundation, which every year recognizes courageous and effective work to further human rights with one or two major awards to individuals or organizations. George Schira is executive director. The selection of award winners is made with the advice of representatives of outstanding human rights organizations. The 1988 prize will be awarded in Paris in celebration of the fortieth anniversary of the Declaration of Human Rights.

In addition, the Foundation awards fellowships to human rights activists engaging in research activities. The building in which the Foundation is located also houses the executive offices for the Carter Center, the living quarters and offices of the President when he is in residence, and a large auditorium and separate cafeteria, which can be used by the various organizations located in the Carter Presidential Center.

Jimmy Carter described the function of the multi-purpose Carter Presidential Center as follows: "Through the establishment of the Carter Presidential Center, we can gather thoughtful people from all walks of life and work with them to shape meaningful alternatives to even the most controversial and intransigent problems, and then present these for consideration by policy makers and the general public."[17]

19. Presidential Libraries in the Planning Stage:
The Richard M. Nixon and Ronald W. Reagan Libraries

In 1988, both the Nixon and the Reagan libraries were in the planning stages. The Nixon presidential records, because of Watergate, fall under special provisions of the Presidential Recordings and Materials Preservation Act of 1974 and must be maintained in the Washington metropolitan area. At the time of the final preparation of the manuscript for this book, the Reagan presidency was not completed and its records were being maintained in the White House. The Reagan biographical sketch ends with the 1980 presidential election.

Foundations to raise funds for, and plan the Nixon and Reagan presidential libraries were established in the 1980s, and final sites for these libraries, both in southern California, were selected in late 1987 and early 1988. The establishment of the Nixon Presidential Materials Project and the plans for the Nixon and Reagan presidential libraries are presented in this chapter.

RICHARD M. NIXON
Thirty-seventh President—Republican
1969–1974

Born on January 9, 1913, in Yorba Linda, California, Richard Milhous Nixon moved at the age of nine with his parents and four brothers to Whittier, California, where his father operated a combination general store and gas station. He graduated from Whittier College in 1934, and went to Duke University Law School on a tuition scholarship, graduating in 1937, third in his class. After returning to Whittier, he entered a law firm and joined a dramatics club where he met Pat Ryan, to whom he proposed on the evening they met; they married two years later.

Shortly after the attack on Pearl Harbor, Nixon left Whittier for Washington, where he worked for a few months in the Office of Price Administration. During that time he developed a strong dislike for the federal bureaucracy. In September 1942, he received a navy commission as lieutenant, j.g. He became an operations officer for an air transport unit in the South Pacific, spent some time on U.S. shore duty, and retired at the end of the war as lieutenant commander. After returning to California, he decided to run for Congress, and defeated Democratic Congressman Gerry Voorhis, whom he had labelled as a left-wing socialist, in the 1946 election. During his first term in the House, Nixon's major contribution was to assist in the effort to pass, over President Truman's veto, the Taft-Hartley bill. Assigned to the House Un-American Activities Committee, he gained national attention as a skillful cross-examiner in the Alger Hiss-Whittaker Chambers case regarding Hiss's alleged communist tendencies; Hiss was indicted for perjury.

In 1950, Nixon ran for the Senate seat of Helen Gehagen Douglas and won the election as the youngest Republican senator. When Dwight Eisenhower won the Republican presidential nomination in 1952, he chose Nixon as his vice presidential running mate. A vigorous campaigner, Nixon contributed significantly to both Eisenhower elections with his appeal to party regulars and extreme conservatives, while Eisenhower gained the support of many middle of the road voters from both parties. During Eisenhower's three illnesses between 1955 and 1957, Nixon presided skillfully over many cabinet meetings. In 1954, he supported the sending of U.S. troops to Vietnam when France started to pull out of its former colony. In 1959, he successfully engaged in a debate with Party Secretary Nikita Krushchev in Moscow by comparing the American and Russian types of government.

When Nixon ran for president in 1960, his prestige was such that he ran unopposed in all Republican state primaries, while John F. Kennedy faced several Democratic opponents. At the Republican presidential convention, on the suggestion of President Eisenhower, Nixon was nominated by acclamation. Somewhat reluctantly, he agreed to participate in four televised debates with Kennedy. It is generally believed that Nixon's performance in the debates helped Kennedy win the election. After his defeat, Nixon joined a Los Angeles law firm, wrote his book *Six Crises,*[1] and decided to run for the California governorship in 1962. He lost this election to Democratic Governor Edmund G. (Pat) Brown and moved to New York City where he joined another law firm. However, he continued to support Republican candidates on the state and national levels, including Senator Barry Goldwater in his 1964 presidential race against Lyndon B. Johnson. Nixon entered the 1968 presidential campaign and captured the New Hampshire and Oregon primaries. At the Republican convention he was nominated on the first ballot and chose Spiro Agnew, the former governor of Maryland, as running mate. He won the election with 301 electoral votes against Hubert Humphrey's 191 and George Wallace's 46; the popular vote was much closer, with Nixon leading Humphrey by only 0.7 percent.

In his presidential campaign Nixon had promised to accomplish a speedy resolution of the Vietnam conflict. His slow progress towards this goal resulted in new anti-war protests in the spring of 1969, which intensified after the U.S. invasion of Cambodia and the killing by National Guard troops of seven protesting Kent State University students in

1970. The 1970 congressional elections continued Democratic majorities in both Houses of Congress. Anti-war demonstrations in Washington in May 1971 resulted in the mass arrests of over 13,000 students, an action eventually judged by a federal court to have been illegal. In 1971 the Senate passed a bill calling for American troop withdrawal from Vietnam.

In June 1971, the Nixon administration obtained injunctions to prohibit the publication of the "Pentagon Papers", documents about the Vietnam War, by the *New York Times, Washington Post,* and other newspapers for reasons of national security. The Supreme Court upheld the newspapers' right to publish these documents by a vote of six to three. In 1972, President Nixon brought about normalization of relations with Communist China and developed friendlier relations with the Soviet Union, while the conflict in Vietnam continued. The improvement of relations with China and the Soviet Union promised well for the President's re-election.

Nixon's campaign organization, the "Committee to Re-elect the President," was responsible for the wire-tapping and break-in of the Democratic National Headquarters in the Watergate building in June 1972. While newspapers carried stories tying the Watergate break-in to the White House, the administration denied any connection with the affair. The Nixon-Agnew ticket won the election by a 60.7 percent plurality, but again left both Houses of Congress under Democratic control. On January 27, 1973, formal peace agreements with Vietnam were signed in Paris.

The trial of the seven Watergate burglars began on January 8, 1973. On February 7, the Senate voted to organize a Select Committee chaired by Senator Sam Ervin of North Carolina to study the Watergate scandals. On April 30, President Nixon announced the resignations of presidential assistants Ehrlichman, Haldeman, and Dean, and of Attorney General Kleindienst; on July 7, 1973, Nixon refused to turn over papers to Senate investigators; on July 16 the taping of meetings in the White House was made public; on July 26 subpoenas for turning over requested tapes were refused by the President. In August 1973, the press released news that Vice President Agnew had accepted bribes from contractors while governor of Maryland. On October 10, 1973, Agnew resigned; 10 days later the President ordered Watergate prosecutor Archibald Cox to cease his efforts to obtain the Watergate tapes. When Cox refused, Nixon requested that Attorney General Richardson fire Cox, which Richardson refused. Consequently Richardson and Deputy Attorney General Ruckelshaus resigned. Finally, Acting Attorney General Robert H. Bork fired Cox.

In November 1973, Leon Jaworski, the new Watergate prosecutor, obtained grand jury indictments of former Attorney General John Mitchell, presidential assistants Haldeman and Ehrlichman, and many others. The Watergate Grand Jury named President Nixon as an unindicted co-conspirator in the Watergate proceedings in June 1974 and forwarded its evidence to the House Judiciary Committee, which was considering the President's impeachment. On July 24, 1974, the House Judiciary Committee started to debate the articles of impeachment. On the final count, 27 members voted for and 11 against the first article of impeachment—followed by votes of 28 for to 10 against on the second and 21 to 17 on the third article of impeachment. Barry Goldwater, as the leading Republican senator, informed Nixon that there were not enough Senators to stave off his impending impeachment.

On August 5, Nixon released the June 23, 1972 tape that showed he had ordered the Watergate cover-up long before he had admitted that he knew anything about it. Three days later, Nixon called Vice President Gerald Ford to the Oval Office. Nixon was at his desk, looking down. For a few seconds, he continued to study the papers in front of him. Then he looked up and said "Jerry, I know you'll do a good job."[2] President Nixon resigned from office on August 9, 1974, and Vice President Gerald Ford became president. A month later, Ford granted Nixon "a full, free and absolute pardon". In accepting the pardon, Nixon made no admission of guilt, but said: "Looking back . . . .I can see clearly that I was wrong in not acting more decisively and more forthrightly in dealing with Watergate. I know that many fair-minded people believe that my motivation and actions in the Watergate affair were intentionally self-serving and illegal. I now understand how my own mistakes and misjudgements have contributed to that belief and seemed to support it . . . . That the way I tried to deal with Watergate was the wrong way is a burden I shall bear for every day of the life that is left to me."[3]

Before his retirement in September 1986, Senator Barry Goldwater summarized his feelings about half a dozen presidents whom he had known. His comment about Nixon was: "I wouldn't trust Nixon from here to that phone. He had a good foreign-policy head on him, but he was dishonest. Anybody that would lie to his wife and lie to his children and then lie to his country, I have no use for."[4]

THE NIXON PRESIDENTIAL RECORDS

The records and memorabilia of the Nixon presidency are stored in the Nixon Presidential Materials Project facility, a National Archives warehouse in Alexandria, Virginia. The private, pre-presidential and vice presidential papers, which Nixon turned over to the Archives shortly after his election in 1968, are stored in the Federal Archives and Records Center at Laguna Niguel, California. A privately planned Nixon Library will be built in Yorba Linda, California. At the beginning of his presidency, Nixon was very much concerned with the preservation of his records and was actually the first president to establish a formal White House liaison office with the National Archives to preserve and organize his administration's records so that they would be ready for transfer to his presidential library as soon as he left office. After the Nixon resignation in 1974, large quantities of documents, files, tapes, and other materials accumulated by the President and his staff remained in government custody. While archivists, in accordance with Nixon's instructions, compiled these materials for shipment to California, President Ford requested the advice of William B. Saxbe, his attorney general, concerning the ownership of the records. On September 6, 1974, Saxbe concluded, that the papers were owned by Nixon, but were "peculiarly affected by a public interest" which might justify the imposition of "certain limitations directly related to the character of the documents as records of governmental activity."[5]

In the meantime, Arthur Sampson, the General Services Administrator, executed a depository agreement with Nixon under which the former president would retain title to his papers but would donate, at a future date, a substantial portion of them to the United States for research and study. Under the Nixon-Sampson agreement, the materials would be stored by the GSA in a California Archives warehouse in locked areas. Neither GSA nor Nixon could gain access to them without mutual consent. Nixon would be able to withdraw papers after a waiting period of three years and tapes after five years. Materials that were neither withdrawn nor destroyed would then be donated to the government with restrictions regarding public access. The materials under discussion consisted of about 40 million pages and 950 reels of White House tapes. In addition, it was also stipulated that all tape recordings would be destroyed after 10 years, or upon Nixon's death, whichever would occur first. The U.S. archivist had not been consulted regarding this agreement.

Congress acted quickly to forestall the Nixon-Sampson Agreement by passing the Presidential Records and Materials Preservation Act of 1974 (PL93-526), which President Ford signed on December 19, 1974. The day after President Ford signed the act, Nixon challenged it in court as being unconstitutional because it invaded executive privilege, infringed on his right to privacy, and amounted to unconstitutional search and seizure of his property. A three-judge district court rejected the claims in *Nixon v. Administrator of General Services* (408 F. Supp. 321 (DDC 1976)) and the Supreme Court affirmed this decision in 1977 (*Nixon v. Administrator of General Services*, 433 U.S. 425 (1977)), thereby eliminating the Nixon-Sampson Agreement.

After the Supreme Court validation of the Presidential Records and Materials Preservation Act, the National Archives drafted and attempted to publish regulations concerning public access to the Nixon materials, as mandated by the law. The first two sets of regulations were disapproved by the Senate; the third set was withdrawn by the GSA Administrator in order to reconsider the regulations in light of the Supreme Court decision in *Nixon v. Administrator*. The fourth set became effective in 1977; Nixon filed suit to challenge the validity of these regulations, and the GSA Administrator withdrew them as part of a settlement with Nixon. The fifth set became effective in March 1980 but was successfully challenged in a lawsuit filed by former Nixon staff members in *Allen v. Carmen*, 578 F. Supp. 951 (DDC 1983).[6]

Following the *Allen v. Carmen* decision, the archivist established the Nixon Materials Review Group to study the regulations, and to make recommendations on possible changes or alternatives. The group, consisting of federal employees experienced in the archival processing of presidential materials, issued a report in March 1984, recommending that the set of regulations challenged in *Allen v. Carmen* remain unchanged. With minor alterations, the Archives proposed this sixth set of regulations to the Office of Management and Budget. In February 1986, the Office of Legal Counsel of the Department of Justice issued the opinion that the regulations were valid and adequate, and they were published in the

Federal Register of February 28, 1986, as "Preservation and Protection of and Access to Historical Materials of the Nixon Administration; Repromulgation of Public Access Regulations; Final Rule."[7] However, claims of violations of executive privilege and violation of privacy by the Archives in releasing records continue to be pursued by Nixon's lawyers in the courts. The National Archives processed and began to release Nixon administration papers and tapes in May 1987 in accordance with the regulations of the 1974 Presidential Recordings and Materials Preservation Act, which vested control of the papers in the Archives. In April 1987, Nixon lawyers objected to certain parts of the papers planned for release; as a result, these papers must be examined by the archivists as to whether they may infringe on Nixon's executive privilege or personal privacy rights, and Nixon's personal representatives may spotcheck access limitation decisions. In 1988, Nixon lawyers were still suing the government to obtain compensation for the legal costs of the lawsuits disputing the release of the records; these costs are estimated to exceed $1.5 million.

RESEARCH MATERIALS IN THE NIXON PRESIDENTIAL MATERIALS PROJECT

The Nixon Presidential Materials Project in Alexandria, Virginia, operated by the National Archives, is housed in a brick and concrete warehouse located between other structures of the same size and type. (One of the neighboring buildings was used to store the TOW missiles that were secretly shipped to Iran in 1985.) The building contains about 80,000 square feet of office and storage space. Well lighted, secure rooms are filled with steel shelves stacked with acid-free document boxes containing folders of presidential papers. The document boxes are arranged numerically to facilitate their quick location. Other storage areas are filled with cardboard boxes in which gifts from Americans and foreign dignitaries are stored. There are no museum objects on display. A small research and reading room is available to visitors where documents that have been opened and declassified can be studied and duplicated on request, following the same procedures as in other presidential libraries. Finding aids to the open collections in the documents are available. Card files help to identify people or subjects of interest. There is a separate listening room for the Nixon White House tapes. Other audiovisual materials, such as still pictures, records, films, and audio- and videotapes, are stored in separate rooms. Work and laboratory space is available for the staff to examine, sort, clean, and arrange the vast quantity of still unexamined written, taped, and photographed records.

The Nixon Presidential Materials Project holds approximately 40 million pages of textual records; a large number of audiovisual materials, including 950 reels of White House tapes; and more than 30,000 gift items. The following descriptions are based on "Holdings of the Nixon Presidential Materials Project," "Availability of the Nixon Presidential Materials," and interviews with the project staff.[8]

Manuscripts

The papers, documents, and correspondence in the Alexandria depository cover the period from 1969 to 1974. The largest part of the collection are the White House Central Files. From 1972 to 1974, there also existed a Special Files Unit that handled only sensitive materials. These files contained the President's diary and files from key staff members, such as Haldeman, Ehrlichman, Colson, and Dean, and selections from about four dozen other staff members who held sensitive positions. In addition there are files from various government departments and agencies, and donated collections of papers of cabinet members, other government employees, and private citizens. A collection unique to the Nixon period is the Watergate files from the special prosecutor's office.

The Papers of Richard M. Nixon

Files	*Cubic Feet*
White House Central (WHCF)	6,794
White House Staff (165 collections)	11,000
White House Special (61 collections)	628
National Security Council (11 collections)	622

Donated Materials

	Cubic Feet
137 collections	349

Federal Government Records (1968–1977)

	Cubic Feet
Task Force, Board and Commission Records	367
Files of the Office of Presidential Materials	20
Watergate Special Prosecutor Project	13

As of March 1988, approximately 1,200 cubic feet of textual materials were available for public research, consisting of the White House Special Files, and segments from the White House Subject Files and Staff Office Files. The first 250,000 pages of Nixon documents were opened in June 1987; these included the files of John Ehrlichman, John W. Dean, and the papers of Alexander M. Haig, Jr., Nixon's chief of staff at the time of his resignation. The papers opened since then include those of H. R. Haldeman; Patrick Buchanan, a speechwriter in the Nixon and the Reagan White House; Dwight Chapin, Nixon's appointment secretary; and Ronald Ziegler, Nixon's press secretary.

Oral History Project

Staff members of the National Archives conducted exit interviews of 249 departing members of the White House staff between 1970 and 1974, as part of the Nixon oral history program. The files include audiotapes, transcripts, clippings, notes, and correspondence. These materials are not available to the public.

Audiovisual Materials

The most controversial part of the Nixon Presidential Collection are the White House tapes made by recording devices installed in 1971 by the White House Secret Service Technical Services Division, and operational until 1973. On July 13, 1973, the existence of the taping system was revealed by Alexander Butterfield, R.H. Haldeman's deputy. When he was asked by two staff members of the Ervin Committee how notes were taken during White House meetings, he told them about the taping system. The sound activated system had over a dozen recording devices in various locations. The sound system in the White House was disconnected on March 18, 1973, and the Camp David device on July 18, 1973. In 1977, the tapes were turned over to the Archives, which prepared topical outlines of the tapes and enhanced their quality through sound improvement techniques that increased the volume and filtered out noises. In July 1978, Judge John Sirica gave the National Archives copies of 31 conversations used as evidence in the trials of John B. Connally, John D. Ehrlichman, H.R. Haldeman, Robert Mardian, John N. Mitchell, and Kenneth Parkinson. About 4,000 hours of recordings on 950 tapes are stored in the Alexandria facility. Twelve and one half hours of the White House tapes had been fully transcribed and indexed and were available to the public as of the end of 1987. The slow process of transcribing and indexing additional tapes is being continued by the archivists.

Most of the other items in the audiovisual collection are open; they contain close to one half million photographs taken by the White House photographers during the Nixon presidency. A separate file numbering about 1,200 pictures covers 18 pre-presidential years, from 1950 to 1968. The White House Communications Agency produced sound recordings of the Presidential campaigns and speeches, of Vice Presidents Agnew and Ford, of Mrs. Nixon, and of other family members. They also recorded in full the Watergate hearings.

The Naval Photographic Center produced films of some of the diplomatic and social events of the Nixon presidency. Other films from various sources were given to the White House. Private television stations donated nearly 4,000 hours of broadcast time. The Public Broadcasting System contributed videotapes of its public affairs programs and the major television networks gave tapes of their morning and evening news programs. The Nixon-Agnew Committees to Elect (and Re-elect) the President deposited their sound and video recordings with the Project.

Published Materials and Gifts

The Nixon Project holds 16,000 printed volumes in the Reference Books Collection, which dates from 1969 to 1984. The Government Printing Office Publication's Collection, covering the period Nixon was in office (1969–74), contains 2,800 cubic feet of material, one copy of every government publication printed by GPO during the Nixon administration. The Presidential Gift Book Collection (1969–74) contains 10,000 volumes. The collections of gifts received by President Nixon while in office include 951 official gifts from foreign governments and 20,000 gifts from domestic sources.

THE RICHARD NIXON PRESIDENTIAL ARCHIVES FOUNDATION

The Richard Nixon Presidential Archives Foundation, incorporated in 1983, is planning the Nixon Presidential Library in a manner comparable to organizations that have served other presidents to collect funds, employ architects, acquire land, and contract for building construction and the acquisition of furniture and equipment. William E. Simon, Nixon's former secretary of the Treasury, is the President of the Nixon Archives Foundation, and John C. Whitaker, former secretary of the Nixon cabinet and former undersecretary of the department of the interior, its executive director. The Foundation wants to continue the tradition of individual presidential libraries. However, many administrative and legal questions, such as which of the more sensitive papers will be made public, and when, remain to be resolved. The facilities, services, hours of operation, and accessibility of resources of the private Nixon library are planned to be about the same as if it were operated by the U.S. government. The library, as planned, will be operated from a trust fund of the Foundation. For this reason, the Foundation is collecting about $5 million beyond the cost of the library itself. The Nixon Foundation plans to donate the facility to the government if and when the government will be permitted to accept it.

By early 1987, the Foundation had collected pledges for over $24 million, and held title to a 13-acre site in San Clemente, a few miles north of the former Western White House. The site had been made available by the John D. Lusk Company, which was in the process of developing a large residential tract in the area. Preliminary architectural plans had been prepared by the firm of Langdon, Wilson and Mumper of Newport Beach and Los Angeles, California. In March, the Foundation was negotiating final designs and construction bids for the library. However, difficulties with San Clemente planning guidelines and the California Coastal Commission arose, and the Foundation announced in October 1987 that it had accepted the offer of a nine-acre site by the city of Yorba Linda to build President Nixon's library next to his birthplace. The reasons given by the Foundation for these changes were:

> We can build much sooner than if we have to put up with the long delays and uncertainties we have encountered at the San Clemente site . . . . President and Mrs. Nixon and their two daughters have enthusiastically endorsed the move. The President, because his roots

are in Yorba Linda, feels more strongly about locating his Library next to his birthplace than he does another location . . . . Much of the original furniture will be placed in the renovated Nixon family home so that visitors will have a vivid sense of not only President Nixon's early years, but also the way people lived in California just after the turn of the century. The combination of the Nixon Library/Museum and the family home will function as a harmonious setting telling the story of the President's life, both public and private.[9]

The city of Yorba Linda purchased a nine-acre site adjacent to Nixon's home and deeded it to the Nixon Library in the summer of 1988; ground breaking at the site was scheduled for December 1988.

The design of the library is a compromise between Spanish style architecture and a modern library structure; it consists of two parts joined by a long arcade or corridor. When completed, the library will have an area of 82,000 square feet, 68,000 of which will make up the library, consisting of reading rooms, staff offices, and storage areas for documents, published materials, audiovisual materials, and museum objects, assuming that all materials now stored in the Nixon Presidential Materials Project will eventually be transferred to California. The rest of the floor space is dedicated to exhibits and an auditorium for lectures, meetings, and film presentations. Since congressional action will be required to move the Nixon archival materials from the Washington area to a presidential library facility in California, construction will progress in two phases. The first phase will contain the museum area and possibly the pre-presidential materials from the warehouse in Laguna Niguel, and the personal papers and memorabilia accumulated during the post-presidential period. The National Archives are cooperating with the Foundation in these plans. The second phase will accommodate the official presidential materials, if and when an agreement is reached between Nixon and the National Archives.[10]

The exhibits are planned to make extensive use of audiovisual techniques. Topics will include domestic policy, preparation for the presidency, the war in Southeast Asia, U.S.-Soviet relations, relations with China, the moon landing, and Watergate, as well as areas of Nixon's pre-presidential career, such as the Pumpkin Papers and the Alger Hiss trial. In President Nixon's words, the library will not be "a monument to the career of one man, but a place where visitors and scholars will be able to recall the events of the time when he served as President, and to measure and weigh the policies his Administration pursued."[11]

RONALD REAGAN
Fortieth President—Republican
1981–1989

Ronald Wilson Reagan was born on February 6, 1911, in Tampico, Illinois, the second son of John and Nellie Reagan. John Reagan was a shoe salesman who changed jobs frequently. Ronald Reagan grew up in several small midwestern towns; he went to high school in Dixon, Illinois, where he played football and was employed as a swim instructor. He worked his way through Eureka College, a small Disciples of Christ school in Illinois. After graduation in 1932, he became a radio sports announcer. In 1937, he passed a screen test and won his first movie contract in Hollywood. During the next 27 years, Ronald Reagan appeared in many, mostly grade B, movies. In 1940, he married actress Jane Wyman, with whom he had a daughter and an adopted son.

During World War II, Reagan served in the U.S. Army Air Force; his poor vision kept him out of active military duty, but he worked on the preparation of military training films and rose to the rank of captain. After the War, he returned to Hollywood, became active in the Screen Actors Guild, and served from 1947 to 1952 as its president, gaining his first experience in labor relations and politics. He was a liberal Democrat and supported Harry Truman in 1948. Reagan and Jane Wyman were divorced in 1948; in 1952, he married Nancy Davis, also an actress. They had two children. When his movie career declined, he switched to television. From 1954 to 1962, he hosted the General Electric Theater series and was public relations representative for the company, making personal appearances throughout the country.

In the 1950s, Reagan adopted an increasingly conservative political outlook. As spokesman for General Electric, he emphasized conservative principles, and, in 1962, he changed his voter registration from Democrat to Republican. A nationally televised campaign speech for Barry Goldwater in 1964 brought him to the attention of conservatives as a potential political candidate. He ran for governor of California in 1966 and defeated incumbent Democrat Edmund (Pat) Brown. During his two terms as governor, from 1967 to 1975, he learned a great deal about practical politics when he had to cope with Democratic majorities in both houses of the California legislature. In 1976, his attempt to win the Republican nomination for president failed when the party supported the nomination of Gerald R. Ford. Reagan was nominated as the Republican candidate in 1980 and won a landslide victory against President Carter, carrying 42 states with 489 electoral votes.

THE RONALD REAGAN PRESIDENTIAL LIBRARY PLANS

The Ronald Reagan Presidential Foundation was created in 1985 to fund the design, construction, endowment, and supervision of a presidential library and a center for public affairs, with William French Smith, Ronald Reagan's first attorney general, as chairman; Edwin Meese III, his second attorney general, as vice chairman; and W. Glenn Campbell, the director of the Hoover Institution, as a board member. Ronald Reagan was nominated as an honorary fellow in 1975; the papers of his two terms as California's governor were deposited at the Institution. In a 1981 letter, Campbell invited the President to locate his presidential library on the Stanford Campus in close proximity to the Hoover Institution. In 1983, a faculty committee of Stanford University decided that the Reagan Library would be a valuable academic resource, but that a public affairs center, run by the Hoover Institution and therefore outside of University control, would not be acceptable. In February 1985, the trustees of Stanford University approved a site for the library and museum on campus, subject to environmental impact studies. The plans at that time called for a separate site for the Ronald Reagan Center for Public Affairs to be built in the San Francisco area. In the 1986 annual report of the Hoover Institution, Campbell wrote that the Stanford trustees decision to accept the Reagan Library meant that the "entire university could boast of a Reagan connection."[12] This statement prompted faculty and student criticism that the Reagan Library, when added to the Hoover Institution, would compromise the University's independence and open it up to accusations of partisanship towards right-wing Republican causes.

At the beginning of 1987, architect Hugh A. Stubbins unveiled the design of the library. The proposed building, in California's attractive mission style with red tile roofs and stone finish, was expected to accommodate an unprecedented volume of presidential documents and to occupy 115,000 square feet, making it the largest presidential library. Faculty and student opposition to the library was strengthened by a petition of 3,500 local area residents who objected to the size of the facility, which would tower over the campus, and to the increase in traffic it would bring to Palo Alto. Finally, Gary L. Jones, the executive director of the Ronald Reagan Presidential Foundation, announced in April 1987 that the trustees had decided that it would be preferable to build the library and the public affairs center on the same site; since these facilities could not both be accommodated at Stanford, the Foundation would consider a different location, preferably in southern California, where construction could proceed without further delays.[13]

In response, the Foundation received more than 30 site proposals. The University of Southern California and other educational institutions were under consideration, but in November 1987, the decision was made to accept a 100-acre site, donated by the California real estate development firm Blakeley Swartz, in the Thousand Oaks area of Ventura County. Nancy Reagan had inspected the site in August 1987 and found it very acceptable. It is on an isolated hill top, with beautiful views of the mountains and the Pacific Ocean, about an hour's drive from the Bel Air section of Los Angeles where President and Mrs. Reagan plan to settle after he leaves office. The design of the proposed Stanford library would have to be changed only slightly. Ground breaking was planned for November 1988, and fund raising efforts towards an estimated cost of $70 million were well under way. The Public Affairs Center will be constructed later and funded separately.[14] When Ronald Reagan leaves office, he plans to use the office provided for him at the new location of the Foundation on the 34th floor of the Fox Plaza Tower in Century City, California, the site of the former 20th Century Fox film studios.[15]

Appendixes

1. Statistics for Presidential Libraries

The statistics presented in this Appendix were prepared by the Office of Presidential Libraries of the National Archives in the fall of 1987. FY stands for the federal fiscal year, which now runs from October 1 through September 30 of the next calendar year. Costs for the Nixon Presidential Materials Project are mainly for the declassification of materials; there are no operations and maintenance costs because the facility is housed in an Archives warehouse in Alexandria, Virginia.

Table 1: Actual Costs of Presidential Libraries, FY 1987 (in Thousands)

LIBRARY	Program Costs	Operations & Maintenance Costs	Repair & Alteration Costs	Recurring and Nonrecurring Reimbursables[1]	Common Distributable[2]	Rent	Total Costs
Hoover	$518	$ 223	$ 80	$ 0	$ 0	$ 0	$ 821
Roosevelt	593	529	21	0	0	0	1,143
Truman	743	730	330	0	0	0	1,803
Eisenhower	719	703	186	0	0	0	1,608
Kennedy	783	1,073	511	0	0	33	2,400
Johnson	936	1,092	28	0	0	0	2,056
Nixon	714	0	0	39	0	57	810
Ford	637	828	253	0	0	0	1,718
Carter	726	748	76	0	0	0	1,550
Central Office, Planning & Direction, & White House Liaison	877	87	0	0	416	248	1,628
TOTALS	$7,246	$6,013	$1,485[3]	$39	$416	$338	$15,537
Less: NARA Operations & Maintenance		−87					
		$5,926					

[1] Building services in addition to rent
[2] Proportionate share of central office support services
[3] Repair and Alteration Costs includes $485K for Kennedy Library from the 114X account

Table 2: Holdings of Presidential Libraries, Total as of October 1987 (in Units)

	HOOVER	ROOSEVELT	TRUMAN	EISENHOWER
ACCESSIONS & HOLDINGS				
PAPERS (Pages)				
Personal Papers	6,578,850	16,449,678	13,411,624	19,284,851
Federal Records	108,167	716,000	709,600	689,300
Presidential Records	0	0	0	0
MICROFORMS (Rolls/Cards)				
Personal Papers	703	657	3,221	965
Federal Records	663	13	32	0
Presidential Records	0	0	1	0
AUDIOVISUAL				
Still Pictures (Images)	34,279	131,094	86,269	193,028
Film (Feet)	151,591	309,476	325,604	603,945
Video Tape (Hours)	14	28	71	42
Audio Tape (Hours)	240	1,024	265	909
Audio Discs (Hours)	73	1,107	240	238
ORAL HISTORY				
Pages	11,245	3,120	46,733	30,574
Hours	0	84	1,349	766
MUSEUM OBJECTS	4,501	23,363	24,384	29,218
PRINTED MATERIALS				
Books (Volumes)	24,669	44,637	40,456	22,076
Serials	27,637	32,089	73,223	35,445
Microform	1,402	2,457	1,464	5,151
Other	1,562	86,107	91,481	24,017

In this table, personal papers are defined as the materials that presidents deeded to the government in perpetuity. Federal records are the documents of presidential committees, commissions, and other federal agency correspondence. Presidential records refer to the Nixon papers, which were not deeded to the government, but were transferred to the Archives as a result of federal legislation.

Table 2: Holdings of Presidential Libraries, Total as of October 1987 (in Units) (cont.)

KENNEDY	JOHNSON	NIXON	FORD	CARTER	TOTAL HOLDINGS TO DATE
26,753,486	28,678,254	784,000	17,539,555	26,194,030	155,674,328
641,880	2,837,888	912,000	403,000	131,000	7,148,835
4,000	0	44,414,000	0	0	44,418,000
20,447	572,729	0	23	0	598,745
1,972	5,962,000	0	0	0	5,964,680
0	0	5,312	0	0	5,313
125,985	608,122	435,000	311,474	1,500,000	3,425,251
7,038,422	824,746	2,200,000	778,100	1,120,080	13,351,964
1,017	6,736	3,900	1,073	1,434	14,315
6,893	12,566	1,490	1,053	2,000	26,440
711	802	0	3	0	3,174
36,437	51,034	2,200	173	606	182,122
1,654	2,247	228	8	148	6,484
16,802	35,870	21,750	4,466	40,000	199,554
70,733	15,352	9,000	8,767	1,350	237,040
11,692	3,938	0	40	3,247	187,311
3,591	3,732	0	545	6,453	24,795
10,448	13,958	0	2,026	7,409	237,008

Table 3: Space Allocations in Presidential Libraries, FY 1987

LIBRARY	PROGRAM AREAS (Net Usable Square Feet)							SUPPORT & SERVICE AREAS (Unassigned Square Feet)	TOTAL SQUARE FEET
	OFFICE SPACE	HOLDINGS STORAGE	EXHIBIT SPACE	RESEARCH AREA	STAFF WORK AREAS	OTHER PUBLIC AREAS	TOTAL PROGRAM SPACE		
Hoover	1,749	8,397	6,530	2,331	2,049	2,924	23,980	6,020	30,000
Roosevelt	4,649	16,576	9,739	1,344	2,479	3,358	38,145	12,855	51,000
Truman	8,743	8,201	18,572	2,926	8,273	8,843	55,558	40,442	96,000
Eisenhower	5,653	18,013	22,145	2,932	3,414	12,865	65,022	22,978	88,000
Kennedy	4,411	13,729	15,980	4,759	5,087	24,557	68,523	26,477	95,000
Johnson	6,975	37,140	22,272	5,000	7,690	14,550	93,627	23,373	117,000
Ford Library	4,647	13,158	0	5,088	2,691	7,266	30,850	7,471	38,300
Ford Museum	4,200	2,000	16,000	0	3,300	9,000	34,500	5,200	39,700
Carter	3,380	19,818	15,269	1,900	2,527	9,682	52,576	17,424	70,000
Average	4,934	15,226	14,056	2,698	4,168	10,338	51,420	18,027	69,444

NOTES:
Office Space: staff offices, staff conference room, and Presidential office, if any.
Holdings Storage: archival, audiovisual, and museum object storage.
Research Areas: document and audiovisual research rooms.
Staff Work Areas: document processing and preservation areas, photo labs, exhibit preparation areas.
Other Public Areas: main lobby, auditorium, meeting rooms.
Support & Service Areas: corridors, stairways, elevator shafts; lunchrooms, restrooms,
    first-aid station; security guard room; mechanical space.

Table 4: Researcher Daily Visits to Presidential Libraries, FY 1946–87

Fiscal Year	Hoover	Roosevelt	Truman	Eisenhower	Kennedy	Johnson	Nixon	Ford	Carter	Total
1946-1964		9,341								9,341
1958-1964			2,217							2,217
1965		669	794							1,463
1966	41	862	514	12						1,429
1967	225	1,089	603	97						2,014
1968	327	1,094	921	35						2,377
1969	452	1,066	826	99						2,443
1970	598	1,112	996	144	36					2,886
1971	509	1,192	808	209	316					3,034
1972	563	1,604	283	173	389	185				3,197
1973	609	1,345	767	342	461	484				4,008
1974	616	1,278	1,051	336	868	1,116				5,265
1975	498	1,361	880	390	682	1,243				5,054
1976 & TQ	949	2,274	1,663	756	957	1,564				8,163
1977	427	1,303	886	484	1,123	1,297				5,520
1978	528	1,535	985	496	878	1,797				6,219
1979	958	1,097	785	527	785	1,533		122		5,807
1980	614	1,603	973	625	1,419	1,618	84	119		7,055
1981	672	1,243	1,306	676	2,975	1,687	121	74		8,754
1982	686	1,439	918	648	2,196	2,257	124	234		8,502
1983	656	1,283	1,378	802	2,251	1,848	87	496		8,801
1984	582	1,415	1,361	718	2,251	1,804	259	863		9,253
1985	604	1,016	1,211	748	2,110	2,301	852	977		9,819
1986	564	1,358	975	779	1,834	1,673	427	977		8,587
1987	616	1,172	1,369	784	2,016	2,455	819	625	569	10,425
TOTAL	12,294	38,751	24,470	9,880	23,547	24,862	2,773	4,487	569	141,633

In 1976 there was an extra transition quarter which changed the beginning of the fiscal years thereafter from July 1 to October 1.

Table 5: Museum Visitors to Presidential Libraries, FY 1947–87

Fiscal Year	Hoover	Roosevelt	Truman	Eisenhower	Kennedy	Johnson	Ford	Carter	Total
1947–1961		3,005,289							3,005,289
1958–1961			474,555						474,555
1962		138,802	150,161	131,000					419,963
1963		161,190	140,538	106,792					408,520
1964	39,362	161,469	155,053	101,988					457,872
1965	78,857	177,537	179,890	91,891					528,175
1966	95,713	180,915	193,045	93,496					563,169
1967	73,577	159,363	180,824	139,427					553,191
1968	81,056	157,116	170,671	148,179					557,022
1969	80,751	164,298	165,384	364,750					775,183
1970	91,083	162,423	182,823	449,631					885,960
1971	70,648	160,295	186,174	263,234		85,240			765,591
1972	81,989	181,520	186,866	318,684		676,116			1,445,175
1973	82,822	191,194	340,818	299,741		704,190			1,618,765
1974	84,002	194,314	264,230	215,586		542,717			1,300,849
1975	106,109	188,106	291,180	197,727		520,985			1,304,107
1976 & TQ	148,099	223,673	510,584	295,532		905,244			2,083,132
1977	91,324	371,514	321,136	177,332		657,907			1,619,213
1978	95,418	276,865	264,714	170,172		502,115			1,309,284
1979	69,775	215,582	219,067	127,026		480,521			1,111,971
1980	64,088	241,459	201,642	143,910	563,470	446,062			1,660,631
1981	70,337	226,238	211,864	125,458	358,554	384,884	22,476		1,399,811
1982	61,227	202,048	197,477	131,961	318,845	368,289	423,886		1,703,733
1983	59,637	206,147	200,913	117,420	255,474	409,304	83,071		1,331,966
1984	58,487	186,833	210,149	109,720	283,568	357,390	139,529		1,345,676
1985	50,310	194,578	188,552	115,103	252,617	402,768	114,214		1,318,142
1986	51,958	193,150	176,578	101,232	222,327	447,714	92,526		1,285,485
1987	53,690	189,335	168,645	95,895	256,790	419,595	97,812	190,388	1,472,150
TOTAL	1,840,319	8,111,253	6,133,533	4,632,887	2,511,645	8,311,041	973,514	190,388	32,704,580

In FY 1976 there was an extra transition quarter which changed the beginning of the fiscal years thereafter from July 1 to October 1.

Table 6: Staff Positions in Presidential Libraries as of October 1987

Library	Number of Employees On-Board			Number of Vacant Positions
	Full-Time	Part-Time	Intermittent	
HOOVER (19):				2
Administration	4			
Archives	8			
Museum	2	1	2	
ROOSEVELT (29):				2
Administration	5			
Archives	10	1		
Museum	7		4	
TRUMAN (34):				1
Administration	6			
Archives	11		2	
Museum	9	3	2	
EISENHOWER (33):				0
Administration	7			
Archives	10			
Museum	11	5		
KENNEDY (64):				6
Administration	5	3	1	
Archives	15	1	3	
Museum	9	14	7	
JOHNSON (28):				1
Administration	7			
Archives	12	1	1	
Museum	6			
NIXON (27):				2
Administration	3	1		
Archives	18	2	1	
Museum				
FORD (28):				3
Administration	6			
Archives	8	1		
Museum	7	2	1	
CARTER (39):				6
Administration	5			
Archives	8	1	5	
Museum	11		3	
CENTRAL OFFICE (22):				2
Administration	9			
Archives	10		1	
TOTALS (323):				25
Administration	57	4	1	
Archives	110	7	13	
Museum	62	25	19	

2. Directory of Major Presidential Records Collections

The following directory gives the locations of the major portions of the records of the presidency from Washington to Reagan. Other papers are dispersed among various libraries, historical societies, and private collections; information on these, if available, is given in the relevant chapters of this book. The address for all collections of presidential papers in the Library of Congress is the same and is given in full only once, under George Washington.

George Washington
Division of Manuscripts
Library of Congress
Madison Building
Washington, DC 20540

John Adams
Massachusetts Historical Society
1154 Boylston Street
Boston, MA 02215

Thomas Jefferson
Library of Congress

James Madison
Library of Congress

James Monroe
Library of Congress

John Quincy Adams
Massachusetts Historical Society

Andrew Jackson
Library of Congress

Martin Van Buren
Library of Congress

William Henry Harrison
Library of Congress

John Tyler
Library of Congress

James K. Polk
Library of Congress

Zachary Taylor
Library of Congress

Millard Fillmore
Buffalo and Erie County Historical Society
25 Nottingham Court
Buffalo, NY 14202

Franklin Pierce
Library of Congress

James Buchanan
Historical Society of Pennsylvania
1300 Locust Street
Philadelphia, PA 19107

Abraham Lincoln
Library of Congress

Andrew Johnson
Library of Congress

Ulysses S. Grant
Library of Congress

Rutherford B. Hayes
Hayes Memorial Library
1337 Hayes Avenue
Fremont, OH 43420

James A. Garfield
Library of Congress

Chester A. Arthur
Library of Congress

Grover Cleveland
Library of Congress

Benjamin Harrison
Library of Congress

William McKinley
Library of Congress

Theodore Roosevelt
Library of Congress

William Howard Taft
Library of Congress

Woodrow Wilson
Library of Congress

Warren G. Harding
Harding Memorial Library
Ohio Historical Society and
Archives Library
I-71 and 17th Avenue
Columbus, OH 43211

Calvin Coolidge
Library of Congress

Herbert Hoover
Hoover Institution on War,
Revolution and Peace Library
Stanford University
Stanford, CA 94305
Herbert Hoover Library
Park Side Drive
West Branch, IA 52358

Franklin D. Roosevelt
Franklin D. Roosevelt Library
259 Albany Post Road
Hyde Park, NY 12538

Harry S. Truman
Harry S. Truman Library
U.S.-24 and Delaware Street
Independence, MO 64050

Dwight D. Eisenhower
Dwight D. Eisenhower Library
4th Street Southeast
Abilene, KS 67410

John F. Kennedy
John F. Kennedy Library
Columbia Point
Boston, MA 02125

Lyndon B. Johnson
Lyndon Baines Johnson Library
2313 Red River Street
Austin, TX 78705

Richard M. Nixon
Nixon Presidential Materials Project
Office of Presidential Libraries
National Archives
Washington, DC 20408

Gerald R. Ford
Gerald R. Ford Library
1000 Beal Avenue
Ann Arbor, MI 48109

Jimmy Carter
Jimmy Carter Library
1 Copenhill
Atlanta, GA 30307

Ronald Reagan
Reagan Presidential Materials
Project
Office of Presidential Libraries
National Archives
Washington, DC 20408

3. Directory of Presidential Historic Sites

by Mark Carroll

Listed below are the main historic sites associated with each president, along with the current proprietor and mailing address of each site. The National Park Service is given in the addresses as NPS.

George Washington
Mount Vernon
Mount Vernon Ladies' Association
Mount Vernon, VA 22121

Birthplace
NPS
Washington's Birthplace, VA 22575

John Adams
The Old House
NPS
Quincy, MA 02269

Thomas Jefferson
Monticello
Jefferson Memorial Foundation
Charlottesville, VA 22901

James Madison
Montpelier
National Trust for Historic
Preservation
Orange, VA 22960

James Monroe
Ash Lawn
College of William and Mary
Williamsburg, VA 23185

Oak Hill
(Private: not open)
Leesburg, VA 22075

John Quincy Adams
The Old House
NPS
Quincy, MA 02269

Andrew Jackson
The Hermitage
Ladies' Hermitage Association
Hermitage, TN 37076

Martin Van Buren
Kinderhook
NPS
Kinderhook, NY 12106

William Henry Harrison
Grouseland
Vigo Chapter, D.A.R.
Vincennes, IN 47591

John Tyler
Sherwood Forest
(Private: but open)
Charles City, VA 23030

James K. Polk
Home
State of Tennessee, Polk Memorial
Association, Polk Memorial Auxiliary
Columbia, TN 38401

Zachary Taylor
Springfield
(Private: not open)
Louisville, KY 40207

Millard Fillmore
Home
East Aurora Historical Society
East Aurora, NY 14052

Franklin Pierce
Home
State of New Hampshire
Hillsboro, NH 03244

James Buchanan
Wheatland
James Buchanan Foundation for the
Preservation of Wheatland
Lancaster, PA 17603

Abraham Lincoln
Birthplace
NPS
Hodgenville, KY 42748

Boyhood Home
NPS
Lincoln City, IN 47522

Home
NPS
Springfield, IL 62703

Andrew Johnson
Home
NPS
Greeneville, TN 37744

Ulysses S. Grant
Home
City of Galena
Galena, IL 61036

Rutherford B. Hayes
Spiegel Grove
Hayes Family, Ohio Historical Society
Hayes Foundation
Fremont, OH 43420

James A. Garfield
Lawnfield
Western Reserve Historical Society,
Lake County Historical Society, and
NPS
Mentor, OH 44060

Chester A. Arthur
Birthplace
State of Vermont
North Fairfield, VT 05455

Grover Cleveland
Westland
(Private: not open)
Princeton, NJ 08540

Benjamin Harrison
Home
Benjamin Harrison Foundation
Indianapolis, IN 46202

William McKinley
Home
(Private: not open)
Canton, OH 44708

Theodore Roosevelt
Birthplace
NPS
New York, NY 10003

Sagamore Hill
NPS
Oyster Bay, NY 11771

William H. Taft
Home
NPS
Cincinnati, OH 45219

Woodrow Wilson
Birthplace
Wilson Birthplace Foundation
Staunton, VA 24401

Home
National Trust
Washington, DC 20008

Warren G. Harding
Home
State of Ohio
Marion, OH 43302

Calvin Coolidge
Birthplace
State of Vermont
Plymouth Notch, VT 05056

Herbert Hoover
Birthplace
NPS
West Branch, IA 52358

Franklin D. Roosevelt
Home
NPS
Hyde Park, NY 12538

Harry S. Truman
Home
NPS
Independence, MO 64075

John F. Kennedy
Home
NPS
Brookline, MA 02146

Dwight D. Eisenhower
Home
NPS
Gettysburg, PA 17325

Lyndon B. Johnson
Ranch
NPS
Johnson City, TX 78636

Property designations for subsequent presidents are being considered by Congress.

4. Overview of the White House Filing System*

Fred W. Shipman, first director of the Franklin D. Roosevelt Library, undertook a study of the workings of the White House offices, the results of which were published by the FDR Library in 1945 as "Report on the White House Executive Office." Parts of Shipman's "Report" were incorporated into the introduction for various finding aids to materials in the FDR Library. Since this description of White House files and the functioning of the White House Office applies also to administrations that followed that of Franklin Roosevelt, portions of the introduction are reproduced here.

Franklin D. Roosevelt, as administrative head of the Executive Branch of the United States Government, had the assistance of several secretaries, administrative assistants and special assistants as well as a personal secretary. Mail addressed to the White House was routed by the Assistant Executive Clerk either to the President, through his personal secretary; to an assistant with a specific area of responsibility; to the Office of the Chief of Correspondence for the preparation of a routine reply; or, if appropriate, was routinely referred to another government agency for action. The correspondence which went to the President directly was either answered personally by him or sent to another agency for the preparation of a draft reply. After the White House mail had been answered, it was routed to the Office of the Chief of Files for filing. At this time a record was also kept of all correspondence referred elsewhere. This White House office maintained what was known as the White House Central Files; the filing system used was that originally developed in 1906 during the presidency of Theodore Roosevelt.

The Central Files were divided into four categories of material. The ALPHABETICAL FILE contained copies of letters of acknowledgment for mail referred elsewhere, copies of forwarding letters, lists of forwarded mail, abstracts of documents placed into the other filing categories, as well as some routine correspondence. Material in this file was arranged alphabetically by correspondent or subject.

The OFFICIAL FILE was intended to consist of correspondence and other material related to the policy-making activities of the President. It included correspondence, memoranda, and reports from government officials and other public and private individuals. Within this group of papers are files on government departments and agencies; subjects of concern to the President; important organizations and individuals; as well as files on less important persons or subjects. These files are arranged numerically by subject or individual concerned.

The PRESIDENT'S PERSONAL FILE was set up to contain correspondence concerned with matters in which the President took a personal interest. The files vary in size according to subject matter and include incoming and outgoing correspondence, memoranda, printed material, and newspaper clippings; records of telephone calls kept by the President's personal secretary; diaries and itineraries compiled by the appointments secretary; transcripts of

*"Roosevelt, Franklin D., Papers as President, 1933–1945," Introduction to finding aids to various files at the FDR Library.

Roosevelt's press conferences prepared by the office of the press secretary; and a master file of speeches given by the President. One of the largest files contains public reaction mail to a number of Roosevelt's speeches and government programs; there are also files on gifts, honorary memberships, fraternal organizations and philanthropic societies as well as files on personal friends and political associates of the President.

The CONFIDENTIAL FILE contained material similar to that found in the other filing categories which had been designated confidential by the President or one of his secretaries or assistants. It was arranged alphabetically by subject.

The boundaries between these file groupings were often vague and similar material can be found in both the Official File and the President's Personal File. In many cases both groups of papers will contain files on a particular subject or individual. Researchers should thus consult both files to be assured of seeing all the material on their topic.

To facilitate the use of the Central Files, the Office of the Chief of Files prepared an index of important individuals and subjects and also adopted a system of inserting cross reference sheets in other related files throughout the four groups of papers. When correspondence was received by the Office a classifier determined the appropriate file for the original document and so marked the covering letter. Notations were also made on the document to indicate the other files where abstracts of the particular correspondence would be placed. The correspondence then passed to a typist for the preparation of the required number of abstracts. Subsequently, clerks would file both the original papers and the abstracts. With a few exceptions, all of the mail received at the White House (or a record thereof) would thus end up in the Central Files. Occasionally, large amounts of correspondence concerning a particular subject would be referred to another agency without a record being kept. Secretaries and administrative assistants might also retain small amounts of correspondence in their own files. An index of the titles to the name and subject files and a numerical listing of files is available in the research room.

The President's personal secretary, while sending ordinary correspondence to the Central Files, also maintained a PRESIDENT'S SECRETARY'S FILE of documents deemed special and confidential by the President. The correspondence retained by the personal secretary was arranged alphabetically by subject into a DIPLOMATIC FILE, containing confidential reports from American representatives abroad; a DEPARTMENT FILE, containing material from various government agencies; a FAMOUS PEOPLE FILE; a SECRET FILE with correspondence from individuals such as Winston S. Churchill and Joseph Stalin; a SPECIAL STUDIES FILE; and a GENERAL FILE. This material plus the Confidential File of the Central Files has been incorporated into what is known as the President's Secretary's File.

Chapter Notes

CHAPTER 1. Agencies Responsible for the Maintenance of Presidential Records

1. *Index to the George Washington Papers* (Washington, DC: Library of Congress, Manuscript Division, 1964), p. v.
2. John Y. Cole, *For Congress and the Nation: A Chronological History of the Library of Congress* (Washington, DC: Library of Congress, 1979), p. 3.
3. Ibid.
4. David C. Mearns, *The Story Up to Now: The Library of Congress 1800–1946* (Washington, DC: Library of Congress, 1947), p. 2.
5. Ibid., p. 6.
6. Lucy Salamanca, *Fortress of Freedom: The Story of the Library of Congress* (Philadelphia, PA: Lippincott, 1942), p. 35.
7. Cole, *For Congress and the Nation*, p. 4.
8. Thomas Jefferson, Letter to Library Committee of Congress, Sept. 21, 1814.
9. Cole, *For Congress and the Nation*, p. 9.
10. Ibid., pp. 9–10.
11. Ibid., p. 69.
12. Ibid., p. 39.
13. John Cole, "The Library of Congress and the Presidential Parade, 1800–1984" *Library of Congress Information Bulletin* 43:42 (Oct. 15, 1984): 343–48, p. 343.
14. Cole, *For Congress and the Nation*, p. 75.
15. *The Annual Report of the Librarian of Congress, 1986* (Washington, DC: Library of Congress, 1987), pp. A-4-7, A-23-24.
16. Cole, *For Congress and the Nation*, p. 32.
17. Ibid., p. 45.
18. Houston Gwynne Jones, *The Records of a Nation: Their Management, Preservation and Use* (New York: Atheneum, 1969), p. 5.
19. Claude H. Van Tyne and Waldo G. Leland, *Guide to the Archives of the Government of the United States,* 2nd ed. (Washington, DC: Carnegie Institution, 1907).
20. Victor Gondos, Jr., *J. Franklin Jameson and the Birth of the National Archives 1906–1926* (Philadelphia, PA: University of Pennsylvania Press, 1981) pp. 20–21.
21. Jones, *The Records of a Nation,* p. 8.
22. Waldo G. Leland, "The National Archives: A Program" *American Historical Review* XVIII (Oct. 1912): 1–28.
23. Jones, *The Records of a Nation,* p. 10.
24. Ibid., p. 12.
25. Ibid., p. 144.
26. Donald R. McCoy, *The National Archives: America's Ministry of Documents 1934–1968* (Chapel Hill, NC: University of North Carolina Press, 1978), p. 24.
27. Ibid., p. 291.
28. General Services Administration, ADM 5450.3, CHGE 124, Jan. 31, 1964, p. 131.
29. *Presidential Libraries Manual* (Washington, DC: National Archives and Records Administration, 1985).

CHAPTER 2. Legislation Relating to Presidential Libraries

1. David D. Lloyd, "The Harry S. Truman Library" *American Archivist* 18 (Apr. 1955): 99–110, p. 107.
2. U.S. Congress, House, *Hearing before House Committee on Government Operations to Provide for the Acceptance and Maintenance of Presidential Libraries and for Other Purposes* (84th Congress, 1st Session, June 13, 1955), p. 58.
3. Ibid., p. 28.
4. Ibid., p. 2.
5. Ibid., p. 6.
6. Ibid., p. 48.
7. Larry Berman, "The Evolution and Value of Presidential Libraries" in *The Presidency and Information Policy*, Harold C. Reyla et al eds. Vol. IV:1 (New York: Center for the Study of the Presidency, 1981), p. 84.
8. 433 U.S. 425 (1977).
9. U.S. National Study Commission on Records and Documents of Federal Officials, *Final Report* (Washington, DC: U.S. Government Printing Office, 1977).
10. U.S. Congress, House, *Presidential Records Act of 1978, Brooks Report* (95th Congress, 2nd Session, Aug. 14, 1978), pp. 10–24.
11. U.S. Congress, Senate, *Cost of Former Presidents to U.S. Taxpayers, FY 1980; Senate Hearing before the Committees on Appropriations and Governmental Affairs* (96th Congress, 1st Session, Nov. 6, 1979), p. 3.

CHAPTER 3. Guides to Presidential Records

1. Thomas Jefferson, *The Life and Selected Writings of Thomas Jefferson*, edited by Adrienne Koch and William Peden (New York: Modern Library, 1944), p. 502.
2. George Washington, *The Writings of George Washington: Being the Correspondence, Addresses, Messages*, edited by Jared Sparks, 12 vols. (Boston: American Stationers'; J.B. Russell, 1834–1837).
3. James Madison, *The papers of James Madison, purchased by order of Congress; being his correspondence and reports of the debates during the Congress of the Confederation*, 3 vols. (Washington, DC: Langtree & O'Sullivan, 1840).
4. *A Compilation of the Messages and Papers of the Presidents*, edited and compiled by James Daniel Richardson, 20 vols. (New York: Bureau of National Literature, Inc, 1917).
5. Houston Gwynne Jones, *The Records of a Nation: Their Management, Preservation and Use* (New York: Atheneum, 1969), p. 118.
6. Claude H. Van Tyne and Waldo G. Leland, *Guide to the Archives of the Government of the United States,* 2nd ed. (Washington, DC: Carnegie Institution, 1907).
7. Jones, *The Records of a Nation*, p. 120.
8. *The National Union Catalog of Manuscript Collections: 1959–1961* (Ann Arbor, MI: J.W. Edwards, 1962).
9. Franklin D, Roosevelt, *The Public Papers and Addresses of Franklin D. Roosevelt*, compiled by Samuel I. Rosenman, with a special introduction and explanatory notes by President Roosevelt, 13 vols. (New York: Random House, 1938–1950).
10. Warren R. Reid, "Public Papers of the Presidents" *American Archivist* 25:4 (Oct 1962), p. 435.
11. Ibid., p. 436.
12. *Guide to the National Archives of the United States* (Washington, DC: U.S. Government Printing Office, National Archives and Records Service, 1974).
13. Philip M. Hamer, *A Guide to Archives and Manuscripts in the United States* (New Haven, CT: Yale University Press, 1961).
14. *Directory of Archives and Manuscript Repositories in the United States* (Washington, DC: U.S. Government Printing Office, National Historical Publications and Records Commission, 1978); *Directory of Archives and Manuscript Repositories in the Unites States,* 2nd ed. (Phoenix, AZ: The Oryx Press, 1988).
15. Dennis A. Burton, James B. Rhoads, and Raymond W. Smock, *A Guide to Manuscripts in the Presidential Libraries* (College Park, MD: Research Materials Corp., 1985).

CHAPTER 4. Presidential Book Collections at Historic Sites

1. Since 1935, the National Park Service has exercised federal responsibility to preserve significant components of our national heritage. This is carried out by a variety of programs involving Landmarks, Historic Sites, and the National Register of Historic Places.
2. National Park Service, "Presidential Sites: An Inventory of Historic Buildings, Sites and Memorials Associated with the Former Presidents of the United States. A Report to the United States Congress by the Secretary of the Interior" (Washington, DC., 1982), p. ii.
3. The author circulated a questionnaire in June 1985 to public and private presidential sites. Many returned descriptive materials with their questionnaires.
4. The Mount Vernon Ladies' Association of the Union, "Annual Report 1984" (Mount Vernon, VA, 1985), p. 4.
5. Robert G. Ferris, ed., *The Presidents: From the Inauguration of George Washington to the Inauguration of Gerald Ford. Historic Places Commemorating the Chief Executives of the United States* (Washington, DC: U.S. Department of the Interior, National Park Service; Government Printing Office, 1976), pp. 447–49.
6. Annette Melville, comp., *Special Collections in the Library of Congress* (Washington, DC: Government Printing Office, 1980), pp. 189–91, 381.
7. Charles A. Goodrum, *Treasures of the Library of Congress* (New York: Harry N. Abrams, Inc., 1980), pp. 23–24.
8. Charles B. Anderson, ed., "Bookselling in America and the World: Some Observations and Recollections," in *Celebration of the 75th Anniversary of the American Booksellers Association* (New York: Quadrangle Books/The New York Times Book Co., 1975), pp. 78–79.
9. Betty C. Monkman, "White House Libraries," *Encyclopedia of Library and Information Science,* Vol. 33, (New York: Marcel Dekker, Inc., 1982), pp. 148–49.

CHAPTER 5. The Early Presidents

1. David C. Whitney, *The American Presidents* (New York: Doubleday, 1975), p. 5.
2. Ibid., p. 15.
3. Ibid.
4. *Index to the George Washington Papers* (Washington, DC: Library of Congress, Manuscript Division, 1964), p. v.
5. John D. Knowlton, "Properly Arranged and So Correctly Recorded" *American Archivist* 27 (July 1969), p. 372.
6. *Index to the George Washington Papers,* p. vi.
7. Knowlton, *American Archivist,* p. 374
8. *Index to the George Washington Papers,* p. vi.
9. Ibid., p. vii.
10. Ibid.
11. Ibid., p. viii.
12. Ibid., p. vii.
13. Ibid., p. ix.
14. Ibid.
15. George Washington, *The Writings of George Washington: Being the Correspondence, Addresses, Messages,* edited by Jared Sparks, 12 vols. (Boston: American Stationers'; J.B. Russell, 1834–1837).
16. *Index to the George Washington Papers,* p. xiii
17. George Washington, *The Writings of George Washington,* edited by Worthington Chauncey Ford, 14 vols. (New York and London: Putnam, 1889–1893).
18. George Washington, *The Writings of George Washington from the Original Manuscript Sources, 1745-1799,* edited by John C. Fitzpatrick, 39 vols. (Washington, DC: U.S. Government Printing Office, 1944).
19. Thomas Jefferson, *The Life and Selected Writings of Thomas Jefferson,* edited by Adrienne Koch and William Peden (New York: Modern Library, 1944), pp. xviii–xix.
20. Ibid., p. xliv.
21. *Index to the Thomas Jefferson Papers* (Washington, DC: Library of Congress Manuscript Division, 1962), p. vii.
22. Thomas Jefferson, *The Papers of Thomas Jefferson,* edited by Julian P. Boyd, Lyman H. Butterfield, et al., Vol I. (Princeton, NJ: Princeton University Press, 1950–), p. xi.

23. *Guide to the Microfilm Edition of the Jefferson Papers of the University of Virginia, 1732–1828*, edited by Douglas W. Tanner, Microfilm Publication No. 9 (Charlottesville, VA: University of Virginia, Apr. 1977), p. i.
24. Thomas Jefferson, *Memoir, Correspondence, and Miscellanies, from the Papers of Thomas Jefferson*, edited by Thomas Jefferson Randolph, 4 vols. (Charlottesville, VA: F. Carr and Co., 1829).
25. George Tucker, *The Life of Thomas Jefferson, Third President of the United States*, 2 vols. (Philadelphia, PA: Carey, Lea, Blanchard, 1837).
26. T. J. Randolph, Letters to F. A. H. Muhlenberg, Sept. 27, 1846; Muhlenberg Family Papers, Manuscript Division, Library of Congress.
27. *Index to the Thomas Jefferson Papers*, p. ix.
28. Ibid., pp. ix–x.
29. Thomas Jefferson, *The Writings of Thomas Jefferson: Being his Autobiography, Correspondence, Reports, Messages, Addresses, and other Writings, Official and Private*, 9 vols. Published by Order of the Joint Committee of Congress on the Library, from the original manuscripts, deposited in the Department of State, edited by H.A. Washington (Washington, DC: Taylor & Maury, 1853–1854).
30. *Index to the Thomas Jefferson Papers*, p. xi.
31. Ibid., p. xii.
32. Ibid., p. xiii.
33. Ibid.
34. Thomas Jefferson, *The Works of Thomas Jefferson*, collected and edited by Paul Leicester Ford, 10 vols. (New York and London: Putnam, 1892–1899).
35. *Index to the Thomas Jefferson Papers*, p. xiii.
36. Thomas Jefferson, *Papers of Thomas Jefferson*, edited by Julian P. Boyd, Lyman H. Butterfield, et al. 21 vols. (Princeton, NJ: Princeton University Press, 1950–).
37. *The Jefferson Papers at the University of Virginia*, Part I. A calendar compiled by Constance E. Thurlow and Francis L. Berkeley Jr., Part II. A supplementary calendar compiled by John Casteen and Anne Freudenberg (Charlottesville, VA: University of Virginia, 1973).
38. *Guide to the Microfilm Edition of the Jefferson Papers of the University of Virginia*, p. 9.
39. Whitney, *The American Presidents*, p. 43.
40. William Peters, *A More Perfect Union* (New York: Crown Publishers, Inc., 1987), p. 26.
41. Alexander Hamilton, John Jay, and James Madison, *The Federalist: A Commentary on the Constitution of the United States Being a Collection of Essays Written in Support of the Constitution Agreed Upon September 17, 1787, by the Federal Convention* (New York: The Modern Library, 1941), p. x.
42. James Madison, *The papers of James Madison, purchased by order of Congress; being his correspondence and reports of the debates during the Congress of the Confederation*, 3 vols. (Washington, DC: Langtree & O'Sullivan, 1840).
43. Whitney, *The American Presidents*, p. 47.
44. James Madison, *Selections from the Private Correspondence of James Madison from 1813 to 1836* (Washington, DC: J.C. McGuire, 1853).
45. James Madison, *Jonathan Bull and Mary Bull: By James Madison. An Unedited Manuscript* (Washington, DC: Printed for presentation by J.C. McGuire, 1856, 14 p.).
46. James Madison, *Letters and Other Writings of James Madison*, edited by Philip R. Fendall, published by order of Congress, 4 vols. (Philadelphia, PA: Lippincott, 1865).
47. Whitney, *The American Presidents*, p. 54.
48. Ibid., p. 55.
49. "Memoir of James Monroe, Esqu., relating to his Unsettled Claims upon the People and Government of the United States" *National Intelligencer* (Washington, DC: Gales and Seaton, 1826).
50. James Monroe, *The People, the Sovereigns, Being a Comparison of the Government of the United States with Those of the Republics which have Existed Before, with the Causes of their Decadence and Fall*, edited by Samuel L. Gouverneur, Jr. (Philadelphia, PA: n.p., 1867).
51. James Monroe, *The Autobiography of James Monroe*, edited by Stuart Jerry Brown (Syracuse, NY: University of Syracuse Press, 1959).
52. *Index to the James Monroe Papers* (Washington, DC: Manuscript Division of the Library of Congress, 1963.), p. vi.
53. Ibid., p. vii.
54. Ibid.
55. James Schouler, *History of the United States Under the Constitution* (New York, 1882), p. iii.

56. *Bulletin of the Bureau of Rolls and Library of the Department of State*, No. 2, November 1893 (Washington, DC, 1893).
57. James Monroe, *The Writings of James Monroe, including a collection of his public and private papers and correspondence now for the first time printed*, edited by Stanley Murray Hamilton (New York and London, 1898–1903).
58. *James Monroe Papers in Virginia Repositories*, edited by Curtis W. Garrison, Microfilm Publication, No. 7 (Charlottesville, VA: University of Virginia, 1969).

CHAPTER 6. Pre-Civil War Presidents

1. John Spencer Bassett, *Life of Andrew Jackson* (New York: Macmillan, 1925), p. v.
2. Ibid.
3. Henry John Eaton and John Reid, *Life of Andrew Jackson* (Birmingham, AL: University of Alabama Press, 1974).
4. *Index to the Andrew Jackson Papers* (Washington, DC: Library of Congress, 1967), p. x.
5. Ibid., p. xi.
6. Ibid., p. xii.
7. Ibid.
8. Ibid., p. xv
9. Amos Kendall, *Life of Andrew Jackson, Private, Military and Civil* (New York: n.p., 1843–44, nos. 1–7).
10. *Index to the Andrew Jackson Papers*, p. xvi.
11. Ibid.
12. Ibid.
13. Ibid.
14. Thomas Hart Benton, *Thirty Years' View*, 2 vols. (New York and Boston: Appleton, 1854–1856).
15. James Parton, *Life of Andrew Jackson*, 3 vols. (Boston: Houghton Mifflin, 1857–1858).
16. *Congressional Record*, 48th Congress, 1st Session, vol. 15, p. 1480.
17. *Index to the Andrew Jackson Papers*, p. xxi.
18. Ibid., p. xxii.
19. Bassett, *Life of Andrew Jackson*
20. Marquis James, *Andrew Jackson, the Border Captain* (Indianapolis, IN: Bobbs-Merrill, 1933).
21. Arthur M. Schlesinger, Jr., *The Cycles of American History* (Boston: Houghton Mifflin, 1986), p. 389.
22. David C. Whitney, *The American Presidents* (New York: Doubleday, 1975), p. 86.
23. Martin Van Buren, *Inquiery into the origin and course of political parties in the United States* (New York: Hurd & Houghton, 1867).
24. Martin Van Buren, *The Autobiography of Martin Van Buren*, edited by John C. Fitzpatrick (Washington, DC: Government Printing Office, 1920).
25. Martin Van Buren, *Calendar of the Papers of Martin Van Buren*, prepared from the original manuscripts in the Library of Congress by Elizabeth Howard West, Division of Manuscripts (Washington, DC: Government Printing Office, 1910), p. i.
26. *Index to the William H. Harrison Papers* (Washington, DC: Library of Congress, Manuscript Division, 1960).
27. Benjamin Harrison, letter to Reverend Bruce A. Hinsdale, July 9, 1896.
28. Collection of Presidential Wills, Manuscript Division, Library of Congress.
29. *Index to the John Tyler Papers* (Washington, DC: Library of Congress, 1961), p. v.
30. Ibid.
31. Ibid.
32. Lyon Gardiner Tyler, *Letters and Times of the Tylers* (Richmond, VA: Whittet & Shepperson, 1884–1886).
33. Whitney, *The American Presidents*, p. 104.
34. John Quincy Adams, *Memoirs of John Quincy Adams, Comprising Portions of his Diary from 1795 to 1848*, edited by Charles Francis Adams (Freeport, NY: Books for Libraries Press, 1969), p. 103.
35. Thomas A. Bailey, *Presidential Greatness: The Image and the Man from George Washington to the Present* (New York: Appleton-Century, 1966), p. 211.
36. *Index to the James K. Polk Papers* (Washington, DC: Library of Congress, 1969), p. ix .
37. James K Polk, *Diary of James K. Polk During His Presidency, 1845–1849, now first printed*, edited and annotated by Milo Milton Quaife, Vol. 1 (Chicago: A.C. McClury & Co., 1910), p. 7.
38. *Index to the James K. Polk Papers*, p. ix.

39. John S. Jenkins, *The Life of James Knox Polk* (Auburn, NY: J.M. Alden, 1850).
40. *Index to the James K. Polk Papers*, p. xii.
41. Ibid.
42. Whitney, *The American Presidents*, p. 111.
43. *Index to the Zachary Taylor Papers* (Washington, DC: Library of Congress, Manuscript Division, 1960)
44. Whitney, *The American Presidents*, p. 122.
45. *Index to the Franklin Pierce Papers*, (Washington, DC: Library of Congress, 1962).
46. *Calendar of the Papers of Franklin Pierce*, prepared from the original manuscripts in the Library of Congress by W. L. Leech (Washington, DC: Library of Congress, Division of Manuscripts, 1917)
47. *Index to the Franklin Pierce Papers*, p. v.
48. John G. Nicolay and John Hay, *Abraham Lincoln; A History* (New York: The Century Company, 1890).
49. *Index to the Abraham Lincoln Papers* (Washington, DC: Library of Congress, Manuscript Division, 1960).
50. David C. Mearns, "The Story of the Papers," in *The Lincoln Papers*, Vol. 1 (Garden City, NY: Doubleday, 1948), p. 103.

CHAPTER 7. Post-Civil War Presidents

1. David C. Whitney, *The American Presidents* (New York: Doubleday, 1975), p. 152.
2. *Index to the Andrew Johnson Papers* (Washington, DC: Library of Congress, Manuscript Division, 1963), p. v.
3. Ibid.
4. Ibid., p. vi.
5. David M. DeWitt, *The Impeachment and Trial of Andrew Johnson, Seventeenth President of the United States* (New York and London: Mcmillan, 1903)
6. James S. Jones, *Life of Andrew Johnson, Seventeenth President of the United States* (Greenville, TN: East Tennessee Publishing Company, 1901).
7. *Index to the Andrew Johnson Papers*, p. viii.
8. Whitney, *The American Presidents*, p. 163.
9. Ulysses S. Grant, *Personal Memoirs of U.S. Grant* (New York: C.L. Webster & Co, 1885–1886).
10. *Index to the Ulysses S. Grant Papers* (Washington, DC: Library of Congress, Manuscript Division, 1965), p. viii.
11. Ibid., p. vii.
12. Ibid., p. v.
13. Adam Badeau, *Military History of Ulysses S. Grant* (New York: Appleton, 1885).
14. John R. Young, *Around the World with General Grant* (New York: Subscription Book Department, American News Co., 1879).
15. *Index to the Ulysses S. Grant Papers*, p. vii.
16. Ibid., p. v.
17. U.S. War Department, *The War of Rebellion: A Compilation of the Official Records of the Union and Confederate Armies*, published under the direction of the Secretary of War, 70 vols. (Washington, DC: Government Printing Office, 1880–1901).
18. *Index to the Ulysses S. Grant Papers*, p. ix.
19. Ibid., p. v.
20. Whitney, *The American Presidents*, p. 176.
21. *Index to the James Garfield Papers* (Washington, DC: Library of Congress, Manuscript Division, 1973), p. v.
22. Ibid.
23. Ibid., p. viii.
24. James A. Garfield, *The Works of James Abraham Garfield*, edited by Burke A. Hinsdale, 2 vols. (Boston: J.R. Osgood & Co., 1882–1883).
25. *Index to the James Garfield Papers*, p. x.
26. Theodore Clarke Smith, *Life and Letters of James Abraham Garfield*, 2 vols. (New Haven, CT: Yale University Press, 1925).
27. *Index to the James Garfield Papers*, p. xii.
28. Ruth (Stanley-Brown) Feis, *Mollie Garfield in the White House* (Chicago: Rand, McNally, 1963).
29. Lucretia Comer, *Harry Garfield's First Forty Years; a Man of Action in a Troubled World* (New York: Vantage Press, 1965).

30. *Index to the Chester A. Arthur Papers* (Washington, DC: Library of Congress, Manuscript Division, 1961), p. v.
31. Ibid.
32. Whitney, *The American Presidents*, p. 189.
33. *Index to the Grover Cleveland Papers* (Washington, DC: Library of Congress, Manuscript Division, 1965), p. v.
34. R.D.W. Connor, "The Franklin D. Roosevelt Library" *American Archivist*, III:2, (Apr. 1940), p. 82–83.
35. *Index to the Grover Cleveland Papers*, p. vi.
36. Robert McNutt McElroy, *Grover Cleveland, the Man and the Statesman*, introduction by Elihu Root (New York and London: Harper and Brothers, 1925), pp. 387–88.
37. Whitney, *The American Presidents*, p. 203.
38. Benjamin Harrison, *This Country of Ours* (New York: Scribner, 1897).
39. Marcia Wright, "The Benjamin Harrison Papers" *Library of Congress Quarterly Journal of Current Acquisitions* 18:3 (May 1961), p. 124.
40. Harry J. Sievers, *Benjamin Harrison*, 3 vols. (Chicago: H. Regnery Co., 1952–1968).

CHAPTER 8. Twentieth-Century Presidents

1. David C. Whitney, *The American Presidents* (New York: Doubleday, 1975), p. 211.
2. Ibid., p. 214.
3. Charles S. Olcott, *The Life of William McKinley,* 2 vols. (Boston and New York: Houghton Mifflin, 1916).
4. *Index to the William McKinley Papers* (Washington, DC: Library of Congress, Manuscript Division, 1963).
5. Whitney, *The American Presidents*, p. 227.
6. Theodore Roosevelt, *The Naval War of 1812* (New York and London: Putnam, 1903).
7. Theodore Roosevelt, *Life of Thomas Hart Benton* (Boston and New York: Houghton Mifflin, 1887).
8. Theodore Roosevelt, *The Winning of the West* (New York and London: Putnam, 1889–1896).
9. Theodore Roosevelt, *Theodore Roosevelt: An Autobiography* (New York: Macmillan, 1919).
10. *Index to the Theodore Roosevelt Papers* (Washington, DC: Library of Congress, Manuscript Division, 1969), p. vii.
11. Ibid., p. viii.
12. Joseph Bucklin Bishop, *Theodore Roosevelt and His Time,* Vol. 1 (New York: Scribner, 1920), p vii.
13. *Index to the Theodore Roosevelt Papers*, p. xi.
14. *A Sense of History; the Best Writings from the Pages of American Heritage.* Introductory note by Byron Dobell (Boston: Houghton Mifflin, 1985), p. 573.
15. Ibid., p. 580.
16. *Index to the William Howard Taft Papers* (Washington, DC: Library of Congress, Manuscript Division, 1972), p. vi.
17. Ibid.
18. Ibid.
19. Ibid., p. v.
20. Ibid., p. vi.
21. Ibid., p. vii.
22. Ibid., p. x.
23. Woodrow Wilson, *History of the American People,* 10 vols. (New York and London: Harper and Brothers, [1918]).
24. Whitney, *The American Presidents*, p. 248–49.
25. *Index to the Woodrow Wilson Papers* (Washington, DC: Library of Congress, Manuscript Division, 1973), p. v.
26. Ibid., p. vii.
27. Ibid.
28. Ibid., p. viii.
29. Ray Stannard Baker, *Woodrow Wilson and World Settlement*, written from his unpublished and personal material, 3 vols. (Garden City, NY: Doubleday, Page & Co., 1922).
30. Ray Stannard Baker, *American Chronicle: The Autobiography of Ray Stannard Baker* (New York: Scribner, 1945)
31. *Index to the Woodrow Wilson Papers*, p. xii.

32. Ray Stannard Baker, *Woodrow Wilson, Life and Letters,* 8 vols. (Garden City, NY: Doubleday, Page & Co., 1927–1939).
33. John Y. Cole, *For Congress and the Nation: A Chronological History of the Library of Congress* (Washington, DC: Library of Congress, 1979), p. 130.
34. Woodrow Wilson, *Papers of Woodrow Wilson,* edited by Arthur S. Link et al., 40 vols. (Princeton, NJ: Princeton University Press, 1966–1986).
35. Paul F. Boller, Jr., *Presidential Anecdotes* (New York: Oxford University Press, 1981), p. 241.
36. Frank Freidel, *The Presidents of the United States of America* (Washington, DC: White House Historical Association, 1964).
37. Whitney, *The American Presidents,* p. 269.
38. Ibid., p. 271.
39. Calvin Coolidge, *The Autobiography of Calvin Coolidge* (New York: Cosmopolitan Books, 1929).
40. *Index to the Calvin Coolidge Papers* (Washington, DC: Library of Congress, Manuscript Division, 1965), p. v.
41. Ibid., p. vi.
42. Ibid., p. v.
43. Claude M. Fuess, *Calvin Coolidge, the Man from Vermont* (Boston: Little, Brown and Company, 1940).
44. William A. White, *A Puritan in Babylon: The Story of Calvin Coolidge* (New York: Macmillan, 1938), p. vii.

CHAPTER 9. Historical Societies

1. David C. Whitney, *The American Presidents* (New York: Doubleday, 1975), p. 20.
2. Ibid., p. 21.
3. Ibid.
4. Ibid., p. 23.
5. Ibid., p. 58.
6. Ibid., p. 62.
7. L. H. Butterfield, "The Adams Papers: Whatever You Write Preserve," *American Heritage* X:3 (Apr. 1959), p. 31.
8. Ibid., p. 30.
9. John Adams, *The Works of John Adams, Second President of the United States,* with a Life of the Author, Notes and Illustrations by his Grandson, Charles Francis Adams, 10 vols. (Boston: Little, Brown and Company, 1850–56).
10. L. H. Butterfield, "Papers of the Adams Family: Some Account of their History" *Proceedings of the Massachusetts Historical Society* LXXI (Oct. 1953–May 1957), p. 341.
11. Ibid., p. 335.
12. Ibid., p. 331.
13. Butterfield, "The Adams Papers: Whatever You Write Preserve," p. 29.
14. Butterfield, "Papers of the Adams Family: Some Account of their History," p. 342.
15. Ibid., p. 336.
16. Ibid., p. 337.
17. Charles Francis Adams, *Letters of Mrs. Adams* (Boston, 1840).
18. Adams, *The Works of John Adams, Second President of the United States.*
19. John Quincy Adams, *Memoirs of John Quincy Adams, Comprising Portions of his Diary from 1795 to 1848,* edited by Charles Francis Adams, 12 vols. (Freeport, NY: Books for Libraries Press, 1969).
20. Butterfield, "Papers of the Adams Family: Some Account of their History," p. 337.
21. Butterfield, "The Adams Papers: Whatever You Write Preserve," p. 32.
22. Charles Francis Adams II, *Charles Francis Adams* (Boston: Houghton Mifflin, 1900).
23. Butterfield, "Papers of the Adams Family: Some Account of their History," p. 340.
24. Adams, John Quincy, *The Writings of John Quincy Adams,* edited by Worthington Chauncey Ford, 7 vols. (New York: Macmillan 1913).
25. John Adams, *Diary and Autobiography of John Adams,* edited by L. H. Butterfield, 4 vols. (Boston: Belknap Press of Harvard University Press, 1961), p. xxvi.
26. *Guide to the Microfilm Edition of the Millard Fillmore Papers,* edited by Lester W. Smith (Buffalo, NY: Buffalo and Erie County Historical Society and State University College at Oswego, NY, 1975), p. 8.
27. Ibid.
28. J.D. Richardson, *A Compilation of the Messages and Papers of the Presidents,* Vol. 6, (New York, 1907), p. 2704.

29. *Guide to the Microfilm Edition of the Millard Fillmore Papers*, p. 9.
30. Millard Fillmore, *The Millard Fillmore Papers*, edited by Frank H. Severance, Vols. 10, 11 (Buffalo, NY: The Buffalo Historical Society, 1907).
31. *Guide to the Microfilm Edition of the Millard Fillmore Papers*, p. 11.
32. Whitney, *The American Presidents*, p.129.
33. Rexford G. Tugwell, *How They Became President* (New York: Simon and Schuster, 1964), p. 180.
34. Whitney, *The American Presidents*, p. 132.
35. Ibid.
36. *Guide to the Microfilm Edition of the James Buchanan Papers at the Historical Society of Pennsylvania*, edited by Lucy F. West (Philadelphia, PA: Historical Society of Pennsylvania, 1974), p. 16.
37. Herbert R. Collins and David B. Weaver, *Wills of the U.S. Presidents* (New York: Communication Channels, Inc., 1976), pp. 118–19.
38. *Guide to the Microfilm Edition of the James Buchanan Papers at the Historical Society of Pennsylvania*, p. 17.
39. George Ticknor Curtis, *Life of James Buchanan, Fifteenth President of the United States*, 2 vols. (New York: Harper, 1883).
40. James Buchanan, *The Works of James Buchanan Comprising his Speeches, State Papers and Private correspondence*. Collected and edited by John Bassett Moore, 12 vols. (Philadelphia, PA: Lippincott, 1908–11).
41. *James Buchanan and Harriet [Lane] Johnston. A Register and Index of Their Papers in the Library of Congress* (Washington, DC: Library of Congress, Manuscript Division, 1979), p. 4.
42. Tugwell, *How They Became President*, p. 359.
43. Whitney, *The American Presidents*, pp. 262–63.
44. *The Warren G. Harding Papers; an inventory to the Microfilm Edition* (Columbus, OH: Archives and Manuscript Divisions, Ohio Historical Society, 1964), p. 2.
45. Ibid., p. 5.
46. Kenneth W. Duckett, "The Harding Papers, How Some Were Burned" *American Heritage* 16:2 (Feb. 1965), p. 30.
47. *New York Times*, December 25, 1925, p. 1.
48. Duckett, "The Harding Papers, How Some Were Burned," p. 108.
49. Francis Russell, *The Shadow of Blooming Grove: Warren G. Harding in His Times* (New York: McGraw-Hill, 1968).
50. Francis Russell, "The Harding Papers: How Some Were Saved" *American Heritage* 16:2 (Feb. 1965), p. 28.
51. Ibid., p. 106.
52. Ibid., p. 110.
53. Ibid., p. 25.
54. Ibid., p. 110.

CHAPTER 10. Special Libraries

1. David C. Whitney, *The American Presidents* (Garden City, NY: Doubleday, 1975), p. 168.
2. Kenneth B. Davison, *The Presidency of Rutherford B. Hayes*, Contributions in American Studies, Number 3 (Westport, CT: Greenwood Press, 1972), p. 167.
3. Harry Barnard, *Rutherford B. Hayes and his America* (Indianapolis, IN: Bobbs-Merrill, 1954), p. 590.
4. Ibid., p. 503.
5. Samuel C. Townsend, *Spiegel Grove. The Home of Rutherford B. Hayes* (Fremont, OH, 1965), p. 18.
6. Davison, *The Presidency of Rutherford B. Hayes*, p. 167.
7. "Dedication of the Hayes Memorial Library" *Ohio Archaeological and Historical Quarterly* 25:4 (Oct. 1916), p. 401.
8. Ibid., pp. 433–434.
9. Ibid., p. 434.
10. Davison, *The Presidency of Rutherford B. Hayes*, p. 239.
11. Franklin D. Roosevelt, Letter to Webb C. Hayes II, Oct. 27, 1937.
12. Watt P. Marchman and James H. Rodabaugh, "Collections of the Rutherford B. Hayes State Memorial" *Ohio History* 71:151–57 (July 1962), p. 157.
13. Herbert C. Hoover, *Principles of Mining* (New York: Hill Publishing Company, 1909), 199 p.

14. Frank Freidel and Allen Brinkley, *America in the 20th Century* (New York: A.A. Knopf, 1976), p. 205.
15. Herbert C. Hoover, *Memoirs*, 3 vols. (New York: Macmillan, 1951–52).
16. Herbert C. Hoover, *The Ordeal of Woodrow Wilson* (New York: McGraw-Hill, 1958), 318p.
17. Ralph W. Hansen, "Stanford University Libraries" *Encyclopedia of Library and Information Science*, Vol. 29 (New York: Marcel Dekker, Inc, 1980), pp. 1–32.
18. Herbert C. Hoover, *Herbert Hoover, A Register of his Papers in the Archives of the Hoover Institution on War, Revolution and Peace* (Stanford, CA: Hoover Institution Press, Stanford University, 1983), pp. ix–xi.

CHAPTER 11. The Franklin D. Roosevelt Library and Museum in Hyde Park, New York

1. David C. Whitney, *The American Presidents* (Garden City, NY: Doubleday, 1975), p. 288.
2. Ibid., p. 289.
3. Franklin D. Roosevelt, Letter to James Roosevelt, Dec. 26, 1937.
4. Thomas A. Baily, *Presidential Greatness* (New York: Irvington Publishers, Inc., 1978), p. 24.
5. Franklin D. Roosevelt, Letter to Samuel E. Morison, Feb. 28, 1938.
6. William J. Stewart and Charyl C. Pollard, "Franklin D. Roosevelt, Collector" *Prologue* (Winter 1969): 13–28, p. 13.
7. Eleanor Roosevelt, *This Is My Story* (New York and London: Harper, 1937), p.128.
8. Franklin D. Roosevelt, Letter to Dr. Edward J. Winkoop, Dec 15, 1934.
9. Henry J. Toombs, Letter to Franklin D. Roosevelt, Nov. 13, 1937.
10. Franklin D. Roosevelt, Letter to Henry J. Toombs, Nov. 22, 1937.
11. Franklin D. Roosevelt, Letter to Keith Morgan, May 25, 1938.
12. Donald R. McCoy, "The Beginnings of the Franklin D. Roosevelt Library" *Prologue* (Fall 1975): 138–150, p. 139.
13. Franklin D. Roosevelt, Letter of Invitation and Memorandum, Dec. 1, 1938. The Letter was sent to: Charles A. Beard, historian; Julian P. Boyd, Director, Historical Society of Pennsylvania; William E. Dodd, former ambassador to Germany; Alexander C. Flick, New York State Historian; Helen Taft Manning, President of Bryn Mawr College; Samuel Eliot Morison, Harvard University; Frederic L. Paxson, President, American Historical Association; Edmund E. Day, President, Cornell University; Frank P. Graham, President, University of North Carolina; Randolph G. Adams, Librarian, University of Michigan; R.D.W. Connor, Archivist of the United States; Archibald M. MacLeish, poet and future Librarian of Congress; Felix Frankfurter, Associate Justice of the Supreme Court; Samuel I. Rosenman, Justice of the Supreme Court of New York; Stewart Chase, Department of Labor; Ernest Lindley, author; Francis C. Walker, later assistant to the president; and Margaret M. Wells, President, League of Women Voters.
14. Franklin D. Roosevelt, *Public Papers and Addresses of Franklin D. Roosevelt, with a special introduction and explanatory notes by President Roosevelt*, compiled by Samuel I. Rosenman. 13 vols. (New York: Random House, 1938–1950).
15. Press Release, Dec. 10, 1938.
16. Waldo Gifford Leland, "The Creation of the Franklin D. Roosevelt Library: A Personal Narrative" *American Archivist* (1955): 11–29), p. 13.
17. Julian P. Boyd, Letter to to Franklin D. Roosevelt, Dec. 12, 1938.
18. Leland, "The Creation of the Franklin D. Roosevelt Library," p. 21.
19. Eleanor Roosevelt, *Franklin D. Roosevelt and Hyde Park,* Hyde Park Historical Association (n.d.), p. 18.
20. Herbert H. Lehman, Letter to Franklin D. Roosevelt, May 22, 1939.
21. McCoy, "The Beginnings of the Franklin D. Roosevelt Library," p. 147.
22. Fred Shipman, "What Do You Know About the Franklin D. Roosevelt Library?" Unpublished paper. Feb. 1941, p. 3.
23. *Historical Materials in the Franklin D. Roosevelt Library* (Washington: National Archives and Records Administration, The Franklin D. Roosevelt Library, Sept. 1985).
24. Based on Franklin D. Roosevelt memoranda in the President's Personal File.
25. James L.Whitehead, *The Museum of the Franklin D. Roosevelt Library* (Hyde Park, NY, n.d.), p. 15.

CHAPTER 12. The Harry S. Truman Library in Independence, Missouri

1. Harry S. Truman, *Memoirs by Harry S. Truman. Volume One, Year of Decisions.* (New York: Doubleday, 1955), p. 119.
2. David C. Whitney, *The American Presidents* (Garden City, NY: Doubleday, 1975), p. 296.
3. Thomas A. Bailey, *The Pugnacious Presidents* (New York: The Free Press, 1980), p. 411.
4. Whitney, *The American Presidents*, p. 297.
5. Neil M. Johnson and Philip D. Lagerquist, "Resources at the Harry S. Truman Library on Western Issues and Programs" *Government Publications Review,* Vol 7A (1980): 159–66, p. 159.
6. Harry Truman, Letter to Jess Larsen, Jan. 17, 1953.
7. Oral History Interview with Robert P. Weatherford, Jr., June 11, 1976 (Harry S. Truman Library, Oral History Collection), p. 19–22.
8. Address by the Honorable Earl Warren, Chief Justice of the United States Supreme Court, at the Dedication Ceremony of the Truman Library, Independence, Missouri on July 6, 1957. Press Release, p. 2–3.
9. Richard H. Rovere, "Mr. Truman Shows Off His Library," *The New York Times Magazine* (June 30, 1957), p. 22.
10. "The Harry S. Truman Library" (National Archives release, May 1987), p. 2.
11. *Historical Materials in the Harry S. Truman Library* (Independence, MO: Harry S. Truman Library, National Archives and Records Service, General Services Administration, Jan. 1982)

CHAPTER 13. The Herbert Hoover Library and Museum in West Branch, Iowa

1. Ruth Dennison, "The Herbert Hoover Presidential Library" *Encyclopedia of Library and Information Science,* Vol. 10 (1970): 398–400), p. 398.
2. Herbert Hoover, "Presidential Library Address, West Branch, August 10, 1962" *The Palimpsest* 43:8 (Aug. 1962), p. 379.
3. *Historical Materials in the Herbert Hoover Presidential Library* (West Branch, IA: Herbert H. Hoover Presidential Library, Mar. 1985).
4. George H. Nash, *The Life of Herbert Hoover: Volume 1: The Engineer, 1874–1914* (New York: W.W. Norton, 1983).

CHAPTER 14. The Dwight D. Eisenhower Library in Abilene, Kansas

1. Dwight D. Eisenhower, *Crusade in Europe* 2 vols. (Garden City, NY: Doubleday, 1948).
2. Rexford G. Tugwell, *How They Became President* (New York: Simon and Schuster, 1964), p. 448.
3. Thomas A. Bailey, *Presidential Greatness: The Image and the Man from George Washington to the Present* (New York: Appleton-Century, 1966), p. 325.
4. David C. Whitney, *The American Presidents* (New York: Doubleday, 1975), p. 317.
5. Ibid.
6. Dwight D. Eisenhower *The White House Years,* 2 vols. (Garden City, NY: Doubleday, 1963–65).
7. Eisenhower Foundation, Minutes of the Executive Committee Meeting, June 14, 1950, p. 4.
8. "Remarks at the Dedication of the Eisenhower Museum, Abilene, Kansas. Nov. 11, 1954." *Public Papers of the Presidents. Dwight D. Eisenhower, 1954* (Washington, DC: Government Printing Office, 1959), p. 1045.
9. Dwight D. Eisenhower, Letter to Emmett S. Graham, Mar. 8, 1954.
10. "Some Considerations on Presidential Papers and Libraries," National Archives Memo, Jan. 30, 1954, p. 2.
11. 86th Congress, House of Representatives, Government Activities Subcommittee of the Committee on Government Operations, Press Release, April 28, 1960.
12. Dwight D. Eisenhower, Letter to William E. Robinson, May 18, 1965.

13. Memo from Wilton B. Persons to White House Staff, Nov. 18, 1960.
14. *Historical Materials in the Dwight D. Eisenhower Library* (Abilene, KS: Dwight D. Eisenhower Library, National Archives and Records Service, General Services Administration, 1984).
15. *Dwight D. Eisenhower: A Select Bibliography of Periodical and Dissertation Literature* (Abilene, KS: Dwight D. Eisenhower Library, National Archives and Record Service, General Services Administration, 1981).
16. John E. Wickman, "Dwight D. Eisenhower Library" *Encyclopedia of Library and Information Science* 37, Supplement 2 (1984): 73–70, p. 75.

CHAPTER 15. The John F. Kennedy Library in Boston, Massachusetts

1. John Fitzgerald Kennedy, *Why England Slept* (New York: W. Funk, 1940).
2. John Fitzgerald Kennedy, *Profiles in Courage* (New York: Harper, 1956).
3. David C. Whitney, *The American Presidents* (New York: Doubleday, 1975), p. 328.
4. Thomas A. Bailey, *The Pugnacious Presidents. White House Warriors on Parade* (New York: The Free Press, 1980), p. 434.
5. Whitney, *The American Presidents*, p. 330.
6. Thomas A. Bailey, *Presidential Greatness: The Image and the Man from George Washington to the Present* (New York: Appleton-Century, 1966), p. 329.
7. Tip O'Neill with William Novak, *Man of the House. The Life and Political Memoirs of Speaker Tip O'Neill* (New York: Random House, 1987), p. 178.
8. Wayne C. Grover, Letter to John F. Kennedy, Dec. 19, 1960.
9. Nathan M. Pusey, Oral History Interview, June 21, 1967, p. 12–13.
10. Paul Buck, Letter to Arthur Schlesinger, Jr., Feb. 15, 1961.
11. Nathan M. Pusey, Letter to John F. Kennedy, Mar. 28, 1961.
12. John F. Kennedy, Letter to Nathan M. Pusey, May 24, 1961.
13. Bernard Boutin, Oral History Interview, June 3, 1964, p. 43.
14. Arthur Schlesinger, Jr., Letter to cabinet members, May 23, 1962.
15. Pusey, Oral History Interview, p. 17–18.
16. Dan H. Fenn, Jr, "Launching the John F. Kennedy Library" *The American Archivist* 42: 4 (Oct. 1979), p. 430.
17. Richard E. Neustadt to Arthur Schlesinger, Jr., "First Thoughts on the Kennedy Library," Dec. 26, 1963.
18. Edward M. Kennedy to Arthur Schlesinger, Jr., "Views on the John F. Kennedy Memorial and Library," Dec. 30, 1963.
19. William David and Christina Tree, *The Kennedy Library* (Exton, PA: Schiffer Publishing, Ltd., 1980), p. 124.
20. Kennedy to Schlesinger, "Views on the John F. Kennedy Memorial and Library."
21. Wayne C. Grover to Arthur Schlesinger, Jr., "Progress Report on the John F. Kennedy Library," Dec. 19, 1962.
22. *Historical Materials in the John Fitzgerald Kennedy Library* (Boston: John F. Kennedy Library, 1986).
23. David and Tree, *The Kennedy Library*, p. 77.
24. "Reagans Call on Camelot" *Boston Globe*, June 26, 1985, p. 70+.
25. *Historical Materials in the John Fitzgerald Kennedy Library*, p. i.

CHAPTER 16. The Lyndon B. Johnson Library in Austin, Texas

1. Doris Kearns, *Lyndon Johnson and the American Dream* (New York: Harper & Row, 1976), p. 357.
2. Lyndon Baines Johnson, *The Vantage Point: Perspectives of the Presidency 1963–1969* (New York: Holt, Rinehart and Winston, 1971).
3. Kearns, *Lyndon Johnson and the American Dream*, pp. 365–66.
4. Mildred Portner, Oral History Transcript, p. I–14.
5. Horace Busby, Memorandum for the President and Mrs. Johnson, "The Archives Project," Feb. 1965, pp. 3–4.
6. Ibid., p. 7.
7. W.W. Heath, Letter to Lyndon B. Johnson, Aug. 6, 1965.
8. Lyndon B. Johnson, Letter to W. W. Heath, Aug. 9, 1965.

9. Alfred Steinberg, *Sam Johnson's Boy: A Close-Up of the President from Texas* (New York: Macmillan, 1968), p. 821.
10. White House Daily Diary, Friday, Sept. 10, 1965.
11. Gordon Bunshaft, Oral Interview Transcript, p. I–12.
12. *The Lyndon Baines Johnson Library and Museum* (The Lyndon Baines Johnson Foundation, n.d.), p. 5.
13. "Remarks of President Johnson at the LBJ Library Dedication." University of Texas Systems, News and Information Service. Press Release, May 22, 1971, pp. 1–2.
14. Richard M. Nixon, "Remarks at the Dedication of the Lyndon Baines Johnson Library in Austin, Texas" *Public Papers of the Presidents of the United States: Richard Nixon, 1971* (Washington, DC: United States Government Printing Office, 1972), p. 656.
15. Kearns, *Lyndon Johnson and the American Dream*, pp. 363–64.
16. Dorothy Territo, Letter to Lyndon B. Johnson, Sept. 17, 1965.
17. Ibid.
18. Lyndon B. Johnson, Letter to Lawson Knott, Nov. 1966.
19. Based on various status reports about the acquisition of materials for the Lyndon Baines Johnson Library, 1967–1968, by Lawson B. Knott, General Services Administrator, and on a memorandum from Herman Kahn to Dorothy Territo, "Acquisition of Government Printing Office Publications for the Lyndon B. Johnson Library," Mar. 3, 1966.
20. Lyndon B. Johnson, Letter to Lawson B. Knott, May 22, 1968.
21. Joe B. Frantz, Letter to Frank Erwin, June 3, 1968.
22. Kearns, *Lyndon Johnson and the American Dream*, p. 353.
23. *Historical Materials in the Lyndon B. Johnson Library*, 1987 draft obtained from the National Archives, Office of Presidential Libraries.
24. Lady Bird (Claudia T.) Johnson, *White House Diary* (New York: Holt, Rinehart and Winston, 1970), p. 243.
25. Ibid., p. 313–15.
26. George E. Reedy, Letter to Lyndon B. Johnson, Oct. 19, 1968.

CHAPTER 17. The Gerald R. Ford Library in Ann Arbor, Michigan and the Gerald R. Ford Museum in Grand Rapids, Michigan

1. Gerald R. Ford and John R. Stiles, *Portrait of the Assassin* (New York: Simon & Schuster, 1965).
2. Jerald F. terHorst, *Gerald Ford and the Future of the Presidency* (New York: Third Press, 1974), p. 81.
3. Ibid., p. 139.
4. David C. Whitney, *The American Presidents* (New York: Doubleday, 1975), p. 392.
5. Ibid., p. 393.
6. Ibid., p. 395.
7. Arthur M. Schlesinger, Jr., *The Cycles of American History* (Boston: Houghton Mifflin, 1986), p. 289.
8. Whitney, *The American Presidents*, (Garden City, NY: Doubleday, 1982), p. 414.
9. Tip O'Neill with William Novak, *Man of the House: The Life and Memoirs of Speaker Tip O'Neill* (New York: Random House, 1987), p. 262.
10. Robert M. Warner, "The Prologue is Past" *The American Archivist* 41: 1 (Jan. 1978), pp. 6–7.
11. Ibid., p 7.
12. *Ann Arbor News*, Sept. 17, 1974.
13. Thomas G. Ford, Letter to Philip W. Buchen, July 11, 1975.
14. Philip W. Buchen, Letter to Thomas G. Ford, July 29, 1975.
15. Carl H. Morgenstern, Letter to Gerald R. Ford, Aug. 1, 1975.
16. Interview transcript, Gerald Ford Library, Richard Doolen files, Aug. 26, 1975.
17. Philip W. Buchen, Letter to Carl H. Morgenstern, Aug. 26, 1975.
18. GSA News Release, "President Ford Deeds Papers to U.S.; Library, Museum to Be in Michigan" (Washington, DC: U.S. General Services Administration, Dec. 14, 1976).
19. "Ford Library Agreement," July 31, 1978.
20. *Ann Arbor News*, Apr. 28, 1981, p. A5.
21. Arthur F. Sampson, Letter to Gerald R. Ford, Dec. 17, 1974.
22. *Historical Materials in the Gerald R. Ford Library*, compiled by David Horrocks and William McNitt; Audiovisual Section by Richard Holzhausen. (Ann Arbor, MI: Gerald R. Ford Library, Aug. 1986).

CHAPTER 18. The Jimmy Carter Center in Atlanta, Georgia

1. James David Barber, *The Presidential Character,* 2nd ed. (Englewood Cliffs, NJ: Prentice-Hall, Inc., 1977), p. 509.
2. David C. Whitney, *The American Presidents* (Garden City, NY: Doubleday, 1982), p. 410.
3. Ibid., p. 412.
4. Jimmy Carter, *Keeping Faith: Memoirs of a President* (New York: Bantam Books, 1982), p. 17.
5. Tip O'Neill with William Novak, *Man of the House: The Life and Memoirs of speaker Tip O'Neill* (New York: Random House, 1987), p. 297.
6. Whitney, *The American Presidents,* p. 417.
7. Ibid., p. 421.
8. Arthur Schlesinger, Jr., *The Cycles of American History* (Boston: Houghton Mifflin, 1986), p. 293.
9. O'Neill, *Man of the House,* p. 298.
10. Carter, *Keeping Faith.*
11. Donald B. Schewe, "Transfers and Transformations: Processing the Papers of Jimmy Carter" *Georgia Archive* X: 2 (Fall 1982), p. 53.
12. Ibid., pp. 58–59.
13. Hugh Carter, Robert J. Lipshutz, Michael Cardozo to Jimmy Carter, "Disposition of Your Presidential Papers; Establishment of a Carter Library," Aug. 8, 1977, p. 3.
14. Jimmy Carter, Letter to Lynton E. Godwin III, Mayor of Plains, June 8, 1979.
15. Jimmy Carter, Press Release, Oct. 1982.
16. "President Praises Carter at Library" *New York Times,* Oct. 2, 1986, p. 1+.
17. Carter Presidential Center Press Release, 1987.

CHAPTER 19. Presidential Libraries in the Planning Stage: The Richard M. Nixon and Ronald W. Reagan Libraries

1. Richard M Nixon, *Six Crises* (Garden City, NY: Doubleday, 1962).
2. Hugh Sidey, *Portrait of a President* (New York: Harper & Row, 1975), p. 18.
3. David C. Whitney, *The American Presidents* (New York: Doubleday, 1975), p. 382.
4. *Newsweek,* Sept. 29, 1986, p. 27.
5. Charles J. Cooper, *Nixon Paper Regulations,* Memorandum for Robert P. Bedell (U.S. Department of Justice, Office of Legal Counsel, Feb. 18, 1986), p. 2.
6. Ibid., p. 10.
7. National Archives and Records Administration, "Preservation and Protection of and Access to Historical Materials of the Nixon Administration; Repromulgation of Public Access Regulations" *Federal Register* 51:40 (Feb. 28, 1986), pp. 7728–36.
8. "Holdings of the Nixon Presidential Materials Project" (National Archives, Office of Presidential Libraries, Nov. 1986); "Availability of the Nixon Presidential Materials" (Nixon Presidential Materials Project, Oct. 1987).
9. William E. Simon and Maurice H. Stans, Memo to Contributors to the Richard Nixon Presidential Library Project, Oct. 23, 1987.
10. Personal communications with John Whitaker, Executive Director, Richard Nixon Presidential Archives Foundation, Fall 1987.
11. *The Richard Nixon Presidential Library* (Washington, DC: Richard Nixon Presidential Archives Foundation, brochure, n.d.).
12. William Trombley, "Reagan Library Strains Link Between Stanford and Hoover Institution" *Los Angeles Times,* Mar. 8, 1987, Part I, p. 3+.
13. "Southland, Not Stanford, to Get Reagan Library" *Los Angeles Times,* Apr. 24, 1987, p. 1+.
14. "Serene Site for Reagan Library" *Los Angeles Times,* Feb. 13, 1988, p 3+.
15. "The President Heads for Higher Office" *The Washington Post,* Jul. 9, 1988, p. D3.

Bibliography

This bibliography is a selection of published works cited or consulted in the preparation of the manuscript, and works of and by various presidents. The works by the presidents themselves are listed chronologically by date of publication.

WORKS RELATING TO PRESIDENTIAL RECORDS IN GENERAL

Annual Report of the Librarian of Congress, 1986. Washington, DC: Library of Congress, 1987.

Bailey, Thomas A. *The Pugnacious Presidents.* New York: The Free Press, 1980, 504p.

Barber, James David. *The Presidential Character.* 2nd ed. Englewood Cliffs, NJ: Prentice-Hall, 1977, 576p.

Berman, Larry. "Evolution and Value of Presidential Libraries" in Harold C. Relyea et al. *The Presidency and Information Policy,* New York: Center for the Study of the Presidency, IV:1, 1981, pp. 79–91.

Boller. Paul F., Jr, *Presidential Anecdotes.* New York: Oxford University Press, 1981, 410p.

———. *Presidential Campaigns.* New York: Oxford University Press, 1984.

Buck, Elizabeth Hawthorn. "General Legislation for Presidential Libraries." *American Archivist* 18:4 (Oct. 1955): 337–41.

Burton, Dennis A., Rhoads, James B., and Smock, Raymond W. *A Guide to Manuscripts in the Presidential Libraries.* College Park, MD: Research Materials Corp., 1985, 451p.

Cole, John Y. *For Congress and the Nation: A Chronological History of the Library of Congress.* Washington, DC: Library of Congress, 1979, 196p.

———. "The Library of Congress and the Presidential Parade, 1800–1984." *Library of Congress Information Bulletin* 43:42 (Oct. 15, 1984): 343–48.

Collins, Herbert R., and Weaver, David B. *Wills of the U.S. Presidents.* New York: Communications Channels, Inc., 1976.

A Compilation of the Messages and Papers of the Presidents. Edited and compiled by James Daniel Richardson. 20 vols. New York: Bureau of National Literature, Inc, 1917.

Cost of Former Presidents to U.S. Taxpayers. FY 1980. Washington, DC: 96th Congress, 1st Session.

Directory of Archives and Manuscript Repositories in the United States. 2nd ed. Phoenix, AZ: The Oryx Press, 1988, 872p.

Encyclopedia of Library and Information Science. New York: Marcel Dekker, Inc., 1968–.

Ferris, Robert G., ed. *The Presidents; from the Inauguration of George Washington to the Inauguration of Jimmy Carter.* Washington, DC: National Park Service, 1977.

Freidel, Frank, and Brinkley, Allen. *America in the 20th Century.* New York: A.A. Knopf, 1976, 581p.

Gondos, Victor, Jr. *J. Franklin Jameson and the Birth of the National Archives 1906–1926.* Philadelphia: University of Pennsylvania Press, 1981, 232p.

Goodrum, Charles A. *Treasures of the Library of Congress.* New York: Harry N. Abrams, 1980.

Guide to the National Archives of the United States. Washington, DC: U.S. Government Printing Office, National Archives and Records Service, 1974, 884p.

Hackman, Larry J., and Sahli, Nancy. "The NHPRC and a Guide to Manuscript and Archival Material in the United States." *American Archivist* 40:2 (Apr. 1977): 201–05.

Hamer, Philip M. *A Guide to Archives and Manuscripts in the United States.* New Haven, CT: Yale University Press, 1961, 775p.

Jones, Houston Gwynne. "Presidential Libraries: Is There a Case for a National Presidential Library?" *American Archivist* XXXVIII (July 1975): 325–28.

———. *The Records of a Nation: Their Management, Preservation and Use.* New York: Atheneum, 1969, 311p.

Kirkendall, Richard S. "Presidential Libraries: One Researcher's Point of View." *American Archivist* 25:4 (Oct. 1962): 441–48.

Land, Robert H. "The National Union Catalog of Manuscript Collections." *American Archivist* XVIII (Apr. 1955): 99–110.

Magill, Frank N. *The American Presidents: The Office and the Men.* 3 vols. Pasadena, CA: Englewood Cliffs, NJ: Salem Press, 1986.

McCoy, Donald R. *The National Archives: America's Ministry of Documents 1934–1968.* Chapel Hill, NC: University of North Carolina Press, 1978, 437p.

Mearns, David C. *The Story Up to Now: The Library of Congress 1800–1946.* Washington, DC: Library of Congress, 1947, 226p.

The National Archives and Records Administration; Annual Reports for the Years Ended September 30, 1987. Washington, DC: National Archives and Records Administration, 1988, 104p.

The National Union Catalog of Manuscript Collections (1959–1961). Ann Arbor, MI: J.W. Edwards, 1962, 1061p.

O'Neill, James E. "Will Success Spoil the Presidential Libraries?" *American Archivist* XXXVI (July 1973) 339–51.

O'Neill, Tip with Novak, William. *Man of the House: The Life and Political Memoirs of Speaker Tip O'Neill.* New York: Random House, 1987, 387p.

Peters, William. *A More Perfect Union.* New York: Crown Publishers, Inc., 1987, 294p.

"Presidential Sites: An Inventory of Historic Buildings, Sites and Memorials Associated with the Former Presidents of the United States." Washington, DC: National Park Service, 1982.

Public Papers of the Presidents of the United States. Washington, DC: Government Printing Office, continuing series.

"Raiding the White House Files—Papers Sold, Burned, Hidden, Given to the World." *US News and World Report* 35 (Nov. 27, 1953): 29–32.

Reid, Warren R. "Public Papers of the Presidents." *American Archivist* 25:4 (Oct. 1962) 435–39.

Salamanca, Lucy. *Fortress of Freedom: The Story of the Library of Congress.* Philadelphia: Lippincott, 1942, 445p.

Schlesinger, Arthur M., Jr. *The Cycles of American History.* Boston: Houghton Mifflin, 1986, 498p.

Schouler, James. *History of the United States under the Constitution.* New York, 1882.

A Sense of History; the Best Writings from the Pages of American Heritage. Introductory note by Byron Dobell. Boston: Houghton Mifflin, 1985, 832p.

Shelley, Fred. "The Presidential Papers Program of the Library of Congress." *American Archivist* 25:4 (Oct. 1962): 429–33.

Tugwell, Rexford G. *How They Became President.* New York: Simon and Schuster, 1964, 587p.

Van Tyne, Claude H., and Leland, Waldo G. *Guide to the Archives of the Government of the United States.* 2nd ed. Washington, DC: Carnegie Institution, 1907, 327p.

Veit, Fritz. *Presidential Libraries and Collections.* New York: Greenwood Press, 1987, 152p.

Viola, Herman J. *The National Archives of the United States.* New York: Harry N. Abrams, 1984, 488p.

Wallace, David H. "Historic Libraries in National Park Service Areas: Independence National Historical Park." Washington, DC: National Park Service.

Whitney, David C. *The American Presidents.* New York: Doubleday, 1975, 470p.; Doubleday, 1982, 561p.

Wigdor, Alexandra K., and Wigdor, David. "The Future of Presidential Papers." in Harold C. Relyea et al. *The Presidency and Information Policy,* New York: Center for the Study of the Presidency, IV:1, 1981, pp. 92–101.

WORKS RELATING TO INDIVIDUAL PRESIDENTS

George Washington

Index to the George Washington Papers. Washington, DC: Library of Congress, Manuscript Division, 1964, 294p.

Knowlton, John D. "Properly Arranged and So Correctly Recorded." *American Archivist* 27 (July 1969): 371–74.

Washington, George. *The Writings of George Washington: Being the Correspondence, Addresses, Messages.* Edited by Jared Sparks. 12 vols. Boston: American Stationers'; J.B. Russell, 1834–37.

——. *The Writings of George Washington.* Edited by Worthington Chauncey Ford. 14 vols. New York and London: Putnam, 1889–93.

——. *Diaries: 1748–1799.* Edited by John C. Fitzpatrick. 4 vols. Boston: Houghton Mifflin, 1925.

——. *The Writings of George Washington from the Original Manuscript Sources, 1745-1799.* Edited by John C. Fitzpatrick. 39 vols. Washington, DC: U.S. Government Printing Office, 1944.

John Adams

Adams, Abigail. *Book of Abigail and John: Selected Letters of the Adams Family, 1762-1784.* Edited by L.H. Butterfield. Cambridge, MA: Harvard University Press, 1975, 411p.

Adams, Charles Francis. *The Life of John Adams.* 2 vols. New York: Haskell House Publishers, Ltd, 1968.

Adams, John. *The Works of John Adams, Second President of the United States: With a Life of the Author.* Notes and Illustrations by his Grandson Charles Francis Adams. 10 vols. Boston: Little, Brown, 1850–56.

——. *The Adams–Jefferson Letters; the Complete Correspondence.* Edited by Lester J. Cappon. 2 vols. Chapel Hill, NC: University of North Carolina Press, 1959.

——. *Diary and Autobiography of John Adams.* Edited by L. H. Butterfield. 4 vols. Boston: Belknap Press of Harvard University Press, 1961.

——. *Earliest Diary of John Adams.* Edited by L.H. Butterfield. 4 vols. Boston: Belknap Press of Harvard University Press, 1961.

——. *Legal Papers of John Adams.* Edited by Lawrence K. Wroth and Hiller B. Zobel. 3 vols. Boston: Belknap Press of Harvard University Press, 1965.

——. *Papers of John Adams.* Edited by Robert J. Taylor. 4 vols. Boston: Belknap Press of Harvard University Press, 1977–83.

Bowen, Catherine Drinker. *John Adams and the American Revolution.* Boston: Little, Brown, 1950, 699p.

Butterfield, L.H. "The Adams Papers: Whatever You Write Preserve." *American Heritage* X:3 (Apr. 1959): 26–32, 88–93.

Butterfield, L.H. "Papers of the Adams Family: Some Account of their History." *Proceedings of the Massachusetts Historical Society* LXXI (Oct. 1953–May 1957), pp. 328–356.

Microfilms of the Adams Papers. Boston: Massachusetts Historical Society, 1954–56, parts 1–4.

Mugridge Donald H. "The Adams Papers." *American Archivist* XXV (Oct. 1962): 449–54.

Thomas Jefferson

Guide to the Microfilm Edition of the Jefferson Papers of the University of Virginia, 1732–1828. Edited by Douglas W. Tanner. Charlottesville, VA: University of Virginia Library, The Thomas Jefferson Papers, Microfilm Publication No. 9, Apr. 1977, 96p.

Index to the Thomas Jefferson Papers. Washington, DC: Library of Congress, Manuscript Division, 1976, 155p.

Jefferson, Thomas. *Memoir, Correspondence, and Miscellanies, from the Papers of Thomas Jefferson.* Edited by Thomas Jefferson Randolph. 4 vols. Charlottesville, VA: F. Carr and Co., 1829.

———. *The Writings of Thomas Jefferson: Being his Autobiography, Correspondence, Reports, Messages, Addresses, and other Writings, Official and Private.* Published by Order of the Joint Committee of Congress on the Library, from the original manuscripts, deposited in the Department of State. Edited by H.A. Washington. 9 vols. Washington, DC: Taylor & Maury, 1853–54.

———. *The Writings of Thomas Jefferson.* Published in 1853 by Order of the Joint Committee of Congress. Edited by Andrew A. Lipscomb and Albert Bergh. 20 vols. Washington, DC: Memorial Associates of the United States, 1903–04.

———. *The Works of Thomas Jefferson.* Collected and edited by Paul Leicester Ford. 12 vols. New York and London: Putnam, 1904–05.

———. *The Life and Selected Writings of Thomas Jefferson.* Edited by Adrienne Koch and William Peden. New York: Modern Library, 1944, 756p.

———. *Papers of Thomas Jefferson.* Edited by Julian P. Boyd, Lyman H. Butterfield, et al. 20 vols. to date. (Princeton, NJ: Princeton University Press, 1950–.

———. *The Family Letters of Thomas Jefferson.* Edited by Edwin Norris Betts and James Adam Baer, Jr. Columbia, MO: University of Missouri Press, [1966], 506p.

———. *Calendar of the Correpondence of Thomas Jefferson.* 3 vols. New York: B. Franklin, 1970.

———. *The Thomas Jefferson Papers: A Microfilm Edition of the Thomas Jefferson Coolidge Collection of Manuscripts at the Massachusetts Historical Society.* Boston: Massachusetts Historical Society, [1977].

Lafayette, Marie Joseph Yves, Marquis de. *The Letters of Lafayette and Jefferson.* With an introduction and note by Gilbert Chinard. Baltimore, MD: Johns Hopkins Press; Paris: "Les Belles Lettres," 1929, 443p.

Sifton P.G. "Provenance of the Thomas Jefferson Papers." *American Archivist* 40:1 (Jan. 1977): 17–30.

Tucker, George. *The Life of Thomas Jefferson, Third President of the United States.* 2 vols. Philadelphia: Carey, Lea, Blanchard, 1837.

James Madison

Hamilton, Alexander, Jay, John, and Madison, James. *The Federalist: A Commentary on the Constitution of the United States Being a Collection of Essays Written in Support of the Constitution Agreed Upon September 17, 1787, by the Federal Convention.* New York: Modern Library, 1941, 618p.

Index to the James Madison Papers. Washington, DC: Library of Congress, Manuscript Division, Reference Department, 1965, 61p.

Madison, James. *The Papers of James Madison, Purchased by Order of Congress; Being his Correspondence and Reports of the Debates during the Congress of the Confederation.* 3 vols. Washington, DC: Langtree & O'Sullivan, 1840.

———. *Selections from the Private Correspondence of James Madison from 1813 to 1836.* Washington, DC: J.C. McGuire, 1853.

———. *Jonathan Bull and Mary Bull: By James Madison. An Unedited Manuscript.* Washington, DC: printed for presentation by J. C. McGuire, 1856, 14p.

——. *Letters and Writings of James Madison Fourth President of the United States.* 4 vols. New York: A. Worthington, 1865.

——. *Letters and Other Writings of James Madison.* Edited by Philip R. Fendall. Published by order of Congress. 4 vols. Philadelphia: Lippincott, 1865.

——. *The Papers of James Madison.* Edited by William T. Hutchinson and William M.E. Rachal. 6 vols. Chicago: University of Chicago Press, 1962–82.

Rives, William Cabell. *History of the Life and Times of James Madison.* 3 vols. Boston: Little, Brown, 1859–68.

James Monroe

Index to the James Monroe Papers. Washington, DC: Manuscript Division of the Library of Congress, 1963.

James Monroe Papers in Virginia Repositories. Edited by Curtis W. Garrison. Charlottesville, VA: University of Virginia, Microfilm Publication, No. 7, 1969, 63p.

Monroe, James. *The People the Sovereigns, Being a Comparison of the Government of the United States with Those of the Republics which have Existed Before, with the Causes of their Decadence and Fall.* Edited by Samuel L. Gouverneur, Jr. (his grandson and administrator). Philadelphia, 1867.

——. *The Writings of James Monroe, Including a Collection of his Public and Private Papers and Correspondence Now for the First Time Printed.* Edited by Stanislaus Murray Hamilton. 7 vols. New York and London: Putnam, 1898–1903.

——. *The Autobiography of James Monroe.* Syracuse, NY: University of Syracuse Press, 1959.

Schouler, James. *History of the United States under the Constitution.* New York, 1882.

John Quincy Adams

Adams, John Quincy. *Writings of John Quincy Adams.* Edited by Worthington Chauncey Ford. 7 vols. New York: Macmillan, 1913.

——. *Memoirs of John Quincy Adams, Comprising Portions of his Diary from 1795 to 1848.* Edited by Charles Francis Adams. 12 vols. Freeport, NY: Books for Libraries Press, 1969.

——. *The Russian Memoirs of John Quincy Adams.* Edited by Worthington Chauncey Ford. New York: Arno Press, 1970, 602p.

——. *Diary of John Quincy Adams.* Edited by David Grayson Allen. 2 vols. Cambridge, MA: Belknap Press of Harvard University Press, 1981.

Hecht, Marie B. *John Quincy Adams.* New York: Macmillan, 1972, 682p.

Andrew Jackson

Bassett, John Spencer. *Life of Andrew Jackson.* 2 vols. New York: Macmillan, 1925.

Benton, Thomas Hart. *Thirty Years' View.* New York and Boston: Harpers, 1854–56.

Hammond, Bray. "Jackson's Fight with the 'Monster'" in *A Sense of History.* Boston: Houghton Mifflin, 1985.

Index to the Andrew Jackson Papers. Washington, DC: Library of Congress, 1967.

Jackson, Andrew. *The Papers of Andrew Jackson.* Edited by Sam B. Smith and Harriet Chappal Owsley. 2 vols. Knoxville, TN: University of Tennessee Press, 1980–84.

James, Marquis. *Andrew Jackson, the Border Captain.* Indianapolis, IN: Bobbs-Merrill, 1933, 461p.

Kendall, Amos. *Life of Andrew Jackson, Private, Military and Civil.* New York: n.p., 1843–44, Nos. 1-7.

Schlesinger, Arthur Meier. *The Age of Jackson.* Boston: Little, Brown, 1945, 577p.

Martin Van Buren

Calendar of the Papers of Martin Van Buren. Prepared from the original manuscripts in the Library of Congress by Elizabeth Howard West, Division of Manuscripts. Washington, DC: Government Printing Office, 1910, 757p.

Curtis, James C. *The Fox at Bay: Martin Van Buren and the Presidency, 1837–1841.* Lexington, KY: University Press of Kentucky, 1970, 234p.

Niven, John. *Martin Van Buren: The Romantic Age of American Politics.* New York and Oxford: Oxford University Press, 1983, 715p.

Van Buren, Martin. *Inquiery into the Origin and Course of political Parties in the United States.* By the late ex-President Martin Van Buren, edited by his sons. New York: Hurd & Houghton, 1867, 436p.

——. *The Autobiography of Martin Van Buren.* Edited by John C. Fitzpatrick. Washington, DC: Government Printing Office, 1920, 808p.

Wilson, Major L. *Presidency of Martin Van Buren.* Lawrence, KS: University Press of Kansas, 1984, 252p.

William Henry Harrison

Index to the William H. Harrison Papers. Washington, DC: Library of Congress, 1960.

John Tyler

Chitwood, Oliver Perry. *John Tyler, Champion of the Old South.* New York: Russell & Russell, 1964, 496p.

Index to the John Tyler Papers. Washington, DC: Library of Congress, 1961.

Seagar, Robert. *And Tyler Too; a Biography of John and Julia Gardiner Tyler.* New York: McGraw-Hill, 1963, 681p.

Tyler, Lyon Gardiner. *Letters and Times of the Tylers.* 3 vols. Richmond, VA: Whittet & Shepperson, 1884–86.

James K. Polk

Index to the James K. Polk Papers. Washington, DC: Library of Congress, 1969, 91p.

Jenkins, John S. *The Life of James Knox Polk.* Auburn, 1850.

McCormac, Eugene Irving. *James K. Polk; a Political Biography.* New York: Russell & Russell, 1965, 746p.

McCoy, Charles Allan. *Polk and the Presidency.* Austin, TX: University of Texas, 1967, 238p.

Polk, James K. *Diary of James K. Polk During His Presidency, 1845–1849, Now First Printed.* Edited and annotated by Milo Milton Quaife. 4 vols. Chicago: A.C. McClury & Co., 1910.

Sellers, Charles Grier. *James K. Polk, Jacksonian, 1795–1843.* Princeton, NJ: Princeton University Press, 1957, 526p.

Zachary Taylor

Dyer, Brainerd. *Zachary Taylor.* New York: Barnes & Noble, 1967, 455p.

Hamilton, Holman. *Zachary Taylor.* 2 vols. Indianapolis, IN: Bobbs-Merrill, 1941–45.

Index to the Zachary Taylor Papers. Washington, DC: Library of Congress, 1960.

Taylor, Zachary. *Letters of Zachary Taylor, from the Battlefields of the Mexican War.* Rochester, NY: The Genesee Press, 1908, 194p.

Millard Fillmore

Fillmore, Millard. *The Millard Fillmore Papers.* Edited by Frank H. Severance. 2 vols. Buffalo, NY: Buffalo and Erie County Historical Society, 1907.

Guide to the Microfilm Edition of the Millard Fillmore Papers. Edited by Lester W. Smith. Buffalo, NY: Buffalo and Erie County Historical Society and State University College at Oswego, NY, 1975, 47p.

Rayback, Robert J. *Millard Fillmore: Biography of a President.* Buffalo, NY: Buffalo and Erie County Historical Society, 1959, 470p.

Franklin Pierce

Calendar of the Papers of Franklin Pierce. Prepared from the original manuscripts in the Library of Congress by W.L. Leech. Washington, DC: Library of Congress, Division of Manuscripts, 1917, 102p.

Hawthorne, Nathaniel. *Life of Franklin Pierce.* New York: Garrett Press, 1970, (Reprint of 1852 ed.), 144p.

Index to the Franklin Pierce Papers. Washington, DC: Library of Congress, 1962, 16p.

Nichols, Roy Franklin. *Franklin Pierce, Young Hickory of Granite Hills.* 2nd ed., revised. Philadelphia: University of Pennsylvania Press, 1958, 625 p.

James Buchanan

Auchampaugh, Philip Gerald. *James Buchanan and his Cabinet on the Eve of Secession.* Lancaster, PA: Private Print, 1926, 224p.

Buchanan, James. *Messages of President James Buchanan.* Compiled by J.B. Henry. New York, 1888, 328p.

——. *The Works of James Buchanan Comprising his Speeches, State Papers and Private Correspondence.* Collected and edited by John Bassett Moore. 12 vols. Philadelphia and London: Lippincott, 1908–11.

Guide to the Microfilm Edition of the James Buchanan Papers at the Historical Society of Pennsylvania. Edited by Lucy F. West. Philadelphia: Historical Society of Pennsylvania, 1974, 55p.

Historical Records Survey of Pennsylvania. Guide to the Manuscript Collections in the Historical Society of Pennsylvania. Edited by Bernard S. Levin. Philadelphia: Historical Society of Pennsylvania, 1940, 350p.

James Buchanan and Harriet [Lane] Johnston. A Register and Index to Their Papers in the Library of Congress. Washington, DC: Library of Congress, Manuscript Division, 1979.

Klein, Philip Shriver. *President James Buchanan, a Biography.* University Park, PA: Pennsylvania State University Press, 1962, 506p.

Smith, Elbert B. *The Presidency of James Buchanan.* Lawrence, KS: University of Kansas, 1975, 225p.

Abraham Lincoln

Bullock, Helen D. "The Papers of John G. Nicolay, Lincoln's Secretary." *Library of Congress Quarterly Journal of Current Acquisition* 7 (May 1950): 3–8.

——. "The Robert Todd Lincoln Collection of the Papers of Abraham Lincoln." *Library of Congress Quarterly Journal of Current Acquisitions* 5 (Nov. 1947): 3–8.

Index to the Abraham Lincoln Papers. Washington, DC: Library of Congress, Manuscript Division, 1960.

Lincoln, Abraham. *Works of Abraham Lincoln.* Edited by Roy P. Basler. 8 vols. New Brunswick, NJ: Rutgers University Press, 1953–55.

Mearns, David C. "The Lincoln Papers." *Abraham Lincoln Quarterly* IV (December 1947): 369–85.

——. "The Story of the Papers." in *The Lincoln Papers.* 2 vols. Garden City, NY: Doubleday, 1948.

Nicolay, John G., and Hay, John. *Abraham Lincoln; a History.* 10 vols. New York: The Century Company, 1890.

Andrew Johnson

DeWitt, David M. *The Impeachment and Trial of Andrew Johnson, Seventeenth President of the United States.* New York and London: Macmillan, 1903, 646p.

*Index to the Andrew Johnson Papers.*Washington, DC: Library of Congress, Manuscript Division, 1963, 111p.

Johnson, Andrew. *The Papers of Andrew Johnson.* Edited by Leroy P. Greef and Ralph W. Haskins. 6 vols. Knoxville, TN: University of Tennessee Press, 1967–83.

Jones, James S. *Life of Andrew Johnson, Seventeenth President of the United States.* Greeneville, TN: East Tennessee Publishing Company, 1901, 400p.

Lomask, Milton. *Andrew Johnson: President on Trial.* New York: Farrar, Strauss, 1960, 376p.

Steele, Robert V.P. *First President Johnson: The Three Lives of the Seventeenth President of the United States.* New York: Morrow, 1968, 676p.

Stryker, Lloyd Paul. *Andrew Johnson; a Study in Courage.* New York: The Macmillan Co., 1929, 881p.

Ulysses S. Grant

Badeau, Adam. *Military History of Ulysses S. Grant.* 3 vols. New York: D. Appleton, 1885.

Grant, Ulysses S. *Personal Memoirs of U.S. Grant.* 2 vols. New York: C.L. Webster & Co, 1885–86.

Index to the Ulysses S. Grant Papers. Washington, DC: Library of Congress, Manuscript Division, 1965.

U.S. War Department. *The War of Rebellion: A Compilation of the Official Records of the Union and Confederate Armies.* Published under the direction of the Secretary of War. 70 vols. Washington, DC: Government Printing Office, 1880–1901.

Young, John R. *Around the World with General Grant.* New York: Subscription Book Department, American News Co., 1879, 256p.

Rutherford B. Hayes

Barnard, Harry. *Rutherford B. Hayes and his America.* Indianapolis, IN: Bobbs-Merrill, 1954.

Davison, Kenneth B. *The Presidency of Rutherford B. Hayes.* Westport, CT: Greenwood Press, 1972.

Hayes, Rutherford B. *Diary and Letters of Rutherford B. Hayes.* Edited by Charles R. Williams. 5 vols. Columbus, OH: Ohio State Archaeological and Historical Society, 1922-26.

Marchman, Watt P., and Rodabaugh, James H. "Collections of the Rutherford B. Hayes State Memorial." *Ohio History* 71:151–57 (July 1962).

Smith T.A. "Before Hyde Park: The Rutherford B. Hayes Library." *American Archivist* 43:4 (Fall 1980): 485–88.

James A. Garfield

Coffin, Charles Carleton. *The Life of James A. Garfield.* Boston: J.H. Earle, 1880, 379p.

Comer, Lucretia. *Harry Garfield's First Forty Years; a Man of Action in a Troubled World.* New York: Vantage Press, 1965, 270p.

Feis, Ruth (Stanley-Brown). *Mollie Garfield in the White House.* Chicago: Rand, McNally, 1963, 128p.

Garfield, James Abraham. *The Great Speeches of James Abraham Garfield.* St. Louis: J. Burns, 1881, 751p.

———. *The Works of James Abraham Garfield.* Edited by Burke A. Hinsdale. 2 vols. Boston: J.R. Osgood & Co., 1882–83.

———. *The Diary of James A. Garfield.* Edited by Harry James Brown and Frederick D. Williams. 3 vols. East Lansing, MI: Michigan State University, 1967–73.

Index to the James Garfield Papers. Washington, DC: Library of Congress, Manuscript Division, 1973.

Smith, Theodore Clarke. *Life and Letters of James Abraham Garfield.* 2 vols. New Haven, CT: Yale University Press, 1925.

Chester A. Arthur

Index to the Chester A. Arthur Papers. Washington, DC: Library of Congress, Manuscript Division, 1961, 13p.

Reeves, Thomas C. *Gentleman Boss; the Life of Chester Alan Arthur.* New York: Knopf, 1975, 500p.

Grover Cleveland

Cleveland, Grover. *Letters of Grover Cleveland, 1850–1908.* Selected and edited by Allan Nevins. Boston and New York: Houghton Mifflin, 1933, 640p.

Index to the Grover Cleveland Papers. Washington, DC: Library of Congress, Manuscript Division, 1965, 345p.

McElroy, Robert McNutt. *Grover Cleveland, the Man and the Statesman.* Introduction by Elihu Root. 2 vols. New York and London: Harper and Brothers, 1925.

Nevins, Allan. *Grover Cleveland; a Study in Courage.* New York: Dodd, Mead & Company, 1932, 832p.

Benjamin Harrison

Harrison, Benjamin. *The Speeches of Benjamin Harrison.* New York: United States Book Company, 1892, 580p.

———. *The Constitution and Administration of the United States of America.* London: D. Nutt, 1897, 360p.

———. *This Country of Ours.* New York: Scribner, 1897, 360p.

Index to the Benjamin Harrison Papers. Washington, DC: Library of Congress, 1964.

Myers, Elizabeth P. *Benjamin Harrison.* Chicago: Reilly & Lee Books, 1969, 165p.

Sievers, Harry J. *Benjamin Harrison.* 3 vols. Chicago: H. Regnery Co., 1952–68.

Wallace, Lewis. *The Life of General Benjamin Harrison.* Philadelphia: Hubbard Brothers, 1888, 578p.

William McKinley

Index to the William McKinley Papers. Washington, DC: Library of Congress, Manuscript Division, 1963.

Olcott, Charles S. *The Life of William McKinley.* 2 vols. Boston and New York: Houghton Mifflin, 1916.

Theodore Roosevelt

Bishop, Joseph Bucklin. *Theodore Roosevelt and His Time: Shown in His Own Letters.* 2 vols. New York: Scribner, 1920.

Index to the Theodore Roosevelt Papers. 3 vols. Washington, DC: Library of Congress, Manuscript Division, 1969.

Lorant, Stefan. *The Life and Times of Theodore Roosevelt.* Garden City, NY: Doubleday, 1959, 640p.

Roosevelt, Theodore. *Life of Thomas Hart Benton.* Boston and New York: Houghton Mifflin, 1887, 372p.

——. *The Winning of the West.* 4 vols. New York and London: Putnam, 1889–96.

——. *The Naval War of 1812.* New York and London: Putnam, 1903, 549p.

——. *Theodore Roosevelt: An Autobiography.* New York: Macmillan, 1919, 647p.

——. *Selections from the Correspondence of Theodore Roosevelt and Henry Cabot Lodge: 1884-1918.* 2 vols. New York: Scribner, 1925.

William Howard Taft

Hess, Stephen. "Big Bill Taft" in *A Sense of History.* Boston: Houghton Mifflin, 1985.

Index to the William Howard Taft Papers. Washington, DC: Library of Congress, Manuscript Division, 1972.

Mason, Alpheus Thomas. *William Howard Taft, Chief Justice.* New York: Simon and Schuster, 1965, 354p.

Woodrow Wilson

Baker, Ray Stannard. *American Chronicle: The Autobiography of Ray Stannard Baker.* New York: Scribner, 1945, 531p.

——. *Woodrow Wilson and World Settlement.* Written from his unpublished and personal material. 3 vols. Garden City, NY: Doubleday, Page and Company, 1922.

——. *Woodrow Wilson, Life and Letters.* 8 vols. Garden City, NY: Doubleday, Page and Company, 1927–39.

Index to the Woodrow Wilson Papers. 3 vols. Washington, DC: Library of Congress, Manuscript Division, 1973.

Link, Arthur. *Wilson.* Princeton, NJ: Princeton University Press, 1947–65.

Wilson, Woodrow. *History of the American People.* 10 vols. New York and London: Harper and Brothers, [1918].

——. *Crossroads of Freedom, the 1912 Campaign Speeches.* Edited by John Wells Davidson. New Haven, CT: Yale University Press for the Woodrow Wilson Foundation, 1956, 570p.

——. *Priceless Gift; the Love Letters of Woodrow Wilson and Ellen Axson Wilson.* Edited by Eleanor Wilson McAdoo. New York: McGraw-Hill, 1962, 324p.

——. *Papers of Woodrow Wilson.* Edited by Arthur S. Link, et al. 40 vols. Princeton, NJ: Princeton University Press, 1966–86.

Warren G. Harding

Duckett, Kenneth W. "The Harding Papers, How Some Were Burned." *American Heritage* 16:2 (Feb. 1965): 24–31, 102–09.

Murray, Robert K. *The Harding Era: Warren G. Harding and His Administration.* Minneapolis, MN: University of Minnesota Press, 1969.

——. *The Politics of Normalcy: Governmental Theory and Practice in the Harding-Coolidge Era.* New York: Norton, 1973.

Pitzer, Donald E. "An Introduction to the Harding Papers" *Ohio History* 75:2–3 (Spring–Summer 1966): 76-81.

Russell, Francis. "The Harding Papers: How Some Were Saved." *American Heritage* 16:2 (Feb. 1965): 24–31, 102–09.

——. *The Shadow of Blooming Grove: Warren G. Harding in his Times.* New York: McGraw-Hill, 1968.

Sinclair, Andrew. *The Available Man.* New York: MacMillan, 1965, 344p.

Warren G. Harding Papers; an Inventory to the Microfilm Edition. Columbus, OH: Archives and Manuscript Divisions, Ohio Historical Society, 1970.

Calvin Coolidge

Abels, Jules. *In the Time of Silent Cal.* New York: Putnam, 1969, 320p.

Coolidge, Calvin. *The Autobiography of Calvin Coolidge.* New York: Cosmopolitan Book, 1929, 246p.

Fuess, Claude M. *Calvin Coolidge, the Man from Vermont.* Boston: Little, Brown, 1940, 522p.

Index to the Calvin Coolidge Papers. Washington, DC: Library of Congress, Manuscript Division, 1965, 34p.

McCoy, Donald R. *Calvin Coolidge: The Quiet President.* New York: Macmillan, 1967, 472p.

White, William A. *A Puritan in Babylon: The Story of Calvin Coolidge.* New York: Macmillan, 1938, 460p.

Herbert Hoover

Best, Gary Dean. *Herbert Hoover, the Post-Presidential Years 1933-1964.* 2 vols. Stanford, CA: Hoover Institution Press, 1983.

Danielson, Elena C., and Palm, Charles G. *Herbert C. Hoover; A Register of his Papers in the Hoover Institution Archives.* Stanford, CA: Hoover Institution Press, 1983.

Historical Materials in the Herbert Hoover Library. West Branch, IA: Herbert Hoover Presidential Library, 1985.

Hoover, Herbert C. *Principles of Mining.* New York: Hill Publishing Company, 1909, 199p.

——. *Memoirs.* 3 vols. New York: Macmillan, 1951–52.

——. *The Ordeal of Woodrow Wilson.* New York: McGraw-Hill, 1958, 318p.

——. *An American Epic.* 3 vols. Chicago: H. Regnery Company, 1959–61.

——. *The Hoover-Wilson Wartime Correspondence.* Ames, IA: Iowa State University Press, 1974, 297p.

Lyons, Eugene. *Herbert Hoover, a Biography.* Garden City, NY: Doubleday, 1964, 444p.

Nash, George H. *The Life of Herbert Hoover: Volume 1, The Engineer, 1874-1914.* New York: W.W. Norton, 1983.

Franklin D. Roosevelt

Connor, R.D.W. "The Franklin D. Roosevelt Library." *American Archivist* III:2 (Apr. 1940): 81–92.

———. "FDR Visits the National Archives." *American Archivist* XII (1949): 323–32.

Historical Materials in the Franklin D. Roosevelt Library. Hyde Park, NY: The Franklin D. Roosevelt Library, 1985.

Leland, Waldo Gifford. "Creation of the Franklin D. Roosevelt Library: A Personal Narrative." *American Archivist* 8 (1955): 11–29.

McCoy, Donald R. "Beginnings of the Franklin D. Roosevelt Library." *Prologue* (Fall 1975): 138–50.

Roosevelt, Eleanor. *This Is My Story.* New York and London: Harper & Brothers, 1937, 365p.

Roosevelt, Franklin D. *Public Papers and Addresses of Franklin D. Roosevelt.* With a special introduction and explanatory notes by President Roosevelt, compiled by Samuel I. Rosenman. 13 vols. New York: Random House, 1938–50.

——— *FDR: His Personal Letters.* Edited by Elliott Roosevelt, foreword by Eleanor Roosevelt. 4 vols. New York: Duell, Sloan & Pearce, 1947–50.

———. *Roosevelt and Churchill, Their Secret Wartime Correspondence.* Edited by Harold D. Langley and Manfred Jonas. New York: Saturday Review Press, 1975, 805p.

Sherwood, Robert Emmet. *Roosevelt and Hopkins, an Intimate History.* New York: Harper, 1950, 1002p.

Stewart, William J., and Pollard Charyl C. "Franklin D. Roosevelt, Collector." *Prologue*, Winter 1969): 13–28.

Harry S. Truman

Historical Materials in the Harry S. Truman Library Independence, MO: Harry S. Truman Library, 1984 (Truman Centennial Edition), 66p.

Lagerquist, Philip D. "The Harry S. Truman Library as a Center for Research in the American Presidency." *College and Research Libraries* 25:1 (Jan. 1964): 320–36.

Morrissey, Charles T. "Truman and the Presidency—Records and Oral Recollections." *American Archivist* 28:1 (Jan. 1965): 53–61.

Truman, Harry S. *Memoirs by Harry S. Truman.* Volume 1, Year of Decisions. Volume 2, Years of Trial and Hope. Garden City, NY: Doubleday, 1955, 1956.

———. *The Autobiography of Harry S. Truman.* Edited by Robert H. Ferrell. Boulder, CO: Colorado Associated University Press, 1980, 154p.

Truman, Margaret. *Harry S. Truman.* New York: William Morrow & Co., 1973, 602p.

Dwight D. Eisenhower

Ambrose, Stephen E. *Ike: Abilene to Berlin; The Life of Dwight D. Eisenhower.* New York: Harper & Row, 1973, 220p.

———. *The Supreme Commander; The War Years of General Dwight D. Eisenhower.* Garden City, NY: Doubleday, 1970, 732p.

Childs, Marquis W. *Eisenhower; Captive Hero: A Critical Study.* New York: Harcourt and Brace, 1958, 310p.

Eisenhower, Dwight D. *Crusade in Europe.* Garden City, NY: Doubleday, 1948, 559p.

———. *The White House Years* 2 vols. Garden City, NY: Doubleday, 1963–65.

———. *At Ease: Stories I Tell to Friends.* Garden City, NY: Doubleday, 1967, 400p.

———. *The Papers of Dwight David Eisenhower.* Edited by Alfred D. Chandler, Jr. Baltimore, MD: Johns Hopkins Press, 1970–78, vols 1–9.

———. *Letters to Mamie.* Edited and with commentary by John S. Eisenhower. Garden City, NY: Doubleday, 1978, 282p.

——. *The Eisenhower Diaries.* Edited by Robert H. Ferrell. New York: Norton, 1981, 445p.

Eisenhower, John S. *Strictly Personal.* Garden City, NY: Doubleday, 1974, 412p.

Historical Materials in the Dwight D. Eisenhower Library. Abilene, KS: Dwight D. Eisenhower Library, 1984.

John F. Kennedy

Historical Materials in the John Fitzgerald Kennedy Library. Boston: John F. Kennedy Library, 1986.

Kennedy, John Fitzgerald. *Why England Slept.* New York: W. Funk, 1940, 252p.

——. *Profiles in Courage.* New York: Harper, 1956, 266p.

——. *The Burden and the Glory.* Edited by Allan Nevins. New York: Harper & Row, 1964, 293p.

Manchester, William Raymond. *Portrait of a President: John F. Kennedy in Profile.* Boston: Little, Brown, 1967, 266p.

Schlesinger, Arthur M. *A Thousand Days: John F. Kennedy in the White House.* Boston: Houghton Mifflin, 1965, 1087p.

Sidey, Hugh. *John F. Kennedy, President.* New York: Atheneum, 1964, 435p.

Sorenson, Theodore C. *Kennedy.* New York: Harper & Row, 1965, 783p.

White, Theodore H. *The Making of the President, 1960.* New York: Antheneum, 1964, 401p.

Lyndon B. Johnson

Goldman, Eric Frederic. *The Tragedy of Lyndon Johnson.* New York: Knopf, 1969, 531p.

Johnson, Lady Bird (Claudia T.). *A White House Diary.* New York: Holt, Rinehart and Winston, 1970.

Johnson, Lyndon Baines. *To Heal and to Build: The Programs of President Lyndon B. Johnson.* Edited by James McGregor Burns. New York: McGraw-Hill, 1968, 506p.

——. *The Vantage Point: Perspectives of the Presidency, 1963-1969.* New York: Holt, Reinhart and Winston, 1971, 636p.

Kearns, Doris. *Lyndon Johnson and the American Dream.* New York: Harper & Row, 1976, 432p.

LBJ: A Bibliography Compiled by the Staff of the LBJ Library. Austin, TX: University of Texas Press, 1984, 275p.

Steinberg, Alfred. *Sam Johnson's Boy: A Close-Up of the President from Texas.* New York: Macmillan, 1968, 871p.

White, Theodore H. *The Making of the President, 1964.* New York: Atheneum, 1965, 431p.

Richard M. Nixon

Drew, Elizabeth. *Washington Journal: The Events of 1973-1974.* New York: Random House, 1975, 428p.

Jaworski, Leon. *The Right and the Power: The Prosecution of Watergate.* New York: Reader's Digest Press (distributed by Crowell), 1976, 305p.

National Archives and Records Administration, "Preservation and Protection of and Access to Historical Materials of the Nixon Administration; Repromulgation of Public Access Regulations." *Federal Register* 51:40 (Feb. 28, 1986): 7728-36.

Nixon, Richard M. *Six Crises.* Garden City, NY: Doubleday, 1962, 458p.

——. *The White House Transcripts: Submissions of Recorded Presidential Conversations to the Committee of the Judiciary of the House of Representatives.* Edited by Gerald Gold. New York: Viking Press, 1974, 877p.

——. *The Memoirs of Richard Nixon.* New York: Grosset & Dunlap, 1978, 1120p.

Sirica, John J. *To Set the Record Straight: The Break-in, the Tapes, the Conspirators, the Pardon.* New York: Norton, 1979, 394p.

White, Theodore H. *Breach of Faith: The Fall of Richard Nixon.* New York: Atheneum; Reader's Digest Press, 1975, 374p.

Gerald R. Ford

Ford, Gerald R. *A Time to Heal: The Autobiography of Gerald R. Ford.* New York: Harper & Row, 1979, 454p.

Ford, Gerald R., and Stiles John R. *Portrait of the Assassin.* New York: Simon & Schuster, 1965, 508p.

Historical Materials in the Gerald R. Ford Library. Compiled by David A. Horrocks and William H. McNitt. Ann Arbor, MI: Gerald R. Ford Library, 1986.

Nessen, Ron. *It Sure Looks Different from the Inside.* Chicago: Playboy Press, 1978, 367p.

Sidey, Hugh. *Portrait of a President.* With photos by Fred Ward. New York: Harper & Row, 1975, 189p.

terHorst, Jerald F. *Gerald Ford and the Future of the Presidency.* New York: Third Press, 1974, 245p.

Warner, Robert W. "The Prologue is Past." *American Archivist* 18:1 (Jan. 1978): 5–15.

Jimmy Carter

Carter, Jimmy. *A Government as Good as Its People.* New York: Simon & Schuster, 1977, 262p.

——. *Why Not the Best?* Nashville, TN: Broadman Press, 1977, 208p.

——. *Keeping Faith.* Toronto and New York: Bantam Books, 1982, 622p.

——. *Making the Most of the Rest of Your Life.* New York, Random House, 1987.

Germond, Jack. *Blue Smoke and Mirrors.* New York: Viking Press, 1981, 337p.

Hamilton, Jordan. *Crisis.* New York: Putnam, 1982, 431p.

Johnson, Haynes B. *In the Absence of Power: Governing America.* New York: Viking Press, 1980, 339p.

Powell, Jody. *The Other Side of the Story* New York: Morrow, 1984, 322p.

Ronald Reagan

Boyarski, Bill. *Ronald Reagan: His Life and Rise to the Presidency.* New York: Random House, 1981, 205p.

Cannon, Lou. *Reagan.* New York: G. P. Putnam, 1982, 464p.

Edwards, Lee. *Ronald Reagan: A Political Biography.* Houston, TX: Nordland, 1980, 307p.

Evans, Rowland, and Novak, Robert. *The Reagan Revolution.* New York: E.P. Dutton, 1981, 257p.

Reagan, Ronald. *Sincerely, Ronald Reagan.* Edited by Helene Von Damm. New York: Berkeley Books, 1980, 224p.

——. *America's New Beginning: A Program for Economic Recovery.* Washington, DC: The White House, Office of the Press Secretary, 1981.

Reagan, Ronald, with Huber, Richard G. *Where's the Rest of Me?* New York: Duell, Sloan and Pearce, 1965, 316p.

Trombley, William. "Reagan Library Strains Link Between Stanford and Hoover Institution." *Los Angeles Times,* Mar. 8, 1987, Part I, p. 3+.

Index

by Linda Webster

Abedi, Agha Hasan, 237
Adams, Abigail Smith, 117, 120
Adams, Brooks, 122, 123
Adams, Charles Francis, 27, 120,
  121–22
Adams, Charles Francis, II, 122, 123
Adams, Charles Francis, III, 122, 123
Adams, Ephraim D., 145
Adams, George Washington, 120
Adams, Henry, 122, 123
Adams, John
  bibliography of, 281–82
  biography of, 46, 47, 117–18
  book collection at home of, 27
  Jefferson's comments on books, 28
  papers of, 6, 21, 88, 119–24
  presidency of, 2, 42, 46, 54, 68,
    118
Adams, John, II, 120
Adams, John Quincy
  bibliography of, 283
  biography of, 57, 118–19
  book collection at home of, 28
  Monroe's papers and, 58
  papers of, 6, 21, 88, 119–24
  Polk and, 72
  presidency of, 68, 119
Adams, John Quincy, II, 122
Adams, John Quincy, IV, 123
Adams, Louisa Catherine Johnson,
  119
Adams, Randolph G., 156, 157
Adams, Sherman, 189
Adams, Thomas Boylston, 123
Adams Manuscript Trust, 122–24
Adams National Historic Site, 27
Adams Papers, 123–24
Agnew, Spiro, 209, 218, 219–20, 240,
  241, 246
Albert, Carl, 218
Allen v. Carmen, 243

Alsop, Joseph, 189
American Antiquarian Society, 106
American Association for State and
  Local History, 22
American Historical Association, 8,
  21, 103
American Legion, 9, 184
American Philosophical Society, 52
American Relief Administration, 147
American Revolution, 42
American State Papers, 20–21
Andrew Jackson, the Border Captain
  (James), 65
Archives of the United States
  Government (Flippin), 21
Arnold, Benedict, 40, 47
Around the World with General Grant
  (Young), 86
Arthur, Chester A.
  bibliography of, 287
  biography of, 91, 140
  book collection at home of, 31–32
  Library of Congress collection of
    papers, 91–92
  papers of, 91–92
  presidency of, 4, 91, 105
Arthur, Chester A., Jr., 91
Arthur, Chester A., III, 92
Ash Lawn, 28, 57
Audiodiscs. See Audiovisual materials
Audiotapes. See Audiovisual materials
Audiovisual materials
  Carter Center, 236
  Eisenhower Library, 190
  Ford Library, 226
  Hoover Archives, 147
  Hoover Library and Museum, 180
  Johnson Library, 214
  Kennedy Library, 201
  Nixon Presidential Materials
    Project, 246

Audiovisual materials (continued)
  Roosevelt (Franklin D.) Library
    and Museum, 164
  Truman Library, 175

Badeau, Adam, 86
Bahmer, Robert, 11
Baker, Howard, 227
Baker, Ray Stannard, 111–12
Baldinger, Ora M., 134
Bancroft, George, 63, 73–74
Barnard, Harry, 140
Bassett, John Spencer, 65, 74
Bayard, Thomas F., 44
Beckley, John J., 3
Belgium, 147
Bell, John, 80
Benedict, E.C., 95
Benson, Ezra Taft, 189
Bentley Library. *See* University of
  Michigan
Benton, Thomas Hart, 64, 175
Bicentennial celebration, 227
Billington, James H., 5
Birchard, Sardis, 139, 140
Bishop, Joseph B., 103–04
Bixby, William K., 51
Blaine, James G., 85, 91, 93, 96
Blair, Francis, 63–64, 65
Blair, Mary Elizabeth, 65
Blair, Montgomery, 64
Blair, Woodbury, 65
Blair (Montgomery) Collection, 65
Bloom, Sol, 9
Bohlen, Charles, 189
Bolton, Robert, 189
Bonaparte, Napoleon, 211
Booksellers' Association, 36
Boone, Joel T., 180
Boorstin, Daniel J., 4
Booth, John Wilkes, 80
Bordin, Ruth, 220
Bork, Robert H., 241
Boston Athenaeum Library, 27
Boston Public Library, 92
Boutin, Bernard, 195–96
Bowdoin College, 79
Boyd, Julian P., 51–52, 156
Brand, Katherine E., 112
Breckenridge, John C., 79, 82
Brennan, William Joseph, Jr., 16–17
Britton, Nan, 133
Brooks, Jack, 186, 208
Brooks, R. Max, 208
Brown, Edmund G. (Pat), 240, 249
Brown, Stuart Gerry, 58

Brown University, 80
Bryan, William Jennings, 93, 99, 100
Bryce, Lord, 107
Buchanan, Annie, 130, 131
Buchanan, Edward Y., 130–31
Buchanan, James
  bibliography of, 285
  biographers of, 73, 131
  biography of, 128–30
  book collection at home of, 30
  Jefferson papers and, 48
  Library of Congress collection of
    papers, 132
  Madison papers and, 55
  papers of, 6, 130–32
  Polk and, 72
  presidency of, 129
  presidential campaign, 77
  presidential election of, 125
  Tyler and, 71
Buchanan, Patrick, 245
Buchanan Foundation, 131
Buchen, Philip, 217, 221–22, 226
Buck, Paul H., 195
Buffalo and Erie County Public
  Library, 127
Buffalo Historical Society, 6, 95,
  126–28
Bundy, McGeorge, 212
Bundy, William P., 213
Bunshaft, Gordon, 208, 209
Burns, Arthur, 225
Burr, Aaron, 61
Burton, Dennis, 24
Burton, Theodore E., 97
Busby, Horace, 206–07
Bush, George, 227
Butterfield, Alexander, 246
Butterfield, Lyman H., 120

Cabot, Edward C., 122
Cadell and Davies, 2
Cadwalader, John, 73, 131
Calhoun, John C., 21, 57
Califano, Joseph, 212
Camp David Accords, 231, 236
Campbell, W. Glenn, 146, 249
Cardozo, Michael, 233
Carey, Matthew, 42
Carmen, Gerald P., 223
Carter, Amy, 36
Carter, Hugh, 233, 234
Carter, Jimmy
  bibliography of, 292
  biography of, 229–32, 249
  book collection at home of, 35

Ford Library and, 228
papers of, 12, 23, 24, 235–36
presidency of, 11, 219, 230–32
Presidential Records Act, 17
Carter, Rosalynn Smith, 36, 229, 233,
236
Carter Center of Emory University,
232, 235, 237
Carter-Menil Human Rights
Foundation, 235, 238
Carter Museum, 236–37
Carter Presidential Center
automation in, 25
building, 235
establishment of, 232–34
Georgia Department of
Transportation, 235
research materials in, 235–36
site on university campus, 15
Cartoons, 201, 228
Casals, Pablo, 202
Cass, Lewis, 75, 77
Casselman, William, 224
Chambers, Whittaker, 240
Chapin, Dwight, 245
Charles Francis Adams (Adams), 123
Chase, William, 152
Chicago Historical Society, 55, 66, 74
Chiles, Lawton, 18
Christian, George B., Jr., 134, 135, 136
Christopher, Warren, 235
Churchill, Winston, 170, 180
Civil War, 86–87, 100, 101, 142
Clark, Charles E., 156
Clark, Edward T., 115
Clark (Edward T.) papers, 115
Clarke, Robert, 140
Clay, Henry, 21, 62, 119
Clayton, John M., 59
Clements (William L.) Library *See*
University of Michigan
Cleveland, Frances Folsom, 93, 94–95
Cleveland, Grover
bibliography of, 287
biographers of, 95
biography of, 93, 97
book collection at home of, 32
Library of Congress collection of
papers, 94–96
papers of, 94–96
presidency of, 4, 44, 93
presidential campaign, 91
Clifford, Clark, 213, 214
Cohen, Wilbur, 189
Coleman, Ann, 129
Coleman, George P., 51

Coleman, L.V., 156
College of Oswego, 127
College of William and Mary, 28, 52,
60, 72
Columbia County Historical Society,
67
Columbia University, 112, 207
Comer, Lucrecia, 90
Commission for Relief in Belgium,
145, 147
Concord Public Library, 79
Congressional Library. *See* Library of
Congress
Connally, John B., 246
Connell, Richard, 165
Connor, Robert D.W., 9, 10, 13, 21,
152, 154, 155, 156, 158, 159
Constitutional Convention, 55
Continental Congress, 4, 7, 103, 117
Coolidge, Calvin
bibliography of, 289
biographers of, 115
biography of, 114–15
book collection at home of, 33
election of, 149
Library of Congress collection of
papers, 115–16, 136
papers of, 52, 115–16, 136, 180
presidency of, 9, 114–15, 144
Coolidge, Grace Anna Goodhue, 114,
115
Coolidge, Thomas Jefferson, 51
Coolidge, Thomas Jefferson, Jr., 51
*Correspondence of the Late President
Adams,* 120
Cortelyou, George B., 100
Cortelyou, George B., Jr., 100
Cortez, Fernando, 211
Cox, Archibald, 241
Cox, James, 149
Crusade in Europe (Eisenhower), 183
Curtis, George Ticknor, 131
Cushing, Caleb, 55
Cutts, James Madison, 55
Czolgosz, Leon F., 100

*D-Day: Normandy Invasion in
Retrospect,* 191
Dandridge, Bartholomew, 42
Dandridge, Betty Taylor Bliss, 76
Darby, Harry, 185
Daughters of the American
Revolution, 9, 184
Daugherty, Harry M., 133, 134, 135
Davidson, John W., 112
Davis, David, 80

Davis, Jefferson, 75, 78
Day, William R., 100
De Menil, Dominique, 238
Dean, John W., 241, 245
DeBakey, Michael E., 211
Delaware Canal, 132
Democratic National Committee, 198, 213
Detroit Public Library, xiii, 44, 95
Devers, Jacob L., 189
Dewey, Thomas E., 169, 180, 183
DeWitt, David M., 83
Diary of James K. Polk (Quaife), 73
Dickinson College, 131
Directory of Archives and Manuscript Repositories in the United States, 24
Docking, George, 185
Documentaries. *See* Films
Donithen, Alfred, 135
Donithen, Hoke, 135, 136
Doubleday, Charles N., 135
Douglas, Helen Gehagen, 240
Douglas, Stephen A., 79
Douglas, William O., 218
Duckett, Kenneth, 137
Duke University, 72
Dun, Robert G., 92
Dutch immigration and settlement, 163
Dutchess County, N.Y., 163

East Aurora Historical Society, 30
Eaton, Henry John, 62
Ehrlichman, John, 241, 245, 246
Einstein, Albert, 165
Eisenhower, Doud Dwight, 186
Eisenhower, Dwight D.
  bibliography of, 290–91
  biography of, 182–84
  book collection at home of, 34
  mural of, 215
  oral histories of, 180, 189
  papers of, 11, 23, 187–90
  photographs of, 190
  presidency of, 4, 16, 144, 171, 183–84, 193, 194, 205, 240
  presidential papers and, 23
Eisenhower, Ida Stover, 184
Eisenhower, Mamie Doud, 182, 186, 187, 191
Eisenhower Center, 186–87, 207
Eisenhower Doctrine, 184
Eisenhower Foundation, 184, 185, 191
Eisenhower Home and Museum, 186

Eisenhower Library
  audiovisual materials, 190
  educational programs at, 191
  establishment of, 184–87
  manuscripts, 187–88
  microfilm collection, 189
  oral history transcripts, 189
  printed materials collection, 190
  research materials in, 12, 187–90
Eisenhower Museum, 184–85, 190–91
Eisenhower Presidential Library Commission, 185–86
Elsey, George M., 22
Emerson, William R., 166
Emory University, 15, 232, 235, 237
Ervin, Sam, 241
Erwin, Frank C., Jr., 207, 208, 211
Evans, Luther H., 4

Fair Deal, 169
Fairfax, Lord, 39
Fall, Albert B., 133–34
Fall, Mrs. George W., 74
Farley, James E., 180
FDR Library. *See* Roosevelt (Franklin D.) Library and Museum
Federal Bureau of Investigation, 181
Federal Power Commission, 181
Federal Property and Administrative Services Act, 10, 14, 170, 171
Federal Records Act, 10–11, 14, 21, 170
Federalist (Madison), 54
Feinberg, Charles A., 92
Feis, Ruth, 90
Fendall, Philip R., 55
Fenn, Dan H., 199
Field, Marshall, 55
Fillmore, Abigail Powers, 30, 36, 125
Fillmore, Millard
  bibliography of, 285
  biography of, 125
  book collection of, 30, 127
  papers of, 6, 126–28
  presidency of, 125
  presidential election of, 129
Fillmore, Millard Powers, 126, 127
Films. *See* Audiovisual materials
Finder, Leonard, 183
Finley, John H., 94–95
Fish, Hamilton, 50
Fitzpatrick, John C., 44
Fleming, Robert W., 221, 223
Flippin, Percy Scott, 21
Floete, Franklin G., 171
Forbes Library, 116

Force (Peter) Collection, 5, 44, 139
Ford, Betty Bloomer Warren, 217, 220, 225, 227, 228
Ford, Gerald R.
  bibliography of, 292
  biography of, 217–20
  book collection at home of, 35
  book donations to, 36
  Nixon papers and, 242
  papers of, 23
  presidency of, 4, 12, 16, 218–19, 242, 243, 249
  speeches of, 246
Ford, Paul Leicester, 50
Ford, Thomas, 221–22
Ford, Worthington C., 44, 74, 84, 86, 123
Ford (Gerald R.) Commemorative Committee, 222, 227
Ford (Gerald R.) Congressional Collection, 226
Ford (Gerald R.) Foundation, 227
Ford (Gerald R.) Library
  audiovisual materials, 226
  building, 223–24
  establishment of, 220–23
  manuscripts, 225–26
  oral histories in, 226
  PRESNET demonstration site, 25, 225
  printed material in, 226
  research materials in, 224–26
  site on university campus, 15
Ford (Gerald R.) Museum, 35, 227–28
Ford's Theater, 30, 80
Forster, Rudolph, 107
Francis, Charles, 88
Frankfurter, Felix, 158
Franklin, Benjamin, 4, 5, 21, 46, 103
Franklin and Marshall College Library, 131
Franklin D. Roosevelt Library. *See* Roosevelt (Franklin D.) Library
Frantz, Joe B., 211
Fremont, John C., 125, 129
Friends of the LBJ Library, 215–16
Fuess, Claude M., 115

Gadsden, James, 62
Galbraith, John Kenneth, 215
Gardiner Family Papers Collection, 72
Garfield, Abraham, 90
Garfield, Harry, 89, 90

Garfield, James A.
  bibliography of, 287
  biographers of, 89
  biography of, 87–88
  book collection at home of, 31
  Library of Congress collection of papers, 89–90
  papers of, 88–90
  presidency of, 88
  presidential nomination, 85, 91, 96
Garfield, James R., 89, 90
Garfield, Lucretia Rudolph, 88, 89
Garfield, Mrs. James R., 89
Garner, John Nance, 156
Gates, Horatio, 47
Gates-Wallace-Truman house, 34
Gavin, James M., 189
General Services Administration, 10, 11, 14, 144
Gerald R. Ford Library. *See* Ford (Gerald R.) Library
Gerald R. Ford Museum. *See* Ford (Gerald R.) Museum
Gerry, Elbridge, 2
Gilded Age, 142
Gilder, Richard Watson, 94
Gillet, Ransom Hooker, 73
Global 2000, 235, 237–38
Goldstein, Ernest, 212
Goldwater, Barry, 189, 205, 240, 242, 249
Goodpaster, Andrew, 189
Gordon, William, 42
Gouverneur, Maria, 57, 58, 59
Gouverneur, Marian Campbell, 59
Gouverneur, Mary Diggs Lee, 59
Gouverneur, Mrs. Samuel L., Jr., 60
Gouverneur, Samuel L., 57, 58–59, 60
Gouverneur, Samuel L., Jr., 59
Graham, Emmett S., 185
Grand Rapids Public Library, 221
Grand Rapids Public Museum, 221
Grant, Frederick D., 86
Grant, Mrs. Rollin P., 74
Grant, Ulysses S.
  bibliography of, 286
  biographers of, 86
  biography of, 80, 85–86
  book collection at home of, 31
  Library of Congress collection of papers, 86–87
  memoirs of, 85–86
  papers of, 86–87
  presidency of, 85, 91, 140
Grant, U.S., III, 86
Great Society, 215

Greenspan, Allan, 227
Griffiths, John L., 97
Grouseland, 29
Grover, Wayne C., 10, 11, 15, 22, 194, 196
GSA. *See* General Services Administration
Guggenheim, Charles, 198
Guide to Archives and Manuscripts in the United States (Hamer), 24
Guide to Manuscripts in the Presidential Libraries (Burton), 24
Guide to Records in the National Archives, 24
Guide to the Archives of the Government of the United States (Van Tyne and Leland), 8, 21
Guiteau, Charles J., 88

Hagedorn, Herman, 104
Hagerty, James C., 189
Haig, Alexander, 218, 245
Haldeman, H.R., 12, 241, 245, 246
Halford, Elijah W., 97
Hallek, Henry W., 86
Halstead, Murat, 89
Hamer, Philip M., 24
Hamilton, Alexander, 4, 21, 40, 46, 53, 57, 59, 103, 118
Hamilton, Mrs. Alexander, 43
Hancock, John, 1, 40, 117
Hannigan, Robert, 169
Harding, Florence Kling DeWolfe, 133, 134–36
Harding, Warren G.
  bibliography of, 289
  biographers of, 136–37
  biography of, 133–34
  book collection at home of, 33
  historic sites of, 138
  Library of Congress collection of papers, 137
  papers of, 6, 107, 134–38, 180
  presidency of, 106, 133–34, 143–44
  presidential campaign of, 114
  presidential election of, 149
Harding Memorial, 135–36, 138
Harding Memorial Association, 33, 135–36, 137
Harger, Charles M., 184, 185
Harlan, Laura, 134
Harriman, Averell, 215
Harris (Seymour) collection, 201

Harrison, Benjamin
  bibliography of, 287
  biographers of, 97, 98
  biography of, 69, 96–97
  book collection at home of, 32
  Library of Congress collection of papers, 97–98
  papers of, 97–98
  presidency of, 97, 106
  presidential campaign, 93
  presidential nomination, 99
  W.H. Harrison's papers and, 69
Harrison, John Scott, 69, 98
Harrison, Mary Scott Lord Dimmick, 69, 97, 98
Harrison, William Henry
  bibliography of, 284
  biography of, 68–69, 70
  book collection at home of, 29
  defeat of Van Buren, 67
  Library of Congress collection of papers, 69–70
  papers of, 69, 98
  presidency of, 68
Harrison (Benjamin) Foundation, 32
Harry Garfield's First Forty Years (Feis and Comer), 90
Harry S. Truman Library. *See* Truman Library
Harvard University, 104, 146, 195
Haven, Mrs. S.G., 126
Hay, Elizabeth, 58, 59
Hay, John, 80
Hayes, Lucy Ware Webb, 139, 142
Hayes, Rutherford B.
  bibliography of, 286
  biographers of, 140
  biography of, 99, 139–40
  book collection of, 31, 140–41
  Monroe papers and, 59
  papers of, 140–43
  presidency of, 7, 91, 140
  Taft and, 106
Hayes, Webb C., 6, 31, 141
Hayes, Webb C., II, 142
Hayes (Rutherford B.) and Lucy Webb Hayes Foundation, 31, 141
Hayes (Rutherford B.) Library, 6, 31, 90, 92, 98, 101, 131, 141, 142–43
Hayes Presidential Center, 140–43
Hazard, Ebenezer, 20
Heath, W.W., 207, 214
Hechler, Kenneth, 22
Hemingway, Ernest, 199

Hemingway, Mary, 199
Hemmeter, Christopher, 234
Henry E. Huntington Library. *See*
    Huntington (Henry E.), Library
Henry, Patrick, 54, 57
Herbert Hoover Library and Museum.
    See Hoover (Herbert) Library
    and Museum
Hermitage, 61
Hinsdale, Burke A., 89
Hirst, David W., 112
Hiss, Alger, 240, 247
Historic sites. *See* Presidential historic
    sites
Historical Collections (Hazard), 20
Historical societies. *See* names of
    specific states, counties, and
    cities
History of the American People
    (Wilson), 109
Hoes, Laurence G., 60
Hoover, Herbert
    bibliography of, 289
    biographers of, 181
    biography of, 133, 143–44
    book collection at home of, 33
    book donations to, 36
    Harding Memorial and, 136
    papers of, 11, 12, 23, 145–47,
        178–80
    presidency of, 4, 9, 144
    presidential election of, 150
    presidential library and, 1
Hoover Birthplace Foundation, 177,
    178
Hoover Institution and Library on
    War, Revolution and Peace, 6,
    145–47, 177
Hoover (Herbert) Library and
    Museum
    administration of, 33
    audiovisual materials, 180
    establishment of, 177–78
    manuscripts, 179–80
    microfilm and microfiche
        collections, 180
    museum area in, 181
    oral history transcripts, 180
    printed materials in, 180
    research materials in, 6, 11, 23,
        146, 178–80
Hoover (Herbert) National Historic
    Site, 178
Hoover Presidential Library
    Association, 178, 181
Hoover War Collection, 145

Hoover War Library, 145
Hope, Bob, 227
Hopkins, Harry, 158, 159, 159, 161
Hopkinson, Charles, 114
Howell, John, 36
Howells, William Dean, 142
Hudson Valley, 163
Hughes, Charles Evans, 110, 133
Human rights, 12, 235, 238
Humphrey, Hubert, 193, 240
Hungary, 147
Hunt, Gaillard, 76, 91, 97, 107
Huntington (Henry E.) Library, 44,
    52, 56, 76, 78–79, 84, 87
Hutchinson, Edward, 225

Illinois Historical Society, 80
Immigration, 163
*Impeachment and Trial of Andrew
    Johnson* (DeWitt), 83
Indiana Historical Society, 69
Indiana State Library, 98
Inquiery (Van Buren), 67
Institute of Latin American Studies,
    209
Iran hostage crisis, 237

Jackson, Andrew
    bibliography of, 283
    biographers of, 62–64, 65
    biography of, 61–62
    book collection at home of, 28–29
    Johnson and, 82
    Library of Congress collection of
        papers, 65–66
    papers of, 62–66, 74
    Polk and, 72
    presidency of, 7, 61–62, 68, 119,
        129
    Tyler and, 70, 71
    Van Buren and, 62, 63–64, 66–67
Jackson, Andrew (grandson), 65
Jackson, Andrew, Jr., 61, 62, 63, 65
Jackson, Rachel Donelson Robards,
    61
James, Marquis, 65
Jameson, J. Franklin, 8, 9, 9, 21, 65,
    74, 90, 111, 115, 135–36
Jaworski, Leon, 241
Jay, John, 51, 53–54, 158
Jefferson, Martha Wayles Skelton, 46
Jefferson, Thomas
    bibliography of, 281–82
    biographers of, 48
    biography of, 28, 40, 45–47, 53, 54,
        57, 117–18

Jefferson, Thomas (continued)
  book collection of, 3, 27–28, 35
  Library of Congress collection of
    papers, 49–53
  papers of, 4, 20, 21, 47–53, 59, 103
  presidency of, 2–3, 46, 54, 57
  University of Texas holdings on,
    211
Jefferson (Thomas) Memorial
  Association, 28
*Jefferson Papers of the University of
  Virginia,* 52
Jenkins, John S., 73
Jesup, Thomas S., 76
Jewish Joint Distribution Committee,
  147
JFK Library. See Kennedy (John F.)
  Library
Joerg, W.L.G., 156
John F. Kennedy Library. See
  Kennedy (John F.) Library
Johnson, Andrew
  bibliography of, 286
  biographers of, 83–84
  biography of, 82–83
  book collection at home of, 30–31
  Library of Congress collection of
    papers, 84–85
  papers of, 21, 83–85
  presidency of, 82, 85, 88
Johnson, Eliza McCardle, 82
Johnson, Claudia Taylor (Lady Bird),
  34, 204, 206, 207, 208, 210, 214,
  215, 216
Johnson, Lyndon B.
  bibliography of, 291
  biographers of, 208
  biography of, 204–06
  book collection at home of, 34
  Eisenhower Library and, 186
  Hoover Library and, 177
  oral history tapes of, 180
  papers of, 11, 23, 210–14
  presidency of, 176, 205–06, 217
  presidential election of, 240
  Truman Library and, 172
Johnson, Robert, 83
Johnson (Lyndon B.) Foundation,
  211, 215–16
Johnson (Lyndon B.) Library
  audiovisual materials, 213–14
  buildings, 209–10
  educational programs at, 215–16
  establishment of, 206–08
  manuscripts, 212
  museum areas in, 214–15

  oral history interviews, 211, 213
  printed materials in, 213
  research materials in, 12, 210–14
  site on university campus, 15
Johnson (Lyndon B.) Ranch and
  National Historical Park, 216
Johnson (Lyndon B.) School of Public
  Affairs, 146, 207, 209, 216
Johnston, Harriet Lane, 129, 130–31,
  132
Johnston, Henry E., 130, 132
Jones, Gary L., 250
Jones, James S., 84
Jones, Paul C., 5
Jonge, Maury de, 222
Jordan (Arthur) Foundation, 32

Kahn, Herman, 11, 160, 196
Keeping Faith (Carter), 232
Kefauver, Estes, xiii, 193
Kendall, Amos, 62–64, 65
Kennedy, Edward, 196, 197, 198, 199,
  202, 227
Kennedy, Jacqueline Lee Bouvier,
  36–37, 192, 199. *See also*
  Onassis, Jacqueline Kennedy
Kennedy, John F.
  bibliography of, 291
  biography of, 192–94, 217
  book collection at home of, 26, 34
  mural of, 215
  papers of, 11, 23, 198–201, 210
  presidency of, 193–94
  presidential election of, 205, 240
Kennedy, Joseph P., 180
Kennedy, May S., 132
Kennedy, Robert F., 196, 199, 200,
  202
Kennedy, Rose Fitzgerald, 180
Kennedy (John F.) Institute of
  Government, 202
Kennedy (John F.) Library
  audiovisual materials, 201
  building, 198
  educational programs at, 202–03
  establishment of, 194–98
  manuscripts, 199–200
  Metropolitan Boston Transit
    Authority (MBTA), 196–97
  museum area in, 201–02
  oral history interviews, 200
  printed materials in, 200–01
  purpose of, 207, 209
  research materials in, 198–201
Kennedy (John F.) Library
  Foundation, 202

Kennedy (John F.) School of
Government, 146, 197, 209
Kennedy (Robert F.) book awards, 201
Kentucky Historical Society, 76
Keyes, Henry, 9
Killian, James R., 189
King, Martin Luther, 206, 229
Kissinger, Henry, 215, 224–25, 227
Kleberg, Richard, 204
Kleindienst, Richard, 241
Knott, Lawson, 210
Knowland, William F., 172
Koerner, Hazel, 127

LaClaire, David B., 227
Lafayette, General, 43
Laguna Niguel, Federal Archives and
Records Center, 242, 248
Lake County Historical Society, 31
Lamont, Daniel Scott, 94
Lancaster County Historical Society,
131
Lance, Bertram, 230
Landon, Alfred M., 150
Langford, Laura Carter Holloway, 83,
84
Larned, Daniel R., 71
Larson, Jess, 170
Latin American Collection, 209
Lawnfield, 31
LBJ Library. *See* Johnson (Lyndon B.)
Library
League of Nations, 145
Lear, Tobias, 42–43
Lee, Charles, 42
Lee, Henry, 40, 62
Lee, Light Horse Henry, 62
Lee, Robert E., 80, 85
Legislative, Executive and Judicial
Appropriations Act, 4
Lehman, Herbert H., 158
Leland, Waldo G., 8, 9, 21, 155, 156,
157, 158
*Letters and Other Writings of James
Madison* (Rives and Fendall), 55
Letters and Times of the Tylers
(Tyler), 72
Letters of Mrs. Adams (Adams), 122
Lewis, Robert, 42
Libraries. *See* Presidential libraries
Library of Congress
Arthur papers, 91–92
Buchanan papers, 132
Cleveland papers, 94–96
congressional records in, 8
Coolidge papers, 115–16, 136

Fillmore's support of, 126
Force (Peter) Collection, 5, 44, 139
functions of, 2
Garfield papers, 89–90
Grant papers, 86–87
Harding papers, 135, 136, 137
Harrison (Benjamin) papers, 97–98
Harrison (William Henry) papers,
69–70
Hayes's support for, 139, 140
history of, 2–5, 28
Jackson papers, 64–65, 65–66
Jefferson papers, 4, 49–53, 103
Johnson (Andrew) papers, 84–85
legislation pertaining to, 2–4
legislative reference services of, 110
Lincoln papers, 80–81
McKinley papers, 100–01
Madison papers, 4, 55–56, 103
Manuscript Division, 4, 5
*Master Record of Manuscript
Collections,* 22
microfilming project of presidential
papers, 5–6
Monroe papers, 4, 59–60, 103
Montgomery Blair Collection, 65
*National Union Catalog of
Manuscript Collections,* 22
Office of Register of Copyright, 4
Pierce papers, 78–79
Polk papers, 74–75
presidential book collections in,
35–36
presidential papers in, 1
Presidents' Papers Index Series, 24
Roosevelt (Theodore) papers,
103–05
Taft papers, 106–08
Taylor papers, 76–77
Tyler papers, 72
Van Buren papers, 67–68
Washington papers, 4, 44–45, 103
Wilson papers, 110–14
Wilson's personal library, 2, 112
*Life and Letters of James Abraham
Garfield* (Smith), 89
Life of Andrew Jackson (Bassett), 65
Life of Andrew Jackson (Eaton), 62
Life of Andrew Johnson (Jones), 84
Life of Herbert Hoover (Nash), 181
Life of James Knox Polk (Jenkins), 73
Life of Thomas Hart Benton
(Roosevelt), 103
Life of Thomas Jefferson (Tucker), 48
Life of William McKinley (Olcott), 100

Lincoln, Abraham
bibliography of, 285–86
biographers of, 80
biography of, 79–80
book collection at home of, 26, 30
Garfield and, 88
letter to Grant, 86
Library of Congress collection of
papers, 80–81
papers of, 80–81
presidency of, 4, 80, 82, 129
Tyler and, 71
Lincoln, Mary Todd, 79
Lincoln, Nancy Hanks, 30
Lincoln, Robert T., 80–81
Lindenwald, 29
Link, Arthur S., 112
Lippmann, Walter, 114
Lipshutz, Robert, 233
Livermore, Samuel, 2
Lloyd, David D., 22, 171, 172
Lloyd (David D.) Prize, 176
Longstreet, James, 83
Longworth, Alice Roosevelt, 104
Lyndon B. Johnson Library. *See*
Johnson (Lyndon B.) Library

McAdoo, Eleanor Wilson, 112
MacArthur, Douglas, 147, 182, 190
McClellan, John, 208
McCormack, John, 14
McElroy, Robert McNutt, 95
McGuire, James C., 55
McGuire, James C., II, 56
McHenry, James, 42
McKee, Mary Harrison, 97
McKellar, Kenneth, 9
McKinley, Ida Saxton, 99
McKinley, William
bibliography of, 288
biographers of, 100
biography of, 99–100
book collection at home of, 32
Library of Congress collection of
papers, 100–01
papers of, 100–01
presidency of, 4, 99–100, 102, 106
presidential campaign, 93
McLane, Louis, 7, 43–44
McLaughlin, James A., 63, 65
McLean, Edward, 134
McLean, Evalyn Walsh, 134
MacLeish, Archibald, 4, 158
McPherson, Harry, 213
McShain, John, 158
Maddox, Lester, 229

Madison, Dolley Payne Todd, 28,
54–55
Madison, James
bibliography of, 282–83
biographers of, 55
biography of, 46, 53–54, 57
book collection at home of, 28
Library of Congress collection of
papers, 55–56
papers of, 4, 20, 21, 48, 54–56, 59,
103
presidency of, 3, 54, 57, 119
Taylor and, 75
Washington papers and, 43
Magruder, Patrick, 3
Manning, Helen Taft, 108, 156
Mansure, Edmund F., 15
Marcy, William L., 73
Mardian, Robert, 246
Marshall, Charles D., 127
Marshall, George C., 182
Marshall, John, 43
Martin, Joseph W., Jr., 14, 172
Martin, Thomas P., 9, 92
Massachusetts Historical Society, 6,
27, 51, 52, 67, 119–24
Masten, Arthur H., 91
*Master Record of Manuscript
Collections,* 22
Mearns, David C., xiii
Meese, Edwin, III, 249
Mellon, Andrew, 133
*Memoir, Correspondence, and
Miscellanies from the Papers of
Thomas Jefferson* (Randolph), 48
Memoirs (Truman), 168, 170
Memoirs of John Quincy Adams
(Adams), 122
Messages and Papers of the Presidents
(Richardson), 21, 23
Mexican War, 79
Mexico, 132
MHC. *See* Michigan Historical
Collections
Michener, Louis T., 97
Michigan Historical Collections,
220–21
Military History of U.S. Grant
(Badeau), 86
Millard Fillmore Papers (Severance),
127
Milligan, Fred J., 137
Milligan, Joseph, 3
Milliken, William G., 223, 227
Mischler, Wendell W., 107
Missouri Historical Society, 51, 52

Mitchell, John N., 241, 246
Mitchell, Louise Reed, 92
Mollie Garfield in the White House
   (Feis and Comer), 90
Monaghan, Frank, 158
Mondale, Walter F., 230
Monetary reforms, 142
Monroe, James
   bibliography of, 283
   biography of, 56–58
   book collection at home of, 28
   Library of Congress collection of
     papers, 59–60
   papers of, 4, 20, 58–60, 103
   presidency of, 54, 57, 119
Monroe Doctrine, 57
Monroe (James) Law Office and
   Memorial Library, 59, 60
Monticello, 27–28, 51
Moore, Charles, 89, 91–92, 107–08,
   110–11, 134–35
Moore, John Bassett, 131
Morgenstern, Carl H., 222
Morison, Samuel Eliot, 152, 155, 157,
   158
Morris, Stuyvesant Fish, 67
Moses, Raphael J., 83
Motion pictures. *See* Audiovisual
   materials
Mount Vernon, 27
Muhlenberg, Frederick A.H., 48
Mumford, L. Quincy, 4, 206
Museum of the Presidents, 19

Nash, George H., 181
National Archives, 1, 7–12, 13, 14,
   23, 24, 52, 107, 144, 170
National Archives Act, 9–10, 14, 21
National Archives and Records
   Administration Act, 10
National Archives and Records
   Service. *See* National Archives.
National Archives Trust Fund, 18
National Capital Planning
   Commission, 19
National Historic Landmarks, 26
National Historical Publications and
   Records Commission, 24
National Historical Publications
   Commission, 10, 21, 22, 23, 24
National Park Service, 26, 216
National Security Council, 188
National Study Commission on
   Records and Documents of
   Federal Officials, 16, 17

*National Union Catalog of Manuscript
   Collections,* 22
Naval history, 12
Naval paintings, 163, 166
Naval Photographic Center, 226, 246
Naval War of 1812 (Roosevelt), 103
Navy Department, 161
Nelson, Judson, 227
Nesbitt, Jack, 12
Nessen, Ron, 227
Neustadt, Richard, 196
Nevins, Allan, 73
New Deal, 150, 160, 163, 164
New Hampshire Historical Society, 78
New Jersey Historical Society, 79
New York Historical Society, 52, 66,
   69, 87, 92, 95, 131
New York Public Library, 56, 60, 66,
   79
New York State Library, 67, 92
Newman, J. Wilson, 92
Newsreels. *See* Films
NHPC. *See* National Historical
   Publications Commission
Nichols, Roy F., 78
Nicolay, John G., 80
Niederlander Gift Collection, 127
Nixon, Edgar B., 160
Nixon, Pat Ryan, 239, 246
Nixon, Richard M.
   bibliography of, 291–92
   biography of, 219, 239–42
   book collection at home of, 35
   book donations not made to, 36
   Johnson Library and, 209–10
   papers of, 11–12, 16–17, 23,
     242–47
   presidency of, 11–12, 13, 16, 206,
     218, 219, 224, 227, 231, 240–42
   presidential campaign, 193
Nixon (Richard) Archives Foundation,
   247–48
Nixon Birthplace Foundation, 35
Nixon Presidential Library, 35, 16,
   247–48
Nixon Presidential Materials Project
   audiovisual materials, 246
   manuscripts, 245
   oral history project, 246
   ownership of Nixon papers, 242–44
   printed materials in, 247
   published materials and gifts, 247
   research materials in, 244–47
*Nixon v. Administrator of General
   Services,* 16, 243
Northwest Ordinance, 56

NPS. *See* National Park Service
NSC. *See* National Security Council
Oak Hill, 28
O'Connor, Basil, 157, 171
Office of Economic Opportunity, 211
Office of Presidential Libraries, 10–12
Office of Presidential Papers and
    Archives, 11–12
*Official Records of the War of the
    Rebellion*, 86
Ohio Historical Society, 6, 31, 90,
    101, 108, 134–38, 141
Ohio State Archaeological and
    Historical Society, 141
Ohio State Library, 140
Olcott, Charles S., 100
Old Executive Office Building, 37
Old House, 27, 28, 120–21, 123
Onassis, Jacqueline Kennedy, 198,
    199. *See also* Kennedy,
    Jacqueline
O'Neill, Tip, 231, 232
OPPA. *See* Office of Presidential
    Papers and Archives
Oral histories
    Carter Center, 236
    Eisenhower Library, 189
    Ford Library, 226
    Hoover Archives, 147
    Hoover Library and Museum, 180
    Johnson Library, 211, 213
    Kennedy Library, 200
    Nixon Presidential Materials
        Project, 246
    Roosevelt (Franklin D.) Collection,
        162
    Truman Library, 174
Ordeal of Woodrow Wilson (Hoover),
    144
Oregon, 132
O'Reilly, Henry, 58–59
Oswald, Lee Harvey, 194

Page, John, 47
Panama Canal Treaty, 236
*Papers of the Continental Congress
    Relating to Jefferson*, 52
Papers of Thomas Jefferson (Boyd),
    51–52
Papers of Woodrow Wilson (Link), 112
Paris Peace Conference, 147
Parkinson, Kenneth, 246
Parton, James, 64
Patterson, Andrew Johnson, 84
Patterson, Martha Johnson, 83–84

Pei, I.M., 196, 198, 202
Pendergast, T.J., 168
Pennsylvania Historical and Museum
    Commission, 131
Pennsylvania Historical Society, 6, 44,
    52, 56, 69, 79, 130–31
People, The Sovereigns (Monroe), 58
Pershing, John, 182
Personal Memoirs of U.S. Grant
    (Grant), 86
Persons, Wilton B., 187
Phillips, Carrie, 133, 136–37
Phonograph records. *See* Audiovisual
    materials
Pierce, Benjamin, 77
Pierce, Frank H., 78
Pierce, Franklin
    bibliography of, 285
    biographers of, 78
    biography of, 77–78
    book collection at home of, 30
    Library of Congress collection of
        papers, 78–79
    papers of, 78–79
    presidency of, 78, 129
    presidential election of, 125
Pierce, Kirk D., 78
Pierpont Morgan Library, 67, 72, 95,
    131
Polk, James K.
    bibliography of, 284
    biographers of, 73–74
    biography of, 72–73
    book collection at home of, 29
    Library of Congress collection of
        papers, 74–75
    papers of, xiii, 74–75
    presidency of, 72–73, 77, 82
    presidential election of, 129
    presidential nomination of, 71
Polk, Samuel, 29
Polk, Sarah Childress, 72, 73–74
Porter, Horace, 86
Portrait of the Assassin (Ford and
    Stiles), 218
Poverty programs, 211
Presidential book collections
    Hayes Memorial Library, 142
    Jefferson, 3, 27–28, 35
    Library of Congress, 35–36
    presidential homes, 27–35
    presidential sites, 26–27
    Roosevelt (Franklin D.), 163
    Truman Library, 174
    White House libraries, 36–37
    Wilson, 2

Presidential historic sites, 26–27, 260–62
Presidential homes, 27–35
Presidential libraries. *See also* names of specific libraries
  administration of, 10–12
  costs of, 11, 251
  holdings of, 252–53
  legislation, 14–16, 18–19
  limits to, 13, 18–19
  museum visitors to, 256
  researcher daily visits to, 255
  size of, 18, 19
  space allocations of, 254
  staff positions in, 257
  universities as sites for, 15
Presidential Libraries Act (1955), xiii, 1, 11, 13, 14–16, 146, 171, 185, 194
Presidential Libraries Act (1986), 12, 18–19
Presidential Libraries Manual, 12
Presidential papers
  bibliographic guides to, 20–25
  bibliography of, 279–81
  database for, 25
  definition of, 233
  directory of, 258–59
  legislation, 16–18
  microfilming project, 5–6
  ownership of, 13, 94
  Supreme Court cases concerning, 232
Presidential Recordings and Materials Preservation Act, 12, 13, 16–17, 243
Presidential records, definition of, 233
Presidential Records Act, 12, 13, 17–18, 232–33
Presidents. *See* names of specific presidents
Presidents' Papers Index Series, xiii–xiv, 5, 24
PRESNET, 25, 212, 225
Preston, Mrs. Thomas J., Jr., 95
Price (Arthur) Collection, 201
Princeton University, 51, 56, 95, 108, 112, 131, 146
Pringle, Henry, 158
Prison reforms, 142
Profiles in Courage (Kennedy), 192
Pryor, David, 18
Public Papers and Addresses of Franklin D. Roosevelt (Rosenman), 22

Public Papers of the Presidents of the United States, 22–24
Puritan in Babylon (White), 115
Pusey, Nathan M., 195–96
Putnam, Herbert, 3, 8, 65, 74, 80, 103, 111

Quaife, Milo M., xiii, 73

Ramsay, David, 62
Ramsey, Maurice M., xiii
Randall, Henry Stephens, 73
Randolph, Caroline Ramsey, 50, 51
Randolph, John, 66
Randolph, Mrs. William Mann, 51
Randolph, Sarah N., 50
Randolph, Thomas Jefferson, 47, 48–49, 50
Randolph family papers, 52
Ransom, Harry, 207
Rayburn, Sam, 172, 204
Reagan, Nancy, 202, 235, 249, 250
Reagan, Ronald
  bibliography of, 292
  biography of, 219, 248–49
  book collection at home of, 35
  book donations to, 36
  Carter Center and, 235
  Ford Museum and, 227
  Kennedy Library and, 202
  papers of, 13, 17, 23, 24
  presidency of, 4, 5, 12
  presidential election of, 232
Reagan (Ronald) Center for Public Affairs, 250
Reagan (Ronald) Home Restoration and Preservation Association, 35
Reagan (Ronald) Presidential Foundation, 249–50
Reagan (Ronald) Presidential Library, 249–50
Reconstruction, 142
Reconstruction Finance Corporation, 181
Reed, Albert, 184
Reed, Daniel, 136
Reedy, George, 207, 215
Rees, Edward H., 14
Reid, John, 62
Relief programs, 12, 147, 178, 181
Revolutionary War. *See* American Revolution
Rhoads, James B., 24, 223
Rice, Stuart A., 156
Richardson, Elliot, 241
Richardson, James Daniel, 21, 23

Richardson, Sid W., 209
Rickover, Hyman, 229
Rinelander, Mrs. Philip M., 56
River Brethren, 182
Rives, William C., 55, 56
Roberts, Clifford, 189
Robinson, William E., 186
Rochambeau, Jean Baptiste, Comte de, 5
Rockefeller, Nelson Aldrich, 219
Roosevelt, Alice Hathaway Lee, 101
Roosevelt, Claes Martenszen, 152
Roosevelt, Eleanor, 32, 152, 157, 158, 162, 163, 164, 166, 169, 237
Roosevelt, Franklin D.
  bibliography of, 290
  biography of, 149–51
  book collection of, 33–34, 163
  mural of, 215
  papers of, 12, 22, 23, 159–64, 180
  presidency of, 4, 9, 10, 147, 150–51, 169, 182, 204
  presidential election of, 144
  presidential library and, 1, 13
  view of Connor, 10
Roosevelt, Jacob, 152
Roosevelt, James, 34, 149, 152
Roosevelt, Mrs. Theodore, 103–04
Roosevelt, Sara Delano, 149, 158
Roosevelt, Theodore
  autobiography of, 103
  bibliography of, 288
  biographers of, 103–04
  biography of, 101–02, 110
  book collection at home of, 32
  correspondence with Taft, 107
  Library of Congress collection of papers, 103–05
  papers of, 103–05
  presidency of, 4, 8, 102–03, 106
Roosevelt (Franklin D.) Four Freedoms Awards, 166–67
Roosevelt (Franklin and Eleanor) Institute, 166–67
Roosevelt (Franklin D.) Library and Museum
  administration of, 10
  audiovisual materials, 163–64
  authorization for, 16
  building, 159
  costs of, 11
  establishment of, 8, 13, 157–59
  Hayes Library and, 6, 142
  legislation concerning, 157–58
  manuscripts, 162
  museum area of, 165–66

oral history interview transcripts, 162
  planning of, 151–57
  printed materials collection, 163
  recorded speeches in, 164
  research materials in, 159–64
Roosevelt Study Center in The Netherlands, 166
Roosevelt (Theodore) Association, 32
Roosevelt (Theodore) Memorial Association, 104
Roosevelt (Theodore) National Park, 32
Rosenman, Samuel I., 22, 23, 155, 156, 157, 159, 162
Ross, Harry E., 115
Rostow, Walt W., 212
Ruckelshaus, William D., 241
Rush, Benjamin, 68
Rusk, Dean, 213, 215
Russell, Francis, 136–38
Russia, 147
Rutherford B. Hayes Library. *See* Hayes (Rutherford B.) Library

SALT II Treaty, 236
Sam Johnson's Boy (Steinberg), 208
Sampson, Arthur, 16, 224, 243
Sandburg, Carl, 211
Sasakawa, Ryoichi, 237
Sawyer, Carl, 136
Saxbe, William B., 242
Schira, George, 238
Schlesinger, Arthur M., Jr., 195, 196, 232
Schlesinger, Arthur M., Sr., 151
Schmidt, Helmut, 231
Schuyler, Philip, 40
Scott, Winfield, 77, 125
Scowcroft, Brent, 224–25
Screen Actors Guild, 249
Selections from the Private Correspondence of James Madison from 1813 to 1836 (McGuire), 55
Sellers, Charles G., 73
Seminole War, 61
Severance, Frank H., 127
Shadow of Blooming Grove (Russell), 136
Shelby, Senator, 99
Shepard, C. Sidney, 127
Sherman, John, 51
Sherman, William Tecumseh, 235
Sherwood Forest, 29, 71
Shipman, Fred, 10, 156, 158, 160, 165

Shouler, James, 59
Sid Richardson Hall, 209
Siever, Harry J., 98
Simon, Louis A., 156, 157
Simon, William E., 247
Sioussat, St. George, 115
Sirica, John, 246
Smith, Alfred, 144, 149–50
Smith, Theodore Clarke, 89
Smith, William French, 249
Smithsonian Institution, 19
Smock, Raymond W., 24
Smoot, Reed, 9
Snyder, John W., 175
Society of American Archivists, 22
Sorenson, Theodore, 196
Southwest Texas State University, 206
Spanish-American War, 142
Sparks, Jared, 20, 43–44
Special libraries. *See* Hayes (Rutherford B.) Library and Hoover (Herbert) Library and Museum
Spiegel Grove, 140–41
Spofford, Ainsworth Rand, 4, 5, 50, 51, 74, 140
Sprague, William, 43
Stanford University, 6, 144, 145, 146, 177, 249–50
Stanley-Brown, Joseph, 89
State Department, 37, 180
Stauffer, Mrs. Walter R., 76
Steinberg, Alfred, 208
Stelle, Edward, 49
Stephens, Thomas E., 175
Stevenson, Adlai E., 183, 193
Stickney, William, 64
Stiles, Jack, 217–18
Stone Library, 122, 123
Stubbins, Hugh A., 250
Supreme Court, 16–17, 107, 129, 147, 150, 183, 232, 243
Swarr, Hiram B., 130, 131

Taft, Alfonso, 105
Taft, Charles P., 108
Taft, Helen Herron, 106, 108
Taft, Robert A., 108, 180
Taft, William Howard
  bibliography of, 288
  biographers of, 158
  biography of, 105–06, 110
  book collection at home of, 33
  Library of Congress collection of papers, 107–09
  papers of, 106–09, 111, 135
  presidency of, 106

presidential nomination, 102, 133
Taft (William Howard) Memorial Association, 33
Taft-Hartley Bill, 240
Taylor, Betty, 76
Taylor, Hugh P., 48
Taylor, John R.M., 76
Taylor, Margaret Smith, 75, 76
Taylor, Richard, 76
Taylor, Zachary
  bibliography of, 284
  biography of, 75–76
  book collection at home of, 29–30
  Library of Congress collection of papers, 76–77
  papers of, 76–77
  presidency of, 75–76, 125
Temple, Larry, 213
Tennessee Historical Society, 66, 74
Tennessee State Library, 66, 74, 84
Terrell, William G., 64, 65
Territo, Dorothy, 210
Texas Collection, 209
Thirty Years View (Benton), 64
This Country of Ours (Harrison), 97
Thomson, Charles, 7
Thurber, Henry T., 94
Thurmond, Strom, 169
Tibbott, Frank E., 97–98
Tilden, Samuel, 139
Todd, John Payne, 55, 56
Toner, Joseph M., 5
Tonkin Resolution, 205
Toombs, Henry J., 152–53
Trevor, Karl L., 11
Trudeau, Pierre, 227
Truman, Bess Wallace, 34, 168, 175
Truman, Harry S.
  bibliography of, 290
  biography of, 168–70
  book collection at home of, 34
  Eisenhower Library and, 185
  Hoover Library and, 177
  mural of, 215
  papers of, 10, 11, 14, 23, 170, 173–75
  personal book collection of, 174
  photographs of, 175
  presidency of, 4, 144, 169–70, 183, 192, 240, 249
  presidential papers and, 22–23
Truman Doctrine, 169
Truman (Harry S.) Institute for National and International Affairs, 172, 176

Truman (Harry S.) Library
    audiovisual materials, 174
    building description, 172–73
    coin collection, 175
    completion of, 16
    educational programs at, 215
    establishment of, 14, 170–72
    and Kennedy Library, 207
    manuscripts, 173–74
    microfilm collection, 174
    museum area in, 175–76
    oral history interview transcripts,
        174
    printed materials collection, 174
    research materials in, 12, 173–75
Tucker, George, 47, 48, 51
Tugwell, Rexford G., 162
Tully, Grace, 159
Tumulty, Joseph P., 110
Twain, Mark, 86
Tyler, John
    bibliography of, 284
    biography of, 68, 70–71
    book collection at home of, 29
    Library of Congress collection of
        papers, 72
    papers of, 71–72
    presidency of, 70–71
Tyler, Julia Gardiner, 70
Tyler, Letitia Christian, 70, 70, 71
Tyler, Lyon G., 71–72
Tyler, Mason, 71

United Nations, 166, 169, 175, 183
Universal Declaration of Human
    Rights Trust, 166
University of Kentucky, 76
University of Michigan, 15, 56,
        220–23
    Bentley Library, 220–21
    Clements (William L.) Library, 52,
        56, 69, 79
University of North Carolina, 69, 76
University of Southern California, 250
University of Texas, 15, 146, 206,
        207–08, 209, 211
University of Virginia, 28, 51, 52, 56,
        60, 112

Val-Kill, 158
Van Buren, Martin
    autobiography of, 67
    bibliography of, 284
    biography of, 62, 66–67
    book collection at home of, 29

correspondence with Jackson,
        63–64
    Library of Congress collection of
        papers, 67–68
    papers of, 5, 67–68
    Polk and, 72
    presidency of, 20, 67
    presidential campaign, 68, 75
Van Buren, Mrs. Smith Thompson, 67
Van Buren, Smith Thompson, 67
Van Tyne, Claude H., 8, 21
Vander Velde, Lewis G., 220
Vantage Point (Johnson), 206
Varick, Richard, 40–42
Videotapes
    Carter Center, 236
    Ford Library, 226
    Hoover Library and Museum, 180
    Johnson Library, 214
    Kennedy Library, 201–02
    Nixon Presidential Materials
        Project, 246
    Roosevelt (Franklin D.) Library
        and Museum, 163
    Truman Library, 175
Vietnam War, 205, 214, 219, 240–41
Virginia Historical Society, 44, 56, 69
Virginia State Library, 44, 52, 60
Volwiler, Albert T., 97–98
Voorhis, Gerry, 240

Walker, Frank C., 154, 155, 156, 157
Wallace, George, 240
Wallace, Henry, 169
Walsh, Robert, 48
War Department, 37, 161
Warner, Robert M., 220, 224
Warren, Earl, 172, 183
Warren Commission, 217
Washington, Bushrod, 27, 42–43
Washington, George
    bibliography of, 281
    biographers of, 43
    biography of, 39–40, 117
    book collection at home of, 27
    correspondence with Jefferson, 47
    Library of Congress collection of
        papers, 44–45
    papers of, 1, 4, 13, 20, 40–45, 48,
        103
    presidency of, 40, 46, 54, 57, 118,
        119
Washington, George Corbin, 43–44
Washington, Henry A., 47, 49, 50, 51
Washington, Lawrence, 39

Washington, Martha Dandridge
Custis, 43
Washington Bonus March, 147
Watergate, xiii, 13, 16, 218, 221,
241–42, 245, 246, 247
Watson, Douglas A., 36
Watterston, George, 3
Weatherford, Robert C., Jr., 171
Webster, Daniel, 70, 76, 126
*Weekly Compilation of Presidential
Documents,* 24
Weinberger, Caspar, 227
Welliver, Judson C., 135
Wells, Lillian A., 127
Western Reserve Historical Society,
31, 101
Western Reserve University, 108
Westland, 32
Wheatland, 30, 130, 131
Whitaker, John C., 247
White, Andrew D., 145
White, William Allen, 115
White House
filing system, 25, 160, 263–64
gift collection, 201
law library, 37
library, 4
Map Room, 161
research center, 37
White House Diary (Johnson), 214
White House Years (Eisenhower), 184,
188
Whitman, Ann, 188
Whitman (Ann) File, 188
Why England Slept (Kennedy), 192
Wickman, John A., 186
Wilbur, Ray Lyman, 145
Wilcox, Ansley, 32
Wild, General, 71
William L. Clements Library. *See*
University of Michigan
Williams, John J., 211
Williamson, Don, 136–37
Willkie, Wendell L., 151
Wilson, Edith Bolling Galt, 36, 110,
111–12
Wilson, Ellen Louise Axson, 109, 110,
112
Wilson, Harold, 215
Wilson, James Grant, 126

Wilson, Woodrow
bibliography of, 288
biographers of, 111–12
biography of, 109–10
book collection of, 2, 26, 33, 112
books in Library of Congress,
35–36
correspondence with Hoover, 147
Library of Congress collection of
papers, 110–14
papers of, 107, 110–14, 135
presidency of, 102, 106, 109–10,
133, 143, 149
presidential election of, 149
Wilson (Woodrow) Birthplace
Foundation, 33
Wilson School for Public and
International Affairs, 146
Winning of the West (Roosevelt), 103
Wisconsin Historical Society, 69
Woodrow Wilson: Life and Letters
(Baker), 112
*Woodrow Wilson and World
Settlement* (Baker), 111
Woodruff, Robert, 233
Works of James Abraham Garfield
(Hinsdale), 89
Works of John Adams (Adams), 120,
121, 122
World War I, 145, 147, 178, 181
World War II, 12, 145, 147, 151, 160,
161, 164, 165, 169, 190–91, 227
Wright, Frank Lloyd, 172, 223
Writings of George Washington
(Ford), 44
Writings of George Washington
(Sparks), 43
*Writings of George Washington from
the Original Manuscript Sources*
(Fitzpatrick), 44
Writings of John Quincy Adams
(Adams), 123
Writings of Thomas Jefferson, 49
Writings of Thomas Jefferson (Ford),
50
Wyman, Jane, 249
Wythe, George, 45

Yale University, 44, 72, 74, 108
Young, Andrew, 230–31
Young, John Russell, 4, 86

Ziegler, Ronald, 245

FRANK L. SCHICK is an author and consultant with a distinguished government and academic career in the library and information science field. His special interests include American history and politics, the history of books and publishing, and library research and statistics. He holds a Ph.D. from the University of Michigan and has contributed widely to the professional literature. He is the editor of *Statistical Handbook on Aging Americans*, also published by The Oryx Press.

RENEE SCHICK is an information services consultant specializing in microcomputer-based bibliographic information storage and retrieval. She has many years of writing and editorial experience.

MARK CARROLL is director of George Mason University Press, Fairfax, Virginia. In his 40-year publishing career, he has worked at Yale University Press and Harvard University Press, as well as the National Park Service, where he was responsible for professional publications. He was the founding president of the Society for Scholarly Publishing and has had a continuing interest in international publishing and copyright.

R. B. Hayes

Franklin D. Roosevelt

John Tyler

Wm H. Taft

Jimmy Carter

Th. Jefferson

Millard Fillmore

Woodrow Wilson

Andrew Johnson

M Van Buren

A. Lincoln

Harry Truman

Calvin Coolidge

James Monroe

James Madison

J. A. Garfield

John F. Kennedy

Richard Nixon

W. H. Harrison

C. A. Arthur